ROGER /

Kmas
2024

kes , (T)

with warm
regards
as aks

Ken

Clarissa

Hugo Vickers is a writer, lecturer and broadcaster, and an acknowledged expert on the British Royal Family. He has written biographies of the Queen Mother, Cecil Beaton, Vivien Leigh, Princess Andrew of Greece and the Duchess of Windsor. His book *The Kiss* won the 1996 Stern Silver Pen Award for Non-Fiction. His recent bestsellers have included *Malice in Wonderland* and *The Sphinx* – the life of Gladys, the Duchess of Marlborough.

Also by Hugo Vickers

We Want the Queen

Gladys, Duchess of Marlborough

Debrett's Book of the Royal Wedding

Cocktails and Laughter

Cecil Beaton

Vivien Leigh

Royal Orders

Loving Garbo

The Private World of the Duke and Duchess of Windsor

The Kiss

Alice, Princess Andrew of Greece

The Unexpurgated Beaton: The Cecil Beaton Diaries

Beaton in the Sixties

Alexis, the Memoirs of the Baron de Redé

Elizabeth, The Queen Mother

Horses and Husbands

St George's Chapel, Windsor Castle

Behind Closed Doors

Coronation

The Quest for Queen Mary

The Sphinx

The Crown Dissected

Malice in Wonderland

A Royal Life (with HRH The Duke of Kent)

Elstree 175

Pining in Paradise

Clarissa

Muse to Power

The Untold Story of Clarissa Eden, Countess of Avon

HUGO VICKERS

HODDER &
STOUGHTON

First published in Great Britain in 2024 by Hodder & Stoughton Limited
An Hachette UK company

1

A CIP catalogue record for this title is available from the British Library

Hardback ISBN 9781399736770
ebook ISBN 9781399736794

Typeset in Bembo MT by Hewer Text UK Ltd, Edinburgh
Printed and bound in Great Britain by Clays Ltd, Elcograf S.p.A.

Hodder & Stoughton policy is to use papers that are natural, renewable
and recyclable products and made from wood grown in sustainable forests.
The logging and manufacturing processes are expected to conform
to the environmental regulations of the country of origin.

Hodder & Stoughton Limited
Carmelite House
50 Victoria Embankment
London EC4Y 0DZ

The authorised representative in the EEA is Hachette Ireland, 8 Castlecourt Centre,
Castleknock Road, Castleknock, Dublin 15, D15 YF6A, Ireland (email: info@hbgi.ie)

www.hodder.co.uk

To Sally Ashburton, with love

Contents

Part Four

Select Family Tree
Churchill – Bertie – Eden

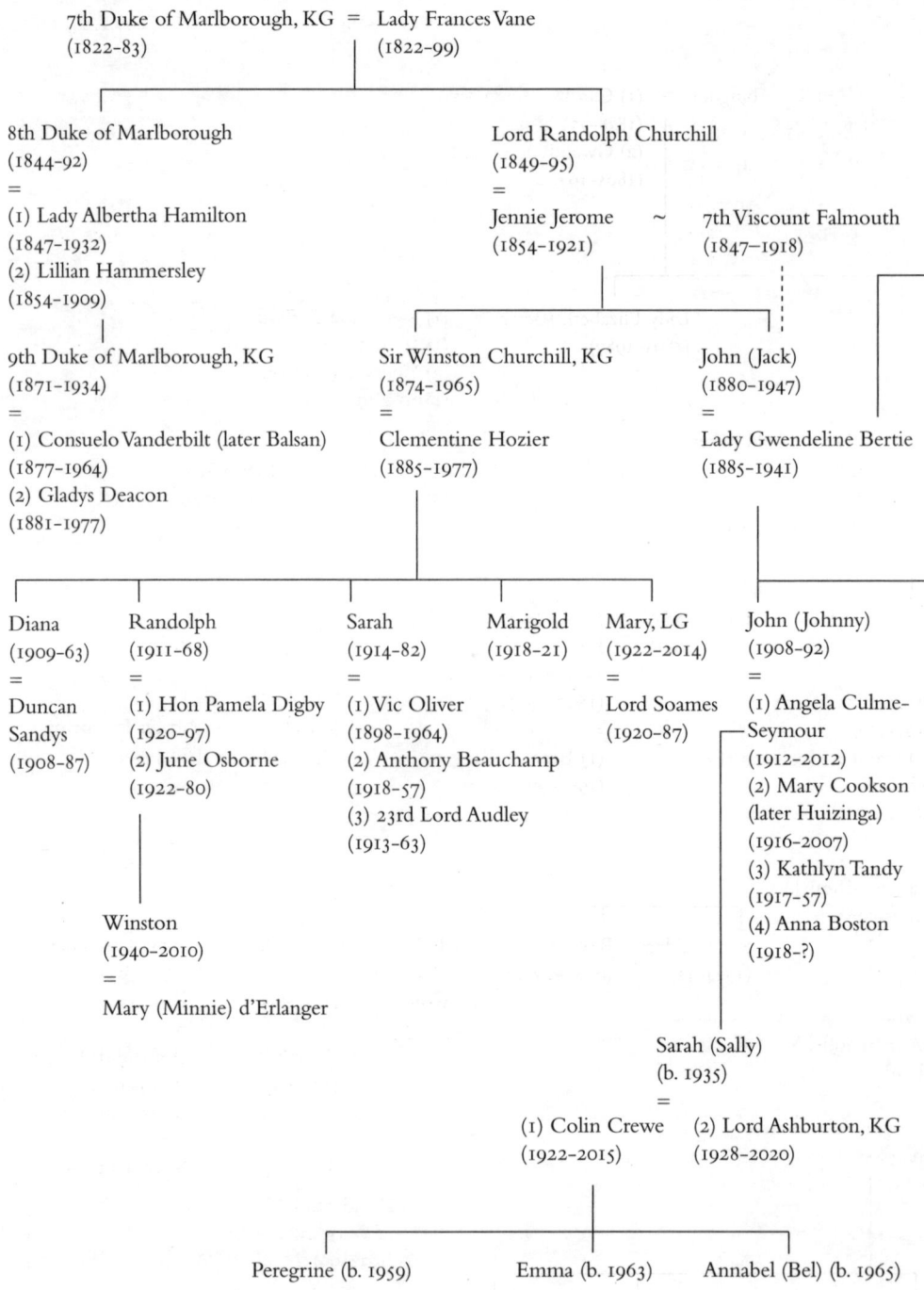

7th Duke of Marlborough, KG = Lady Frances Vane
(1822-83)   (1822-99)

8th Duke of Marlborough
(1844-92)
=
(1) Lady Albertha Hamilton
(1847-1932)
(2) Lillian Hammersley
(1854-1909)

Lord Randolph Churchill
(1849-95)
=
Jennie Jerome   ~   7th Viscount Falmouth
(1854-1921)   (1847-1918)

9th Duke of Marlborough, KG
(1871-1934)
=
(1) Consuelo Vanderbilt (later Balsan)
(1877-1964)
(2) Gladys Deacon
(1881-1977)

Sir Winston Churchill, KG
(1874-1965)
=
Clementine Hozier
(1885-1977)

John (Jack)
(1880-1947)
=
Lady Gwendeline Bertie
(1885-1941)

Diana   Randolph   Sarah   Marigold   Mary, LG   John (Johnny)
(1909-63)   (1911-68)   (1914-82)   (1918-21)   (1922-2014)   (1908-92)
=   =   =   =   =
Duncan   (1) Hon Pamela Digby (1) Vic Oliver   Lord Soames   (1) Angela Culme-
Sandys   (1920-97)   (1898-1964)   (1920-87)   Seymour
(1908-87)   (2) June Osborne (2) Anthony Beauchamp   (1912-2012)
               (1922-80)   (1918-57)   (2) Mary Cookson
                               (3) 23rd Lord Audley   (later Huizinga)
                               (1913-63)   (1916-2007)
                                                                           (3) Kathlyn Tandy
               Winston   (1917-57)
               (1940-2010)   (4) Anna Boston
               =   (1918-?)
               Mary (Minnie) d'Erlanger

                                                           Sarah (Sally)
                                                           (b. 1935)
                                                           =
                                    (1) Colin Crewe   (2) Lord Ashburton, KG
                                    (1922-2015)   (1928-2020)

                   Peregrine (b. 1959)   Emma (b. 1963)   Annabel (Bel) (b. 1965)

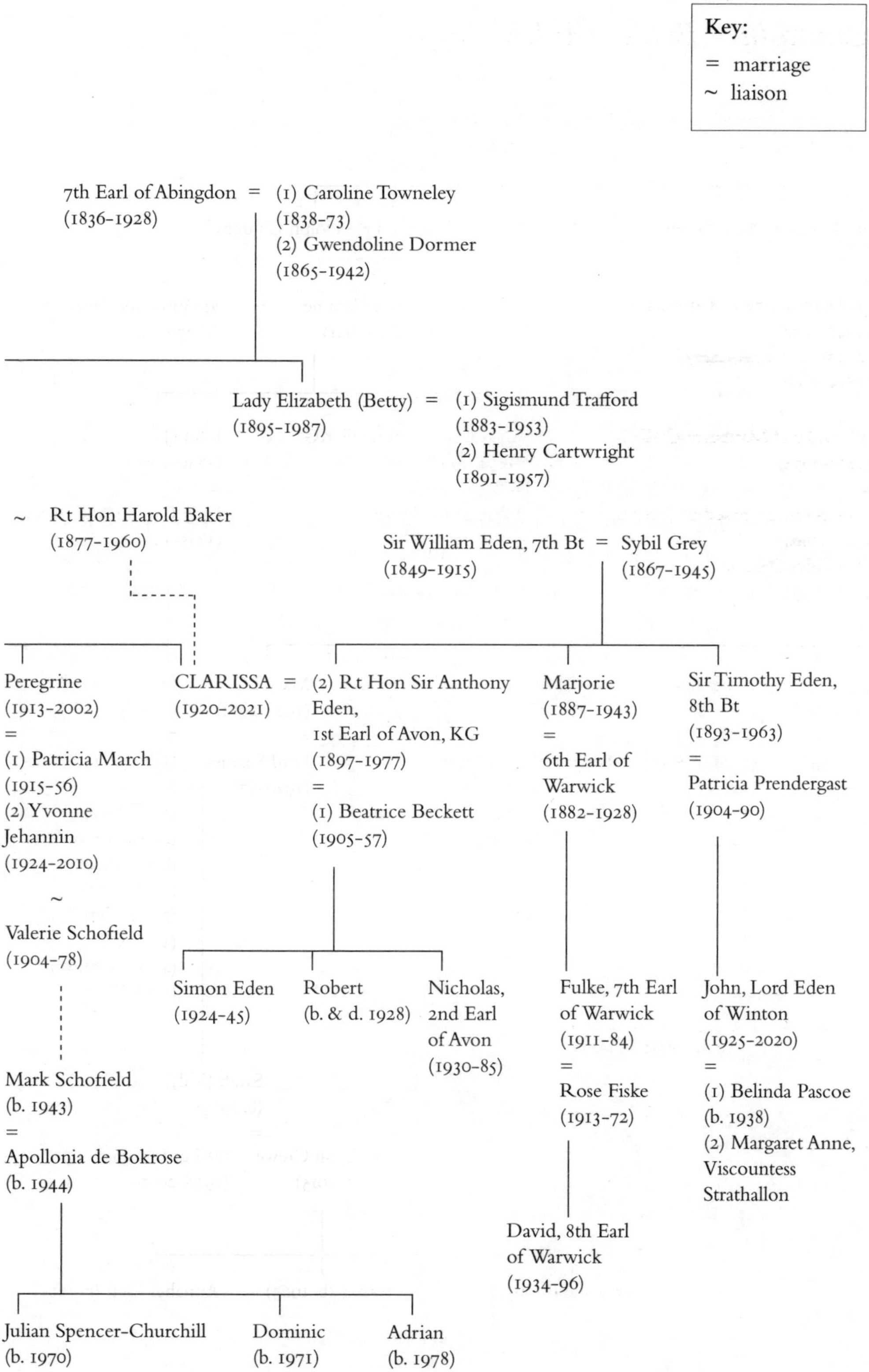

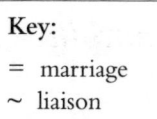

7th Earl of Abingdon = (1) Caroline Towneley
(1836-1928)　　　　　　(1838-73)
　　　　　　　　　　　　(2) Gwendoline Dormer
　　　　　　　　　　　　(1865-1942)

Lady Elizabeth (Betty) = (1) Sigismund Trafford
(1895-1987)　　　　　　　(1883-1953)
　　　　　　　　　　　　　(2) Henry Cartwright
　　　　　　　　　　　　　(1891-1957)

~ Rt Hon Harold Baker
　　(1877-1960)

Sir William Eden, 7th Bt = Sybil Grey
(1849-1915)　　　　　　　　(1867-1945)

Peregrine
(1913-2002)
=
(1) Patricia March
(1915-56)
(2) Yvonne
Jehannin
(1924-2010)

~

Valerie Schofield
(1904-78)

Mark Schofield
(b. 1943)
=
Apollonia de Bokrose
(b. 1944)

CLARISSA = (2) Rt Hon Sir Anthony
(1920-2021)　Eden,
　　　　　　1st Earl of Avon, KG
　　　　　　(1897-1977)
　　　　　　=
　　　　　　(1) Beatrice Beckett
　　　　　　(1905-57)

Simon Eden　Robert　　　Nicholas,
(1924-45)　　(b. & d. 1928)　2nd Earl
　　　　　　　　　　　　　of Avon
　　　　　　　　　　　　　(1930-85)

Marjorie
(1887-1943)
=
6th Earl of
Warwick
(1882-1928)

Fulke, 7th Earl
of Warwick
(1911-84)
=
Rose Fiske
(1913-72)

David, 8th Earl
of Warwick
(1934-96)

Sir Timothy Eden,
8th Bt
(1893-1963)
=
Patricia Prendergast
(1904-90)

John, Lord Eden
of Winton
(1925-2020)
=
(1) Belinda Pascoe
(b. 1938)
(2) Margaret Anne,
Viscountess
Strathallon

Julian Spencer-Churchill　Dominic　　Adrian
(b. 1970)　　　　　　　　　(b. 1971)　　(b. 1978)

Author's Note

I appreciate that the world in 2024 is a different place from what it was in the twentieth century. Clarissa's papers and diaries reflect and record what was said at the time, but the world of Churchill, Eden and Clarissa was one where the notions of gender and race were discussed in ways no longer considered acceptable. Some of the language used in this book when quoting from this source material is authentic to its time and, though potentially difficult to read now, it has been left in, as it is inextricable from Clarissa's life, her social circles, her experiences and her conversations during this period.

Introduction

Clarissa, Countess of Avon, was one of the most unusual women of the twentieth century. Well-connected as the niece of Winston Churchill, a quite extraordinary beauty, an intellectual and a bohemian, she was much loved by the great figures of her age. Yet she was remote and self-sufficient. If she had nothing of interest to say she said nothing. In 1952 she married Anthony Eden. Living at the heart of Britain's political life as wife to the Foreign Secretary and then at 10 Downing Street, she was a far from insignificant political wife.

Ill health and the Suez crisis caused Eden to resign in 1957, and for the next twenty years Clarissa cared for him in beautiful Wiltshire houses, entertained his political friends and wintered with him on Bequia and later in Barbados. After his death in 1977, she returned to her haute-bohemian existence. She selected her friends with care. Had a bomb dropped on her ninetieth birthday party, it would have wiped out a cross-section of the intellectual, aristocratic and artistic world of Britain. She was sharp, discriminating and acerbic. The best of friends, she was dismissive to those who bored her. She lived to be 101.

I was lucky to know her well for more than forty years, and she bequeathed me her private papers with a message that I might publish them if I wished. Essentially private, she dropped her guard with me as she knew I had discovered many of her secrets when writing about Cecil Beaton. I first became aware of her at a young age. I saw the Avons regularly in newspapers, and in real life at St George's Chapel, Windsor, where my interest in that particular world was ignited when I was twelve.

There was another connection. My grandfather, Cecil Vickers, had set up the stockbroking firm of Vickers, da Costa in 1917. Clarissa's father, John (Jack) Spencer-Churchill, was one of his partners, and Sir Winston was a client of the firm. Clemmie Churchill had presented both my aunts at court in the 1920s, and when, in 1936, my elder aunt, Joan Vickers, had wanted to go into politics, she had gone to see Winston Churchill at Chartwell to ask his advice.[*]

When I embarked on my biography of Gladys Deacon in 1975, my aunt contacted Clarissa to see if she had known Gladys. Clarissa invited us over for a drink at Alvediston.[†] So she who had been seen but distantly until then became real. I kept a note of the visit: 'Drove to Alvediston – lovely manor house, Queen Anne, done up by the last owner, white gates. Lady Avon opened the door herself. She is pretty, firm chin, wisps of white hair, otherwise fair. Green cashmere jumper, mass of gold chains, lovely ring with light blue stone on right hand, simple wedding ring on the other hand. Plastic watch (strange), suede shoes, skirt . . .'

Lady Avon poured me a large gin and tonic.

'Is it vodka?'

'You asked for gin so that's what you wanted.' She said: 'Anthony sends his apologies.' They had had a lunch guest and he was tired due to treatment for cancer. 'He doesn't know anything about Gladys Deacon, but thinks he remembers meeting her in the twenties.' She recalled Gladys on a train to Blenheim, her face a little too close to her mother's. It was a 'frightening face, ravaged by the operation.'[‡] When they arrived at Blenheim, the main hall was divided into coops, and each one had Blenheim spaniels and puppies in it. 'The smell was quite horrible.' It contrasted with the Duke who dined privately from gold plate, wearing his Garter riband and star.

She listened to what I had to say about Gladys in St Andrew's Hospital, and then the conversation switched to politics. She asked my aunt how young Winston Churchill was getting on. She showed us the garden, dovecote and outhouses. There were two huge banquettes in the conservatory and I spotted some Ambre Solaire. We stayed about an hour.[1]

---

[*] Dame Joan Vickers (1907–94), MP for Plymouth, Devonport 1955–74, later a life peer.

[†] Years later I looked in Clarissa's appointment diary for the day: 'Joan Vickers & nephew', she had written. Two days earlier Margaret Thatcher, the new leader of the Conservative Party, had come to lunch, arriving by helicopter in a field.

[‡] She had caused paraffin wax to be injected into her nose.

As we drove away, it did not occur to me, or to her, that I would go to her house again – let alone that in 2021, forty-six years later, I would give the eulogy at her funeral in the nearby church.

Lord Avon died on 14 January 1977, just before his eightieth birthday. Later that year I was part of a delegation invited to the Speaker's House at the House of Commons when Sir Lincoln Hallinan, chairman of the Commemorative Collectors' Society, presented a ceramic plate to a group of prime ministers, celebrating those who had served the Queen as such up to the year of the Silver Jubilee. It was a surreal experience to find myself in a room containing three former prime ministers and among them Clarissa and her stepson, Nicholas, 2nd Earl of Avon.*[2]

No sooner had I finished my Gladys Deacon biography in January 1979 than Lord Weidenfeld asked me to a dinner for Dame Rebecca West. I came in to find I knew nobody but recognised everybody.† After dinner Clarissa came on from the opera with some friends.‡ Lord Weidenfeld said: 'Clarissa tells me her father and your grandfather were partners. Go and say hello to her.' I went over. I saw a different side to her from the chatelaine of Alvediston, or the Prime Minister's widow at Westminster. She was frisky, like a skittish young girl. 'Am I hungry enough to eat this?' she asked, pushing the food across the table. She looked at the name card in front of her: Edna O'Brien. 'How very appropriate,' she said enigmatically.

Later that year I helped Laura, Duchess of Marlborough, with her memoirs, *Laughter from a Cloud,* and she filled me in about the characters who were appearing in my life, including Clarissa. It transpired

---

* There was gossip at prime ministerial level. When Harold Wilson came in, Sir Alec Douglas-Home said: 'Ah! Hark the Harold!' and when Harold Macmillan came in he said: 'Here's Harold doing his old man act.' One of the many interesting things that emerged as they talked over lunch was that Macmillan said he always knew if he would win or lose an election by the questions at meetings. If they asked a lot of questions, they were planning to vote for him. If they sat in polite and respectful silence, it was a lost cause. Harold Wilson agreed. I sat next to Wilson at lunch. He never addressed a word to me.

† The other guests included Lord and Lady Quinton, Kenneth Harris, Kenneth Rose, Marcia Falkender, Edna O'Brien, Martin Amis, Mark Boxer, Annabel Goldsmith and Valerie Wade. Princess Maria Gabriella of Savoy came in after dinner.

‡ One of them was Marina Berry, with whom Clarissa later went to the Caucasus.

that Lady Diana Cooper disliked her because they had both loved Raimund von Hofmannsthal, an Austrian of great charm, working with TimeLife in London. There was rivalry between Clarissa and Laura's sister, Ann Fleming, over the powerful and substantially built lawyer, Lord Goodman. Laura had known Anthony Eden – there had been a fling at some point. Both Laura and Clarissa had had homes in Barbados in the 1960s, and while most people thought Clarissa took wonderful care of Anthony in his last years, Laura thought her over-protective.

There was another Weidenfeld dinner in July. When the designer John Stefanides introduced me to Clarissa, she replied: 'I've known him since before he was born.' John invited me to dinner the following night before a dance given by Mark and Arabella Lennox-Boyd. Clarissa was there, the dinner was memorable because, rather late, in walked Bianca Jagger, still wearing the same yellow jacket and black trousers from the front page of the *Evening Standard* that day: she had been attending a hearing relating to her divorce from Mick.

Clarissa wrote to me when the Gladys biography was published in September 1979. I am convinced she played a role in my being asked to write the biography of Cecil Beaton. When getting directions to Beaton's home at Broadchalke in Wiltshire to see if I were to be approved as biographer, I had told his secretary, Eileen Hose, I knew my way to Alvediston. I had lunch with Cecil Beaton on Thursday, 13 December 1979, and at another Weidenfeld dinner the following Sunday, it sounded as though it was going to happen. Clarissa was at that dinner:

Harold Lever fell over which prompted Clarissa Avon to tell the story of how Lord Olivier was about to tell her why *Amadeus* was too long when he collapsed into some china and lay flat on the floor. Then he didn't move an inch. There was a car downstairs so Lady Olivier & the chauffeur put him in it. She returned and the dinner went on. 'And I never heard what he thought about *Amadeus*,' grinned Clarissa.[3]

Later she said: 'I hear you're doing Cecil. I'm so pleased.' She pronounced him 'Sissel'. She also said she hoped that I wouldn't make him too much the centre of it. Cecil Beaton died the following January, two days after I had started work. Clarissa was ashen-faced in the churchyard at Broadchalke as he was laid to rest in Wiltshire ground.

When I was working at Cecil Beaton's house, Eileen Hose said: 'Cecil wouldn't have bothered with her if she hadn't basically been nice.' I found Clarissa's letters, and in particular her startling description of the Profumo affair in 1963.* I detected her antipathy towards Mary Soames and how she hated Randolph Churchill. Then one day she materialised at Reddish House and invited me for a drink.†

I drove over to Alvediston. Clarissa had lots of advice on how to approach the Cecil Beaton book and she spoke of Garbo's 1951 visit, how captivating and mercurial she was.

She said: 'I told George that after this you must do a heavyweight. All right, Cecil. But then you must get away from the Royal Family.' We somehow got on to Mountbatten and she admitted she'd always had an allergy towards him. She said he was perverting the course of history by establishing his enormous, very expensive archive at Broadlands (entirely devoted to his career) because he was rich enough to do it. 'I've somehow managed to avoid going to any of the twenty memorial services for him.' She told me he had persuaded Anthony to go down to be part of the documentary series on his life – then later he asked him to write a letter, saying he congratulated him at London Airport on the work he'd done in India. Allan Noble, Eden's parliamentary private secretary, was consulted and said that that was impossible as they were never at the airport at the same time. 'So around came another Garter ceremony,' said Clarissa, 'and Anthony told Dickie he couldn't do that. Dickie said, "Well, it must have been somewhere else. It doesn't matter." It shows the lengths he'll go to.' Clarissa couldn't understand the way he'd hoodwinked the Queen and Prince Philip: 'Yes, Prince Charles – the great hero figure', but not the Queen, 'who isn't at all easy to convince'. But she said she'd watched the way that the Mountbattens, who were nowhere, suddenly became part of the royal procession. She said that Edwina was a good woman. 'After her death, he went off the rails.'

* *See pages 225–6.*
† I am conscious that I wrote a certain amount about Clarissa in *Malice in Wonderland*, but I excised a lot from the text planning to save it for this book. So most of these diary entries have not been published before.

She offered me space to work at Alvediston if that fitted and then, just as I was leaving, she said: 'Would you like to go to *Lucrezia Borgia* on Tuesday?'[4]

In June Eileen Hose mentioned that Clarissa was looking for a house sitter when she went away in the summer. I said: 'What about me?' So Clarissa and I had lunch in London and it was decided that I would provide my own food and cater for myself and she would provide wine. My duty was to walk the dogs. This fascinated Lady Diana Cooper, who had become a friend. She asked me: 'Are you going to live in open sin with her?' In July she returned to this point: 'But will you be all right?'

'I shan't want anything.'

'But will she want something?'[5] This seemed unlikely. She was then sixty. I was twenty-eight.

And so I arrived to stay at Alvediston. At the beginning we avoided each other by design. I had wondered how Clarissa spent her time. Mainly she listened to fine music and read books. She worked outside, her gardener coming into the library where I was working to say: 'Good morning, sir. Her Ladyship asked me to ask you if you like globe artichokes.'

Clarissa had been meant to go away but actually she didn't. We began to coincide our dinners, and I learnt more about her. It was helpful to have her guidance over Cecil. When I read his book, *My Bolivian Aunt*, I concluded that his exotic aunt was the most interesting of the three sisters. Clarissa said: 'I always thought her a fearful bore'[6] – one of her favourite condemnatory descriptions.

She discussed the problem of finding an official biographer for Lord Avon. Sir Philip Magnus suffered from cataracts and was too old. She wanted a historian who knew the period well, and was contemplating Professor Sir Jack Plumb. Alistair Horne was writing the life of Macmillan and was under Macmillan's thumb with his subject breathing down his neck. She was noncommittal about whether or not she might one day write her own memoir.

She told me that her father was devoted to my aunt, who was spoken of as his girlfriend.* She explained that she had fallen out with

---

* When my aunt was elected to the London County Council in March 1937, Clarissa's father wrote to her: 'Bravo! I am so glad you did it – now the H of C!! All complaints about rates – babies – drains etc will be forwarded in due course.'

her brother Johnny over some remarks he had made about the British Empire when she was nineteen. That situation deteriorated later.

She said that in India, lately, she had smoked hashish with Teddy Millington-Drake. She told me how the Christies had had Margaret Thatcher to dinner at Glyndebourne. Edward Heath had been there the same evening, but they could not invite him: 'He'd painted himself into a corner.'

Many of the characters that feature in this biography materialised or were discussed. She described how Ali Forbes,* had overtaken a lorry and trailer at great speed on his way to Glyndebourne. As he was being breathalysed, he spluttered about being in a dinner jacket. 'I should have kept a tweed jacket in the car!' His combative manner led to him accompanying the police to the station and he didn't get home until 6 a.m.[7]

Clarissa took me to a production of *Der Rosenkavalier* at Glyndebourne. She loved opera, though she hated Glyndebourne: the theatre was bad; it was full of businessmen entertaining their clients and, if anything remotely funny happened, they roared with laughter. More figures from her past appeared that night – Lord and Lady David Cecil: he had been at Oxford when she was there in 1939. We spotted Lord and Lady Hutchinson. Clarissa said that June Hutchinson (whom Cecil Beaton had tried to marry) did not speak to her as Jeremy had been her first great love, and as she said: 'Ever since Anthony died, she has viewed me with suspicion.' We ran into him in the interval, but not June. Clarissa had longed to tell her I was writing about Cecil and watch her reaction.[8]

At the end of my stay in Alvediston, Clarissa was going to Italy and I was going to France. I ventured: 'What a pity that our paths don't cross on this holiday.'

'Well, perhaps they do . . .'

Hardly had I spoken than she had worked out that it was possible for me to meet her in Siena. She telephoned Lord Lambton and I was invited to accompany her to his villa, Cetinale. By then, following his resignation from politics in a sex scandal in 1973, he was living a kind of *Brideshead Revisited* Lord Marchmain exile with his mistress, Claire

---

* Alastair Forbes (1918–2005), Anglo-American journalist, exhaustive book reviewer and man about town.

Ward. In preparation for the visit, she loaned me his unpublished (and unpublishable) novel with a 'hero' based on George Weidenfeld. She asked, 'Are you tough? Yes, you are,' before letting me have it. I read it, in considerable astonishment, with its evil depiction of the Baron. One scene had him about to marry into an aristocratic family. The family were in the garden and heard a sound. Looking up, they saw him testing the attic windows. He was conducting a private survey of the house to see how financially sound the family was; he tricked his authors out of their royalties, and worse. He held a girl's hands in 'a cold, sweaty paw'.

I caught up with Clarissa in Siena on 27 August. She had been travelling with the Salisburys.* It was typical of her to say that they were her oldest friends, but she couldn't have stood another day of them. After lunching with them, we drove to Cetinale.†

Tony Lambton was a great tease. He was intrigued by how much I knew about Clarissa. One evening I mentioned that I knew she found Mary Soames difficult at the breakfast hour. They all thought I knew more than I did and that nothing escaped me. Tony was relishing a row that had occurred between Ann Fleming and her granddaughter Mary, who had been staying in a house down the hill. Philip Ziegler was also there and wanted to see Cetinale. He tried to press Clarissa as to when Philip Magnus would be starting work on the Eden biography. She was dismissive. Ziegler was writing about Mountbatten. Clarissa told him how he cooked the books (in his archives). 'I must be careful not to overreact against that, certainly,' he said.[9]

When we left, Tony told Clarissa that I was 'the most sinister character. He doesn't forget a single thing you say. It's all filed away in the recesses of his mind.' Coming from him, I took this as a rare compliment. She was entertained that I had 'rattled' him.[10]

After house sitting and the Italy visit, Clarissa and I became great friends. I frequently stayed with her at Alvediston, she would come to dinner in my flat in Lexham Gardens, and we travelled together. Needless to say, mischievous figures such as Ali Forbes tried to insinuate that the relationship was more than that. At a book launch at the

* Robert, 6th Marquess of Salisbury (1916–2003), and his wife Mollie (1922–2016).
† I described this visit at length in *Malice in Wonderland* (pages 58–63).

Ritz he dived in with 'Not just house sitting, but also the Grand Tour . . .' and later asked about Laura: 'Or have you given her up in favour of Clarissa? Everyone is talking about it.' Diana Cooper nodded. I was horrified.[11]

I was lucky to have known many of the protagonists in this story – in particular Lady Diana Cooper, Laura, Duchess of Marlborough, Ali Forbes, but also Lady Gladwyn, Valentine Lawford and others. Cecil Beaton was a key figure whose life ran parallel with Clarissa's from 1940 to 1980. I got to know Sir Martin and Lady Charteris in the year of the Silver Jubilee (1977), Gay Charteris having been at Oxford with Clarissa in 1940.

In 1979 Laura had taken me to stay at Faringdon with Robert Heber Percy ('Mad Boy') who had inherited the house from Lord Berners. I had met Priscilla Bibesco in Paris, and her somewhat dodgy husband, Simon Hodgson. I had also met Clarissa's brothers, Johnny and Peregrine, and Sir Winston Churchill's daughter, Sarah. Winston and Minnie Churchill became friends as did Mary Soames, with whom I had worked on the International Year of the Child. Diana Cooper produced Harold Macmillan at lunch at Warwick Avenue.

Clarissa took me to the opera with Lord Goodman, followed by dinner at his table in the Savoy Grill. We visited the Metropolitan Museum in New York with Nin Ryan. Nin co-opted me onto her summer party list, invariably mustering three former prime ministers in the room. Thus many of the characters in this book are real to me.

My favourite stories centred around Clarissa's take on life. In Patmos in 1983 the way she expressed her wish to go home at the end of a dinner party was to say to me: 'We've rather exhausted the social possibilities of this meal, don't you think?'[12]

Many years later I told her that James Fairfax, an Australian philanthropist we both knew, had heard that I was in Canberra and intending to fly to Sydney. He invited me to lunch and sent a car to collect me, bring me to Bowral where he lived, and then on to Sydney later, a journey of at least 175 miles. Did she say: 'How nice of him'? Not at all. She said: 'He must have been desperate for company.'

She possessed a quality of positive negativity. In March 1982 I gave a dinner for the Emanuels, who had designed Diana, Princess of Wales's wedding dress the year before. Clarissa was older than the other guests but on top form. She arrived dressed in a black velvet suit with ecclesiastical gold on the shoulders and wonderful Elizabethan puff sleeves.

Clarissa told us she thought the Barbican centre unspeakably awful. Round pieces of wood for the floor, suspended lamps looking like steel poles with upturned goldfish bowls on the end, a ceiling made entirely of Meccano, and walls of sprayed rough concrete that tore your clothes – the only good thing about it was the acoustics. She made it sound deadly.

The conversation flitted over ballet, *Brideshead Revisited*, and found its most satisfactory outlet in *Dallas*. Clarissa said that in China she was always eating things 'that looked like Sue Ellen's lips'. She preferred shows like *Dallas* to *Brideshead*, which she thought less authentic.[*]

One of the guests was Nicholas Shakespeare[†] in 'smart mufti', a scarf thrown round his neck. He dominated the evening, steering the conversation the way he wished. He fell for Clarissa. She said later that he thought her a relict from history, even Asquith's widow. 'I was in the nursery then,' Clarissa said, more than once. Nicholas had worked on a BBC chat show that had required him to research statistics on the purchase of vibrators. He clearly dined out on this topic, telling us that a million were sold each year. If I was anxious about where this conversation was going, I need not have worried. Clarissa came out with: 'You mean you can get circumcised ones and uncircumcised ones?'[13]

[*] *Dallas* greatly amused Clarissa, perhaps surprisingly. She enjoyed all the grown men like J.R. talking about their 'daddies'.
[†] Nicholas Shakespeare (born 1957), novelist and later biographer of Bruce Chatwin and Ian Fleming.

PART ONE

I. WINSTON, JACK AND GOONIE

Clarissa described her background as a mixture of 'high aristocracy and bohemian',[1] by which she meant her mother's family, the Berties. Her father's family, the Churchills, descended from William Churchill in Devon at the time of Edward IV, and from the Spencers, originally from Wormington in Lancashire at the time of Henry VIII. Her father, Jack, more formally Major John Strange Spencer-Churchill DSO, was born at Phoenix Park, Dublin, on 4 February 1880, the younger son of Lady Randolph (Jennie) Churchill at a time when Lord Randolph was secretary to his father, the 7th Duke of Marlborough, Lord Lieutenant of Ireland from 1876 to 1880. The elder boy was Winston Churchill.

Jack went to Elstree School and Harrow, served in the Second Boer War, and the First World War, in which he was awarded his DSO. He went into the Stock Exchange, becoming a partner with Paul Nelke* in Nelke, Phillips & Bendix in 1906. All those of German origin were drummed out of the Stock Exchange in 1917 due to anti-German feeling towards the end of a long war. My grandfather, Cecil Vickers, had also been a partner of Nelke, Phillips. He mustered backers (including Sir Ernest Cassel) and started his own firm, Vickers, da Costa, in 1917, taking Jack with him and making him one of the six partners in 1921. In 1938 a new partnership was formed, my grandfather holding 45.5 per cent of the shares, and Jack 12 per cent.

---

* Paul Nelke (1860–1925), a larger-than-life figure, who worked arduously in the City, had brilliant success on the turf, and was a formidable opponent in a card game. When he died, it was noted: 'Of German birth, there was no more loyal citizen of the adopted land in which he lived his life.' His daughter Maud (1891–1982) married Gilbert Russell, and they lived at Mottisfont Abbey, where she commissioned Rex Whistler to paint the murals. Her war diaries were published – *A Constant Heart* (Dovecote Press, 2017).

Clarissa said little about Jack, other than that he left for the office early and returned late, retreating into his study with the *Evening Standard*. She was allowed about fifteen minutes with him. She saw more of him on holiday. Her brother Johnny was more forthcoming: 'Father . . . had elegance and charm. He was slightly better-looking than my uncle, with a more clearly cut mouth, blue eyes and the same distinctive cranium as all Churchills. People sought his company, but frankly he was not what I would call intelligent.'[2] Father and son shared a passion for Wagner, and although Jack had a first-class library, he spent more time admiring the covers and bindings than reading the books. Johnny's first wife, Angela Culme-Seymour, described Jack as 'friendly, talkative, and mildly flirtatious . . .'[3]

Jack had a splendid moustache. Winston's children used to call him 'Uncle Well I Know But . . .' due to his frequent use of that expression and they teased him for the number of 'whats' in his conversation. He dismissed things he did not like as 'playing the ass'. When Johnny wanted to leave Vickers, da Costa to be an artist, Jack's response was 'Why slave for a few pence when for doing nothing except sign a few documents you can drink champagne and smoke cigars for the rest of your life?'[4] Johnny thought his parents got on well enough, yet with 'no intellectual communication between them'.[5] They played mah-jong after dinner while scarcely speaking. They loved the opera, but more for social reasons than the music. His father closed windows; when he left for the office, his mother reopened them. Peregrine was closest to his father, admiring him and taking an interest.

Jack may have had a Churchillian cranium, but was he a Churchill? There was a long gap between the birth of Winston and Jack in 1874 and 1880. Some suggested that this was because Lord Randolph suffered from syphilis. That and the rumours as to Jack's biological parentage found their way into books, and were fiercely and litigiously denied by his younger son, Peregrine. In 1975 Gladys, Duchess of Marlborough, married to Jack's first cousin, told me that the reason Jack was so in awe of his brother Winston was because they had different fathers, and she had no reason to invent that.[6]

Jennie had many lovers. There were numerous candidates for Jack's biological father. In 1940 James Pope-Hennessy was told that Jack had Austrian blood, his father being Prince Karl Kinsky.[*7] Other candidates were the Earl of Roden and Earl Cowley.[†] Anita Leslie and the Leslie family (not always accurate) advanced Evelyn Boscawen, 7th Viscount Falmouth (1847–1918), known as 'Star'. His father had been a keen racing man and won the Derby with Fred Archer in the saddle. Johnny told Chips Channon that it was him.[8] The Leslie theory was supported by Anne Sebba in her 2007 biography of Jennie, and in 2023, DNA tests undertaken by Julian Schofield (now Spencer-Churchill) in Canada – he discovered he descended from Peregrine – added weight to this idea.[9]

★ ★ ★ ★ ★

There are numerous descriptions of Jack's wife, Lady Gwendeline Bertie. Goonie, as she was known, came from a Catholic family. She was the daughter of the 7th Earl of Abingdon, and his second wife, Gwendoline Charlemagne-Dormer. As a child she lived with her parents at Wytham Abbey, three miles north-west of Oxford, originally a fifteenth-century abbey.

Goonie's father had been the Earl since 1884. She descended from the Berties, of Bearsted, Kent, in 1501, later Dukes of Ancaster and Earls of Lindsey, and from the Norreys family, seated in Lancashire at the time of Henry III. They owned Rycote in Oxfordshire, where Elizabeth I and Charles I had stayed, but the 3rd Earl pulled most of it down to enrich Wytham Abbey in the 1700s. Clarissa's grandfather had to sell Rycote in 1913, and by 1920 he found Wytham Abbey too expensive, so he sold it and settled at Oakden Holt, near Oxford. He was an officer in the Oxfordshire Yeomanry, a magistrate, a convert to Roman Catholicism, and in retirement penned occasional letters to *The Times*, 'marked by sound sense on current topics'.[10] He lived to be ninety-one.

Goonie married Jack on 8 August 1908. In the early years of her marriage she was present at many society events at the highest level – the opera, being presented at court by her sister-in-law Clemmie in

---

* Prince Karl Kinsky (1858–1919) was the one Chips Channon favoured.
† Gladys suggested Earl Cowley, but the 2nd Earl would have been too old, and the 3rd Earl too young.

1910, and at the Duke of Marlborough's house party at Blenheim for King Manoel of Portugal in 1911. Winston invited her to launch the battleship *Marlborough* at Devonport in October 1912, and she dined with the Asquiths at 10 Downing Street.

In 1915 Goonie introduced Winston to painting when he was staying at a rented farm in Surrey, when he resigned from the Cabinet. He did not take to watercolours so she steered him to oils. He painted her after the First World War in what William Rees-Mogg described as 'a study in that mild but chronic depression that some women suffer in middle life . . . One half sympathises with her and half regrets her mood of frustration.'[11] She was also painted by Sir John Lavery and Ambrose McEvoy.

There are many tributes to Goonie's other-worldliness, written in the style of the day. Margot Oxford wrote that she was 'an example of all that was tender, affectionate and feminine. She had the dangerous quality of charm. But with her "charm" had no danger . . . She had a feeling mind . . .'[12] Lady Cynthia Asquith was yet more lyrical: 'Her alluring mermaid beauty has a strange translucent quality; her wide-opened eyes are like blue flowers.'[13] Another friend described her as 'a living poem . . . Her personality combined the greatest distinction and sweetness with a truly original, almost fastidious mind . . . She had a way of illuminating people by her sudden enchanting comments.'[14] Lord David Cecil was a friend of long standing, who later tutored Clarissa at Oxford:

> Lady Gwendeline Churchill's extraordinary charm was implicit in her appearance, her subtle twilight beauty, the fastidious grace of her dress. But it disclosed its power fully only in intimate conversation . . . Pensive, dreamy, with an intense refinement of feeling and a delicate sensibility to the beautiful, she exhaled romance. But unexpectedly mingled with the romance was a touch of eighteenth century elegance, clear-eyed shrewdness, an amused scepticism, expressing itself in an enchanting mischievous irony which flickered over every phase of her talk . . . She was like the single final flower of a high civilisation, bred through generations to bloom once only, for the wonder and delight of mankind.[15]

Clarissa's godmother, Anne, Lady Islington, thought Goonie 'an enchanting spirit who seemed to belong partly to another and more romantic age and partly to a world above the one we live in – a blending of Mary Stuart and Botticelli's *Spring* . . . The learned, the frivolous, the sad, the gay, the great, and the obscure were thus all the same to her. Though spiritually remote – the little intrigues and ambitions of men would bring a look of wondering pity to her calm blue eyes – she was also strengthening and comforting'.[16] Angela Culme-Seymour found her 'gracious and rather distant'.[17]

★ ★ ★ ★ ★

Jack and Goonie married in 1908. But it could all have been very different. The previous summer, Goonie was unmarried and unengaged. Winston Churchill was thirty-seven and already a well-known politician. He had dabbled in several love affairs, notably with Pamela Plowden, Muriel Wilson, and the American actress Ethel Barrymore. He had met Pamela in India in 1896, declaring her 'the most beautiful girl I have ever seen'.[18] He was still professing his love in 1898, though she had told him he was incapable of affection. In 1901 he told his mother: 'There is no doubt in my mind that she is the only woman I could ever live happily with.'[19] It seems that he proposed to her that year at Warwick Castle. She turned him down and in 1902 she married Victor, 2nd Earl of Lytton. She and Winston remained life-long friends. The Winston-Pamela relationship floundered due to his – and her – lack of money, and his tunnel-vision devotion to politics.

None of the biographers is forthcoming about Muriel Wilson, a great Edwardian beauty, and the love of Winston's cousin, Sunny, 9th Duke of Marlborough, before he was made to drop her in favour of Vanderbilt money. Winston seems to have proposed to her in 1904, but she did not consider he had a great future. Somewhere in this mix he proposed to Ethel Barrymore, who told his son Randolph that, like Pamela, she could not have coped with 'the great world of politics'.[20]

There was unquestionably a flutter of romance with Goonie in August 1907. They met at Salisbury Hall, Lady Randolph Churchill's 1668 manor house near St Albans, invited there by Jack. This was shortly before Winston set off on his 'African journey', later to be the subject of an entire book. This romance has not been entirely overlooked. Mary Soames accepted that Winston and Goonie took to each other: 'and a flirtatious "jokey" relationship sparked between them at which – to judge from the three light-heartedly teasing letters extant* she wrote to him in late August – Goonie set the pace'.[21]

Writing in *Citadel of the Heart*, a composite history of later Churchills, John Pearson took the line that Winston could not wait to score off his brother. He wrote that Jack 'hero-worshipped Winston – but even Jack's powers of hero-worship would have been severely tested had he realised that something more than innocent affection was developing between his brother and the girl he loved'. Pearson did not know 'how far or how consciously Churchill encouraged Goonie.'[22] Neither Mary Soames nor Pearson, nor any other Churchill biographer, saw Winston's letters to her because Clarissa never released them. But in 2005 she told Anne Sebba, then researching Jennie: 'It is quite clear that Winston was in love with Goonie when he was young.'[23]

After the first meeting, Winston sent Goonie a telegram, keen to know what penance she suffered as a result of her precipitous departure from Salisbury Hall. From Coombe Abbey, she wrote that she had left when 'the early morning dew was still on the ground, shining like as many crystals, do you remember?' She had endured a long day of travel, it being a bank holiday, and on her return had been rebuked by her mother. She told him:

> I loved my Sunday at Salisbury Hall. It was a well organised day, by nature & by weather. It was lovely, it was interesting, it was enjoyable, to me at least. I do hope that it will be repeated again, but such heavenly days never are & why? It is a shame. It really is.[24]

On 11 August Winston replied from Tring Park, home of Lord Rothschild, teasing her for leaving them:

> I enjoyed Sunday immensely. It must be repeated. But how? But where? These are questions to wh you must help & find an answer. I

* In all there are seven letters.

hope indeed I shall see you again before I start on my journeys. Do try to make a plan; for five months is an age – & you will have forgotten that I exist before I return.

   Alas! Alas!

He launched into a long description of his field day at Tidworth on Sir Ian Hamilton's staff, his stay at Tring, mentioned failing to visit his earlier love, Pamela Lytton, and his plans to attend the French manoeuvres:

> I am so glad you were not bored on Sunday. You sit so silent & demure at table that no one can tell whether the conversation is indifferent to you; & I always get drawn into stupid arguments about politics & forget all the claims of others to have their own special interests talked about – nay more – to talk about their own special interests. So I was afraid afterwards that perhaps you had formed the poorest opinion of my manners.

He urged her to tell him her plans, '& also the plan wh will enable us to meet again, because I would like to see you so much before I go away.'[25]

Was that a love letter? Winston's love letters were invariably about himself. His letters to Pamela Plowden were similar and he had been staggeringly unsympathetic to her in 1900 when her half-brother died aged four: 'I am as full of sympathy as I can be. Poor Bird . . . Babies' deaths are the least sad of all partings: but women feel them most. A strong man full of hope and enthusiasm seems to me a greater cause for sorrow when he is stricken down.'[26]

On 14 August Goonie wrote:

> My dear Mr Winston,
>   Yes, we must meet again, before you leave us on your long long travels, but when, and how? That is what you ask me to answer, and that is what you want me to make a plan for, and that is what I cannot do without your help; how can I!?

She gave him a run-down of her plans and wondered if there was a chance he might be at Blenheim before the French manoeuvres.

She was at Eaton Hall, home of the Grosvenors, listening to Lord Hugh Cecil's conversation:

> I love listening to good talkers, that is why I sit so demure & silent when you are there! I have just got a letter from Pamela, a very happy letter, but poor darling she complains that pillows give no news! Perhaps I might be going up to London for the day some time next week. May I let you know if I do, & perhaps you could come & lunch or something.[27]

He urged her to come to London to 'see Parliament prorogued & dine with me. I will try & make a pleasant dinner with some of your friends, & somebody to look after you.' He had been caught with all-night sittings in the House of Commons and was about to set off for the Transvaal, or so he thought: 'So do come & dine on Wed & let us see each other to say goodbye like Christians. I expect before I return you will be married & I shall have converted to the faith of Islam. One never knows.'[28]

The reference to her being married implies some interest in that direction. But Goonie could not come to London, due to 'a chain of impossibilities'. She had wanted to:

> Dear Mr Winston,
>
> It is positively cruel of Fate to determine that we should not say goodbye, not to allow us the opportunity of bidding each other a friendly farewell, for it is a long time to lose sight of someone, five months, it is five months that you will be away for, is it not, & that is a long time, & I really do think it might have been allowed us – I can not help rebelling against fate, for how utterly unreasonable it can be, considering what pleasure it would have given us, I made the assertion in the plural, why I can not think, but all the same you would have liked me to have come & dined & I would have liked to have done so . . .

She hoped he would not convert to Islam and was sure he would have a 'wildly interesting' trip.[29] As it happened, Winston's trip was postponed. He sent his next letter on the same day, 27 August, telling her he was going to stay with Lady Crewe at Crewe Hall and going to Paris on Sunday night, 1 September, but he resigned himself to not seeing her, thus:

A solitary scapegrace – or should it be scapegoat? – wanders out into the wilderness: And not even one feminine pocket handkerchief salutes his departure with a wave – let alone – a tear . . . Still it is nice of you to say you want to, & would like to see me again & I like you vy much. So don't obliterate me from your mind because I am going away for a long time, but write me some [a line torn from the original letter] all beginning and no end – but with a ring of comradeship & understanding in them, such as has of late crept into *my* mind at least, so far as our correspondence is concerned.[30]

On 28 August Goonie told him she had hoped to come to London: 'I wish I could go with you to Paris on Sunday . . .'[31] – hardly in tune with the growing love she was meant to have for his brother. On 7 September she wrote again: 'Where are you? Where have you been? Where are you going to? What are you going to do? I have lost you for a whole week. I want to find you again. You have effaced yourself from my horizon.'

She wanted to know about his forthcoming trip, and hoped he was not going to Uganda since it was 'a country of fevers, man killing country, full of pestilentious insects and poisonous marshes, you really must not go there.' She bade him farewell.[32]

Winston and Goonie did not meet again before he set off on his African journey. On 10 September Pamela Lytton told him that Goonie had been at Doncaster races – 'ever more beautiful and nice. We talked about you.'[33] In Venice he ran into his cousin, the Duke of Marlborough.* As he sailed past Aden, to Camp Thika, near Nairobi, he continued to write to Goonie. Oblivious to developments back in England, he wrote on 15 October from HMS *Venus*, on the Red Sea, answering her last letter. He apologised if she had found him 'an awful bore – always haranguing everyone on my own particular subjects, & always thinking about amusing my own mind & not

---

* The Duke was skulking following his recent separation from Consuelo Vanderbilt. Gladys Deacon was there too. She became his second wife when Consuelo finally deigned to grant the Duke a divorce.

unfolding others! . . . I confess it & am so sorry. I never feel at ease in conversation. Either I am silent or no one else can talk. These are great faults: but you cannot say I have not confessed them frankly. Now give your blessing.'[34]

Winston wrote again on 18 November, while at sea on the Great Lake, declaring himself envious that his private secretary, Eddie Marsh, had received a letter from her. He asked her: 'And what are you doing all the time? & when are you going to write & tell me about it? I hope I shall find a nice long letter at Gondokoro when – if ever – we arrive there.' He then returned to his more boastful persona: 'You have no idea what a swell an Under-secretary is when he comes to visit these sorts of places. Imagine a combination of Napoleon & the Pope. That will give you some sort of faint idea. How respectful you will all have to be when I come home! & how kind – or I shall go away again & bury myself in the depths of illimitable space – forever', ending his letter: 'Now with best love, my dear, Yours ever, W.'[35]

That letter was written on 18 November. Four days earlier, Jack wrote to him to tell him that 'a wonderful thing' had happened, though Winston did not receive the letter until about 19 December:

> Goonie loves me. I have loved her for a long time – but have always attempted to put thoughts of that kind out of my mind – because I felt that I had nothing to give her – and also chiefly because I never for one moment imagined that she would ever care for me.
>
> About six months ago – I found that she loved me. We had long talks and spoke quite openly to each other. We agreed it was impossible for us to marry – and I promised always to remain a friend to her. Since you went away & until to-night I have not seen her – except on the race-course at Doncaster for a few moments (we were not in the same house). But my love for her was too strong – and at last I wrote and asked if she would wait for me.
>
> She answered that she could not promise to do so. I accepted that. What else could I do? I have nothing in the world to offer her.
>
> But a week afterwards she wrote again and told me her love for

me was stronger than anything else. She said that she would sacrifice anything for her love; and that her ambition for riches and everything else had all vanished and that she would wait for me until I could come and fetch her.

I saw her tonight here in London – and we agreed that our love is too strong to fight against. I have promised to come for her as soon as I can and we are <u>secretly</u> engaged.

<u>This is absolutely secret</u>. Only my mother and George [Cornwallis-West – Lady Randolph's second husband] know about it. Her parents know nothing, nor must they – until I can come up with some proposition.[36]

Jack balanced his joy against the practical issues of money, her being a Catholic, and the reaction of her angry parents. He pointed out to his brother: 'You were in love really once* – and you know what that meant. But you had other things to think of. Your career and your future filled more than half of your life. I love the same way you did – But I have no other thoughts.'[37]

On 21 November Jack wrote again to inform his brother that Goonie had spoken to her mother, who was sympathetic though disapproving. He had approached Paul Nelke, hoping to realise a salary of £1,000 a year. He said: 'I told you – I remember last summer – that I did not believe she would marry a poor man. But that was all wrong.'[38] On the same day, Lady Randolph wrote to Winston: 'I sometimes thought you had designs in that quarter – but not serious ones – & Goonie has always cared for Jack. They are both much in love but will have to wait a long time I'm afraid . . .'[39]

Goonie wrote to Winston on 26 November:

My dear Winston,

Winston 'tout court' I call you, in view of my becoming your sister in law in due time. That is what I am going to become to you. Tell me, do you like the prospect? Is it agreeable to you? I have fallen in love with Jack, and he with me, and we want to marry each other so much – but we have to wait, as we have no money at present – it

---

* Presumably Pamela Plowden.

will come, the money, some day, & that day must be soon, and it will
be soon – & meanwhile we love each other – Winston – Jack is your
brother and you are devoted to him, and of course you are interested
in his welfare. I promise you I will be such a good wife to him, and
always his slave. I will make him happy, and I will try my utmost to
be worthy of him.

She thanked him for writing from the Red Sea: 'It was so nice of you
to write at all, to have remembered that I was existing even! Amongst
all the pomp & ceremony of your state progress . . .'[40] She wrote again
on 16 December:

My dear Winston,

Letters take a long time to come from the Great Lake, you know,
I have only just got yours written from there, today, it has taken
nearly a whole month . . .

Jack & I are so happy; but, Winston, is it not cruel that I am not
allowed to see him, & even writing has been forbidden, though I do
write all the same! Don't you think that it is positively cruel to
impose this on us?

You see, this dreadful financial crisis has upset the City & it has
upset Jack – & though Mother has been told that we want to marry,
Father has not been yet, because nothing definite can be settled
about money, and Jack does not know exactly how much he has got
& how much he will have & all that, and as my Father is – well,
rather difficult to 'tackle' we thought it wd be better to wait & tell
him when everything is absolutely straight & square, which is sure to
be very soon – and meanwhile my Mother does not allow me to see
him; *and we do love so!* I know that you love a woman, Winston, very
much and you know what it means* – you can imagine what I am
going through not being able to visit Jack – I call it positively cruel.[41]

It must have been a considerable shock to Winston when these
letters reached him in Uganda on about 19 December. There had

---

* She must have been referring to Pamela Lytton, who had appeared in their
correspondence from time to time. It could not have been Clementine Hozier in
1907.

been long delays and their messages had crossed. He had been flirting with Goonie, while she was committing herself to his brother. Winston sent Jack a telegram of congratulations and on 22 December he wrote to Goonie:

My dear Goonie,

I am glad to hear your great news. I am more fond of Jack than anybody else I can think of at present in the world. He is a dear – good, brave, honourable & trustworthy. You could not find anyone in whom you could put more confidence. He has not had vy much fun in life, for there has been so little money, & he has not been able to enjoy many of the pleasures, hunting, shooting, polo and other sports wh others in his position in life have had. He has had to deny himself many things, & to work vy hard indeed. I have often felt sad to think of his hard work & long lonely evenings, & wondered whether & how I could do anything to help him. But now that you love him & he loves you & you are going to be married – the whole proportion of things is changed & it is I who look at him with eyes of wistful envy and admiration, because of the great passion by which he is illumined & which he has been able to inspire in you. May you both ever be happy and prosperous is my most sincere and profound desire.

And *of course* be brave. Jack has high abilities – & I think the emergency & your influence will draw from him latent qualities of initiative & construction. You are good & beautiful & strong. Really if you two superior creatures – as creatures go – cannot do what the poorest people in the country do, & what all creation does, namely – create as you choose, what are we to think of the civilisation we asked to be so proud of? I am quite sure ways & means can be arranged on a modest but sufficient scale. In a few years Jack will be making a good income out of his business. Later will come £2,500 a year. There are only a few years of difficulty & struggle. But how well worth while. They will be gilded by your loves for each other; & afterwards they will be another bond between you. I am sure you will be perfectly happy, if only you do not worry about that silly, vain, chattering London, but lead a simple life with all its great joys and true dignity. Even if there was no money at all – & Jack had no prospects – I would urge you

– loving each other as you do – to run all risks. For what is the use of living here below – if stupid social conventions and little petty sordid needs are to be held sufficient to rob men and women of the one golden joy that God meant them to have, and around which all creation plays?

Well God bless you my dear Goonie. I am indeed proud to have such a delightful & fascinating sister-in-law. I am sure you will always be kind to me – for sometimes I am down on my luck – now you are taking Jack – I shall be quite alone. I for my part will do everything in my power to further your wishes & plans, & to wear away any obstacles that may threaten delay. Don't have a long engagement. Insist on having your way, & let the old world change its step to suit your resolves, or run askew. That is the way to win.

Always your friend
Winston[42]

Jack wrote again on 19 December, telling Winston that Paul Nelke was promising a better arrangement for him. Lady Abingdon, Goonie's mother, was in the picture. Lord Abingdon was still in the dark. Jack had managed to see Goonie for two minutes at a railway station: 'Was there ever such a way of making love. She has been at Wytham – and she promised her mother not to see me. So I had to waylay her by accident at the station one day. We write pages to each other all day – but I never see her . . .'[43]

Winston returned from his African journey on 17 January 1908. Goonie, dressed in white crêpe-de-Chine, trimmed with orange blossom, married Jack at the Church of St Aloysius, Oxford, on 8 August. Winston was best man.

Winston and Clementine Hozier began to correspond on 16 April 1908. Three days after Jack's wedding, Winston proposed to her at Blenheim. 'It is done & done forever,' wrote the groom to Jack and Goonie. 'I am to marry Clemmie almost at once. I hope we shall be happy like you are, and always all four of us bound together by the most perfect faith & comradeship.'[44] Winston and Clemmie were married rather more grandly, at St Margaret's, Westminster, on 12 September.

What are we to deduce from this? Winston's letters to Goonie were as near love letters as he was capable of writing. Churchill biographers dismiss the earlier women as mere preludes to his great and lasting love for Clemmie. Fair enough, but it could be that having failed to secure Lady Gwendeline, he simply settled on Clementine Hozier. He certainly wasted no time in so doing.

2. BORED AT BOARDING SCHOOL
1920–35

Jack and Goonie had two sons – John (or Johnny), born in 1909, and Peregrine (or Pebin) in 1913. Observing them in 1918, Clemmie Churchill judged them both charming: 'Pebin has dropped his churlish manners & is most gracious keeping however a shy & dignified reserve. John is very happy at school & is a dear little boy.'[1]

There was a gap until Clarissa was born on 28 June 1920. She was named Anne after her godmother, Lady Islington, Clarissa from the novel *Clarissa* by Samuel Richardson (1748), and Nicolette from a famous poem.* Her grandmother, Lady Abingdon, inspected her and predicted 'a fine tall graceful woman'.[2] Her birth prompted Winston to write to Goonie: 'Beloved Goonie, I am so glad – & that it is a girl too. You wanted that in . . . general outfit. Perhaps it will be another Goonie! At any rate that is something to look forward to. With great love . . .'[3] In his memoirs, Johnny dropped a sly hint about his sister's parentage:

> Among the eminent literary men and scholars who surrounded her [Goonie] at this address [Ebury Street] one stands out more clearly than the rest because of his brain and inscrutable face. He is the Rt Hon. Harold Baker, later the Warden of Winchester College and a lifelong friend of my mother. Even since my mother's death he has remained on close terms with my sister Clarissa. My father once told me that 'Bluey' Baker, as he is known, regards Clarissa as one of the few women in this world with a first-class brain.[4]

---

* Possibly *Aucusson et Nicolette*, a French sung story from medieval times?

So was Clarissa a Churchill? She was always close to her mother, but less so to her father; neither did she ever express a particular affinity with the Churchill family.

Her biological father was Harold 'Bluey' or 'Bluetooth' Baker, a Liberal politician and scholar. She had more in common with him in looks and in brains. An enigma in his schooldays at Winchester, he went on to New College, Oxford, and surpassed all others in promise and achievement, as a Craven Scholar, Hertford Scholar and Eldon Scholar. He devoted himself to classical scholarship, and became President of the Oxford Union. He was called to the bar, served as an MP in Asquith's government from 1910 to 1918, and was sworn as a Privy Councillor in 1915 before he was forty. He opposed granting the vote to women.

Though destined for a great career, Baker's political career ended in 1918. 'Was it deafness, or private means, or some lack of ambition or of physical vigour which held him back?' asked one of his later friends.[5] The world's loss was Winchester's gain for he settled down as Warden of Winchester College from 1936 to 1946, also serving as bursar. Even when ill at the end of his life 'this alert and courteous sage was still able to enchant the pilgrim to Crab Wood (his home near Winchester) with his acute yet gentle questions and comments and his unfailing sympathy, humour and charm'.[6] That great muse to the Pre-Raphaelites, Lady Horner, loved to entertain him at Mells Manor in Somerset, just as she also entertained Clarissa and her mother:

> Through the kaleidoscope of the past so many changing figures come and go, and friends I have known and loved claim a place in the pages of my life. None more so than Harold Baker, who has extended his close and early friendship with Raymond Asquith [her son-in-law] to me and mine, and who for many years has been a cherished guest in my home.[7]

Clarissa saw him throughout her life. She frequently stayed with him at Crab Wood, and even crossed the Channel to France with him when a teenager. He bequeathed her a wood and, at her request, all his books. Clarissa only became certain that he was her father when he died, and she saw the contents of his will. Like many children she could scarcely contemplate her parents having sex with each other, let alone her mother straying to a lover.

In *Citadel of the Heart,* John Pearson shirked writing much about Clarissa's father, Jack, and avoided tackling her parentage. He was aware that Johnny suggested Winston might have cuckolded Jack as Bluey had done. Ali Forbes was categorical that Clarissa was not a Churchill, and as Pearson put it: 'Peregrine alternated between anger at his Uncle over the way he treated his Papa, and a curious lack of knowledge over Pater when one asked him anything precise.'[8]

Johnny wrote that his mother had always longed for a daughter and lavished attention on her. Her brothers became 'the boys' but Clarissa was 'everything to Mother; too much, perhaps, because as frequently happens in such situations, Mother was possessive to a degree'.[9] The family lived at 41 Cromwell Road opposite the Natural History Museum, where at one time Winston and Clemmie had lived with them, family finances being low. Clarissa found it surprising that she acquired any visual taste as she gazed on the massive terracotta Romanesque façade of the enormous museum. However, she relished the proximity of the Victoria and Albert Museum, with its glorious treasures.

Clarissa described her parents as Liberals, though not especially political, and even said that Clemmie was a Liberal at heart, but could not admit it for obvious reasons. All the families Clarissa was brought up with were Liberals – the Asquiths, Sinclairs (later Thursos) and Bonham Carters.

Clarissa was largely raised in the nursery by nannies, but Goonie loved writing to her. Early letters were adorned with fine-coloured writing and beautifully executed drawings – the house where Uncle Winston was staying, or her four-poster bed. Clarissa responded in kind. From her grandparents' house, she wrote: 'I can-not think of anything to say. Here is a picture of me wondering what to say.' She craved her mother's support, but was afraid of being smothered. She had an unemotional Scottish nanny, who left when she was seven, and then two governesses, one of whom taught her cousin Mary. As Clarissa grew older, she found the family atmosphere increasingly oppressive.

For summer holidays her parents took Horsey Hall in Norfolk for a month. That was a smallish brick and flint house with a Georgian stucco front and Victorian bay windows. Not having a country house until 1936, they stayed with relations – the Marlboroughs at Blenheim Palace, or Chartwell in Kent with Uncle Winston.* Clarissa was sometimes sent to stay with her aunt, Lady Betty Trafford (Goonie's sister), at Wroxham Hall in Norfolk, an enormous Georgian house, built around 1790 (since demolished). And she stayed at Breccles Hall, a large Tudor E-plan manor house, enhanced by Detmar Blow and Lutyens. Edwin Montagu† and his wife, the celebrated Venetia Stanley (loved by H. H. Asquith), had lived there since 1917, and in that house they entertained lavishly. One year the Stanleys loaned it to Clarissa's parents. To this litany of houses can be added Rushbrooke in Norfolk, the home of her godmother, Anne, Lady Islington, Pixton Park in Devon, owned by Mrs Auberon Herbert, and Plas Newydd on the Isle of Anglesey, the home of the Marquess of Anglesey and his wife, Lady Marjorie Manners.

Clarissa stayed with her Abingdon grandparents at Oakden Holt, Oxford,‡ and went to Mells with her mother. Goonie was friends with Sir Archibald and Lady Sinclair,§ and every year took Clarissa to Dalnawillan Lodge, Altnabreac, Caithness. They once went to Dieppe to stay with Aunt Clemmie's mother, and another time to Annecy. In the early summers of 1927 and 1928, Clarissa stayed with her mother at the Royal Albion Hotel in Brighton, writing to her father: 'It is terrible here, the whole place is one mass of flags and people. We stay on the balcony all day.'[10]

---

* In September 1925 Clarissa was sent to Overstrand, on the east coast of Norfolk, while her mother took Johnny and Peregrine to Chartwell. There, they dug in the new lake Uncle Winston was making, while she, Aunt Clemmie, their daughters, Diana and Sarah, went blackberry picking.

† The Rt Hon. Edwin Montagu (1879–1924), Liberal politician and Secretary of State for India, and his wife, the Hon. Venetia Stanley (1887–1948). Her daughter, Judy Montagu (1923–72), was a friend of Clarissa, and famously of Princess Margaret.

‡ Lord Abingdon died on 10 March 1928, leaving £226,970. Pictures and other treasures were sold at Sotheby's. His brother died ten days later and his sister in July 1928.

§ Sir Archibald Sinclair (1890–1970), later 1st Viscount Thurso, KT, and his wife, Marigold Forbes (1897–1975). Their daughter Catherine (1919–2007) was a childhood friend of Clarissa and they went to study in Paris together in 1937.

School Days

In April 1926 Clarissa was sent to Kensington High School, nearby at 25 Cromwell Road, founded in 1895 by Miss Edith Lloyd and Miss Maud Cornwell with three pupils to provide them with a sound if conventional education. By the time Clarissa attended, there were 230 pupils.* Miss Cornwell thought Clarissa: 'an intelligent, enthusiastic and capable little girl, always delightful to deal with'. She would have received a school honour had she stayed until twelve fifteen each day.

She loved the school, remembering the teachers as 'wonderful' and 'strict'. She had to work hard, especially when the scholarship girls arrived. She played netball and exercised in the gym. Homework kept her up till bedtime. In 1932 she came third in the Children's Challenge Shield in the Annual Swimming Competition at the Bath Club. But here, as in later schools, the teachers started the history syllabus with the reign of Charles I.

Neville Lewis† painted her at Chartwell. Mary Soames recalled how well behaved Clarissa was and how easy it was 'getting her to sit still.'[11] The picture was exhibited at the Goupil Gallery, though dismissed as not the strongest on display.

In 1929 Clarissa's father accompanied his brother Winston and their respective sons, Johnny and Randolph, on a three-month tour of Canada and the USA, between 3 August and 30 October. My grandfather, Cecil Vickers, joined them in New York with my aunt Joan. On the way home Jack used to splash my aunt in the ship's swimming pool. He frequently took her out in a boat at Horsey Mere when she stayed with them in Norfolk. When he died, my aunt wrote to Winston: 'The holidays at Horsey, Steeple Aston, Catfield & Breccles, the many hours of riding in Windsor Forest and once the Downs, the loan of books will always remain precious memories.'[12] All of this caused Clarissa to say of my aunt: 'She was the bane of my childhood.'

---

* In 1931 Rosalind Wade wrote a novel called *Children Be Happy!*, which was identifiably based on pupils and staff at the school. Miss Lloyd and others sued. All copies and the original manuscript were destroyed.
† Neville Lewis (1895–1972), South African artist.

Johnny

Uncertain of how to pursue his career, Clarissa's brother, Johnny, joined Vickers, da Costa as a clerk in 1930. At first he loved it, heading off to the City in striped trousers and a black jacket, but by the end of 1931 he had decided that the City was not for him. He went to see my grandfather, who supported his choice, adding: 'But you must be honest with yourself and if – only if – you fail, come to me here in this office and I will take you back.'[*][13] Goonie was concerned that this decision would jeopardise his chance of marrying Penelope Chetwode. There had been a possibility that they might marry in 1931. Goonie told Clarissa: 'I am afraid he will never marry Pen now – first because Pen I don't think wants to marry him really[†] – & then there is no money – & secondly Johnny seems so vague & tepid & apparently incapable of really working to make money . . . but somehow I never felt it wd come off – did you?'[14]

Johnny embarked on his career as an artist of some distinction, Clarissa loving the murals he painted at 41 Cromwell Road: 'Johnny has done the <u>most</u> marvellous thing in the sort of hall place outside the drawing room, all with a thick brush & feather.'[15] Mrs Auberon Herbert commissioned him to decorate the enormous hall of her villa, Alta Chiara, in Portofino. There he met Angela Culme-Seymour, who presently moved in with him. They married in Portofino, annoying the mayor by insisting on breaking a plate 'to represent the religious side',[16] thus creating a pagan wedding. At that point Johnny informed his parents. Goonie was glad, and Jack sent him a cheque for £100. However, this was soon followed by demands from Johnny's creditors. 'All this is very tiresome & has put poor old

* The only time Johnny went back was some twenty-three years later when, at the invitation of my father, he decorated the new boardroom in their offices in King William Street, with scenes of Paris, Venice and New York.
† Hon. Penelope Chetwode (1910–86), loosely disguised as 'Sophie' in Johnny's memoirs, the daughter of Field Marshal Lord Chetwode, was toying with three Johns – Sir John Marshall, the archaeologist, being one, Johnny another and, finally, John Betjeman, whom she married on 29 July 1933. Penelope came to see Goonie in October 1934, who found her 'fat, with a fringe, no make-up, terrific vitality – I must say she is a character – & had a lot of pip. She wd have been an uncomfortable daughter-in-law, but very vitalising & stirring.'

Pups in a rage & no wonder I think,' Goonie wrote to Clarissa. 'Johnny is <u>very</u> <u>tiresome</u>.'[17] Goonie worried, not without reason, that though Johnny and Angela were travelling happily around Europe together, they would not be able to live like that for ever.

★ ★ ★ ★ ★

As Clarissa continued her peregrinations through various Norfolk homes in 1930 and 1931, she became more pronounced in her taste. Of Somerleyton Hall she wrote: 'the interior was appalling though rather homely'. There was a squirt fight and for the sports 'the prize was a gaudy case, quite undescribable'.[18] She was frequently a brides-maid. On 15 July 1931 she was one of eleven, in white silk tulle with frilled skirts, to Lady Davina Lytton when she married the Earl of Erne in the Henry VII Chapel, Westminster Abbey.* In the autumn Peregrine gave her records – 'O for the Wings of a Dove' and *The Pirates of Penzance*, and introduced her to *The Gondoliers*.

In January 1932 there was a ball at Wroxham Hall for which Clarissa stayed up till ten thirty, consuming everything on the menu – soup, salad and turkey, orange jelly, whipped cream and chocolate soufflé: 'So I did not do badly.'[19] She danced a polka, her feet hardly touching the floor. In April she went to Portugal, and on 12 December 1932, with her cousins, Mary and Sarah, she was a bridesmaid to Diana Churchill at St Margaret's Westminster, when she married John Bailey, son of Sir Abe Bailey, the South African diamond tycoon.†

1933

Clarissa kept a youthful diary between January and the beginning of May. It is not so different from what other twelve-year-old girls would have

---

* Some of the bridesmaids became close friends – Lady Caroline Paget and Ann Fleming, while Davina, as a war widow, nearly married Anthony Eden during the 1940s.

† The reception was held at 7 Carlton House Terrace, thanks to the 9th Duke of Marlborough, a significant moment in his crumbling marriage to Gladys Deacon. She refused to appear at the wedding to avoid the charade of 'united husband and wife' but came to the reception. Diana and Bailey separated a year later and divorced in 1935. In the same year Diana married Duncan Sandys. They, too, separated and in 1963 she took a fatal overdose.

written, though repeatedly she described her life as dull. On 1 February she speculated: 'Cousin Gladys divorce?', a reference to the failing marriage of the Marlboroughs.* One day she asked her brother Johnny to read to her, but he refused. She decided she liked his friend Angela Culme-Seymour as much as she had Penelope Chetwode. On 2 April, the last entry was bland: 'Antony Knebworth killed. Caroline dished.†'[20]

1933 included a visit to Mary Herbert's villa in Portofino, stays with her grandmother, a three-week Mediterranean cruise with her parents in September and a final family Christmas at Chartwell, where the young cousins enjoyed the requisite 'jollity, special friendships and in-fighting'[21] that made family gatherings such fun.

Downham School

In May 1934 Goonie sent Clarissa to Downham School, Hatfield Heath, near Bishop's Stortford, where she remained until the end of 1935. Goonie declared what she expected:

> What really matters in life is the individual's charm, looks, manners, capabilities & cleverness, sympathy, intuition, & a certain amount of self confidence & assertiveness, vitality & health – certificates or no certificates, matriculations or no matriculations, they don't matter if one is clever, charming, lovely & lovable . . .[22]

The school was housed on an estate that traced its history back to before the Domesday Book, but Down Hall, the sumptuous Italianate building in which the school was housed (and which is now a hotel and spa), was designed by the architect Frederick Pepys Cockerell, for Lord Rookwood, between 1871 and 1873. Whatever the girls thought of it, it was – and is – a handsome building.

---

* Clarissa knew that the 9th Duke wanted to marry Lady Lindsay-Hogg.
† Viscount Knebworth (1903–33), son of the 2nd Earl of Lytton and Pamela Plowden. He was virtually engaged to Lady Caroline Paget. Pamela used to corral Caroline to visit his grave every year. He was killed while serving with the Auxiliary Air Force on 1 May 1933, taking part in a practice flight for an annual air pageant at Hendon.

The school had been founded in 1932 by Mrs Eleanor Craufurd,* the principal until her death in 1950. A one-time Chief Commissioner for the Girl Guides of Scotland, she had played cricket for Scotland. She came to teaching with no experience, but was said to be 'well qualified to lead, to form character and to create the spirit of service and initiative'.[23] Anne Glenconner, a later pupil, recalled her 'gung-ho attitude to life'[24] and how she lived with the co-principal, Miss Beatrice Graham. Goonie thought Mrs Craufurd 'exceptionally full of character, poise & judgement. I like her so very much.'[25] Mrs Craufurd described Clarissa: 'She has of course captivated all their hearts by her charming ways and delightful personality . . . older in appearance & ways than she is in herself . . . She is clever & has a very good brain.' Clarissa dismissed the place as a 'fashionable boarding school . . . orientated to horses'.[26] She said later: 'I was bored to death, very bad teachers . . .'[27]

The school's mission was to prepare girls for a good marriage. They slept four to a dormitory, wore a uniform of grey-green skirt and blazer, with a white shirt and a blue tie. Life was neither Spartan nor comfortable. Like all such schools, it was cold in the winter. Traditional subjects, such as maths, languages, English and some science, were taught in the morning, while later in the day the girls played tennis or other games, rode horses, learnt ballroom dancing, drawing, painting and cooking. A memorable contemporary was Pamela Digby, though Clarissa recalled her as 'a plump unattractive girl', giving no hint to her future, a partly horizontal journey, via many rich men, to becoming US Ambassador Harriman in Paris in the 1990s. Of Pamela she said: 'She was not a precocious child. While we were dreaming of Laurence Olivier, she was dreaming of horses.'[28]

Clarissa was generally unhappy at the school, going about alone while others played. She hated music lessons, wanted to do more drawing and to have extra coaching for tennis. She scored 15/100 for algebra. 'I do hope you will do well at lessons, because you have brains,' her mother wrote to her. By the beginning of 1935, Clarissa

* Mrs Eleanor Craufurd (1875–1950), granddaughter of Admiral Sir John Dalrymple-Hay, Bt, married to Brigadier General John Houison Craufurd, who had died in July 1933.

was acutely unhappy. In May she wrote her mother a 'wailing, sorrow-ing letter', begging to leave. Her mother pleaded:

> It seems to me that you have a lovely life in front of you on the whole & not so bad now – because just stop & reflect. What else cd you be doing <u>now</u> – London wd be intolerable, a governess at Oakden Holt awfully dull – a convent worse. Cheer up & don't be unhappy. Your dormitory is lovely & sunny & airy – it is the best in the school – for a Form Capt . . .'[29]

Goonie admitted that she herself would have 'died' had she been sent to such a school, so she agreed that Clarissa could leave, though she regretted her daughter's lack of a School Certificate – 'a sort of triumphal arch to walk under'.[30] Unlike Pamela Digby, Clarissa did not feel the need to claim she had been head girl or had 'graduated', as Pamela put it, from 'Downham College'.[31]

★ ★ ★ ★ ★

In the summer of 1934 the family moved to 42 Chester Terrace in Regent's Park, a house recommended to them by Pamela Lytton. Clarissa had longed to live there and took her father twice, trying to 'buck him up a bit' but his comment was 'Wuff.'[32] The eventual move and an upsurge in the family finances liberated enough funds for a country house, and in due course they also bought Holworth House in Dorset.

The death of Sunny, 9th Duke of Marlborough, on 30 June 1934 had the unfortunate effect of the 10th Duke and his wife Mary moving into Blenheim and inviting various Churchills for Christmas. Clarissa did not like the idea. 'Darling I'm not looking forward to Blenheim either,' wrote her mother. 'It will be an effort & a strain & after all Mary & Blandford & their children are strangers to us. It won't be at all cosy – & Mary Churchill is sure to be tiresome – but there it is & we will have to make the best of it.'[33] Goonie somehow escaped going and Clarissa hated it:

> Papa wouldn't let me go to church this morning because he wanted to take Pebin round the grounds. Mary B gave me a rotten old book. Aunt Clemmie sent me a 5/- bag like the ones we saw in Marshall &

Snelgrove. Nothing else. Pebin gave me a Kodak camera, one of the kind that fold up. It must have cost a lot, it was very kind of him . . . Mary C is quite nice,* much better than she used to be. The two girls are quite nice, but rather silly.[34]

She dreaded a paperchase the following day. Next she went to stay with the Earl of Dudley at Himley. This appealed more, despite the presence of Lady Victor Paget with '2 motheaten brats' and Billy Ednam's 'horrible' Etonian friends: 'I have got a lovely bedroom, called the Pink bedroom, it is very big with a lot of lights which turn on gradually like in cinema bedrooms. We bathe every evening . . . I have got rather a nice dressing table . . . pink chintz edged with blue cord.'[35]

She enjoyed the luxury: 'I get clean towels every day, and sheets about 3 times a week. And all the lights are left burning in the bedrooms from 4 onwards.'[36] There was hunting and shooting, but she soon wanted to come home.

On 26 March 1935 Johnny's wife Angela produced her daughter, Sally (first called Cornelia).† Goonie kept an eye on Winston and frequently passed on her thoughts to Clarissa. She noted how popular Winston and Clemmie were, invited out everywhere, and wondered why everyone made such a fuss of them 'because except W. himself they surely are not very attractive or amusing or lovely – or are they?'[37] In October 1935 Clemmie gave a 'mammoth' cocktail party at Wimborne House, inviting eight hundred guests, of whom only three hundred turned up. Most of the guests had been friends of Duncan Sandys, then married to Winston's daughter, Diana. Goonie told Clarissa:

Uncle Winston mooned about too surrounded with his Dukes & Duchesses & Prof [Lindemann] & H. G. Wells & Baba Metcalfe.

* Clemmie told Goonie that the new Duke's daughters adored Mary Churchill – 'It's very foolish of them to like such an affected little piece,' she told Clarissa the following June. Mary was brought up in a wing of Chartwell by 'Cousin Moppet', a poor relation of Aunt Clemmie.

† Sally began a life of being passed from one parent to the other and landed with various guardians. In 1957 she married Colin Crewe (1922–2015). After their divorce, she married in 1987 John Baring, Lord Ashburton, KG (1928–2020).

Lord & Lady Wimborne retired to their private apartments, while all this was going on! Aunt Clemmie must have spent hours arranging everything, & pots of money, because it was super, too super really. Well, that's all over, & it seems rather a waste of time on our parts & waste of money on their parts.[38]

In the general election on 14 November that year, Winston's son, Randolph, stood for West Toxteth, Liverpool. His father was heart-broken that he did not get in, but everybody else was delighted: 'All say he is insufferable & bumptious,' wrote Goonie.[39] Some of the electorate threw bananas at him. Clarissa left school at the end of that year and there was another Christmas at Blenheim.

3. THE NARCISSISTIC DIARY
1936–7

Uniquely there exists a full diary for 1936* so we can follow Clarissa closely from the end of 1935 through to 1937, the year when she went to Paris. It is the diary of a surprisingly narcissistic teenager aged fifteen to sixteen.

The new year began at Zürs-am-Arlberg in Austria, for a skiing holiday with Aunt Clemmie, a number of young Churchills, Venetia Montagu and her daughter Judy. Meanwhile Uncle Winston was working in the warmth of Morocco on volume three of his Duke of Marlborough biography, though he felt obliged to return to Britain when George V died.

The stay in Zürs provided more evidence of Clarissa's antipathy towards her cousin Mary. They shared a room, and while Mary never stopped talking, Clarissa seldom spoke. In her memoirs all she said was: 'I was three [in fact two] years older than Mary, which, when one is a child, makes a big difference. However, we got along well enough during the holidays.'[1] Not so. Mary herself was more forthcoming: 'Clarissa was only two years older than me, but our personalities were very different – she was a reserved child, and seemed to have been created "grown-up" all in one fell swoop; I must have seemed odd to her with my more extrovert nature and with my animals and family of dolls, so we were not great companions for one another.'[2]

Clarissa's diary supports this analysis: 'Mary a bore', 'Mary abominable, talks & makes everyone listen to her', 'Mary shows off to

* This diary was found tucked down the side of an armchair by a stranger, who identified Clarissa as the writer, and kindly returned it to her. It is the only diary that exists from that period, though there must have been more. Diaries exist again from 1952 to 1957, and there are some from 2005 to 2011.

Tor-Tor [Gilmour*], who seems to like her.'[3] She resented Mary getting all the attention: 'awful little rat'.[4]

Clarissa was more interested in the effect she had on the other guests than the ski slopes. When Princess Natalie Paley and Edward James turned up, she wrote: 'I'll make them all sit up. I'll make them turn in their seats & stare at me, and want to talk to me & whisper about me. Mary says "Flatterer." I'll flatter them.'[5] She succeeded in getting Natalie Paley's attention before returning home on 19 January.

The next day George V died at Sandringham. 'King dead,' noted Clarissa dispassionately.[6] On 24 January she observed with some pres-cience: 'The King's Imperial Crown fell off the coffin & the Maltese Cross fell off. O God, a bad omen, possibly the prophesy of those ------ prophets. O dear, O dear.'[7] The funeral interested her for the fine uniforms and the sheikhs in flowing robes.

At the end of January she and Catherine Sinclair began attending lectures and drawing lessons at the Byam Shaw art school, finding it full of 'greasy young women in smocks'.[8] They were nervous because a Russian had lifted up Catherine's jumper to find she had nothing on underneath, at which point all the men crowded round her. Clarissa took French and German lessons with a governess; she fenced and took dancing lessons. Like many young girls, she was stage-struck, one night sleeping with a photo of Laurence Olivier she had cut from a newspaper. She went to plays and films. She read copiously and well – *War and Peace* and H. G. Wells.

She attended the Monkey Club, an establishment for debutantes learning to be housewives, partly a members' club, partly educational, founded in 1923 and surviving into the 1950s. It provided general education, music, secretarial training, domestic science and dress-making. There was even a course for brides, teaching them how to give dinner parties and how to cope with leaking pipes and broken armchairs. Clarissa was lucky to be taught by a young woman who was passionate about English literature and thus she discovered her own love for it.

In February her cousin Sarah Churchill announced she wished to

---

* Hon Victoria Cadogan (1901-91), officially the daughter of Viscount Chelsea. Mother of the politician, Ian Gilmour.

marry thirty-seven-year-old Vic Oliver, twice married, of Jewish-Viennese extraction, described by Mary Soames as 'a man of great charm and talent'.[9] Clarissa's mother found Aunt Clemmie in tears and Uncle Winston 'broken up'. When ticked off, Sarah was 'rude to Uncle W. saying she wanted to shake off the cursed name of Churchill!'[10] On 9 July they nearly married but were stopped, so in September Sarah bolted to New York. Clarissa rang Aunt Clemmie when she saw it in the evening paper and found her in hysterics. Randolph was dispatched to America to sort it out, but in vain. 'Great was the dismay of her parents,' wrote Mary. Vic and Sarah married in New York on Christmas Eve 1936, Mary commenting ruefully that Christmas that year at Chartwell was 'very quiet.'[11]

Neither was all well between Clarissa and her mother. Mary Soames wrote: 'Aunt Goonie doted on her lovely flaxen-haired daughter, and showered her with fulsome affection and solicitude: although I was somewhat embarrassed by this (as no doubt Clarissa was too), I remember being considerably shocked by her icy indifference to her mother's displays of affection.'[12] One night at dinner with Goonie and Bluey Baker, there was a row. Goonie rebuked Clarissa: 'Don't be so cockslice,' and Bluey said: 'Yes, and so unkind.' Clarissa bemoaned the situation: 'Blast, he thinks I'm the same as ever, & I have been trying to be better.'[13] She knew she was frequently unkind: 'Oh God, oh God, please stop me wounding her. All her life she slaves for me. Her life is unhappy. She is too good for this world. Yet I am awful to her continually. Please stop me & inflict a punishment on me so I will never do it again.'[14]

Lady Lytton ticked Clarissa off, and she feared that her mother's friends, 'like the old cats they are', would spread the story and 'boys will be shy of me in consequence'.[15] She was equally disdainful of her father. When he bought a new car, she feared he would ruin it and became exasperated: 'Pa awful, jawing & jawing, & so boring. O dear he is a bore. I wish he would drop out of my life.'[16] When my aunt Joan came to dinner with the Churchill family, Clarissa recorded: 'Learn . . . J. Vickers is coming to dine. Comes. I sulk at end of table but P [Peregrine] seems to blossom in her company. Pa jaws.'[17] On 23 November Clarissa noted: 'Vickers boy . . . to dinner.' [My father.]

The other theme that preoccupied Clarissa was her own

considerable beauty. She was particularly irritated that Mary and her brother Johnny teased her about her resemblance to the Swedish film star Greta Garbo, Johnny continually pressing the point. When, at Easter, Sarah Churchill said Clarissa looked 'superior', her brother Johnny chirped in with 'Yes, it's the Garbo touch.' Clarissa commented: 'Oh damn Johnny & the Garbo, Garbo, the *whole* time.'[18] This returned to haunt her when she lunched with Sir Charles Mendl and Elsie de Wolfe at Versailles in May. Lady Mendl said: 'Take off your hat.' She did so. 'There, Greta Garbo, isn't she?' Howard Sturges, a particularly social guest, agreed: 'Yes, definitely. The profile.' And Sir Charles chimed in: 'There, we're having lunch with Garbo.'[19] Even on a train journey to stay with Consuelo Vanderbilt Balsan (former Duchess of Marlborough) – 'very well preserved' – a woman passenger was convinced that Clarissa was the real Garbo. Clarissa could not know, of course, that fifteen years later she and Garbo would become friends.

Uncle Winston said she was too beautiful, while Aunt Clemmie thought everything about her lovely and wondered if she dared take her to Zürs again. Clarissa recorded every tribute to her beauty, Lady Anglesey telling Clemmie: 'I do think Clarissa is <u>perfectly</u> lovely, don't you?' at which point Aunt Clemmie agreed but looked 'sour'[20] – 'Clarissa too striking to go about alone.'[21]

Although she was only fifteen, turning sixteen in June 1936, there was talk of suitors. Lord Leconfield thought she would make a good wife for the young Duke of Norfolk.* Clarissa shuffled with embarrassment, confiding to her diary: 'Catch me marrying a monkey like that!' When she saw the Duke at Cumberland Lodge, she described him as 'charming, but no, very funny little eyes, sweet little nose!'[22] Then there was Lord Howland:† 'sort of Bertie Wooster & eyeglass'[23]. When she discovered he designed dresses 'for a living' she condemned him as 'the big Pansy!'[24]

---

* Bernard, 16th Duke of Norfolk (1906–75). As Earl Marshal he would arrange the funerals of George V and George VI, the Coronations of both George VI and Elizabeth II, and the state funeral of Sir Winston Churchill.
† Ian, Lord Howland, later 13th Duke of Bedford (1917–2002). One of the early peers to make a success of the stately home business, opening Woburn Abbey to the public, with a famous safari park.

On 23 April she actually met the man she would marry while staying with Lord and Lady Cranborne* at Cranborne in Dorset. Given her later involvement, her first impression is startling:

Find Antony [sic] Eden & wife (A.E. in green suit) . . . Great political talk. O save us if England is ever in the hands of Mr Eden. (Mrs E seems to be a dull spot.)²⁵

Later in the year, on a visit to Madame Balsan, Clarissa was subjected to a by no means unique advance from her husband, Jacques, an old aviator whose monkey-gland injections worked all too well:

Ride with Jacques at 8.30. Calls me 'Ma petite Clarisse' & puts arm round waist. Ride on old pudding of a horse in Big Bois. Jacques suddenly amid lots of 'Ma petite Clarisse' kisses my hand & then my arm. I say 'Non vraiment' & he says 'Oh but that is no bad.' Feel depressed for rest of the ride. Why do the drunks & crocks make for me?²⁶

In Somerset at the end of May she found herself in the company of Evelyn Waugh ('What a specimen!'²⁷) and his wife, Laura. Hilaire Belloc criticised her for her silence at dinner. On 24 June she was swimming in another Bath Club competition, the Duchess of York bringing 'the little princesses' along. Later in the year she met them again with their childhood friend, Alathea Fitzalan Howard, Clarissa judging Princess Margaret: 'Younger quite pretty.'²⁸

The family found Holworth House in July and, after a spate of offers and counter offers, her father bought it. Holworth stood about nine miles east of Weymouth, with fine views over the bay to Guernsey in the distance. Seeing it for the first time in August, Clarissa thought it lovely, with a fine dining room and an exquisite

---

* 'Bobbety', later 5th Marquess of Salisbury (1893–1972) and his wife Elizabeth (Betty) Cavendish (1897–1982), daughter of Lord Richard Cavendish. He was a close friend of Anthony Eden, and served with him in several governments. Robert, his heir, was a close friend of Clarissa, and Goonie had noted that his second son, Michael, had died at Eton in 1934. The youngest son, Richard, was killed in the war in 1944.

verandah. She liked her room too. Later she took against the garden's rhododendrons and crazy paving: 'It's like going to a nightmarish picture gallery & in the furthest corner there is one lovely picture, but it doesn't balance the horror all around.'[29] But by the time she wrote her memoirs, the neighbouring countryside had assumed a roseate hue in her memory: 'My heart was always in Dorset from then on.'[30] She explored the county, Weymouth, Chesil Beach, Abbotsbury and Woodsford Castle. In Dorchester she ran into her schoolfriend, Pamela Digby 'v. fat & unmade up'.[31] Pamela allowed her to play tennis at Minterne, the family home.

Throughout the year the deteriorating political situation in Germany, Russia and Spain was a recurring theme, and she worried that her life might be cut short before she had had time to enjoy it: 'We will die in October. Oh God! I am too young to die. I have not tasted of life yet.'[32]

In September Aunt Clemmie pinned her down for Christmas at Chartwell and another trip to Zürs with Mary, prompting Clarissa to wonder how she could escape. She summed up her attitude to life: 'Mum came back just when I was beginning to feel lonely & depressed. I like to be alone but I like someone to be in the next room.'[33] In October she mused about Lady Caroline Paget, then appearing in a Dodie Smith play, *Call It a Day*, as a professional actress. 'I still harbour a slight lesbian feeling for Caroline . . . But I am certainly more attracted to men than I was a year ago. Which is right and normal.'[34]

The year ended in high drama with the abdication of Edward VIII. On 3 December Clarissa noted: 'Mrs Simpson business out, headings 3 ins long in *Daily Mirror*.' Then there was news from Chartwell. Aunt Clemmie shrieked: '& he loves her so much that he crawls round her on hands & knees kissing her feet.' To which Lady Sinclair retorted: 'Well if we are going to have a crawling King, the sooner he goes the better!' On the night when the King went, Clarissa commented: 'Listen to King's abdication speech on wireless: "Oi foind it 'ard to give up moi throwoon" – poor little wretch – has been had every way. Laugh with Mummy & go to bed at 11 in a taut condition.'[35]

They spent Christmas at Holworth, so there were no Blenheim horrors that year. Clarissa had escaped from school. She had fulfilled a year of study in London. Next she escaped to Paris.

Paris Interlude

Clarissa began the new year with her customary pessimism. 'Goodbye 1936. 1937 is here. We are all in 1937, my last year on earth perhaps. Foul day, wind, very rough sea, & mists. Read Emily Dickinson & Boswell in morning. Begin *Gone with the Wind* – good but of a formidable length.' She worried about her lack of religion in the face of what could be imminent war. '1937 came in with a gale & wind and lashings. This is a bad omen.'[36]

Towards the end of January she arrived in Paris to stay at 98 rue Denfert-Rochereau in the XIVe *quartier*, with two friends, Catherine Sinclair and the rebellious but rich Anne Powell.*

'Paris was like the opening of a window on life', Clarissa wrote. 'Being sent there, albeit with two friends and a chaperone, was more than a window – it was a dazzling new world.'[37] Her chaperone was Lady Clerk, the eccentric wife of the British Ambassador, Sir George Clerk. In the embassy, Clarissa met Valentine Lawford and Fitzroy Maclean, both of whom became friends for life.

She arrived in time to see the exhibition of twenty recent works by Georges Braque, mainly still lifes and nudes, at Paul Rosenberg's studio at 91 rue de la Boëtie. This made a lasting impression on her, and for a while she wanted to become a modern artist herself. She attended lectures at the Sorbonne and, with her two friends, took painting lessons from a well-known French artist, Charles Picart Le Doux.† Goonie was keen that Clarissa should read a lot, learn to speak and read French, and play lots of tennis.

There were concerts by the Berlin Philharmonic, *thés dansants*, and parties given by Princess Marthe Bibesco, Comtesse Marthe de Fels, Daisy Fellowes and Elsie Mendl at her home in Versailles. There were dinners with Burnet Pavitt, a highly cultured man with a love of

---

* Anne Powell (1920–2004), younger daughter of Lieutenant Colonel George Powell, Grenadier Guards, a Tory MP and heavy drinker, and of a Roman Catholic mother who had joined the Communist Party; sister of Elizabeth, Lady Glenconner. In 1939 she married Philip Toynbee, and after their divorce, Richard Wollheim. Mother of Polly Toynbee.

† Charles Picart Le Doux (1881–1959), artist and friend of Aristide Maillol. He taught at the Académie de la Grande Chaumière from 1927 to 1959.

music, who went on to be closely involved with Covent Garden and the Royal College of Music. At Lady Mendl's she found herself in potentially dangerous company – 'Indian potentates, remnants of the Austro-Hungarian Empire, playboys and playgirls, writers, painters, musicians, the more bohemian aristocrats and, looming above them all, the amiable face of Grand Duke Dimitri of Russia'.* From London her mother was happy that she was spending time with the Mendls, Valentine Lawford and Burnet Pavitt, but she urged caution:

> I beg of you to use your good sense & don't let those young gentle-men think you are cheap & that they can take you out anywhere – & above all don't let them give you cocktails & drinks. Nothing young gentlemen, both English & French, enjoy more than trying to make pretty young girls slightly tipsy & irresponsible. Do please be on your guard – & also remember that people on the whole, relish to spread stories & damage reputations.[38]

Goonie was glad to know that, although Clarissa was 'moving around in a rather loose crowd', she was using her 'discretion' and being 'discriminating'.[39] When Clarissa went to a ball given by Daisy Fellowes, Goonie made sure she was escorted home.

Goonie came out to visit Clarissa in February and May, and Clarissa came home briefly for Easter. Goonie kept her informed. She had been to Trim Oxford's twenty-first birthday party and Laura Herbert's wedding to Evelyn Waugh. She had seen 'Uncle Winston for a minute, looking so pink like a little sucking pig'.[40] She became exasperated by Johnny's behaviour to his wife Angela: 'Johnny is quite intolerable – I don't like him at all really. The baby is very sweet, poor little thing.'[41] When she went to Chartwell, she caught up with the runaway bride of 1936: 'Sarah & Vic [Oliver] arrived for lunch. She looked ravishing, magnolia skin, red mouth, green eyes, auburn hair & is obviously very happy with Vic, who is frightful, but kind & he loves her.'[42]

Clarissa attended a number of Parisian balls at the end of her stay and returned to London on 27 June. She went to Lady Astor's ball on

---

* Grand Duke Dimitri (1891–1942), a cousin of the Tsar. One-time lover of Coco Chanel, and complicit with Felix Yusupov in the murder of Rasputin.

9 July, spent much time at Holworth, and there were visits to Mells, Plas Newydd, Holker Hall in Cumbria, and Caithness. In October she took classes at the Slade School of Art three days a week, one of them with a Miss Strachey. She attended lectures at the Institute of Philosophy in Gordon Square. Meanwhile Goonie had her heart set on Clarissa undertaking a social season in 1938. She threatened to give a party at the Ritz for young and old, while Duff Cooper suggested Philip Sassoon might lend his house, 25 Park Lane, for a ball.

Clarissa wanted none of it, but she could not entirely escape.

4. ASPIRANT LOVERS

Andrew Billen interviewing Clarissa about her memoirs in 2007:
'. . . she mentions in her book no lovers before Eden.'
Clarissa: 'Maybe there were one or two.'[1]

James Pope-Hennessy
(1916–74)

The latter months of 1937 were a turning point in Clarissa's life. Suddenly, rafts of largely sympathetic and intelligent men began to take an interest in her. What should have been a lifetime's platonic friendship grew at this time. James Pope-Hennessy came on to the scene.

James was a writer of considerable distinction, born into an intellectual Catholic family. His mother, Dame Una, wrote biographies of literary figures, including Sir Walter Scott, Edgar Allan Poe, Charles Dickens and more. His only brother, John, was an art historian who became director of the Victoria and Albert Museum, then the British Museum, and later chairman of European Paintings at the Metropolitan Museum in New York. James was educated at Downside and Balliol College, Oxford. As a youngster he was given a typewriter and his mother paid both brothers to type her manuscripts. He worked for Sheed and Ward, a firm of Catholic publishers, until January 1939, and was then personal secretary to Sir Hubert Young, Governor of Trinidad, for five months. During the war he served in military intelligence. These three phases in his career coincided with his particular friendship with Clarissa, which began in November 1937 when they met at a dinner party, after which she gave him a lift home in her car.

Pope-Hennessy wasted no time in recommending lectures to her, inviting her to his mother's sherry party ten days later, and suggesting a tour round the Wren churches of London. Within four days 'Dear Miss Churchill' became 'My dear Clarissa' (and by July 1938 she was 'Dearest Clarissa'). In her memoirs she was unfairly dismissive of him: 'James attached himself to me from the word go. He was small, with very black hair and heavy eyelids, quick as a lizard and always immensely appreciative and sympathetic.'[2] Their letters give a more enchanting impression of the friendship. She could relate her ideas to him, and in turn he adored her. In a moment of emotional despair in 1940, he wrote: '. . . yr existence is the greatest comfort imaginable in this abrupt world . . .'[3]

She invited him to a lecture on the French poet, Paul Valéry, and he took her to Dr Johnson's house and to many churches, some by Wren – St Paul's Cathedral, St Bartholomew the Great, St Mary-le-Bow and St Martin within Ludgate. Knowing her to be an admirer of John Donne, he showed her the Donne monument 'in his winding sheet by Stone'[4] in St Paul's Cathedral.

By September 1938, James was confiding in her: '. . . as I hope you know I do think of you as one of the people (and there aren't so many, in fact there are few) to whom one is genuinely devoted – and whom one wd do anything for if occasion arose. And the penalty for inspiring that affection is the receipt of these portentous self-revelations . . .'[5] War clouds were threatening, and although war was delayed for another year, Pope-Hennessy advised Clarissa to stay down at Holworth because the atmosphere in London was nerve-racking, and she might not be able to get away again. Gas masks were being issued and there was an 'Armageddon atmosphere'.[6]

Throughout that year, the London expeditions took place, enjoyed by both in equal measure. He celebrated them in his book, *London Fabric*, published in September 1939.* Clarissa had not known that he was writing about their expeditions. She first thought of him as someone entranced by her mother. In *London Fabric* he conducted her, thinly disguised as 'Perdita', on a tour of Wren churches and notably their crypts, then Hampton Court, Dulwich, Hertford House, Greenwich, Stafford House (now Lancaster House), Kensington Palace and Westminster Abbey.

---

* *London Fabric* won the Hawthornden Prize in 1940. James also dedicated *West Indian Summer* to Clarissa, the only time he dedicated two books to the same person.

Though he denied 'Perdita' was a direct portrait of Clarissa, he admitted that it reflected his fascination with her. As such it gives a good impression of Clarissa as a remarkable seventeen-year-old. Gone, or softened by maturity, was the narcissistic diarist of 1936. Instead here was a young woman at home in these historical landmarks, aware of her surroundings and their history. First he described her as she stood in the dark crypt of St Mary-le-Bow Church:

She looked, with her freshness and her swinging golden hair, like a Hans Andersen princess in a dungeon. It was hard to know what she was thinking. There is about her a withdrawn aloofness that just misses being haughty and widely misses being absurd. It is an unmodern quality, and I find it arresting. Yet there is nothing pre-War or Victorian in her; she demands, I think, a French background, the pillared elegance of the Second Empire, or the lofty saloons of Versailles to frame her to perfection . . . But she is not really a shy person, it is only the aloofness she shows at times. She has a fine, small head, and her face is rather round and dimpled, lacking the hungry sculptural lines admired to-day. Her hair, lemon-gold, and glossy like the gilt of a good binding, is combed smoothly to her shoulders and turned in at the ends. She has careful Tissot curls above her forehead. She holds her head straight and high.

The first evening I saw her she had on a white dress; this morning – it was late October – she was wearing a kind of burnt umber colour, which I liked because it made one think of chrysanthemums and the velvety Chinese ducks in St James's Park. She looked so lovely and vivid, standing like that, beneath the blunt brick arches, that I selfishly wanted to stay and gaze at her indefinitely . . .[7]

James was impressed by Clarissa's reactions. She was decisive and unpredictable; she knew what she liked and what she did not. And she matched his erudition with her knowledge and perceptive, sometimes provocative, questions. She did not like crypts, but she would winkle out and admire some alabaster figures tucked away near Wellington's hearse, in those days in St Paul's Cathedral. He was pleased to have her out and about, rather than she studying metaphysical poets in 'the colourless depths'[8] of University College in Bloomsbury.

He relished her 'imagination and the logical swiftness of her mind'.[9] And in *London Fabric* he noted: 'Perdita is one of the few people who write really first-rate letters; not one of the many who write good ones, but, I believe, a perfect example of that phenomenon, the born letter writer.'[10] When they visited Kensington Palace, Pope-Hennessy examined her further:

Again, as at the Queen's House and at the London Museum, I looked critically at Perdita who was fixed in enchantment by the frescoes. No, I thought, she never lets one down. Her appearance was once more up to the mark; the presence with which she stood there gazing at the painted walls, the way she turned her head, the dignity and the lightness which were merged in her pose. She seemed in nothing modern. It was as natural that she should be standing at the brink of the staircase as that Kent should have painted it, or Queen Caroline walked up its treads. The unique power that I had originally felt to be in her, the power which for want of better words I can only call that of fitting in, of becoming part of a scheme of decoration, of emphasising beauty by being in sympathy with it, this indeed is peculiarly her own. And if, I wondered, you are like this at eighteen, what will you be at twenty, or at thirty?[11]

Pope-Hennessy loved Clarissa but he did not aspire to an affair with her. Other admirers were more forthright, but none had a chance because Clarissa had fallen in love with the first great love of her life. She kept him secret from most of them, including from James. Goonie did not always approve of the men who loved Clarissa. However, there was one she did like. 'Trim is a charmer,' she wrote in 1938. 'There is something exceptional about him.'[12] Clarissa had known him since the cradle.

'Trim'
Earl of Oxford and Asquith
(1916–2011)

All Clarissa wrote about Trim Oxford in her memoirs was that he stood by her 'in all [my] transformations, when he might have abandoned me in disapproval'.[13] That does no justice to their relationship.

She had been visiting the Manor House, Mells, in Somerset with her mother since she was tiny, as a guest of the formidable Lady Horner and her daughter Katharine Asquith, Trim's mother. His real name was Julian and he had succeeded his prime ministerial grandfather, H. H. Asquith, as 2nd Earl of Oxford and Asquith in 1928. He was born on 22 April 1916. His father, Raymond Asquith, saw him as a baby when on leave and called him 'Trim', the name he bore all his life – after Trimalchio, a fat, bald character in Petronius's *The Satyricon*. Raymond was killed at the Battle of the Somme on 15 September, when his son was about five months old. Trim was raised as a pious Roman Catholic because his widowed mother, Katharine, converted with grave relief to Catholicism in 1923. After Ampleforth, he went up to Balliol College, Oxford, in 1937.

The Manor House stood on the edge of the village, next to the churchyard, where the church tower famously pealed eight bells. As a child, Clarissa could never sleep through the night as the clock woke her every quarter-hour. Irksome as this was, the peals were melodic and every three hours from midnight, they played one of four tunes, one being Holsworthy, Hanover: 'God Moves in a Mysterious Way'. Yet she wrote to James Pope-Hennessy: 'I do covet this house almost more than any other. You would love it. I suppose I have a very urban outlook on the country. I see it purely as something to be stood away from & beautiful, as a picture.'[14]

Frances Horner was still much in evidence during Clarissa's early visits. She had been the muse and friend to artists such as Edward Burne-Jones and Rossetti, and was close to Tennants such as Margot Asquith. She was one of 'The Souls' like so many of Goonie's friends. Lady Ottoline Morrell judged her 'one of those remarkable and capable Englishwomen who, with a certain amount of artistic and literary culture, can manage society, friends, a family, garden and household with ease and success'.[*][15]

Despite losing one son to scarlet fever in 1908 and the other from wounds at the battle of Cambrai in 1917, she entertained many of the

---

[*] In May 1934 Goonie told Clarissa: 'Yesterday we had a lot of old crows to lunch – Lady Ottoline Morrell, Lady Horner, Lady Birkenhead & the male crows were Eddie Marsh, Sir John Lavery, & Mr Morrell.' (Lady Gwendeline Churchill to C, 41 Cromwell Road, undated but 14 May 1934.)

great figures of the age, including Lord Haldane, J. M. Barrie and even Noël Coward. The youthful Evelyn Waugh heard the staff saying 'Up to a point, Lady Horner' and adapted it for his novel, *Scoop.*

Clarissa remembered her well, bearing 'traces of the features that had made her a muse of the Pre-Raphaelites – large, wide-set eyes, small nose, firm jawbone'.[16] The well-known Irish priest, Canon James Hannay, who wrote novels under the name of George A. Birmingham, was invariably in attendance. He became vicar of Mells, later moving to Holy Trinity, Brompton. Trim was amused by 'the hair breadth margin'[17] by which Clarissa invariably escaped the canon on her visits. Also at Mells was Katharine's friend, Martin D'Arcy, a Catholic priest. He and the canon just tolerated each other. The religious atmosphere of Mells oppressed Clarissa. In November 1939 she quoted Trim's great friend Isaiah Berlin after a visit: 'The grey bats of Popery were whirring round us.' She concluded: 'There is something definitely sinister about rabid Catholics.'[18]

She was also intimidated by Lady Violet Bonham Carter* who, she thought, hated her 'so that I daren't utter in her presence for fear she sd sum me up'. She felt 'a hard aching kernel of suppression inside' her on account of 'the Catholics who cause me to mind my words, & whose watchword anyway is "charitableness" (but such a sour censoring charity), which virtue doesn't come into my make-up! I am a fool to be so inhibited, & it does hurt so.'[19]

Isaiah Berlin was sure that Clarissa was being lined up for Trim as a potential bride. As 1937 gave way to 1938, Trim became increasingly drawn to her and his problem was how to steer a childhood friendship into romance. What he did not know was that she was secretly in love with someone else. She needed Trim as a loving friend and did little to discourage him. They made each other exceptionally happy, which was not the case in her other relationship.

She invited Trim to a skiing holiday in Lenzerheide in Switzerland in January 1938, but he was too busy studying Herodotus to accept. David Wallace, another admirer, and his brother went. During that stay, Clarissa shared a tiny room above a sports shop with Priscilla

---

* Lady Violet Bonham Carter (1887–1969), later Baroness Asquith of Yarnbury, daughter of H. H. Asquith, and sister of Raymond. She is buried in Mells churchyard.

Bibesco. She was annoyed that Priscilla talked incessantly about people she knew. David Wallace was soon in 'such a pitch of hatred over Priscilla that he cannot sit near to her even, let alone spend the evening with her'.[20] Aunt Clemmie and Mary had thirteen 'quite incredibly boring & annoying Forbeses' with them. 'They loathe me with good reason & I can't understand why everyone else likes them,'[21] Clarissa told Trim. The atmosphere was soon strained to breaking point.

By the time she returned on 16 January, Trim was back at Oxford, quoting the *Tablet* on Isaiah Berlin, as 'one of the wittiest Semitic channels flowing through Oxford'.[22] Clarissa invited Trim to Holworth in March, which he described as 'such a luxury of time', with hours spent making coffee, watching the waves, and balancing conversation with 'pools of comfortable silence'.[23] They bought needles and balloons in Weymouth, and made a cake, dripping with raisins. Trim wanted Clarissa to come secretly to Paris with him and invited her to Mells on her own, but she said she could not come unchaperoned. It was one of those 'damning conventions we talked about', which will 'get in your way as well as mine if you have anything to do with me'.[24] She stayed at Holworth, reading Rilke.*

He did persuade her to come to Oxford for canoeing in June. By this time, unlike when at school, she had developed a taste for study. She took an extension course in English and French literature at London University, but she found her family frustrating and told David Wallace she wished they would melt away.

Simultaneously she was bored stiff by the London season, attending balls given by grand ladies in London, at which the American bandleader Jack Harris invariably performed. Sitting next to Lord Howard of Glossop at a dinner, she tried every subject from books, music, travel, through racing, shooting, agriculture, cinema and the Stock Exchange: 'Not once did he make a remark which betrayed promise of a gleam of intelligence or knowledge of the subject.'[25] She preferred to read Stephen Spender, Dylan Thomas, Franz Kafka, René Descartes, George Berkeley and David Hume. She studied Aristotle and modern German ethics, Kant appealing most.

There were girls' luncheons, concerts, balls and dinner parties. She

---

* Rainer Maria Rilke (1875–1926), expressive poet, famed for *The Duino Elegies*.

saw much of Priscilla* and her mother Elizabeth Bibesco. She was spotted at Ascot in 'a grey spotted dress and had a band of grey ribbon on her white coarse-straw hat'.[26] She enjoyed the racing, but thought the rest 'so futile & rich & wasteful'. At a 'ghastly' cocktail party given by the American socialite, Laura Corrigan, the guests, including the Duke of Marlborough and Lady Long, took off their clothes or jumped fully dressed into the swimming pool. And so it continued through the season. Clarissa complained that it was hard to combine ethics with balls every other night. A weekend at Breccles was saved by the presence of Laurence Whistler, who took her to see the Norman arches, but then she had to pull a giant cake into the ball-room at Queen Charlotte's Ball with '500' other debutantes.[27]

Alastair Forbes (already a feature of London life) was a regular lunch appointment in London, and John Merton, later a well-known artist, was in her orbit. Donald Maclean (years later exposed as a spy) was a dance partner. Presently he turned up again in Paris, as third secretary in Sir George Clerk's embassy. By and large she found the young men she encountered immature. She was especially dismissive of Charles Harding, a particularly social figure.[†]

Clarissa gave Trim a lurid description of another ball at Hatfield, telling him it induced in her 'fear, boredom & discomfort alter-nately'.[28] This held particular significance because it was thought at that time that she might marry Robert Cecil (later Viscount Cranborne and Marquess of Salisbury), the goal of many contempor-ary girls of her class being to marry an elder son, the heir to a great estate. This was never Clarissa's plan. When she turned eighteen the following year, Goonie was anxious that she should not marry young. She feared she would miss her, because she loved 'the life & gaiety' she created around herself, but there was another reason: 'Your husband is sure to be someone who does not like me – because anyway so far, the men you seem to prefer are the very ones who seem to despise me.'[29]

---

* In 1939 Priscilla was recruited as a spy by Sir Robert Vansittart, permanent under secretary at the Foreign Office 1930–38.

† James Pope-Hennessy thought she was right about Harding: 'but I so admire perfection in any genre at all that I never feel the least intolerant. But I agree with you about the general dankness.' (JPH to C, 7 July 1938).

More appealing was to meet Trim's friend, the artist David Jones, whom she greatly liked. Despite all this, Aunt Clemmie reported to Goonie: 'On all sides I hear of Clarissa's charm & success, & beauty. I am so glad, becos I love Clarissa, but more glad for you, Goonie Darling, who have <u>lavished</u> so much love, tenderness, thought & <u>intelligence</u> upon her. I hope she will make a brilliant marriage. She is so made to shine.'[30]

With war approaching, Trim shaved off his beard to fit a gas mask and undertook officer training at Tidworth. He wanted Clarissa to visit Mells again, but warned her to avoid the day Queen Mary was coming to lunch as that would not appeal to her. In November he made a tentative step towards moving their relationship to a different plane. 'I have a complicated (but slightly cold-blooded) suggestion which I would like to make. Shall I make it or would you rather not bother?'[31] he asked her. From under the dryer at the hairdresser's Clarissa resisted this move, disapproving of it on principle and in practice: 'I think it is more often fatal to have a mutual self-revelation. Neither do I like it in theory – that is I dislike it done for its own sake as we shall be doing it. Because that inevitably involves lack of all restraint & proportion . . .'

She feared he would find her 'unworthy & little understanding' and reserved the right 'to refuse to disclose anything that has not an active bearing on you & me'. She thought it was inconceivable to resort to guile: 'the <u>only</u> conditions possible are those of complete & solemn honesty & truth . . . I now await instructions as to the 1st stage in the proceedings. It's only fair that you should show the way to move 1st.'[32]

On 17 November Trim elaborated his plan, which involved 'the revelation of certain military secrets on both sides'. He wanted to tell her his 'whole disposition' concerning her and wanted her to reciprocate. He said this was not an ultimatum, adding: 'You see why I said it was cold-blooded but you like drama better than romance so you may not mind.'[33]

Her reply does not survive, but he deduced that she thought he was suggesting a physical relationship for its own sake and protested that he was not an Antoine Bibesco (Priscilla's father, a well-known *coureur* after women, and one of the older men in occasional pursuit of Clarissa). Trim wrote that he had only mentioned it because 'in our peculiar case it was necessary (or soon might be) if we were to go on having any kind of relations at all'. He continued:

> By all means present only a chosen part of your <u>inner</u> self. Our case wouldn't justify me in asking more than that. But at the moment you don't even do that. I mean I don't mind (much) your only presenting to me one facet out of many. What I mind is that you only present the surface even of that facet – reflecting light at odd & original angles, but defying penetration.[34]

He then pursued philosophical theories concerning guile, self-revelation, and the strength of their relations. Later he was more self-revelatory, apologising as to 'how there are some moments when the only terms I cd bear to be on with you seem to involve my making demands which I have no right to make & don't want to make'. He continued:

> You see I love you too much for you ever to be very far from my thoughts & prayers, or for me to be unconcerned about every detail of your behaviour. I get angry sometimes, for instance, seeing you with other people, flashing one of those facets of yours in their faces. It's partly for selfish reasons, I suppose, wanting my facet to be the only one, but partly also because I hate to see you being ingratiating & selling yourself . . . Anyway my concern for you seems to demand a certain amount (not v. large) of self-surrender on your part, which you very naturally don't like the idea of. Whether you do or not, I shouldn't feel justified in asking it unless our love was greater even than it is & I think there are things about your character and mine which makes that difficult.[35]

Trim and Clarissa reached an impasse but they remained close. The exchange of letters did not progress their relationship, but caused no damage.

Charlie
Marquess of Lansdowne
(1917–44)

Another suitor was young Lord Lansdowne, about whom Trim sometimes jokily teased Clarissa, aware that country-house parties held no
appeal for her. Years later Clarissa mused that she might have chosen
to marry him: 'It would have been a good marriage.'[36] She described
him as 'a particular friend . . . a gentle, sensitive boy who, being
unjudgmental and observant, could fit in with anyone'.[37]

Charlie was the grandson of the distinguished 5th Marquess, who
had served as Foreign Secretary, Governor General of Canada and
Viceroy of India. He was born on 9 January 1917. The old Marquess
had died in 1927 and Charlie succeeded his father, the 6th Marquess,
in 1936, when he was nineteen. That was not expected. His father
was a man of scholarly tastes, whose poor health had prevented him
from making a career in public life. In 1933, Charlie's elder brother,
Lord Kerry, a Balliol man, who also suffered from poor health, either
fell or jumped under a tube train; the verdict was left open.

Charlie was educated at Eton and went up to Balliol College, lodging at 89 St Aldate's (the sheets were damp) where Trim was also to
be found. He spent four years at Oxford, the first rather unmemor-
able but when he succeeded to the marquessate he became rich and
fêted. Later he veered away from the smart, rich-minded friends,
members of the Bullingdon Club, feeling he had missed so much of
interest.

He first met Clarissa when staying with Madame Balsan in France
in 1937. Clarissa visited Bowood, his family seat, in December that
year. By November 1938 he was more prominent in her life. A year
later he went to dinner with her and apologised for behaving 'dreadfully badly' to Ali Forbes. He told her that what he liked best was to
slip into a corner with one person and criticise all the others. They
were both at a Blenheim house party, where there had been waltzing.
When war was declared in September 1939, he told her his dream was
to live always at Bowood: 'so absolutely beautiful – to think one
could always live there always, would only be a dream, yet it's a dream
I have day and night'.[38]

The war disrupted Charlie's life as it did everyone else's. In January

1940 he was sent out to Palestine with the Royal Wiltshire Yeomanry. He had a week's leave, 'which was heavenly, but so sad. I said goodbye passionately to everybody – for I am going abroad very soon – thinking I should never see them again'.[39] He asked Clarissa for a copy of Montaigne's *Essays*, which he craved to read, and she sent him one. He did not survive the war. Paying tribute, Trim wrote of his courage, sensitivity, humility and modesty:

> So it was that with his modesty was combined also a confidence, with his gentleness a firmness based on the knowledge that certain things were of enduring value. This knowledge he sought always to extend and deepen . . . Preoccupied at times by his responsibilities, he did not allow their burden to weigh him down, and his moods, grave and gay, succeeded one another so quickly that they often mingled. He was happiest in the country, and had in particular a great love of trees. In the laughter and delicacy of their leaves, the strength and steadfastness of their roots, may be found reflected one of the many rich contrasts of his own character.[40]

David Wallace
(1914–44)

David Wallace met Clarissa at a ball at Knebworth, with the Lyttons, in October 1937. He was the son of Captain Euan Wallace, MP, who died in 1941, and his wife Lady Idina Sackville.* David went up to Balliol from Eton and lodged at 14a Broad Street. His abiding love was for Greece. He was an admirer of Clarissa, though more so of Cressida Bonham Carter. He took Clarissa seriously enough to analyse her character:

> I would not so far disparage your understanding & knowledge of your own nature, as ever to entertain the hypothesis that you picture or even dramatise yourself as a person whose ebullient magnetism

---

* Lady Idina Sackville (1883–1955). She was married five times. At one time she was Countess of Erroll and part of the 'White Mischief' Happy Valley set in Kenya. David called her his 'physical or African mother' or 'carnal mother', as opposed to Barbara Lutyens, his 'other mother'.

and feverishly fulsome ardour compel the most frozen of hearts to melt and the shiest of plants to open fearlessly their petals. But have you never considered that your carefully cultivated froideur, the calm & confident dignity with which you conduct all social & personal relationships, admirable as an intellectual armour, is perhaps not calculated to encourage a facile outburst of unrestrained warmth from the least reticent, that the least defensive will be impelled to raise a counter-barricade, the least pretentious façade, that the most generous may sicken of showing all their hand and the most strenuous tire of making every effort, alone, to return a sullen sneer or a prickly pear, that the most adventurous may hesitate to take risks with so slight a chance of success, the least curious be tempted to try by neglect to strike or spark off the iceberg.

   . . . I have wondered why, granted how very much I like you, I like you no more. The answer is, I think, that I cease to like you where I cease to know you, one needs to be fit & well, to have had a good night's sleep & no worries, fully to enjoy your company; for you cooperate not at all: you make no effort whatsoever, yet you resent neglect; sometimes one cannot make the efforts, your demands are too high . . .[41]

During 1938 they visited Greenwich and he dined with her family, judging that neither 'your mother nor your brother would ever boil an egg by just putting it in their mouth and as such do not help to contribute a combustible atmosphere'.[42] He then went away for seven months, meeting Clive Bell and Gertrude Stein in Paris and Bernard Berenson at I Tatti. He travelled with Ben Nicolson to Arezzo, Cortina, Orvieto and Rome. He failed to meet Clarissa in Europe, but found her photograph, which prompted him to mourn what might have been, 'It seems to incarnate for me all the sorrow and suffering & deception of the world,' and yet he was moving on: 'This picture is the crown of melancholy – the one link with the past, but even that only the echo of a dead world, of a past not that ever was but that might have been, the reflection of a memory of how all dreams were never realised even in that world that has gone.'[43]

A month later, in September 1938, Clarissa went to stay with him and his family at Lavington Park, in Sussex, fascinated by the luxury, the en-suite marble bathroom, white telephone and iced Malvern water in the bedroom. The herbaceous borders contained 'more gardeners than flowers almost'. There was a royal blue swimming-bath in front of the house, which was adorned with a fine Georgian wing, though Clarissa did not care for the hideous 1900 wing or the porch devised by Lutyens. She liked the three Wallace brothers immensely, as she reported to Trim:

> You can imagine I'm not good at boys' chat! and David, in Greek red linen trousers & water green silk shirt, and in a sinisterly dulcet temper towards me & deliciously vindictive about the rest of the world. This crisis is making both of us more bared to the nerve than we usually are with each other, & relations proceed well so far . . . but the meals are the funniest part. Barbie [his mother] seems to consider it *mal convenu* to allow 3 minutes' silence ever. So there is a continual & completely void conversation kept up between her & the 3 *garçons*. I am silent from shyness (& pride in being bored!). David is silent from irritation, emerging from stupor with some highly out of place remark that drives Barbie furious. She in return hits back at him, remarking that neighbours never get on with each other while tow-rows always find something to say to each other etc . . . David has promised never to give me away when I sink low & affirm an adoration of Cole Porter, Lady Castlerosse, the Venetian Lido, Blenheim etc. I hope that I have thus made a more favourable impression than Cressida [Bonham Carter], who, this is strictest confidence for you alone, has been banned from coming here ever again![44]

By the end of the stay she and David were not talking. Within four months, on 24 January 1939 he had married Prudence Magor quietly at St Bartholomew the Great, prompting Isaiah Berlin to say he was no longer 'a rebel by nature'. Four days later David sent Clarissa a postcard from the Élysée Park Hotel, in Paris, thanking her for her congratulatory telegram: 'It was very sweet of you.'[45] And that was the end of that.

In the war he served in the King's Royal Rifle Corps. He did not survive.

Jeremy Hutchinson
later Lord Hutchinson of Lullington
(1915–2017)

The reason that none of the suitors succeeded in becoming a boyfriend of Clarissa was because she had lost her heart to Jeremy Hutchinson. His name appeared in her diaries as early as October 1937 when they lunched together several times in London, and he was invited to dinner with her family. He stayed at Mells when Goonie and Clarissa were there. In her memoirs Clarissa wrote disparagingly of the Paris parties and the London season and how, on her return to London, she proceeded to 'fall for someone who could give me a taste of another side of life.'[46] As was her way, Jeremy was only mentioned as a person with whom she escaped to the music hall in East Stratford or for dinner at the Prospect of Whitby on the Isle of Dogs. She considered these excursions a relief from the social season. As related, she described him to me as her 'first great love'.

There is a significant letter from her mother from Mells in January 1938, at the time when she was staying in Switzerland and David Wallace was in the party. Clarissa had sent her mother a photograph of herself with David in a bar. Her mother responded in a letter that she urged Clarissa to burn:*

> I was so happy to get yr letter & the photos, a bit startled by the one with 'glass in hand' – it looks a bit 'rough'. I use this expression, because Bubbles [Ridley] who is here, said David could be a bit 'rough'. I understood it meant a bit fast, dashing, boisterous? They all laughed here, but Katharine afterwards said Bubbles has a twisted & exaggerated mind. <u>Don't</u> repeat a word of all this to David, because only <u>mischief</u> comes of it. You say Jeremy is in love with you, but I will tell you who <u>is</u> in love with you is Trim. Everybody here noticed Jeremy paying court to you – that is both Katharine & Ly Horner – Trim hardly mentions you.[47]

Jeremy Hutchinson was to become a well-known barrister, described as the finest silk practising at the bar in his day, who might

---

* Fortunately she kept the letter.

have been a Labour Lord Chancellor. He was to defend the spy George Blake, Christine Keeler and publication of books such as *Lady Chatterley's Lover* and *Fanny Hill*. It is suggested that John Mortimer's *Rumpole of the Bailey* was partly based on him. He stood six foot three inches. He was the son of St John Hutchinson, KC, and his wife Mary was a Bloomsbury, a friend of Clive Bell, and the model for Virginia Woolf's *Mrs Dalloway*. From Stowe he went up to Magdalen College, Oxford.

As a correspondent he was considerably more direct than many who wrote to Clarissa, expressing a strong determination to see her at all costs whenever it suited him. As with other admirers, such as Trim and James Pope-Hennessy, the letters began towards the end of 1937. They were more traditional love letters, but as for coming and going, he moved between abject devotion and vacillation.

Clarissa kept friends such as Trim and James Pope-Hennessy in the dark about him, but David Wallace had him in his sights, writing to Clarissa in March 1938: 'As for your row with Jeremy, I know nothing about the details of it or indeed your relations with Jeremy at all. One odd thing about him is that in the last year several of his and my mutual friends have had a bout with him and on each occasion it has not been his fault.'[48]

★ ★ ★ ★ ★

Clarissa had decided to return to Paris and study there. She dined twice with Jeremy in London, then set off on 20 January 1939. One of her motives for going was that it would be easier to continue her affair with Jeremy while in France. He had volunteered for non-combative service in the Royal Navy, so was now in the Royal Naval Voluntary Reserve. There was a clandestine afternoon meeting with Jeremy in Portland, following which he found himself in Glasgow, cold and alone, about to go to sea in a small boat. As so often he vacillated, pronouncing that he was missing her. By February he was in Los Angeles, this time professing that she was the only person he missed.

In March Jeremy was due some leave from the RNVR and arranged to meet Clarissa in Paris, stipulating that his parents should not hear of this. He pictured Clarissa with her medieval manuscripts, philosophy and her transparent white mackintosh. He was delayed until 3 April. But hardly had he appeared than he bolted. From the Hôtel du Quai

Voltaire, he announced his curt departure, not sure if he was being cowardly or courageous, but determined that he 'MUST go'. He told her there was 'nothing more to be done' and asked her forgiveness.[49]

Some days later, from London, when he tried to explain, he based his agony on her having concealed what she was thinking and feeling – in other words that she loved him more than he loved her. And so he felt impelled to go. The rest of his letter was a long wriggle. Nevertheless, the love affair rambled on, albeit haphazardly, and it continued when Clarissa went to live in Oxford in October 1939.

5. PARIS PRE-WAR

As 1938 drew on, Clarissa was pushed into learning German when she would have preferred to take up sculpting. She was reading aesthetics, but wondered to Trim:

> Doubts flit occasionally across my brain as to whether all these people aren't talking a lot of rather sophisticated nonsense from distorted attitudes to things, & esp. from isolating a small part of art & making a philosophical system out of it. The more I look at pictures & the more I read about them the more it seems to me to be impossible, or at any rate dangerous, to dissociate one's attitude about arts from the 1,000s of less pure things that have been so inextricably woven into it since one cd 1st see or think.
>
> Because the theory about pictures & Aesthetics that I've formulated & which I believe in passionately in theory & on paper has so little validity when I actually look at pictures! This shows how hopelessly fake one's meta-physical theories must be, or may be, that look so convincing on paper but which we can never check up in actuality short of instinctive beliefs in direct mysticism.
>
> So Boo.[1]

By December Clarissa was depressed. She spent a 'pagan' Christmas at Blenheim Palace, though enjoyed it more than she expected, despite finding the artist, Paul Maze (who had taught Churchill how to paint) 'a tiresome sponge', and Randolph Churchill, his son, 'most objectionable'.[2]

Partly irritated by her family, and partly for the freedom to be with Jeremy Hutchinson, she returned to Paris. One goal was to study medieval history and art.[3] Clarissa's mother had been concerned about her living in Paris when the European political situation was so fragile. Clarissa told Trim: 'There has been the usual Uncle Winston trouble which is preliminary to all my excursions abroad. But by obstinacy rather than persuasion I think the danger is over.'[4] Goonie told Winston that Jack was depressed and cross, that Clarissa had found England gloomy and dull, and that she was now in Paris 'working hard & blissfully unconcerned'.[5] Winston reassured her that danger was not imminent and that she should write to Lady Phipps, wife of the British Ambassador, who could then warn Clarissa if she needed to leave. He thought she could easily do so via Dieppe or Le Havre if Calais and Boulogne proved too crowded. Goonie was relieved when Clarissa made a plan with the Embassy should such an emergency arise.

Clarissa settled at first at 104 rue de Rennes in a room with yellow organdie curtains and photographs of Rodin sculptures and pictures from the Louvre. She wrote to Trim, telling him she was happy. He replied: 'I didn't realise it had been as bad as all that for you this last year. It's certainly high time you went to Paris for the thought of you being not only bound & pressed but annihilated in London is a distressing one.'[6]

She spent most of her time with the French family, but there were excursions with English friends, Valentine Lawford, 'very pale & nice as ever', and Donald Maclean, 'at the Embassy'.[7] She attended concerts with Pauline Maze, daughter of the painter, a new friend: 'sensitive both to situations & things, in a way that is rare'.[8] She worked on medieval philosophy in the Bibliothèque Nationale. Princess Marthe Bibesco took her up:

I admire her very [much], she has terrific space & breadth of intellect & I have become very fond of her. Hers is the salon world – badinage, politics, fencing, & good breeding, a feeling of enamel & civilisation – no, more culture, the feeling of civilisation belongs to the journalists . . . Marthe's flat on the Île St Louis stands like the bow of a ship against the Seine. It has Bouchers & tapestries & windows every way . . .[9]

There she met the Abbé Mugnier, 'age 85 or 95, stone deaf & blind but terribly witty & making *mots* the whole time like one always hears the famous wits make. He looks like Voltaire.'[10] She went to a lecture by Paul Valéry, without being enrolled at the Sorbonne – 'he speaks very low & it seems very obtuse, something to do with muscular sensations & the intellect I gathered'.[11] She was soon deep into studying the Middle Ages, working at the Louvre on primitive pictures and medieval manuscripts.

Presently Clarissa decided she was not happy with her Paris family, telling Trim: 'I am so miserable in this family. They hate me & I hate the rue de Rennes.'[12] Trim warned her: 'You're hard to please, you know, & unless the family you're with are as insensible as granite, it must be your fault they don't like you – if it is true they don't.'[13] Her mother quoted Mary Herbert to her: 'What fun for C. being in Paris, freed from the tyranny that surrounds those who are being finished by school or governesses.'[14] Goonie was thrilled when Clarissa wrote: 'I am blissfully happy. I wish you cd realize how much & how different to what I ever have been in London. I feel balanced, content, free & satisfied.'[15] One Sunday she even went to church: 'It had that terrible assembly-room-Anglican atmosphere of *bienveillance* – with a slick beloved parish priest reeling off sentiments from the pulpit.' She enjoyed reading Peter Quennell's *Byron* but condemned Gertrude Stein's book on Picasso as 'bogus'.[16]

In March, she escaped to the Massif Centrale on a cultural tour, travelling first with Mrs Margesson,* in her Rolls-Royce. Priscilla Bibesco joined her, but this meant her lasciviously inclined father Antoine was there too: 'I had an overdose of Prince Antoine all last week – <u>he</u> is like an over-lived in room if you like. The people who lived in it may have been very intelligent & witty, & the scent they wore very good, but even so.' When the Margessons left Avallon in a blizzard, Clarissa found herself stuck at the Hôtel de la Poste at Saulieu. Vézelay had been wonderful, Saulieu 'too ugly'.[17] She felt unbalanced in her work in Paris and wished some teacher would inspire her.

---

* Frances Leggatt (1896–1977), wife of David Margesson (1890–1965), then government chief whip, later 1st Viscount Margesson. Her daughter, Gay (1919–2017), was an Oxford friend of Clarissa. Gay married Sir Martin Charteris (1913–99), Queen Elizabeth II's Private Secretary, later Lord Charteris of Amisfield.

By March Clarissa had moved to 32 avenue Rapp in the 7th arrondissement, with windows giving views over Les Invalides and the Eiffel Tower. Hugh Fraser* turned up and they stayed out until 6 a.m. She met Peter Rose Pulham, 'the man who takes photographs of Picasso & has drooping moustachios & side whiskers'.[18] She walked for hours alone through the Paris streets, relishing their aesthetic quality, though worried that she was only a dilettante. She longed to visit Romania, considering it the country of the future. War looked inevitable. Days passed with grand lunches, which required dressing up, then work, galleries or expeditions, drinking in the evenings at six, possibly a cinema and then sitting out till 1 a.m. She loved Paris 'more & more'. To Trim she wrote: 'I have reached a point – which does happen as summer nears – when I can do nothing but float along & live – but at the same time various happenings in my recent life [an oblique reference to Jeremy] are now preventing me from obliviously enjoying that floating with a benumbed conscience.'[19]

In March, James Pope-Hennessy warned Clarissa that her mother was looking ill. Goonie had been unwell the previous summer, with the doctor, Lord Horder, assuring her that she would soon be cured. When not resting on her sofa, she moved about, visiting Chartwell, though she demurred from telling Clarissa detrimental stories about Aunt Clemmie, because they amused Clarissa too much. Johnny wrote in his memoirs that he knew their mother could only live for about two years. She had developed an aneurysm, a cracked main artery in the intestine. Clarissa's father believed Goonie's case to be 'very bad'. He heard of a new treatment in Paris, the problem being to help Goonie without alarming her: 'Any new drastic treatment will at once arouse suspicion and upset her dreadfully. Her improvement is greatly due to her peace of mind . . . This Paris Clinique seems to have made an advance . . . I am living in a nightmare.'[20] Goonie underwent treatment until the end of May.

At Easter 1939 Clarissa returned to England to be with her mother whose ill health was an ever-growing concern. As she put it to Trim: 'I came to England you know, slunk in and out, for a few days at Holworth & got back here worn out & with some relief.'[21] On her

---

* (Sir) Hugh Fraser (1918-84), politician, later married to Lady Antonia Pakenham.

return to Paris, Trim came to see her on his way to Italy. He loved every minute he spent with her. As her Paris sojourn drew to a close, she savoured the last days 'with the intensity one does when things are so significantly for the last time'. She mused on her situation:

> I seem to want something so very different from other people that it dawns on me I shall have to find it alone. Only, because of this difference I always discover sooner or later, I am beginning to believe everything is made up of compromises. One must compromise if, like me, one hasn't the power to sustain illusions. I never could have illusions for long, because unwittingly in my very act of continuing to exist I seemed to break their veil.[22]

It seemed that war had been put off, though at Chartwell Winston, 'very warlike', told Goonie, 'It's put off for the present & that's about all – but anyway it's off.' Goonie reported that there was 'lots of abuse of old Chamberlain & all those footling Ministers & with reason . . . Uncle W. ought to have been made Minister of Supply, & the House of Commons & the country as a whole would have approved, but Chamberlain wouldn't . . . but there is a feeling that Uncle W. will be in the forefront if anything serious happens now again. He has risen in everybody's estimation as a patriot, & all the fawners & grovellers & place hunters & toadies are hanging around – people writing him fulsome letters etc!'[23]

At this point Churchill was predicting that if there was to be a war, it would be in the late summer: 'He was anxious about the Polish problems – Everything was in the lap of the gods – Hit [Hitler] does not want war. We are in a muddle. The whole world is upside down.' She gleaned that the Germans did not want Winston in the government and had instructed their agents 'to spread rumours about & do everything to prevent it'.[24]

Clarissa returned to London on 1 June, for a spate of weddings, Jasper (Bubbles) Ridley and Cressida Bonham Carter, and balls, the Duchess of Sutherland for her niece, Elizabeth Leveson-Gower, at Sutton Place, attended by the Gloucesters, Queen Victoria Eugenie of Spain and other royal figures. This was to be the last season before the war, and Clarissa elaborated on it to James Pope-Hennessy, then working briefly for the Governor of Trinidad. She prided herself that she wrote to him, as she would to herself: 'truly, unelaborated or unsimplified'.[25] She found London racked by rain and high winds and the ARP mud 'increasingly hideous'. Trenches were being hastily completed, and the debutantes were taking VAD exams. Catherine Sinclair was learning to be a Land Girl in Cornwall, while dances were bereft of men who were all away on manoeuvres. They stocked up on biscuits and tinned food:

> Peregrine has a new & highly paid job, selling steel shelters to Eaton Square – Johnny, my other brother, has an even more highly paid one, head of the camouflage department. And now everyone says Hitler won't march on Danzig, but concentrate on Poland instead. I would write of politics but it will be over by the time it reaches you. Someone has issued thousands of enamel badges with 'Churchill' written on them, & to Chartwell come Germans to assure Uncle W. that Hitler means everything & more. Most of our friends are frayed, & all unhappy about various things. So the parties get wilder & more oblivious, and even the rich, thoughtless Socialites say to each other they won't see Ballrooms again.[26]

Clarissa went to her last ball at Hever Castle where the men smelt of expensive hair oil and Molyneux Le Numéro Cinq. The 'pearl-coloured dawn' rose over the lake, 'twenty rockets soaring simultaneously up to the stars & falling on the soft smoke screen puffed out below. Three cheers for Gavin Astor,* he's 21 today, & sent down from Oxford.' In contrast she went to Ben Nicolson's party in two bare rooms in Guilford Street, off Mecklenburgh Square, then to Philip Toynbee's, similar with 'dozens of models & Bohemians, covered in dirt & uncleanliness, on the floor, Craven A, white wine & beer, bonhomie, drunken affection & incoherence'. Ben's party produced Raymond Mortimer, Harold Nicolson, Stephen Spender, Louis MacNeice, Virginia Woolf, Julian Huxley, Wyndham Lewis, Kenneth Clark 'and two great friends & lovers who had quarrelled & parted & were now meeting again in these rooms. One watched their embarrassment, their understanding,

---

* The Hon. Gavin Astor (1918–84), later 2nd Baron Astor of Hever, owner of Times Newspapers. He joined the Life Guards.

their bitter emotion & sometimes their fatalistic resumption of old relationships'.

Ivan Moffat* gave a party in Fitzroy Square:

A modernised flat, with ancient *objets d'art* set in illuminated vacuums in the wall. Leopard skin cigarette boxes, more intoxication, people setting out to get drunk instead of becoming so. Anne & Philip (newest combination) singing Communist songs on a divan, Caroline Paget, people playing that infernal truth game in the box room. Austrians, Poles . . . After an interminable time I seemed to be making soda water with Ben (incoherent & sentimental & drooping) in the pantry. Later there was an accordionist playing penetratingly . . . Ivan, in enormous loose tweeds, his lock falling forward, his grin, his iron-sprung subtleties. In retrospect it was awful.[27]

The approach of war depressed Clarissa. People jumped if a tyre burst in the street. She could not read, just lay on her bed brooding: 'With people I am bad value, gloomy & sour & paralysed, and I haven't a ray of energy with which to either concentrate on mental pursuits or alternatively go out & play with people.'[28]

Clarissa travelled to Romania with Priscilla Bibesco and her parents, stopping in Venice on the way, enjoying a Veronese exhibition, running into Mr and Mrs Douglas Fairbanks Senior and Charles Harding, who spent every summer on the Lido, 'covered in sunburn oil & practically with a medicine beach ball in his hand!'[29] They arrived in Corcova, where Clarissa wished the ever-amorous Antoine Bibesco would not begin every sentence '*Si on est amoureux*' or '*Quand un homme et une femme s'aiment*'.† She concluded that she would have loved Romania without the Bibescos – 'without Antoine & his *amoureux*, without Elizabeth her *Mein Kampf*, her anecdotes & her Asquithian tricks, & without Priscilla & her jazz'.[30] She found Antoine's amorous attitude repulsive, her Teutonic approach to life conflicting with his Slavic ways: 'I'm fond of Antoine tho' – he has

---

* Ivan Moffat (1918-2002), son of the photographer, Curtis Moffat and Iris Tree. Briefly a Communist, later a film producer.
† 'If one is in love' and 'When a man and a woman love each other'.

nice things, wit & kindness in the long run. Short spasms with him are the least representative.'[31]

Soon afterwards Winston Churchill alerted Goonie that war was now imminent. Marthe Bibesco's husband, an aviator, flew Clarissa to Bucharest in his biplane, and on 26 August she joined her mother in Dorset.

War was declared on 3 September.

6. OXFORD
1939–40

In the autumn Clarissa went to live in Oxford, though not as an undergraduate. While she was there, one of the many authors she tackled was Max Beerbohm. 'I've only read the parodies, & Zuleika D. which wasn't really my cup,'[1] she told Trim, though her effect on many undergraduates was not wholly dissimilar from that of Beerbohm's fictional *Zuleika Dobson*.

She settled at 63 St John Street, where the landlady, Mrs Shepheard, was known for her good omelettes. Clarissa loved the mellow city, her lodging, and the gas-ring atmosphere ('amusing because new to me').[2] She was joined by Anne Powell, which meant her lover, Philip Toynbee,[*] 'hanging about wearing two sweaters', and she resumed studying philosophy. Twice a week she worked in the library at the Radcliffe Infirmary: 'It teaches me to be sunny & amicable, & try to not be aristocratic – & the glimpses of people in oxygen chambers & other things is most interesting – there was one man who had caught Mata Hari![†] (This sounds like a disease – I mean the woman spy.)'[3]

Her Oxford life was made easier by having known Lord David Cecil and his wife Rachel since childhood, David being a great

---

[*] Philip Toynbee was described by Jessica Mitford as 'large, rangy . . . uncoordinated as a wolfhound puppy', and by Patrick Leigh-Fermor as looking like 'a raw-boned aristocratic lumber jack or stevedore' (Jessica Mitford, *Faces of Philip* (Heinemann, 1984), p. 22). He married Anne Powell in November, her mother having agreed reluctantly to this, fearing that if she prevented it and Philip was killed in the war, her daughter would never speak to her again. Secretly, however, she banked on him being killed as the only solution to the unfortunate union, but he survived. Of the wedding Clarissa commented to Trim: 'She is brave & short-sighted I sd have said, but it's unpredictable.'

[†] Mata Hari was arrested in Paris in 1917.

admirer of her mother. Clarissa described him as like a Beerbohm cartoon: 'long, thin legs, long face with the typical Cecil family high-domed forehead, limbs always in movement – elegant but not dandy-ish, sitting in his red sweater, drumming with his nicotine-stained fingers'.[4] He had the absent-mindedness of the academic and was of a nervous disposition. Simon Asquith, son of Lady Cynthia, whom Clarissa had known since childhood, told her that when it seemed there could be a war, 'David Cecil, who usually thinks of suicide at the idea of war, has been comparatively calm.'[5]

The Cecils invited her to tea and dinner regularly and through them she met Roy and Billa Harrod, Isaiah Berlin (again) and Maurice Bowra. Hearing that Clarissa wanted to study philosophy, Roy Harrod, a tutor at Christ Church, recommended her to Professor A. J. 'Freddie' Ayer, also of Christ Church, and by the beginning of November Ayer had taken her on.

Just before she went to Oxford, *London Fabric* was published. Clarissa wrote to James:

> Each time I look at that cover I become more pleased with it – & I have been going over the book itself too. It is good, it's undeniably good, dear James. You are clever to have produced it.
>
> Mummy is <u>delighted</u> with it. She is writing to you about it. She has been rocking with laughter over some of your historical descriptions & reading them out loud with joy.[6]

Two of her admirers read it. Charlie Lansdowne was serving with 26th H/H Battery in Egypt: 'How exciting it must have been for you reading about yourself. I was rather jealous that you said much more interesting things to him when he took you to Greenwich than you did when I took you.'[7] On the other hand, Trim thought the book 'most indecent'.[8]

Soon after arriving in Oxford, Clarissa dined with Isaiah Berlin: 'It was one of the most invigorating & enchanting dinners I've ever had. He talked of the Slavs – of Moore* & Price† & Wittgenstein &

---

* Presumably George Edward Moore (1873–1958), professor of philosophy, Cambridge 1925–39.
† Professor H. H. Price (1899–1984), Wykeham professor of logic and fellow of New College. His main interest in philosophy concerned problems connected with knowledge of the external world by sense-perception. He was interested in mysticism.

many other things – also brilliant analyses of Philip [Toynbee] & Wallace, & the Beaumont St. coterie. He promised to communicate with me again about Moore & Price's lectures but so far no word (I'm afraid you've given him rather a conscience about me!) Old Fisher* is agitating to get me a job somewhere.'[9] She loved the 'divine chaos' of papers in Berlin's room. He proved a staunch ally. In time he came to describe her as 'upright & downright',[10] which she enjoyed. Sometimes he could be disconcerting: 'He was very severe with me, & kept on popping questions out of the blue & asking me what I thought about them – which I can't do. Also I get muddled with my language. He has given me Price to read this week.'[11] Trim commented: 'He does adore telling about himself doesn't he?'[12]

Before leaving Oxford to serve in the Welsh Guards, Freddie Ayer recommended her to Professor Tony Peck,† Roy Harrod sponsored her and Isaiah Berlin sanctioned the plan. Peck set her many books to read and told her he would set her a BA paper the following term, though she was not sure she could cope with that. Peck gave her tutorials. When she told him she hadn't read Kant, he said: 'And, indeed, why should you have?' He sent her to Henry Price's class on Hume, deciding she needed to do Hume thoroughly before tackling Kant. Then, to her intense fury, Peck announced that she could no longer attend his lectures or go to the Bodleian. She asked Price if she could attend his and he agreed. Very often she wore a gown, but when Isaiah Berlin asked Price if it was all right for her to wear it in his lectures, he replied, in his broad Scottish accent: 'What! A warrking lie?'

The following year, she attended the lectures of Professor Alick Smith‡ of New College to study Kant and Ethics. She admired him: 'I was really absorbed in my work. Naturally it was far more stimulating to be arguing against Smith & his Kantianism than agreeing. He

---

* H. A. L. Fisher, OM (1865–1940), Fellow of New College, and modern history tutor.
† Antony Dylan (Tony) Peck (1914–87), a pupil of H. H. Price, a Fellow 1938-46, and later a civil servant.
‡ Alick Halford Smith (1883–1958), professor of philosophy, and later Vice Chancellor of Oxford University.

is having me again next term I believe – a man of great charm, & with a <u>very</u> aesthetic suite of rooms with Chinese Chippendale chairs & paintings on silk.' The summer term of 1940 had been 'the most exciting & stimulating imaginable'.[13] So involved was she with these professors by the end of her first term that Philip Toynbee told her he considered it 'sacrilege' that on a whim she should 'invade Oxford University' and get 'the best philosophers' to teach her.[14]

★ ★ ★ ★ ★

Clarissa joined her family in London for Randolph Churchill's wedding to Pamela Digby on 4 October 1939. This was a sudden endeavour on Randolph's behalf, as he was convinced he would be killed. He was said to have proposed to some eight women before setting off to war. Clarissa told James she was not pleased:

> The spectacle of the Randolph Churchills revolted me extremely. It is so frightfully immoral, their ménage, or rather what I consider immoral. To have married because you have made a mess of your life; or because you must have a child to leave behind you. I do think that in spite of the fact that throughout the ages people have married for those sort of reasons or *de convenance*, without any conspicuous harm to themselves or their sensibilities (which perhaps are too much talked about nowadays? by me at any rate!) nevertheless. I do think that one of the advances of the present age is the intelligent and sensible application of morals; not the narrow conception of the Victorian era, which still seems to be with one's mother's generation, with the exception of the old Bloomsburys, who knew better, they knew well, those old Bloomsburys. And to me the marriages *à la mode* are very immoral, and not particularly aesthetic either. It's that that really matters. Ivan [Moffat] and his perversions are all right but they are carried out in such a squalid filthy manner. The combination of Ivan, what you told me, and the spectacle of the Randolph marriage has got my goat rather.[15]

The wedding took place at St John's Church, Smith Square. The couple spent the first few months at Beverley, East Yorkshire, where Randolph's regiment was stationed. Trim ran into them both in Northampton, where they dined and argued about religion and politics. He wrote to Clarissa: 'I couldn't help liking him in spite of them & in spite of doing badly in the argument. (You can imagine he's not easy to argue with). His wife I liked too. Do tell me your reasons for disliking her.'[16] Clarissa obliged:

> How upsetting to find the Randolph Churchills as your latest
> friends . . . I should like to hear what exactly R's opinions are about
> Religion, in so many words I mean. I've always had a conspicuous
> failure with him, insomuch as he's never addressed a word to me in
> my life! Pam I agree has improved with marriage but she is still very
> foolish & very insincere. I think you are too easily duped by
> graciousness of manner which often doesn't mean of heart and soul.
> I've noticed that before.[17]

Randolph was elected MP for Preston in September 1940, when the sitting member died. On 10 October his son, another Winston Spencer-Churchill,* was born at Chequers. Randolph went to the Middle East but on his return Pam said: 'We both realised we'd made a mistake.'[18] Randolph proved himself temperamentally unsuited to marriage. Pam continued to live at Downing Street and Chequers, but thought he needed someone like his mother. who lived entirely for her husband. Young Winston, the son, was celebrated as the bright hope of the future, with a front-cover photograph on *Life* magazine, posed with his mother, by Cecil Beaton, and published on 27 January 1941.

It was not long before the bride was diverted towards a procession of rich men, which became her sensational speciality. Her principal lover was Averell Harriman,† sent to Britain by President Roosevelt. As Ali Forbes put it: 'No doubt F.D.R. who, as Harriman was later to remark, was never much upset to learn of other people's discomfitures, rather enjoyed hearing that his Special Envoy had chosen to add to his remit the pleasurable task of cuckolding the PM's son.' Pam and her son soon moved into a large flat in Grosvenor Square ('Wonderfully clever little girl with her modest allowance, isn't she?' nice Lord Digby was believed to have boasted to a friend).[19] In July 1941 Harriman met

---

* Winston S. Churchill, MP (1940–2010).
† Averell Harriman (1891–1986), US special envoy to Europe, later Ambassador to Moscow. He married Pamela in 1971.

Randolph in Egypt. To Pam Randolph wrote: 'He spoke delightfully about you & I fear that I have a serious rival!'[20] He did indeed. In 1942 Clarissa told James Lees-Milne that 'Randolph's wife had no intention of sticking to him,' and that the Prime Minister would be very sad if they parted.[21]

★ ★ ★ ★ ★

In the latter months of 1939 Clarissa stayed at Dyrham Park, near Bath, which had been leased by her godmother, Anne, Lady Islington, since 1938. Back at Oxford, Harold Nicolson came to lecture, as did Beverley Baxter, 'a ghastly Canadian', and the ever amorous Antoine Bibesco threatened to pay her a visit. Clarissa was unimpressed when politicians such as Brendan Bracken lectured – 'politicians in the raw. Conceited, ignorant, thick skinned'. Harold Nicolson she thought better: 'he also has sensibility & many other deep qualities . . . When one says things his little eyes just twinkle & he gives no hint of having seen the point & then suddenly he begins in a charming & confidential way, "Clarissa, tell me . . ." but it always freezes off, or something external stops it, & one begins to suspect that it's just a manner.'[22]

While Clarissa attended lectures, Trim went into the army and was soon training at Shorncliffe. Jeremy Hutchinson came and went as usual on his occasional leaves. There were plenty of admirers. In November she spent a weekend with Jeremy in London and after Christmas was at Mells, then at Dyrham Park again.

At the beginning of 1940 James Pope-Hennessy was stationed with the 83rd Light AA Battery, RA, in Sevenoaks, pushed into it by Harold Nicolson, while Trim was unhappy in the Royal Engineers. Gay Margesson joined Clarissa in Oxford, 'with her Socialism, her swear words and her smile'.[23]

James Pope-Hennessy was a good sounding board. He and Clarissa both enjoyed reading Proust, and testing opinions of friends in common. One such was Stephen Spender, of whom James despaired: 'These large and arid ex-Communist poets looming across their generation and one's own – what is the use of anything, any writing, any effort, how can one suppose this country or these decades have any hope, justification; or possibility or survival and salvation?' Peter Quennell, later a distinguished editor and writer, corrupted his wives:

'he turns them, he told me, from fresh country girls to nymphomaniacs within a year'.[24] Cyril Connolly appeared in Oxford, talking openly of leaving for America if the Germans invaded successfully, and announced that he had 'plans for trimming *Horizon*'s sails towards Fascism, so that when the Germans came it will be spared'. And Stephen Spender turned up, Clarissa reporting: 'I don't like him. I had breakfast with Berlin & he came loafing in. He has charm of manner though, & doesn't seem half so *ingénu* as I'd been given to understand! But B. insists he is.'[25] Clarissa asked James to give his opinion of her. James had always hoped she would make a great marriage:

> For one thing, you know, you have become more beautiful and have more *éclat*; that you see is the use of letters, one can say things in writing one cdnt mouth or more than imply face to face. I think Oxford is excellent in every way – far more than Paris, though it must all be part of the same build-up. You see you have to my mind extreme potentialities of human perfection – and the only thing possibly that I have sometimes feared is brittleness or too much edge. I wonder if sensibilities and apprehensions do not risk becoming too sharpened – and that one finds oneself equipped not with a quiverful of golden arrows but a case of surgical knives? Oh dear do not misinterpret that will you; but I am trying to tell you quite clearly what I think.
>
> When I keep on about a great marriage you know it is largely a wish to make you completely into a Balzac figure, and to put you into a house and a tradition big enough to hold you. Because I remain convinced that you can dominate in our generation; I see every reason to suppose you possible of becoming such a keyword for our bits of this century as the great Duchess of Devonshire for her era, or Mary Sidney in hers. Tell me if you think I exaggerate or romanticise. I think you have hit genius in the combination: that you seem to me to promise one, of the aristocratic traditions of the England that was worth living in, and the film-star synthetic business which almost everybody seems to imitate all wrong but which is, alas, modernity.[26]

★ ★ ★ ★ ★

All was not well at Mells Manor. Trim's grandmother, Lady Horner, died in her sleep on 1 March 1940, shortly before her eighty-sixth birthday. It was impossible to think of Mells without her. Yet there were still some who remembered her arriving 'as the Squire's young bride in '83 . . . and among them the two Miss Horners.'*[27] Trim described the atmosphere to Clarissa:

> It's been so brilliantly lovely here this weekend – as it often is at times of mourning – very wintry, no sign of Spring but bright slant-ing rays on the tower & the most wonderful sunsets from the ramparts. I so wished you cd have been here to see them. By the swimming pool where it's sheltered I lay for a long time in the sun without a shirt while Mama read aloud the life of Michelangelo. She is very upset I'm afraid – more so than I'd hoped & the poor Canon is terribly pathetic.[28]

James Pope-Hennessy read the effusive tribute to Lady Horner from Margot Oxford: 'Frances was built of a larger scale, purer in heart, wider in sympathy, than the women I have known . . .'[29] He was less enthusi-astic: 'I only to my knowledge met her once, at lunch with Gerry Wellesley, a crinkled old woman with a magenta feather in her hat; much too acute, I thought, and quite indefatigable and persistent; we trundled round the V & A with her afterwards till I was ready to drop.'[30]

The immediate effect of Lady Horner's death was that Mells became yet more Catholic. According to Conrad Russell, Canon Hannay was banned; a kitchen maid's bedroom was converted into a chapel and consecrated in July. Conrad Russell wrote eerily about the 'Black Monk'† seated at the end of the Christmas table opposite Katharine.[31] Monsignor Ronald Knox, the great Catholic theologian, arrived after

---

* Sir John's spinster sisters, Caroline (Callie) (1848–1947), and Muriel (1852–1951) then in their nineties, who shared a house on the estate. In 1939 Diana Cooper wrote of them to Conrad Russell: 'On the other hand there are the two Miss Horners aged 90 and 97. They don't go to bed until 1 or 2 in the morning, and I'm told that if you pass their house about then you'll see lights and hear a lot of chuck-ling and low quiet laughter coming from their room. I wonder if it's: "Stop me if you've heard this one!"' (Lady Diana Cooper to Conrad Russell, 20 October 1939, quoted in her memoirs, *Trumpets from the Steep* (Rupert Hart-Davis, 1960), p. 19).
† Father Raphael Williams, of Ampleforth (1891–1973).

Christmas: 'So now there's two ecclesiastical crows there.'[32] By September 1941 Conrad Russell found Trim's mother in a state of 'impenetrable silence', suffering from religious melancholy, and concluded that she should take the veil: 'She has lost all interest in this world.'[33]

★ ★ ★ ★ ★

In February 1940 Clarissa slipped away for a night with Jeremy. A few days later he pressed her to come near where his ship was in Southampton. The affair was not helped by the changes of plans of the RNVR. They met again later that month and in March. Communication was difficult and presently he regretted that he had not spent the last three days and nights with her, for all he had achieved on board. Soon afterwards Jeremy became edgy, due to these occasional meetings, long separations and the demands of wartime. He tried to explain that his feelings towards her had always been a mystery. Clarissa's letters to him were sweet and passionate. He was attracted, but they were not feeling the same things. The crunch was that he was not in love with her. He felt that 'short passionate meetings' were leading neither of them anywhere and was consequently 'utterly miserable'.[34] She replied, concluding: 'What a waste it all is that you whom I love being with more than anyone on earth should be perpetually out of my life like this.'[35]

But, as it turned out, he was not so miserable. On 14 September 1940, in the midst of his vacillating and wriggling, he married the actress Peggy Ashcroft. She was eight years older than him and had already run through two husbands. She had been performing in Clemence Dane's play, *Cousin Muriel*, at the Imperial Theatre, Brighton, in May. Some days later he wrote a letter to Clarissa that would do him no credit if quoted in full. He said he had got married, had wanted to tell her, but it had been sudden. He assured her that his actress bride had not been the cause of difficulties between them, but that Peggy's arrival had eliminated his distaste for the idea of marriage. It had occurred to him that Clarissa might have been caused pain by seeing the announcement of the marriage. He went on to ask her blessing and hoped that she and Peggy would meet so that she could see why he loved her so much.[36]

Clarissa must have been shocked, but she coped. She wrote to

James Pope-Hennessy: 'Of course the pain of it being irrevocably <u>over</u> is better in a way than the pain of when he used to leave me. No, what is difficult is having to completely rearrange my life, having to focus the most important parts of my being somewhere else after all this time. No better, no worse than the sensations of a plant being uprooted I suppose!'[37]

James was sympathetic and wrote twice at some length. Despite the closeness of their friendship Jeremy had not been mentioned by name. A few weeks later the main anguish had passed for Clarissa, but then reappeared just as she had thought she was controlling it. James was encouraging:

> Anyway you have in front of you all the 20's, for which you shd care-
> fully prepare: Oh God how silly that sounds as though you and I
> were *d'accord* that yr best moment had passed . . . But actually I mean
> you have got through a dominating emotion <u>satisfactorily</u> <u>soon,</u> and
> nothing can ever disrupt you so totally again. You are therefore to be
> envied: and I am pretty well certain that in time (the word you hate)
> a kind of tranquillity and smoothness (different to hardness, which is
> obviously never produced by the experience of suffering, but only by
> the sight of it) will appear.[38]

Clarissa wrote to Trim: 'Will you accept that now is the time of reflection and balance when my eye is not distorted or my heart strung, & that now, by letter, if nothing else is possible, we must proceed. And yet how can you trust me, I who have given you so little, so little happiness even?'[39]

Later she was more forthcoming:

> I do hope the Jeremy thing is going to be all right. I so want him to
> be happy, not to be hurt. I'm sure it will be a success though all
> accounts of her are rather disturbing. I mind, & I do wish he hadn't
> made me love him so – I've never wished that until now.*
>
> I know I've owed this to you long ago, and that all the affection &

---

* In 1941 Jeremy survived the sinking of Mountbatten's HMS *Kelly* off Crete. Eventually he proved unfaithful to Peggy Ashcroft. They divorced in 1965 and he married June Osborn, whom Cecil Beaton had tried to marry in the early 1960s.

sympathy you've given me has been poorly returned, but your interest in me has always been so personal, & so <u>active,</u> while at the same
time I wanted to keep you that I couldn't bear to have to be
estranged, or else be dishonest. And anyway you know my attitude
towards the significance of confidences. Oh Trim I know I've made
a poor case; Jeremy felt the same way too, so perhaps that strength-
ened me against your offensive! I hope this will enable you to piece
things together that must have seemed odd. Please give me a little of
your love & sweetness. I need you, for all my apparent selfish
self-sufficiency.

   I try not to give way to Accidia, but it's hard. Write to me soon
darling

    X C X[40]

Trim replied:

Darling, darling C,

   I've only just got your letter. My last 4 must have seemed unsympathetic & matter of fact, but it was only that they were uninformed.
I can't help admiring your skill in concealment – however sad it's
often made me & however strange it still seems when you cd have
been so sure of my loyalty. My love or 'active interest' as you call it
wasn't as selfish as all that. Now you've lifted the veil so far, you
might lift it <u>farther,</u> for I can sympathise more the more I understand
– but oh my darling, I do already understand & sympathise. My
devotion's yours – to be guided as you want – & if you need me
you've only the word to say.[41]

He visited her in Oxford and then wrote:

I wish there was anything I could do – but you seem to set your face
against it & so I sit faithfully on a sand dune in the distance. I feel
somehow the sands are running out. Probably you've been wiser
about me than I have about you – We can't tell that yet, & maybe
like your uncle & Mr Chamberlain, we shall rejoice together in the
better days that are to come.[42]

7. DRIFTING
1940–41

Winston Churchill became Prime Minister on 10 May 1940, follow-ing Chamberlain's resignation. After that Clarissa became a frequent visitor to 10 Downing Street and Chequers, the Prime Minister's country residence near Aylesbury. Chequers she found 'less awful than I had anticipated. Rather the stockbroker-with-taste's place all the same. Very much Tudor, and set in the folds of the Chilterns, very much Bucks. But the luxury was heavenly, quantities of rare foods, fires, lights, drinks etc . . . W. was in terrific form, if not exactly spir-its. And oozing charm, gosh he has it. The house heavily guarded, and the password "Athens".'[1]

Shortly before this, Clarissa caught up with James Pope-Hennessy, at Long Barn, in Kent, the home of Harold Nicolson and Vita Sackville-West:

> The weekend at the Nicolsons' was enormous fun, but Vita, whom I imagined as moody, aloof, gaunt etc – was fat, jolly & cosy! I liked her enormously tho'. And Nigel, whom everyone says is dull, I thought <u>exactly</u> like Ben. I admire their great integrity don't you, their great honesty & goodness.
>
> The house, Long Barn, was . . . a revelation of the evolution of their taste, because everyone says how lovely Sissinghurst is, & this was too awful.[2]

Clarissa was in Oxford when the Germans advanced on Paris in June 1940. She listened to Churchill's speech in the House of Commons on 4 June, 'We shall fight them on the beaches . . . We shall never surrender . . .' and wrote to James: 'Each night I have nightmares, but nothing like this. Uncle W's speech was intensely moving, & seemed to me the most brilliant piece of oratory I've ever heard.'[3]

During some days in London in 1940, Clarissa became drawn to what she called the Charlotte Street gang, the group who worked on the literary magazine *Horizon* and talked of nothing save the last edition published. She watched as Stephen Spender told Philip Toynbee that his story was not good enough to be published in *Horizon*.[4] Clarissa and James Pope-Hennessy disparaged various friends between them.

James met Peter Watson, then *Horizon's* principal backer, Watson telling him he hated *Horizon* but thought he should support it, disliked the *New Statesman,* was a republican and hated the monarchy.[5] Clarissa told Watson that she thought the poetry in *Horizon* was 'a great let-down compared to the rest'. He replied that he only liked 'stuff he could understand' and left it all in the hands of Cyril Connolly and his team. James described Lucian Freud as 'hell and so dirty looking'. Clarissa responded with two *bons mots* from Maurice Bowra: of the critic, Raymond Mortimer: 'Lady into Fox'; and of the less than handsome Cyril Connolly: 'He's not as nice as he looks.'[6]

Had Peter Watson not been obviously homosexual, Clarissa could have 'fallen in love with him', she told me in 1980. To James she wrote: 'To have anything to do with him would be asking for trouble . . . Probably without heart or soul, but *tant pis* to meet – What I liked, and I'm sure you'll see my point, was his good manners. All this charm and politeness wasn't just sucking up, nor did it signify that he really liked one exceptionally, but I could tell it was innate well-bred manners.'[7]

The Pakenham family (later the Earl and Countess of Longford) lived in Oxford, in a different set. Their daughter Antonia (later Lady Antonia Fraser) remembered meeting Clarissa at a christening: 'She just looked different from everybody. And she was so beautiful, extraordinary skin, and sort of luminous and then all the old Dons weren't beautiful at all.' While some found Clarissa intimidating, Antonia was not frightened of her: 'I wasn't because I'd grown up with her. I thought of her as a fairy tale princess. I was quite happy thinking of her as a fairy princess. I don't think that if we'd been on a desert island we would have been intimate friends. I think I wasn't quite glamorous enough for her. She was very glamorous.'[8]

Frank Pakenham asked Clarissa to lunch. She decided she liked him, despite finding him 'rather disintegrated'. Presently she joined his London Defence Volunteers (LDV), working with Maurice Bowra's friend, the poet and teacher Audrey Beecham, evidently making bombs for potential Germans and omelettes for Bowra and Eric Dodds, Regius Professor of Greek.

In July 1940 Clarissa took a job at Chatham House, working every day in an office-boy role, and with a perpetual headache from proof-reading and sub-editing. She summarised reports from outdated Romanian papers, which seemed irrelevant after the Russians had marched in. Sometimes she was asked her opinion about the content of various reviews. In the end she found it all a dreary waste of time. In October she returned to studying Kant with Professor Alick Smith. She found she could now read Proust. Trim had found him 'steamy' but she thought: 'You mistake for steam what is in fact a ray of pene-trating light illuminating all the dust particles in the air.'[9]

Clarissa took enormous pleasure from her studies as well as her social life. Among the undergraduates there was Simon Asquith who enjoyed 'amused skulking'. And there was his friend, Raymond Carr, a forceful presence at the university, who would be a lifelong friend. He once visited Clarissa and finding her out, scribbled a note on the nearest piece of paper to hand, as it happens the envelope of one of Trim's letters. He sloped along the high street, 'expounding his views in a loud voice'.[10] He later became Warden of St Antony's College.

All of a sudden a new element entered her life.

Lord Berners

At David Cecil's parties Clarissa observed a small man with a bald head. He rarely spoke and sat with his head bowed. Clarissa asked David who he was. 'He's called Lord Berners. He's having a nervous breakdown.' One night he walked back with her. They began to chat and this became a habit. He told her: 'I have a place not far from Oxford. We could take a taxi and visit it.' Thus Clarissa discovered Faringdon, an eighteenth-century house with a large lake, set in an extensive park, a house as eccentric as the depressed though jesting peer who owned it. The doves that flew outside were dyed different colours, and guests were summoned to dinner by a music box. Clarissa was entranced.

Gerald Berners was a composer, novelist and painter. He was also a tease. He had been a diplomat in Rome before inheriting Faringdon and becoming immensely rich. He knew the Sitwells, Harold Nicolson, Siegfried Sassoon and others. At Faringdon he entertained Evelyn Waugh, Cecil Beaton and Rex Whistler. He was immortalised by Nancy Mitford as Lord Merlin in her novel *The Pursuit of Love*. He could be mischievous while being reserved and shy. One of his teases was directed at the tireless hostess, Lady Colefax. She had a habit of scribbling on invitation cards: 'To meet N.C. and W.S.M.' The recipient guessed these would be Noël Coward and Somerset Maugham. So Gerald sent her an enticing card: 'To meet the P. of W.' and when she arrived, he introduced her to the Provost of Worcester. During the war he wore a green woollen skullcap that made him look like Ali Baba.

On another occasion a pugnacious-looking young man was walking around outside the house. Clarissa asked who he was: 'Oh, that's my agent.'[11] He was Robert Heber Percy, Lord Berners' boyfriend, who lived there with him and later inherited his estate. Known for his wild antics, which were excessive, he was nicknamed the Mad Boy. At this time Robert was a private in the army and was sometimes away, serving in Shropshire.

Faringdon House

Clarissa spent many weekends at Faringdon throughout the 1940s. She described Lord Berners to James Pope-Hennessy: 'He is a very attractive character I find. This fascinating background of a life spent in the most refined pleasure. His accounts of life with Diaghilev, Stravinsky, and Gertrude S [Stein] as his friends, Palazzo in Rome, etc . . . and the very subtle malice and humour without any pettiness. We were having dinner the other night and he called the revolting hash we were eating a scavenger's pot-pourri.'[12] She was less amused when, due to the fear of a German invasion, he went round asking the best way to commit suicide. In her view, the house was pretty, with many good points: 'much that is trashy, but amusing'.[13]

She was treated with reserve and suspicion by the Mad Boy, who was anxious not to surrender his role as the favourite. Although some, like Billa Harrod, speculated that Lord Berners was in love with Clarissa and that there might soon be a Lady Berners, there was never a chance of that. Years later she told Mark Amory that had he proposed she would have been 'very surprised'.[14]

It did not take Lord Berners long to put Clarissa into a book. His mischievous and entertaining novel, *Far From the Madding War* was published in 1941. The naughty author wrote that he would be 'obliged if his friends will not attempt to recognise themselves or each other in these pages'. The heroine, Miss Emmeline Pocock, was based on Clarissa:

> The first impression was one of gentleness and modesty. Then you began to realize that she was extremely pretty. Some even considered her beautiful. But her features were too retroussé to conform with the canons of classical beauty. Emmeline herself believed that it was better, for all practical intents and purposes, that a young woman should be pretty rather than beautiful, and made no attempt to assume the airs that so often accompany the fatal gift. She was of rather diminutive stature, but her body was so well proportioned that she appeared taller than she really was. Her hair, as a poetical undergraduate had once said, was reminiscent of a cornfield at daybreak. Her complexion was of that fairness that invites freckles, but as she never exposed herself to the sun this was not a serious defect. Her type was more suggestive of the eighteenth century than of the present day. She looked like a nymph in one of the less licentious pictures of Fragonard. Her manner was aloof and dignified. In fact she was not the sort of girl with whom you might be tempted to take liberties without encouragement. And encouragement in this respect was one of the things Emmeline never gave.[15]

Other characters were Lord FitzCricket (Gerald Berners himself), Caroline Paltry (Penelope Betjeman), Mr Jericho (Isaiah Berlin), Mrs Postlethwaite (the promiscuous wife of a don), and the Provost of Unity (Maurice Bowra). Harold Nicolson took enormous offence at being portrayed as 'Lollypop' Jenkins. The novel also contained references to Cheatham House, the psychoanalysis of Lord FitzCricket, and other vignettes drawn from life.* David Cecil professed that Emmeline was Miss Janet Gordon, daughter of George Stuart Gordon, President of Magdalen College. But the description of Emmeline seated in a soundproofed room in 'All Saints' fits Clarissa perfectly. Besides, in August 1941 Gerald Berners wrote to her: 'The *New Statesman* compared Emmeline to André Gide's Isabelle, "Woman as the frustrater and destroyer of men and all his works"! Did you ever!'[16]

In January 1941 Clarissa wrote from Faringdon that she was keen that James should endear himself to the peer, 'if only for the reason that you & I wd be so <u>perfectly</u> happy here on weekends'. Lord Berners himself was 'so cute – he scuds about whistling, & blows his nose like a pantomime trumpet'. In March she was actually invited by the Mad Boy: 'Now I'm here on Heber's invitation. I gather he's suddenly taken a fancy to me, but I haven't yet made out how or why. Always asking me to come & talk to him while he puts his shoes on or something.'[17]

Another frequent guest was her friend Valentine Lawford. Lady Cunard was in love with him and instructed Daisy Fellowes to keep an eye on him to make sure he was not getting 'mixed up' with Clarissa. Much in the spirit of the house, Valentine took long walks all over the park, obliging Daisy to 'pursue him through bogs and under barbed wire'.[18]

Colly Barclay

Clarissa's relationship with Jeremy Hutchinson had unravelled during the summer of 1940. She then did what many do and entered precipitously into a rebound relationship, which she soon regretted. Clarissa

---

* Clarissa was also said to be a character in Rose Macaulay's *The Towers of Trebizond,* published in 1956. She never read the book, so she was not convinced. Nor was Ann Fleming convinced.

had a habit of noting lovers in her appointment diaries by a sole initial. 'C' was first mentioned on 11 October 1940, when he visited Oxford. She lunched with him on 6 November, then stayed with him in London from 29 November until about 2 December. She stayed with him again on 6 December.

'C' was Sir Colville Barclay, then living at 24 Yeoman's Row, just off Brompton Road. He was the son of the diplomat the Rt Hon. Sir Colville Barclay, a former Ambassador to Sweden, Portugal and Hungary. 'Colly', as he was known, had succeeded his uncle as 14th Baronet in 1930. He had been reading PPE at Trinity College, Oxford, and studying part-time at the Ruskin School of Art, before joining the diplomatic service in 1938. His widowed mother, Sarita, was the daughter of the sculptor Herbert Ward, and had remarried in 1931, the same Sir Robert Vansittart,* mentioned from time to time by Clarissa's mother. Colly was well off, having inherited a sugar plantation in Mauritius, and was able in later life to manage the family's investment portfolio, while enjoying painting and studying botany in Crete. He specialised in conventional landscapes and later in abstract oils with luminous colours.

Clarissa was with Colly at his house in Yeoman's Row from 16 to 18 December, but doubts began to settle in as she confided to Gay Margesson:

> My dress from [Victor] Stiebel's came today. It's rather heavenly, voluptuous & not too fattening. I pined to go to the 400 tonight, but here we are in front of the fire, me writing to you & reading Pater, the gramophone playing Mozart quartets & Schumann – & I say to myself, what oh <u>what</u> is the matter with this scene? Why don't [I] enjoy it, & since I don't enjoy it, <u>why</u> do I go on with it? What curious psychological kink dating from adolescence makes me want to go on, so that nothing wd induce me to stop? Our relationship hasn't progressed since the day he came down & we went sailing, and (& this is what upsets me rather, the purely arbitrary & <u>wholly</u> subjective & unintuitive character of pleasure) I was so ecstatically happy,

---

* Sir Robert (later Lord) Vansittart, GCB, GCMG (1881–1957), formerly permanent under secretary of state for Foreign Affairs, an opponent of appeasement, a poet, novelist and playwright.

<u>happier</u> than ever I'd been with J [Jeremy], d'you see, thru ignorance & the egotistical combination of feeling well, the lovely day, & being with someone I <u>imagined</u> I <u>would</u> find *sympathique* & a little admirable. If one had the power to dupe oneself a bit more often, one would have numerous times of acute pleasure, off one's own steam so to speak (also it's terrifying – as you've often observed with yr men, how C can feel when there's <u>nothing</u> there).[19]

Clarissa then mused to Gay about marriage:

Having affairs is too easy & too pleasant (& so delightfully <u>boring</u>) to want to get married for reasons of sex or companionship or even *désoeuvrement*, which is about what most of our friends get married for isn't it – & anyway I have faith like a fool in my lucky star – I <u>can't</u> believe that for me, the chosen one, the perfect man will not turn up. I believe in my <u>luck</u>, don't you in yours? I suppose at 26 I shall have to get married (The whole dream-man theory rests on a gross overestimation of oneself, even for us! For Priscilla, of course, it's even grosser for I do think she ought to get off while the going's good. No dream-man will come her way.)*[20]

While in London she had had tea with James Pope-Hennessy, about to embark on *History Under Fire,* a book about bombed London, with photographs by Cecil Beaton. She relished spending time with someone 'who saw what I saw & savoured what I savoured'. James was dressed as a dandy, with an eighteenth-century shaped waistcoat and white lawn shirt, influenced in his taste by Cecil. Clarissa did not like the sartorial effect, but she enjoyed the three brioches, the four cups of *café au lait* and the gossip.[21] She returned to Colly's house:

I had an even more cracking row with C., (the 1st one about poetry & this one about whether or not we sd go to the 400! On the 1st occasion I was infuriated by his unsubtle & bad taste, & on the 2nd

---

* Clarissa was right. Priscilla Bibesco married first, in 1944, Mikhail Padev, a Bulgarian who worked for the BBC. They divorced in 1946. Then in 1958 she married a dodgy man called Simon Hodgson, who spent a year in prison for obtaining credit as an undischarged bankrupt. He died in 1992.

occasion by what I am convinced was avarice. He said (I ask you) that we'd been told not to spend money, & he'd rather put his money in defence bonds – this coming from him, so rich, when little James & his £100 had just been standing me a pound's worth of drinks & a box of 100 expensive Russian cigarettes, seemed to crumble, so I blew up. I'm still incensed; how petty of me. Never, never have I quarrelled with a man before & God it's hell. I flounced out of the house & off to Anne's & spent the evening drinking whisky in night-clubs & when I'd struggled myself into a reconciliatory mood went back home – & of course the reconciliation builds up a layer of sentiment between us that has no natural right there at all. It just falsifies & makes something synthetic & that night I dreamt that I was Vansittart's mistress! which only makes matters worse in an unconscious sort of way.[22]

Soon afterwards, Clarissa went down to Crab Wood to spend Christmas and some of the new year, 1941, with her mother. She reported to Gay:

The visit to London became progressively more & more wretched – & I am now in an acute state of depression & unbalance. Oxford has become the centre of gravitation for me. By it I make my stand-ards – and unless I can constantly refer to you, & possibly Shyah [Isaiah Berlin], I do feel myself becoming lost & unbalanced & wretched. (Especially living with C., who is no ballast, rather more a flea in one's pants.)[23]

James was sympathetic to the Colly situation: 'God, how I know the feeling of having rushed into an error.'[24] Clarissa was confused. She did not want to give Colly up: 'I like the ménage too much, & you see there's always J. in the background.* (Of course I decided that J. was the only true Epicurean I'd ever met!! but even he is coarse-textured & pleasure loving).'[25] Nor did she give up Colly entirely, her pocket diaries recording occasional dinners with him during 1941 and 1942.

Clarissa had also seen Robert Cranborne, the man many thought she was destined to marry. Having been brooding at Oxford she went

* Jeremy had by then married Peggy Ashcroft, of course.

out for an enjoyable evening with him – drinks at the Ritz, dancing at the Dorchester and ending up at the 400. The next day they lunched at Quaglino's, after which he gave her a box of chocolates, a jar of *marrons*, 100 cigarettes and eight cigars. She told Gay of another suitor, Eric Duncannon:*

I had a letter from Eric a few days ago. It's terrifying the effect he has over me. When I saw the handwriting my whole being began to pulsate vigorously & for 2 days I was ecstatic & read it every 3 hours! He said he was sorry he'd never written to thank me for the perfect few weeks at Oxford – that it had been a joy to see so much of me after so long a gap, that it had been the happiest period of his life – then a long rigmarole abt how he'd been foolish about bringing people with him the last time (the one I came panting round to you), that he'd written me a note the next day but never sent it as it was too involved, that he'd telephoned Chester Terrace but I wasn't there as I'd said I wd be. Then he asked me to write & say how I was as it wd make him very unhappy to lose touch with me.[26]

During her holiday, while the Blitz raged in London, Clarissa read Turgenev's *First Love* and some Rimbaud. Her mother was happy that they could spend time together: 'You can't imagine what a pleasure it was to have you here by yourself all to myself. I loved your mind, your wit, your sensitiveness & sensibility. I discovered depths I did not know of, & your companionship is enriching & satisfying. I will always long for it & enjoy & appreciate it when I get it.'[27]

But time was running out for Goonie.

* Eric, Viscount Duncannon (1913–93), later 10th Earl of Bessborough, junior minister in several Conservative administrations. He was much in Clarissa's life in 1942. He once proposed to Mary Churchill and was turned down.

8. LONDON
1941–4

Goonie enjoyed hearing about Clarissa's Oxford life – the visits from James Pope-Hennessy, and how Clarissa's father had visited her and reported: 'The trio, Clarissa, Gay & Berners are the talk of Oxford.'[1] In January 1941 Clarissa stayed with the Vansittarts, where Sir Robert, 'a real lady-killer in a yellow pullover & Russian boots',[2] lent her books called *Dead Heat* and *Eleven Were Brave.*

There remained considerable fear that Britain might be invaded, in which case Clarissa was set on hiding at Faringdon. Goonie was still moving between different houses, visiting London or her aged mother, Lady Abingdon,* at Hamstead Marshall, or staying at Blenheim.

James Pope-Hennessy appeared on leave in Oxford. Jeremy Hutchinson had disliked him earlier. Now Tony Lambton met him, while on the sad mission of collecting his brother's effects, following his suicide.† He upbraided Clarissa for knowing someone as 'frightful' as James. Clarissa was pleased that Cecil Beaton was no longer influencing James's dress style. A while before James had been mocking poor Cecil for remarks such as: 'I'm going to Loelia Westminster this Saturday and she told me to bring *tenue de soir.*'[3] Now he thought Cecil suburban.

---

* Clarissa's grandmother outlived Goonie. She spent her last years at Albert Court, London, and died in a London nursing home on 16 September 1942.
† His elder brother, John, Viscount Lambton (1920–41), shot himself on the lawn of Fenton, the family's home in Northumberland. The verdict was a self-inflicted fatal wound, when temporarily of unbalanced mind.

Cecil Beaton

Clarissa had been aware of Cecil Beaton since at least 1936, when she had been drawn to some photographs in *Vogue* of Caroline Paget and David Herbert, and of Caroline's sister Liz, reflected in a broken mirror. She first met Cecil with James in 1940. 'She is quite astoundingly worth noticing and one of the human beings I like and know best in the world,'[4] James wrote to Cecil, in December that year. In March 1941 she reported to Gay Margesson:

> Travelled back to Oxford with Cecil B. He is <u>frightfully</u> funny I think, & knows it, not a buffoon. We got stranded at Oxford Station in howling wind & rain, missing taxi after taxi as efficient women grabbed them all, & he made it all so amusing and enjoyable whereas I sd have been quite un-humorous about it. Eventually rang up Gerald [Berners], his leopard skin scarlet lined rug over his arm. "Gerald, it's Cecil, my dear, STRANDED' in a contralto crescendo . . .
>
> This morning Cecil came round to me & I took him to see the Boucher tapestries & he took literally <u>dozens</u> of photographs of me posed against them, & thru glass cases etc.[5]

At first Cecil found Clarissa 'slightly timid & difficult to get to know',[6] but so appreciative of all the entertainment he offered that they began to see a lot of each other. They remained lifelong friends.

By this time Trim was serving in the Middle East. He wrote to ask after her mother, and to wonder if Clarissa was making omelettes for Lord Berners or resolving problems with Professor Price:

> I have an awful fear you may end up as stenographer (& confidante) to Harold Nicolson. Please don't do that unless you very much want to, tho' I think I shd prefer it to your being too involved with the Vansittarts.
>
> Forgive me for expressing any preference about what you do. It never made much difference when I was with you & I can't suppose it will now I'm 3,000 miles away, but it shows I think of you still & love you so you mustn't mind.[7]

★ ★ ★ ★ ★

In March 1941 there was danger that Clarissa might be conscripted into a Liverpool munitions factory or the WAAF, so she immediately left Oxford. She obtained a 'vital war job' in the cypher department of the Foreign Office, decyphering or decoding, which she started on 15 April. Though she was unqualified and found the job menial, it could involve going overseas. Instead of training for three months in the Locarno Room of the Foreign Office, she worked alongside Anthony Nutting* in a dismal basement, or the 'catacombs' as Lord Berners dubbed it. Clarissa walked across St James's Park to the Foreign Office and ate her lunch in the war-workers' canteen in the National Gallery, 'served by irate ladies from Kensington'.[8] She was determined to involve herself fully 'in current events and the dope generally' but as she wrote to Trim: 'It was a sad change from St John Street and Mr Smith.'†[9]

She asked if she might be sent to Cairo, Tehran or Lisbon, but then went to Chequers for a weekend, where Leo Amery‡ proposed sending her to Washington, which she felt she could not refuse. This was made more difficult by what she called 'the idealistic tension that Aunt Clemmie ... created in the family, a sort of Lady Violet [Bonham Carter] fanaticism'.[10] Her mother's serious illness put an end to that plan.

Clarissa lived in a cut-price room on the fourth floor of the Dorchester in London making her feel 'disintegrated and miserable'. She hardly ever left the hotel, as she quite often had night work, needing to eat at 3 a.m. With the noisy air raids, she found it easier to stay there. If she did emerge, it was to see David Jones painting happily, or the group she described as 'the Anthony Blunt set, the best of the Cambridge type that is'. The presence of Lady Cunard and Lady Colefax at the hotel meant that social life continued apace. Pamela Churchill was on the fourth floor too. Nightly she and Clarissa would go down to the foyer. One night Pamela said she would go and visit Averell Harriman on the first floor. The next day, as she crunched

---

* (Sir) Anthony Nutting (1920-99), then in the Foreign Office, later an MP. He was closely involved with Suez and one of the ministers who resigned.
† Ironically her friend Valentine Lawford was working upstairs for the Foreign Secretary, Anthony Eden, but she never went up there.
‡ Leo Amery (1873-1955), Cabinet Minister, then Secretary of State for India.

through broken glass from a raid, Clarissa spotted Pamela and Averell coming in the other direction. It occurred to Clarissa that: 'It was at this point that [Pamela] realised the possibilities of power and the exercise of her charm. She was not an intellectual and she lacked irony, but she had a clever and shrewd mind, knowing exactly what she wanted. There was no blundering or being the victim of her emotions.'[11]

Goonie lived long enough to see Clarissa settled into her decoding work. She never complained about her health, despite suffering from 'a long tormenting and recurring illness'.[12] She stayed at Cumberland Lodge, in Windsor Great Park, with her widowed brother-in-law, Viscount Fitzalan of Derwent. Then she was moved to the Princess Christian Nursing Home in Windsor. Clarissa went to see her: 'I went there & broke down in tears & asked her not to leave me.'[13] Goonie died on 7 July 1941. Writing in sympathy, Clarissa's godmother, Anne Islington, wondered if Clarissa had realised 'how slender a hold your darling Mother had on life here'.[14]

There was a private burial in the Catholic graveyard at St Michael's Church, Begbroke, not far from Blenheim. Clarissa was there with her father and brothers, as were Winston and Clementine Churchill, their daughters Diana and Sarah, with the Duke and Duchess of Marlborough, Lord Ivor Churchill, the Countess of Lytton, Lord Fitzalan and his granddaughter, Alathea Fitzalan Howard, Katharine Asquith and a few others. 'Poor old Jack, what a gap it will make in his life . . .' wrote George Cornwallis-West to Winston. 'She was quite one of the sweetest women I have ever known, and to know her was to love her.'[15]

Numerous tributes were published in *The Times* and many wrote to Clarissa. Margot, Countess of Oxford wanted her to come to lunch or dine to talk about Goonie. Pamela Lytton told her that 'always to be loved was the mainspring of happiness'[16] and hoped great things lay in store for her. Further sympathy came from Katharine Asquith, Lady Cynthia Asquith, Lady Juliet Duff, Lord and Lady David Cecil, Dame Una Pope-Hennessy, Cecil Beaton, Valentine Lawford, Jock Colville, her Scottish nanny and more.

Goonie's death was a devastating blow to Clarissa. Trim wrote to her from Syria: 'It must be some consolation simply to know how much she loved you & how much by that alone you increased her happiness. You increased it so much too by all your sweetness to her. I know that as well as you do, perhaps better than most people.'[17] She wrote back: 'The pain lasts and must go on lasting for so long, and there is so little to be said, so much to be endured. But I have needed you.'[18]

Isaiah Berlin thought Clarissa blamed herself for embittering her mother's last hours. Of the next years, he wrote, not entirely accurately, that Clarissa fell ill 'with some mysterious sickness and spent two years in bed'. When he visited her from America in 1942, he found her 'very handsome in bed, pining to get away from this mysterious sickness which the doctors could not diagnose'.[19]

Not long after her mother's death, Clarissa was walking back to the Dorchester from the Foreign Office in the pouring rain. Her aunt Clemmie was coming out of Downing Street and gave her a lift in her car. The next day Clemmie sent Sir Charles Wilson (later Lord Moran), Churchill's doctor, to see her. Clarissa was diagnosed with inflammation of the kidneys and instantly 'packed off' to the Lindo Wing of St Mary's Hospital, Praed Street, for several weeks. In August she went to stay with her Oxford friends, David and Rachel Cecil at Rockbourne, their house in Fordingbridge. She loved the peace of the countryside, read Flaubert and Dostoevsky, though found the house damp:* 'The Cecils are being delightful,' she wrote to James Pope-Hennessy. 'In these surroundings they look more like a couple by Zoffany than ever & the little boy [Jonathan]† has a beautiful intelligent face, & is dressed like an early 19th C print, with pleated linen skirts and blouses, cut wide at the neck almost to the shoulder blades (I can't think of children except in relation to their clothes – a child naked is to me almost obscene, like a woman without her wig!).'[20]

In September Clarissa went to stay with Winston at Chequers, but felt 'worse than ever' and took to her bed in a tower where Lady Jane Grey's sister had been imprisoned by Queen Elizabeth I: 'one hears the soldiers tramping up and down on guard all night long'.[21] Venetia

---

* In the 1980s Clarissa visited Lord David and was horrified at the discomfort – the linoleum floor of the glacial bathroom, a lone toothbrush on the basin with but a few strands left, toothpaste squeezed to the last drop, bent double like a ballerina.
† Jonathan Cecil (1939–2011), later an actor, well-known in films and on television.

Montagu saw her and pronounced her as 'looking like Undine with drowned hair'.[22] Clarissa then moved to a series of hotels in Sonning and Crowthorne, Cecil Beaton worrying that she had fallen into the hands of some strange healer, like 'some monkey business of Gerald's'.[23] He was surprised when, in 1942, she settled at the Étoile Hotel, in Charlotte Street.

Clarissa's correspondence with Trim was curtailed because he was away in the Middle East, but she gave him what he described from afar as 'a blood-curdling description'[24] of her illness. In December 1944 he wrote sadly: 'You lost me in the Lebanon three years ago or more, & I think you were then bedridden somewhere in Regent's Park.'[25]

She made a new friend in Alice Astor and moved briefly into one of her two bungalows at Hanover Lodge, in Regent's Park, but after five months, Alice wanted it for her former lover, the choreographer Frederick Ashton. On 4 December Clarissa moved into a flat on the seventh floor of 124 Rossmore Court, Park Road, London NW1, her home until she married Anthony Eden. It overlooked the white Windsor Castle pub, with its castellations, and the distant domes of Sussex Place.

Alice Astor had been married to Serge Obolensky, and then, significantly, to Raimund von Hofmannsthal until they divorced in 1939. Her third husband was Philip Harding, a journalist then serving in anti-aircraft. They would divorce in 1945. Her fourth marriage in 1946 was to David Pleydell-Bouverie, of whom Cecil Beaton wrote: 'The new husband looks like one of the many offspring & adds nothing to the general conversation. He was on his best behaviour & made a good impression, but Alice says he is incredibly contradictory – yet she is determined to overcome all odds & make a success of it at all costs.'*[26] Two years later Alice took up with John La Touche, the lyricist – 'a runt & a second rate egomaniac', according to Cecil.[27] Clarissa judged Alice 'exceptionally <u>nice</u>, earnest,

---

* When I met him in New York in 1981, he had become a disagreeable character in a red velvet jacket who cursed Cecil Beaton for 'lying' about Garbo. He kept saying: 'You talk to Garbo. You ask her. She was so hurt.' And later: 'You're going to propound the myth, are you?' (HV diary, 20 November 1981). Truman Capote and others were convinced that Alice's death was suspicious.

battered, foolish & beautiful,'[28] though Cecil considered that she was motivated by dissatisfaction in life.

In April 1942 Clarissa spent Easter at Faringdon, 'a thoroughly neurotic weekend, Gerald on the hop the whole time, the Mad Boy misanthropic & packing us off to see the neighbours the whole time'.[29] Alice Astor kept Clarissa up till three each morning spilling out her supposed woes. In July Robert Heber Percy and Jennifer Fry, of the chocolate-making family, got married. This alliance was an enormous shock to Gerald, who could not believe what had been going on under his nose. Not only was the Mad Boy marrying, but the bride was pregnant and there was considerable speculation as to who the biological father might be, the bride having been known as 'a kind girl' with several men.*

The daughter was born on 28 February 1943 and christened Victoria. Lord Berners adapted to a grandfatherly role, walking alongside the pram, pushed by Robert and Jennifer. Robert never discussed the paternity of Victoria, then or later, but he was soon frustrated by the shackles of marriage and longed to wriggle out of it. It was an on-off business until finally, in April 1943, Jennifer was ejected from Faringdon and went to live at Oare.†

There were occasional sightings of Clarissa. James Lees-Milne would run into her due to his close alliance with James Pope-Hennessy, when attending lectures given by James or Kenneth Clark. In August 1942 he described her as 'very pale, and white and listless',[30] and a year later as 'extremely white and pale',[31] dressed in a brocade dress to her ankles and reclining on a Récamier sofa, given to her by Lord Ivor Churchill. In November 1943 he was surprised that she took a hired car to go to *An Ideal Husband* at the theatre.

Clarissa also mixed with Chips Channon, 'much to my shame, and very little to my pleasure'.[32] He described her: 'like a water lily, or perhaps gardenia . . . calm, intelligent and independent. I like her

---

* Among the candidates was Lord Edward (Ned) Petty-Fitzmaurice, Charlie Lansdowne's younger brother. In the end DNA proved the biological father to be a dark, heavy-drinking and struggling actor, Ian Lubbock, whose wife Lys went on to be the much-belittled mistress of Cyril Connolly.

† The Heber Percys divorced and in 1949 Jennifer married Alan Ross, editor of the *London Magazine*.

enormously. She is the young girl of the present age, a milder Diana Cooper.'[33] But later in the decade he called her 'a lovely bitch',[34] whom he mistrusted. Other than at the WVS, Clarissa was not employed, but she helped Alice in a factory in Euston Road, where they wielded red-hot irons soldering parts for submarines.

At Rossmore Court, Clarissa found herself near the novelist Elizabeth Bowen, with whom she made friends, and presently Cyril Connolly moved to nearby Sussex Place. Elizabeth Bowen lived in Clarence Terrace where she presided over small parties for tea, drinks and dinners to which Clarissa went. Clarissa enjoyed the intellectual stimulation of Connolly and his friends, though noted his greed and sloth. In February 1944 she had her appendix removed and recuperated at Chequers:

> W. . . . was as loving, humorous, great & utterly seductive as ever, & in a series of quilted Chinese dressing-gowns, & champagne for every meal. Clem was less bloodshot than usual, also in a quilted dressing-gown. (I don't wonder, the house was icy, & I slept in my fur coat). Pam was there too, with green sequins in her hair, doing a mother-act over her child who had bronchitis.[35]

In April 1944 Clarissa stayed at Faringdon, with Alice Astor and Isaiah Berlin as somewhat incompatible guests. On one visit the Mad Boy found a decanter and zigzagged all the way back on the drive home.[36] Clarissa described to Lord Berners how Robert had once driven her 'hell-for-leather' to the station at Didcot: 'I remember screaming, "Not another dog," as we nearly killed a second one. We caught the train by a quarter of a second.'[37]

Killed in Action

In just over a month in the summer of 1944 Clarissa lost four close friends to war. Rex Whistler was killed by a mortar bomb on 18 July, when he left his tank to help men in his unit. David Wallace died in Menina, shot in the neck by German machine-gun fire, on 17 August, aged thirty. After Balliol, he had spent much of his life in Greece, studying Byzantine art. He joined the 60th Rifles as a rifleman, won the Sword of Honour, and a regimental boxing competition, and rose to be a major. Anthony Eden wrote a tribute to him: 'He was destined to be one of the leaders of his generation. Had he lived to take up that political career upon which he had set his heart, no position would have been beyond his reach.'[38] His Greek comrades carved an epitaph on his tomb: 'The soil of Greece is proud to offer hospitality to this hero.'[39]

Four Wallace brothers are commemorated on the Wallace memorial in St Peter's Churchyard at East Lavington. Gerard had been killed in action with the RAF on 20 August 1943. Edward died, also with the RAF, on 4 November 1944, and John died serving with the Life Guards, after the war, on 15 August 1946. The youngest brother, Billy Wallace, survived and was well known in the 1950s as a suitor to Princess Margaret.

Nor was the war kind to the Lansdowne family. Charlie was severely burned when his tank caught fire in the battle of Alamein in 1942. Depressed in hospital, he wrote to Clarissa: 'One's mind must be affected if one is one of the very few who don't look on the war as a riotous lark . . .' He saw Trim, then administrator of an all-Arab area of Palestine and thought him happy: 'Before he has always had to pay the penalty of brilliance – the English mob say "an odd sort of chap" or "a queer fish", can't make him out.'[40] Away from England for five years, he took joy in the Lebanese mountains at Bloudane and the spring flowers of Palestine. His younger brother, Ned (Lord Edward Petty-Fitzmaurice), was killed in Normandy on 11 August 1944, and soon afterwards Charlie went missing in Italy. His death was confirmed nine days later. Trim wrote of him: 'A warmth faded, like the soft warmth of an English afternoon'.[41] To Clarissa's letter of sympathy, his mother replied: 'You realised more fully than most of his friends what Charlie was, and what it is that we have lost. He gave us such untold happiness. He was <u>so</u> fond of you.'[42]

9. RAIMUND
1943–51

In 2007 John Stefanides lent Clarissa Charlotte Mosley's edition of the Mitford letters. It contained a quote from the Duchess of Devonshire that the standard of beauty at the Beistegui Ball in Venice was very high – Diana Cooper, Liz Hofmannsthal & Clarissa Churchill . . .'[1] As Clarissa noted in her diary: 'A triple bulls-eye for R.'[2]

The man in question was Raimund von Hofmannsthal, one of the many figures who flitted randomly through Clarissa's memoirs, without due explanation. Clarissa first saw him at Plas Newydd in 1938 when he was engaged to Lady Elizabeth Paget. She recalled: 'He kept fixing his eyes on me in an extraordinary way. I was in love [with Jeremy Hutchinson] so didn't think about it.' Her mother said to her: 'That man is very dangerous. If he rings up, you're not to answer the telephone.'[3] According to Cecil Beaton, she met him when he had the Cárcano sisters* for a drink in 1943 at Pelham Place, his London home. As he put it:

> A romance started – an abortive, clandestine romance of which I thoroughly disapproved for no good would come of it. R. married happily with children would never marry her. Meanwhile the romance continued. Furtive visits to Homburg, dinners in secret restaurants – Clarissa seemed rather frustrated, often bad tempered. We got along well whenever this secret existence was not discussed.[4]

---

* Miguel Cárcano, Argentinian Ambassador to Britain from March 1942 until March 1946, had two beautiful daughters, Stella (Baby) who married Viscount Ednam, son of the Earl of Dudley, in 1946, and Ana Inez (Chiquita), who married the Hon. John (Jakie) Astor in 1944. Both marriages were dissolved.

Raimund was born on 26 May 1906. His father was Hugo von Hofmannsthal, Austria's most distinguished poet, alongside Rilke, and particularly known today for the librettos for Richard Strauss's operas – *Der Rosenkavalier*, *Arabella* and more. Hugo von Hofmannsthal died in 1929 while dressing for the funeral of Raimund's elder brother, who had committed suicide. The family had Jewish origins. At various times they owned properties in Austria, at this time renting part of Schloss Kammer on Lake Attersee, near Salzburg (bought by Raimund's wife, Alice Astor, and Eleanora von Mendelssohn) and Schloss Prielau,* a seventeenth-century former hunting lodge on the shores of the lake at Zell am See, which Raimund found in the 1930s.

Raimund's sister detected an interest in girls from a very young age and 'the ability to relate to a variety of human beings was quite outstanding in him'.[5] He made his way to Hollywood, Rudolf 'Kaetchen' Kommer finding him work on Max Reinhardt's *The Miracle* as a way of working his passage to California. In 1926 he met Lady Diana Cooper who found him 'shy and strange' and in need of 'protection and affection'.[6] The poor, almost starving Austrian boy was soon besotted by love for Diana; she was thirty-four to his twenty. He cabled his father: 'If you met Helen of Troy and she asked you to go to Troy with her, would you send your son a hundred dollars?'[7] His father obliged and he became Diana's companion, happy to tie her shoes, brush her hair, run her bath and bask in her company. The association caused jealousy on the American tour and did not much appeal to Duff Cooper, Diana's husband, back in London.

Raimund employed his limitless charm to good advantage. He took up with the immensely rich Alice Astor, wife of Prince Serge Obolensky. It is accepted that he was the father of their daughter Sylvia. In 1933 he married Alice, who lived in considerable style at Rhinebeck, New York, and, as mentioned, at Hanover Lodge, in Regent's Park, London. They had one daughter, Romana McEwen, and divorced in 1939.

In 1935 Diana Cooper introduced him to her niece, Lady Elizabeth Paget, daughter of her sister, Marjorie, Marchioness of Anglesey, and

---

* Prielau was confiscated by the Nazis. Winthrop Aldrich, then President of the British War Relief Fund (backed by Chase Manhattan) and later American Ambassador to the UK, helped the family get their chattels back after the war.

considered one of the most beautiful girls of her generation. According to Chips Channon, they were soon deeply in love, but her parents were horrified, since they had dynastic matrimonial hopes for her and were suspicious of Raimund. The Angleseys prevailed on the Duff Coopers to take Liz on a Mediterranean cruise in their yacht, *Enchantress*, for the summer. But Raimund was to be found at every port, armed with a bunch of flowers. Following his divorce from Alice, he married Liz quietly at St Ethelburga's, Bishopsgate,* in May 1939.

Raimund joined *Time* in 1938, his role being 'amorphous but invaluable' as T. S. Matthews, editor of *Time*, wrote – 'for more than thirty years as ambassador, scout, mender of fences, social mentor and guide, interpreter, defender of the faith – faith in Luce† . . .'[8] Despite a tricky start, both Duff Coopers became the greatest friends of 'the Hoffs', spending time with them in England and France. In the tangled web of interconnections, Diana continued to love Raimund, and among his many mistresses, Duff counted Liz's sister, Caroline, who also had an affair with Anthony Eden.‡ Duff's son, John Julius Norwich, greatly admired Raimund and, with his Panglossian approach to life, judged that he never heard Raimund say an unkind word about anyone.

In a book of tributes, printed after Raimund died, his friends assessed his character. Isaiah Berlin respected his love for his Austrian heritage, Mozart, Austrian baroque and neo-classicism, and the world of Strauss. He wrote that Raimund viewed English life 'through a haze of uncritical admiration', was 'a delightful companion, a generous host, an ideal guest, with a gay and unwounding wit'.[9] David Cecil detected his 'special quality of intellectual thoughtfulness' and how he was 'wholly lacking in the conventional Englishman's stiff, self-conscious, disappointing reticence in personal matters'.[10] A. J. Ayer wrote that 'Underneath his hedonism, there was a strong vein of

---

* Neither Clarissa nor her mother was at the wedding, but a great many people who appear in this book were, including the Earl of Dudley, the Countess of Lytton, David Herbert, Cecil Beaton and Rex Whistler.

† Henry Luce (1898–1967), founder of *Time* and *Life* magazines.

‡ Charles Duff wrote that, as time went on, Caroline found sex with Duff irksome: 'I'm dreading tonight. That little pot belly!' (*Charley's Woods*, Zuleika, 2017), p. 25.

seriousness and even of melancholy, which increased as he grew older.'[11]

Others commented later. Charles Duff, Caroline Paget's adopted son, wrote: 'He combined a sensualist's appreciation of all the pleasures of life with an almost innocent good nature and a belief in the inherent goodness of humanity. He had a charm which seemed to come from a *belle époque*, an earlier and more benevolent age.'[12] A fellow Austrian émigré, George Weidenfeld, described him as 'a pampered pet of grand ladies and beautiful heiresses who lived largely on his wit'. He wrote that the Hofmannsthals played 'a distinctive role in London life after the war. His cosmopolitan manner and her looks and provenance radiated an aura of elegance and sophistication.' Furthermore he described Raimund as 'fascinated by his life' and with 'a romantic vision of it. He worshipped the English upper classes and saw himself as a bridge between them and Europe.'[13] Charles Duff added:

Unless you were in the warm and heady embrace of Raimund's civilised and uplifting aura, Mozart, beautiful and elegant women, manners, and surprisingly frank conversation, his life must have looked a bit pampered and trivial. But he seemed to me, his nephew by marriage, European Jewish sophistication at its finest. Although he could be sad at the state of the world and feared for the future of the young, he trod his path lightly. Raimund was a believer in Bildung, that untranslatable German word which means that listening to great music, reading great literature, seeing great art, and being exposed to civilised living, will make a person morally and spiritually a better human being. The maître d's of every great restaurant in Europe knew him by name, and he was, as a host, incredibly generous. He really liked the ladies and he knew what the ladies liked. Gay men felt so at ease with him too. He was a wonderful listener and had perception and empathy.[14]

The impression was romantic, even conventional. But it was not. Perhaps Raimund was too romantic. He was known to be a great ladies' man. His son Octavian related that one day, in White's (or Veit's, as Raimund pronounced it), a fellow member accused him of being a terrible womaniser. Irritated, he retorted: 'I am not a womaniser. I have been faithful to the same two women for the last twenty-five years.'[15] Laura, Duchess of Marlborough, said that Raimund specialised in 'hotting up cold women. He found that paid dividends.'[16] She had in mind Diana Cooper, Liz Paget and Clarissa.

For nine years Raimund conducted a clandestine affair with Clarissa, his wife, Liz, ignorant of his activities. The affair began in 1943 and explains why such a beautiful woman remained unmarried in the prime of life. The many letters he wrote to her, often beginning 'Darling Child', do not shine light into his soul. Sometimes he wrote of his feelings, and occasionally he mentioned people he had seen socially. He was forever expressing his keen wish to see Clarissa, and eager to get a letter from her when he was away. There were the traditional anguished times between lovers, when he considered she was neglecting him, and he pleaded misery until he heard from her. Since the affair endured, any silences were momentary, possibly even arbitrary. Sometimes she was away. Wartime added its dimension of difficulty with letters held up and four arriving all at once.

At the beginning of the war Raimund and Liz were living in New York. Their daughter Arabella was born there in 1942. Liz modelled hats and they returned to Britain in 1943. Liz took her children to the safety of Plas Newydd in Anglesey, while Raimund remained in London, when not stationed elsewhere. In December 1943, as a US citizen, he joined up as a GI in Lichfield, Staffordshire, serving with the American Red Cross alongside his friend, Ivan Moffat. They used to go off to the British camp at night, and eat bacon and eggs with the same enjoyment as if it were a late supper at the Savoy.

On meeting Clarissa, Raimund commended her for her wit and beauty, and there is evidence that she wrote to him wishing she could be with him for ever. He addressed that in 1944:

> Darling, You say you think you would be alright if you could be with me all the time. Perhaps you would – because you love – and if your love is stronger even than your other passions, and because with the help of this love you might even find your way to the unquestioning simplicity of my life, I understand that. But is being together the essential? Am I not alive, and with you all the time? And don't you feel that I *won't* let you go, and must see you through and be

with you always, because such were my dreads when I first met you, and to break them would land me on a sofa in Rossmore Court?[17]

It was a brazen claim for he was also in harmony with his wife. In the same letter, he discussed Clarissa's atheism, hoping she was strong enough to cope with life without God's help. Clarissa might well have hoped he would leave Liz for her. The letters gave her no encouragement. Nor was she without admirers during these years. Years later, she recorded in her diary:

I read a book about Ldy Desborough ... The last time I saw 'Ettie' was when Robert Cecil took me to Panshanger that time he had reappeared, in uniform, & decided he wd probably marry me! When he didn't succeed, he soon married Mollie, who had been the girlfriend of Dickie* before he was killed on leave going to Cranborne.[18]

Raimund was away for eight weeks, early in 1944, training in camp, but there was a walk in the park and lunch with Clarissa. By now Clarissa was writing openly to Cecil Beaton about her affair (something she regretted in later life). In February 1944 she waited for Raimund in the midst of dramatic bombing raids that both scared and impressed her as the red flares and searchlights hit the clouds: 'Meanwhile I am quite happy – or intend to be when R. comes & hope soon the effects of the op will have worn off. I don't think anyone can have loved him as I do, & have so few illusions at the same time. I hope not, for it's often not very pleasant.'[19]

He returned in March 'very thin & subdued at first', much disliking his job in Grosvenor Square, wearing a private's uniform and sleeping

---

* Robert Cecil married Mollie Wyndham-Quin on 18 December 1945. He became Viscount Cranborne in 1947, and Marquess of Salisbury in 1972. His brother, the Hon. Richard Cecil (1924–44), who had been a sergeant pilot and was at Christ Church, died as the result of an accident on 12 August 1944. He had given a lift to an American soldier on his motorcycle, travelling at 85 m.p.h. He dropped the soldier at his camp and set off on the Blandford road at 40 m.p.h. He crashed into a telegraph pole. (*The Times*, 16 August 1944) Dickie was described as 'a personality of arresting distinction ... big and rugged, and yet with such sensitiveness in the noble brow and dark eyes aglow with expressiveness. (*The Times*, 18 August 1944).

on a straw palliasse in Green Street, 'consequently desperately tired &
dejected'.[20] Occasionally Liz appeared in London and then no meetings were possible. In April Clarissa explained to Cecil:

> R. is a wonderful person for me, but really exceptionally so. No one
> could have been sweeter, more intelligent or more sensible with me
> than he, besides the charm & spirits etc you speak of. It was lucky I
> found him.
>
> It isn't at all the sort of relationship I enjoy – other people's
> husbands. I hate it & it makes me unhappy, & I wd never have gone
> on with it, or be doing so now, if I had not grown too fond. I hope
> it won't end in tears. It seems an intrinsically fatal situation, that is
> why I live from day to day & never think of the future, & conse-
> quently am very happy.[21]

Clarissa saw Raimund every day in 1944 from 6 to 16 March, and
again from 20 March to 15 April. She went to Faringdon between 15
and 17 April, then saw him every day from 17 to 29 April. She saw
him daily in May and from 1 to 10 June, and then as often as possible
through June and July, a great deal in August until on 6 September he
went to Paris. And so it continued day after day through October,
November and December, with a few extraneous appointments on
both sides, Clarissa dining with the novelist, L. P. Hartley, her father
or Duff Cooper, and then spending Christmas at Chequers. This was
still wartime, but that does not appear to have impinged on the affair,
other than keeping Liz in Anglesey.

Raimund normally wrote to her from the St James's Club. By July
he was professing: 'You should know how much happiness you are
giving me.'[22] When he did not see her, he missed 'the music that I can
hear when I look into your eyes'.[23] In September he spent seven
nights in London without seeing her and was miserable.

This love affair greatly upset James Pope-Hennessy. Having behaved
in a 'tart and short' manner with Clarissa, he voiced his opinion:

> You see it is that I so hate, hate, hate this love affair. I persuaded
> myself into compliance because I knew it would make you well: but
> for *you* to be involved in a situation that's banal and unattractive and
> clandestine is something I can't stomach . . . It is the old burden of

idealisation that people place upon each other's shoulders: I'm not annoyed because you are something (yr phrase) but because you are not, or because you seem to be behaving in a way you are not meant to behave. This will be unintelligible I suppose. You see I am not without instincts about you and I know you must be really in love and by now really capable of jealousy and all that. Which makes my protests disloyal and futile and offensive; but there it is. I have tried so hard to keep it all down and I thought I'd done so . . .'[24]

Despite this, he remained a faithful friend, though they saw each other less. On Good Friday 1946, when Clarissa was in Paris, he wrote: 'I wonder if you know how much I love you, your presence here is such a pillar of fact in my existence that I hate you to be away.'[25]

The love affair continued with letters exchanged, and occasional unexplained silences. Clarissa kept a flower from Raimund's button-hole from a party given by Tanis Phillips on 11 July 1945. She noted: 'This flower is from his buttonhole, because we waltzed together. I was very happy.' More separations followed – his summer in Austria, and his visit to New York in the autumn, causing another 'ghastly silence'.

At the end of November 1945 Raimund announced his imminent return; Clarissa was at the British Embassy in Paris with the Duff Coopers on her way to Germany. His son, Octavian, was born in February 1946. Clarissa told Cecil: 'Raimund has a son, so now he can stop.'[26] Raimund returned to his job with Time-Life International, acting as ambassador at large for Henry and Clare Boothe Luce, and he and Liz moved into 15 Connaught Square. C. D. Jackson,* his managing director, praised him for his public relations and advertising skills, and ability to promote circulation in Europe, thanks to the languages he spoke: 'von Hofmannsthal has found his niche.'[27]

In 1946 Cecil Beaton was preoccupied with his ill-fated romance with Greta Garbo and horrified that this had become the subject of gossip. He mentioned to Clarissa that she had been wise to take Emerald Cunard into her confidence about Raimund and that in her case her appeal for discretion had been respected. This was far from the case. Clarissa told

---

* C. D. Jackson plays another role in this story. He ran off with Beatrice Eden, Anthony's first wife.

Cecil she had shouted at Emerald and told her she was ruining people's lives: 'She only stopped because I was so rude and worked up about it.'[28] In September Clarissa planned a secret holiday in Switzerland with Raimund, but despite weeks of plotting, he could not get away: 'This sort of thing leaves me utterly exasperated,' she told Cecil.[29]

Instead she went to Paris on 14 September on her way to Lunel to stay with the painter, Jean Hugo, to interview him. From there she wrote to Isaiah Berlin: 'R. has a quality of humility, not the Christian humility which is imposed on pride, nor self-abasement, but a natural humility that I have only seen in one of two other people in my life, and which seems to me fabulously precious and wonderful. For this quality alone I would place him above all other human beings.'[30] Clarissa was 'ruffled' when Berlin cast aspersions on Raimund and warned that 'a great cancer of resentment really <u>will</u> grow inside me!'[31]

In June 1947 Clarissa and Raimund snatched three days in Paris. The letters from Raimund kept the flame alive, with the usual mixture of professing love, ruing absences, and feeling lonely. The clandestine nature of the love affair prompted a telegram announcing: 'Darling suddenly frightened your letters may reach wrong hands. Please don't write Paris neither office nor embassy safe. Will advise Brussels address soonest.'[32] Occasionally Raimund was more informative. In June 1950 he told Clarissa: 'Alice madder than ever, Sylvia, poor Sylvia very plain. Romana *much* nicer.'[33]

And yet, during these years, Clarissa became involved with Anthony Eden and, despite protestations to the contrary, she was also close to Duff Cooper. There is a letter from Duff to Clarissa, written after her marriage: 'Darling, you are the only woman I have ever loved without asking much or indeed anything except a peck on the cheek in return – And now you tell me that you love me "most dearly and tenderly". I feel that I have been over-rewarded and I am proud.'[34]

Yet when she was at the Ritz in Paris in the late 1940s he asked: 'I wish you loved me just a little bit now – Perhaps you will one day? Too late?? Never.' The same letter ends: 'Why not stay here next week? I shall be all alone, would take you out every night? No rape.'[35] Soon afterwards Clarissa suggested she visit him in Cannes, 'provided you are there & that you are not buried in officialdom'.[36]

Duff Cooper's diaries include graphic details of his love affairs with many women – Louise de Vilmorin, Gloria Rubio, Hélène Blasselle,

Ghislaine de Polignac and an eager Hungarian called Anci Dupré (whose husband owned the Hotel Georges V) – 'We lunched and made love with great ardour . . . At making love she is superb. I have never known a better. . .'[37] There was Daphne, Marchioness of Bath: 'We had a pleasant evening and then returned to the Dorchester where we enjoyed ourselves enormously. I had never really made love to her before although I had always wanted to . . .'[38]; and Caroline Paget: 'I made love to her until five in the morning. Sometimes she slept. I never did, accounting myself too happy to lose a moment of consciousness. For the first time she denied me nothing . . .'[39]

At no time did he write about Clarissa in that way. Having got to know her in December 1944, he was soon describing her as 'a rare and charming creature'[40], though aware that there was 'very little sentiment on either side'.[41] When she stayed at the Embassy in November 1945, he wrote: 'Diana doesn't like Clarissa – thinks her cold, aloof and bad-mannered. I do like her, but I don't love her at all. They say she is heart-less. She may be.'[42] In February 1948 he wrote: 'Clarissa is always some-thing of a disappointment to me. I feel that she should somehow be a little more interesting than she is.'[43] He knew she loved Raimund. He was concerned that she had been in Zurich with him (in February 1948): '. . . a very dangerous proceeding. I think that Liz would be quite capable of divorcing him if she were to find out. I am sorry for Clarissa. I fear she is not happy.'[44] In March 1949 Duff was in her London flat when the doorbell rang. Duff recorded:

> I telephoned first and she asked me to come. I had been in the flat
> only a few minutes when the door-bell rang. She went to open it
> and returned immediately. The door was only a few yards away but I
> had heard not a word. It had been Raimund, who afterwards
> confessed. She had dismissed him with a gesture. I asked why. She
> said it would have been embarrassing and I think she was right,
> although neither of them conceal their liaison from me.[45]

This affair was still an issue as late as March 1951. Clarissa asked Duff:

> Darling Duff – something tiresome and unpleasant. Someone has
> told Diana (at least I suppose they have since she says she 'knows')
> that I still see R. and that Liz knows this. Diana seems to have rather

been making hay with this. I don't want to involve you, or even discuss it, beyond asking you to tell me whether it was you who told her this (it is odd, because nobody *knows* whether Liz knows or not, unless *you* have some exclusive information?). If it's not you then it must I think be Grace Radziwill whom I told about R. simply and solely to stop her thinking her husband was my lover, damn her eyes.* I think she might have blurted it out, not from malice, but in the intoxication of a new friendship.

Will you tell me truly? We think it's time to do a firm propping up operation all round.[46]

Before he had time to reply, Clarissa wrote again saying she wished she had never burdened him with that: 'I am so sorry, Duff, but what am I to do? I believe only in love, it's the only thing on earth worth living for – and I'm unfortunately a great sticker.'[47]

Duff replied that Diana may have asked, 'Does that affair still go on?' and that he may have replied, 'I suppose so' – nothing more than that. Duff assured her: 'I certainly did not say that Liz knew because I don't believe for a moment that she does. What a bore it all is. Almost enough to make one give up illicit love – almost, but not quite, thank God.'[48]

If Raimund's wife, Liz,[†] did not know about the affair, plenty of other people did. Ali Forbes recalled berating Raimund after a dinner party when, all too audibly, he hailed a taxi and commanded the cabby to take him to Rossmore Court. Forbes ticked him off, suggesting he might have been more discreet.[49]

One day the relationship had to end. It did so when Clarissa finally accepted a proposal of marriage from Anthony Eden. Looking back years later, Clarissa described Raimund's attitude as 'desire & admire'.[50] She never regretted it, and she kept a copy of the little *Rosenkavalier* memorial volume in her bedroom at Alvediston, and later in London, until the day she died.

---

* This was a rumour that Chips Channon heard in December 1948, Stas Radziwill's infidelity confirmed in his cynical view by his having given her a solitaire diamond worth £8,000. And Duff Cooper wondered if Radziwill had produced £3,000 to buy Clarissa her Wiltshire cottage.
† Liz had an affair with Winthrop Aldrich (1885–1974), American Ambassador to the United Kingdom, 1953–7; and later with the 11th Duke of Devonshire (1920–2004).

10. CONDÉ NAST, KORDA AND WEIDENFELD
1945–52

The war ended and an uneasy peace settled in the land. To some degree life returned to a form of normality, different from pre-war Britain, in a country suffering financial hardship and rationing, with Churchill out of power and a Labour government in charge. Soon after VE Day in July 1945, Clarissa began work at *Vogue,* encouraged by Cecil Beaton, despite Clarissa thinking it 'a sinking ship'. She was paid eight pounds a week. She began her work with enthusiasm, producing one article a month. Her brief was to cover cultural matters, rather than fashion, which gave her the chance to write about artists, authors and poets. Her photograph appeared in the January 1946 edition of *Vogue,* posed behind Stella Cárcano (about to marry Viscount Ednam), a glamorous double portrait by Cecil.

She reported to James that Cecil was trying 'to force food' down her throat, because he thought her too thin. She was happier with hip-bones sticking out, though she found it attracted 'a lot of undesirable men'. Champagne was arriving from Paris, as did Prince Stas Radziwill, Eric Duncannon, 'very good looking & more intelligent', and Duff Cooper, for whom her affection was 'unbounded.'[1]

There were raffish dinners with Emerald Cunard, Daisy Fellowes and Hugh Seely, and Gerald Berners. She dived into the world of the Dudleys* – 'rich, loud, coarse, comfortable, worldly – great fun, swimming pools, gin rummy, stimulating crude admiration for one's looks'. She stayed with Sir Robert and Lady Diana Abdy at Newton Ferrers, in Cornwall: 'I thought it absolutely perfect – exactly the

* Eric, 2nd Earl of Dudley (1894–1969), then married to Laura Charteris (1915–90).

way I have always meant to decorate my house if ever I had one.'² She endured 'a dreadful dinner at the height of the cold spell at Elizabeth Bowen's calico-windowed house', contrasted with a 'tremendous' dinner given by Daisy Fellowes for fifty guests.³ She revisited Mells 'very nice, very satisfying – salt of the Catholic Earth ... a nice contrast to the sort of people I've been seeing so much these last few years. I lay in the grass & bathed in the pool.'⁴

Towards the end of 1945 Nicolas Nabokov, the Russian composer and cousin of Vladimir Nabokov, suggested she should visit Berlin. He had become a friend through Isaiah Berlin, and was working with the US Control Commission in Germany. He was the only man that Raimund ever warned her about. Clarissa obtained two commissions to write about the trip, one from *Vogue* and the other from *Horizon*. She and Nabokov travelled via Paris, staying at the embassy. Her Paris days were packed with lunches, dinners and concerts, Nabokov much present. She lunched with Jean Cocteau, had tea with Gertrude Stein, saw much of Duff Cooper, and was entertained by Marie-Louise Bousquet, Jean Hugo, Carlos de Beistegui and others. Then she and Nabokov went on to Brussels and she arrived in Berlin on 14 December, staying there until the nineteenth.

Vogue published her Berlin diary in which, at one point, she described the Russian guards as wearing 'khaki "Queen Mary" toques'.⁵ Cyril Connolly published a longer article in *Horizon* in March 1946. She was twenty-five, and her article appeared alongside works by Matisse, A. J. Ayer, Alan Pryce-Jones and Maurice Richardson.

Clarissa's report gave a chilling account of Berlin as a post-war city in ruins. Many of the houses in the suburbs were empty shells, and the city centre was 'a jumble of rocks on barren soil'. She was lodged in an ex-Nazi's home, requisitioned by the military on the outskirts of the city. As she put it: 'Studying his shelf of books, even those simple experiences gave me a warning twinge of conqueror's delirium, which a short walk in the streets or a visit to an unheated German flat quickly dissipated.' More Allies arrived daily and more Germans were forced to sleep in halls, stairways and cellars. The able-bodied sought employment with the Allies as this ensured adequate rations. A black market was in clandestine and sometimes open operation. Clarissa managed to track down some cultural life, 'dragged to its feet' and supported by the Allies – the State Opera, plays at the newly named Teatr Pamyati Reinhardta, and the Berlin Philharmonic Symphony Orchestra conducted by Sergio Celibidache, a young Romanian who took over from Leo Borchard* (accidentally killed by a sentry). She found an exhibition of sculptures and paintings in a half-gutted house, but fundamentally culture was dead: 'There is no cultural life in Berlin, in the sense of an exchange of ideas . . . If it existed before, then it was smashed by the Allied raids and battle for the city. With the fall of the Nazi party, many of the executives, actors, musicians, etc., were implicated and have had to be dismissed.' She continued: 'It is rare to find a self-assured and independent-thinking person among the German intellectuals, and the few that exist are generally in the Communist camp.' And she concluded: 'The Germans now see cultural life in terms of trying to please their conquerors.'[6] To Duff Cooper she expressed it differently:

> It's the utter chaos that's so striking; physical & mental – it must be virtu-
> ally impossible to administer a country with everything necessary lacking
> – except if you do it in the Russian way (& that's the most successful
> way there's no doubt). The Russians don't need to impose Communism
> in their zone – they just send their Moscow-trained Germans & it
> happens inevitably . . . The Germans are longing to be 'organised' again,
> whether by gauleiter or commissar, to get them out of the present mess.
> Most of them are completely apathetic about everything except food &
> fuel (though the Communists I saw were active and clever enough) &
> only think not 'What do we want?' but 'What do the Allies expect of
> us?' & they are pretty bewildered trying to find out . . .[7]

Back in England, Clarissa wrote features for *Spotlight* about Rodney Ackland's stage adaptation of Dostoevsky's *Crime and Punishment*, Eisenstein's film *Ivan the Terrible*, Bertrand Russell's book, *History of Western Philosophy*, the exhibition of treasure from the Sutton Hoo

---

* Leo Borchard (1899–1945), German-Russian conductor, who took over from Furtwängler when he fled to Switzerland in January because the Gestapo were pursuing him. After a concert on 23 August 1945, he was invited to dine with a British colonel. He was being driven back late by a British man when a sentry tried to stop them. The driver misinterpreted the signal and drove through, at which point the sentry opened fire and Borchard was killed.

ship burial at the British Museum, the merits of abstract ballet, the new opera season at Sadler's Wells, Laurence Olivier's *King Lear* at the Old Vic, Ralph Richardson's *An Inspector Calls*, Peter Ustinov's new play about Simon Bolivar, *The Man Behind the Statue*, and the burgeoning of theatre in Bristol. She wrote of Cocteau's 'monkey-quick imagination' in the ballet *Le Jeune Homme et la Mort*.

By September Clarissa was finding her work with *Vogue* 'irksome' and the annual salary of £500 inadequate. Condé Nast wanted her to be a feature editor, and the editor, Audrey Withers, did not want her writing the *Spotlight* column. Clarissa had not left London for weeks – 'this beastly, beastly town, which is battered by gales & hail & cloudbursts day after day'. However, she pressed on and in October she wrote about the tapestries of the Cuban painter Jean Lurçat, an exhibition of Gwen John's paintings, the return of Oscar Homolka to appear in the film *The Shop at Sly Corner*, Sid Field on stage in *Piccadilly Hayride*, Bruno Walter back at the Royal Albert Hall, and the inaugural concert of the Royal Philharmonic Orchestra, created by Sir Thomas Beecham, performing in Croydon 'rather defiantly'. Finally she reviewed Arthur Koestler's novel, *Thieves in the Night*, judging that he presented all sides of the Jewish case 'with detachment'.

As ever, in these articles, Clarissa was incisive. She praised John Gielgud as Raskolnikov in *Crime and Punishment* for creating 'terrible, cumulative tension', Ustinov's portrayal of the chief of police, Petrovitch as 'a minutely perfect character sketch and Dame Edith Evans's performance as Katerina Marmeladov as 'beyond all praise . . . wholly credible and incredibly moving'. She was disparaging about contemporary theatre, describing it as 'a mixture of reportage with a few pseudo-philosophical homilies about life; dull dough with a few currants stuck in'. She was especially critical of the Americans – Thornton Wilder and Paul Vincent Carroll with their 'slick, fat dialogue'.[8]

In November 1946 Clarissa left *Vogue* on the grounds that she wanted to write articles independently rather than work in an office. Cecil Beaton was not surprised, convinced that Condé Nast would have been exploiting her for her social contacts. He said that the photographer, Horst 'who used to be a German lout & as such had physical success, has been made into a tired grey cipher of a man,' and that Margaret Case in New York, 'goes on using the same *Vogue* patter until the blood runs cold in one's veins'.[9]

Clarissa aged sixteen

Clarissa's mother, Goonie

Winston Churchill – enthralled by Goonie in 1907

'Bluey' Baker – Clarissa's biological father

Clarissa with her adoring mother – by Marcus Adams

Clarissa as a youngster

A family dinner in Cromwell Road – Jack, Goonie and Clarissa

'Trim' Oxford

James Pope-Hennessy with
Nigel Nicolson in 1940

Mells – a group including Isaiah Berlin and Conrad Russell

Clarissa by Fayer

Clarissa

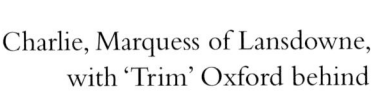
Charlie, Marquess of Lansdowne,
with 'Trim' Oxford behind

Clarissa, a reluctant debutante, with her friend, Priscilla Bibesco, 1939

Lord Berners at Faringdon

Clarissa at Faringdon

Orson Welles & Alexander Korda
on the set of *Anna Karenina*, 1947

Cecil Beaton with Clarissa

Clarissa by Raimund

Raimund by Clarissa

Bad Homburg, 1951

Clarissa's Father, Jack

Since 1944 Clarissa's father had been declining. In September 1940 the bombing of 42 Chester Terrace had left him homeless. For a time he lived in an annexe of 10 Downing Street, at the invitation of Winston. In July 1944 James Pope-Hennessy spotted him in a London club, 'looking so ill and old I didn't recognise him till he'd gone by . . . His collar hung round his neck.'[10] Clarissa and her father went to Chequers to join Uncle Winston and his family for Christmas that year, giving Mary the chance to cast a critical eye on her cousin: 'Clarissa who has regained her glamorous looks – but I find her *so* heavy & dreary . . .'[11]

In 1945 Lord Horder examined Jack and noted 'a little pleurisy',[12] and a large aneurysm in the upper abdominal area. Jack's illness over-shadowed VE Day on 8 May 1945. In June he went to Chequers, but Clemmie was determined to ease him out. She succeeded and he went to the Ritz in London.* In due course Johnny found his father a flat. Jack still took the tube into the city, and he achieved his ambition of becoming a member of the Turf Club. Clarissa saw her father day after day in the early months of 1947, until he died on 23 February with Winston at his side. That winter was so bitter that Lord Moran forbade Winston to attend the burial at Bladon, where Jack was laid to rest next to Lord and Lady Randolph Churchill. Clarissa, Johnny and his second wife, Mary, Peregrine, Duncan and Diana Sandys, Hugo and Lady Caroline Waterhouse were among the mourners.

Winston was able to attend the memorial service at Holy Trinity, St Marylebone, also attended by Lord Ivor Churchill, James Pope-Hennessy, my father, the widowed Mrs da Costa, and many members of the staff of Vickers, da Costa. My aunt Joan wrote to Winston: 'I have lost a very precious friend and one who gave me many hours of happiness . . .'[†13] Duff wrote to Clarissa and she replied: 'death is

---

* This was something of a Pyrrhic victory, since Winston lost the general election on 5 July 1945, and Attlee took over Chequers.

† In 1990 Minnie Churchill urged me to ask my aunt Joan about Jack. Was he in love with her? My aunt was in Odstock Hospital at the time. I have seldom received such a fierce look – which certainly precluded my asking her any further questions of that nature. But she realised that she had not satisfied my curiosity and told me the story of him splashing her in the ship's swimming-pool in 1929. Conclusive, I thought.

always shattering & I think one never feels quite the same again afterwards. But Papa had been ill for so long, & although he was brave & simple & contrived to get happiness out of the small things that were left to him, it was unbearably sad to watch him living.'[14]

In the settlement of his estate, Peregrine identified an insuperable distance between Clarissa and their elder brother, Johnny. One issue, according to Johnny, was that Clarissa had nipped down to Holworth and collected various chattels before they met to divide them. The three siblings inherited Holworth House jointly. Peregrine bought out the others and lived there for some years.

Clarissa panicked about her future. January 1947 found her writing 10,000 words on Anatole de Grunwald's rendering of the Beau Brummell theme for a film. Raimund produced George Weidenfeld. and Isaiah Berlin introduced her to the American playwright S. N. Behrman. Cecil came to her rescue once more and introduced her to Sir Alexander Korda.

Alexander Korda

Korda took Clarissa on in the publicity department of London Film Productions Ltd in March 1947. She was based at 146 Piccadilly, a large building near Hyde Park Corner. 'I work for a few hours each day in a tiny dark overcrowded room . . .'[15] Clarissa wrote to Isaiah Berlin. She was paid £20 a week, thus £1,000 a year, twice her *Vogue* salary. Suddenly her life was taken over, running round Paulette Goddard – 'one of those film stars who study economics, theosophy & things'[16] – Constance Collier, Sir C. Aubrey Smith and even Cary Grant. There were meetings with the editor of *Picture Post,* lunches and dinners with the director Julien Duvivier.

She confessed to Duff Cooper it was odd that she was doing this:

I loathe, and always will, the film world – the people at the top are, as you say, limited in their interests, & the lower executive types are the scum of the earth, worse than Fleet Street hacks, because while being as vulgar, thick skinned, & cretinous, they are also laxer & more conceited. Nor do I really like films themselves & rarely go to one – so perhaps it is a strange job to have . . . I am finding it hard to maintain much interest in Oscar Wilde. I disapprove of the

prevalence of arbitrary & sentimental coincidences – all those fallen
mothers & long lost children – but perhaps that was just the
Victorian atmosphere & the epigrams are, I suppose, witty.[17]

She had admired Korda's pre-war films, made when he was married
to Merle Oberon. Now she found Korda variously possessing 'a sweet
disposition – charm – & a lot of humour'[18] or 'rather weary and not
happy'.[19] He had divorced Merle and was consorting with a minor
star, Christine Norden.

She worked on four films, only two of which she rated as special
– *The Third Man* and *Fallen Idol*. The other two were *An Ideal Husband*
(which began shooting in March) and *Anna Karenina*. She appeared
at the studio in Denham nearly every day, driven there with Cecil in
the studio Rolls-Royce. He was designing the costumes for *An Ideal
Husband* and 'battling with an army of bad taste'.[20] It did not help that
Anna Karenina was being filmed at the same time, as the two productions competed with rivalry and sometimes enmity. Clarissa watched
the filming with Cecil, both of them 'exhilarated and interested in
Korda's direction, his incredible quickness and perception, subtlety
and flair', as Cecil put it.[21]

Paulette Goddard flew in from America as the star, and caused a
strike at the studio by bringing her own hairdresser. In June Clarissa
spent four days with her in Brussels, and then a week in Paris (one of
many visits that year) to promote her film *Bonnie Prince Charlie*. In
Brussels the star was keen to attend a pornographic show, but fortunately when they found one, she lost her nerve. *An Ideal Husband*
premiered at the Carlton Cinema on 13 November. Clarissa's report
to Cecil, who was in America, gives a picture of the scope of her
activities and her analysis of the situation, though she did not mention
that she had dinner with Anthony Eden before the event:

Thursday all your contract girls climbed into landaus and processed
slowly down Piccadilly to the Carlton where the crowd milled around
and gaped at them. It was very glamorous and very social. Alex
[Korda] stood in the floodlights to receive the Mountbattens as they
posed with Vincent and Zoltan [his brothers]. We saw impressive flash-
backs to all the old Korda films & then *Husband* – bad I'm afraid (and
your credits all wrong . . . I just don't know <u>how</u> it could have been so

bad. It was atrociously developed – each scene a different exposure to the last – extensive cutting seems to have increased the junkiness, & more epigrams are being pruned at this moment. The fact that the sets & costumes were not by the same person seems disastrous. All the time the two are conflicting, not only in pattern and colour but in spirit, though <u>you</u> are not harmed by this, only wasted.

Oddly, the performance which now seems to come out of this as by far the best is Glynis Johns. The audience reacted to her immediately . . .

Alex is a little rueful about his slating in the press – curiously enough the three good reviews came from the 3 most left papers – *Herald*, *Star*, & the *Daily Worker*! Of course Lejeune did her stuff 'the most exquisite arrangements of colour, form and grouping make this the most beautiful picture ever made in this country' & wound up with a tribute to A's exquisite taste.

However, there are queues outside the cinema every day, it's booked there for 10 weeks . . .[22]

She reported that '*Anna* is <u>still</u> on re-takes, the opera sequence etc . . . *Prince Charlie* slogs along . . . marred by high politics between Alex & Sam Goldwyn over [David] Niven's ineffectual body.'[23] The excitement was the arrival of Orson Welles to star in *The Third Man*: 'I must say I am sold on the whole performance. I see him as a modern version of those extrovert, creative, vital Renaissance figures – cruder of course & slightly debased from there – he could only have come out of America in a world sick & decayed as ours is. Also I find him so pleasantly patient, polite and humane.'[24] To Duff Cooper she wrote: 'Less conceited, more intelligent, than I had anticipated – and fantastically funny – an appearance like a very handsome bullfrog, green eyes & black curls.'[25] He tended to make passes at every girl.

Clarissa was promoting *Anna Karenina*, making sufficient impression on the star, Vivien Leigh, that she based her characterisation of Lavinia in *Titus Andronicus* on her in 1955. Inevitably, there were comparisons between Greta Garbo and Vivien Leigh, neither of whom betrayed an iota of maternal love for her child. Simon Harcourt-Smith, the writer and producer, judged that it must have been as embarrassing for both to be compared as it was for him to do it, being 'a devoted admirer of both'.[26] The conclusion was that the film was a beautiful failure. Clarissa was dismissive of the various stars:

Cary Grant she found 'terribly grumpy . . . a complete non-starter', Vivien Leigh 'terribly temperamental', but Myrna Loy 'absolutely sweet'. Joseph Cotten, on the other hand, thought Clarissa was just a 'frivolous debutante' and had to be disabused of this by Cyril Connolly. Even the young 'completely unsuitable' Irish actor, Kieron Moore, knew he was hopelessly miscast as Korda's Vronsky.[27]

Anna Karenina premiered on Thursday, 22 January 1948, a busy day for Clarissa, which included visits from Raimund at 9.30 a.m., the hairdresser at 12, lunch at Claridge's, a fitting at 2.30, Raimund again at 3.30, drinks with a man called Noël Bush at 6.30, then the premiere at 8 p.m., followed by a supper party given by Oggie Lynn, the singer and socialite. Both Hofmannsthals gate-crashed the post-film party.[28]

In February there is evidence of another suitor – Colin Tennant, the handsome son of Lord Glenconner and stepson of Clarissa's friend Elizabeth Glenconner. As with so many of Clarissa's friends, they had always known each other slightly. Colin had been at Zürs in 1938, at that time close to Judy Montagu. He was confident to tell Clarissa he loved her, but was miffed that she was forever changing her plans: 'I so want to see you and feel desperate lest you don't.'[29] He mentioned having seen her but a handful of times in the previous six months and he hated to be alone: 'I wait and wait – there is never anyone when I have nothing to do or feel sad or want someone. I don't think about anybody else, or make any plans in case you can come, & I don't really want anyone else.' He threatened to marry the next person he saw.[30] The following day, aware that she was presently leaving for New York, he announced he was going to Switzerland.*

On 19 March 1948 Clarissa sailed aboard *Queen Elizabeth* to promote *An Ideal Husband*. The visit included a break in the Bahamas, Harbour Island and Eleuthera, before ten packed days in New York in April, staying at the Plaza, and then Washington. She returned to London on 30 April to be met at the airport by Raimund. He scarcely recognised her with her short hair, and a new coat reaching almost to the ground – American luxury in the midst of British clothes rationing.

On 23 September 1948 a certain Mr R. Humphries put his house, Rose Bower, a cottage in Little London, Broadchalke, up for auction.

---

* No other letters survive until July 1952, shortly before Clarissa married, when he suggested an evening of greyhound racing.

There was an entrance hall, two reception rooms, a large kitchen, a larder, three bedrooms, a bathroom, a garage and a 'charming' garden. Cecil Beaton's mother went to see it, as did his secretary, Maud Nelson. On a whim Clarissa bought it, telling Cecil: 'I am so excited that I cannot sleep. I have never owned a bit of the earth before, or anything in the country. I have longed for it so much that it is overwhelming now it has really happened.'[31] She took possession on 12 December, after which Cecil's world of Wiltshire became part of hers. The next years are peppered with dinners with Lady Juliet Duff, patron of the arts, at Bulbridge in Wilton, and with the many artistic and talented neighbours whom that part of Wiltshire attracted.

Rose Bower

She had many guests. Her biological father, Bluey Baker, loved his stay in 1949: 'You . . . proved yourself an admirable hostess. The cooking was perfect and the mixture of herbs, and the bottle of Montrachet one of the best I remember.'[32] Cyril Connolly felt so at home that he left his toenail clippings in his bed.

★ ★ ★ ★ ★

Clarissa left Korda in the summer of 1949 and went to work for George Weidenfeld, on *Contact*, which, though officially a magazine, had to be printed between hard covers to qualify for better paper rationing as a book. The first edition appeared in 1946, launched at a luncheon at the Savoy attended by figures such as Harold Nicolson and Lady Violet Bonham Carter. *Contact* was published from three top-floor rooms at 26 Manchester Street in London. Clarissa first visited the office of *Contact* on 27 September. Her job was to persuade authors to write for the magazine.

George Weidenfeld had been a refugee from the Nazi *Anschluss* of Austria in 1938. He had arrived more or less penniless, was lucky to know Flora Solomon, the first person to improve working conditions and the general welfare of staff at Marks & Spencer. She took George under her wing. When he first arrived in Britain, he slept on her floor. He was intelligent, enterprising and fluent in several languages, and made himself a successful wartime career as an interpreter at the BBC. After the war he realised that foreign correspondents would replace armchair pundits, and a great number of pre-war staff would return to their places at the BBC. He was a great admirer of how the British had stood up to the Germans and was keen to promote Anglo-European relations through publishing. Along with *Contact*, he published a few separate books, most memorably *New Deal for Coal* by a rising Labour politician, Harold Wilson.

George was principally interested in politics but appointed Philip Toynbee to look after the literary side. Six issues a year were published, and by the end of 1948, there had been thirteen. The first edition contained an article by the provocative American journalist Emily Hahn on American tourists in London, a piece on Spanish cooking by Elizabeth David, and contributions from Constantine Fitzgibbon and Alan Ross, and a description of his art school by Denton Welch, who had lately died – *The Earth's Crust*. The fifth edition, *The Public's Progress*, was advertised as being 'as lively as a newsreel, as beautifully produced as a limited edition',[33] with twenty features by well-known British and foreign authors. The magazine soon had a reputation for producing some of the best journalism then available in Britain. Writers such as Elizabeth Bowen, James Pope-Hennessy, Lesley Blanch, Enid Bagnold, Vercors, and Philip Toynbee were all published in the 13th edition.

Clarissa was only very briefly involved with *Contact*. Years later, she was surprised when George Weidenfeld confessed that he had been greatly in love with her at the time. She should, by then, have been used to inspiring that reaction. In August 1949 Clarissa went to Salzburg with him, presumably platonically and, although they both loved the opera, she hated the rest:

> I find it macabre, depressing, boring, unpleasant. I am sunk in furious, sulking melancholia which has spread right through me so that my life, my character, & future seem hopeless & desperate.
>
> I find the town squalid. It is simply an American occupation town. I hate the military signs, the green soldiers & their wives with octagonal glasses & bumptious children. I hate the milling decayed European aristocratic flotsam & jetsam. I hate the Café Bazaar & the rain & the Austrians. As a Festival this must have died at least a decade ago.[34]

Faringdon had remained a port of call during the 1940s. Early in 1950 it was clear that Lord Berners was dying. Robert Heber Percy and Clarissa had never got on well, but he was aware of how much she meant to Gerald. He telephoned her and she came to Faringdon. Lord Berners was lying on the Venetian day-bed in his downstairs room. 'He was completely unlike himself,' Clarissa told Sofka Zinovieff. 'He didn't want to be seen. He was past being interested.'[35] She stayed a few minutes. Lord Berners died on 19 April 1950.

Contact survived until 1951. Then, as George put it: 'We buried it and became book publishers.'[36] He had founded Weidenfeld & Nicolson with Nigel Nicolson in 1948, launching it the following year. Clarissa left the company in July 1951, soon to embark on a different future as Anthony Eden's wife. When Lady Antonia Pakenham went to work there in August 1953, Evelyn Waugh said to her: 'I believe you're going to work for George Weidenfeld.'

'Yes I'm thrilled,', she replied.

He said: 'The last person who had your job married the Prime Minister. See that you do better.'[37]

PART TWO

11. THE PATH TO MARRIAGE
1947–52

'He has conversations with the flowers in his garden,
at the same time he makes me feel very bewildered & green.'
Clarissa to Duff Cooper, 6 June 1948[1]

Clarissa had met Anthony Eden at Cranborne in 1936, at which time he had made an unfavourable impression. She met him again at a dinner party given by Lady Cunard on 2 September 1947, at the end of which he quietly asked her to dine with him.* There was a meeting with him at seven thirty on 8 September, sandwiched between Raimund at six, and dinner with Stas Radziwill at eight thirty. She had dinner with Eden on 11 September and went to stay with him at his seventeenth-century home, Binderton, near Chichester, between 27 and 28 September at which the French Ambassador, René Massigli, had been the other 'incongruous' guest. The Raimund relationship was extant when they met. Cecil Beaton judged her 'rather frustrated – often bad-tempered'.[2]

The preceding years had not been kind to Eden. In the summer of 1945 he heard that the RAF Dakota plane in which his son Simon was flying had gone missing in Burma. For four weeks he awaited news, Simon's death being confirmed on 20 July, just a month after the death of his mother, Sybil (on 19 June). His marriage to Beatrice did not survive the loss of their son. She was already living partly with C. D. Jackson,† a distinguished American. She moved to America in 1946,

---

* On 28 August Clarissa attended Trim's marriage to Anne Palairet at the Brompton Oratory.
† C. D. Jackson (1902–64), served with the Office of Strategic Studies in France from 1943, as deputy Chief at the Psychological Warfare Division of SHAEF from

but did not marry Jackson or the prominent American surgeon with whom she was later associated. When Beatrice was dying in 1957 Clarissa thought Anthony should go and see her. He flatly refused.

By November 1947 Duff Cooper was describing Eden as 'her latest admirer'. Duff did not like Eden and was aware that Eden did not like him. Assessing this new interest in Clarissa's life, he maintained that Caroline Paget had now ended her affair with Eden: 'Clarissa says that he never stops trying to make love to her.'[3]

Anthony Eden

Anthony Eden was one of the most impressive politicians of the twentieth century, acknowledged as a fine foreign secretary, with consummate diplomatic skills. He won a Military Cross in the First World War, spoke Persian and Arabic, had a first-class honours degree from Oxford, a highly developed taste in art, and was noted for his sartorial elegance, his Homburg hats being called Edens. Politicians in his day were often men of considerable achievement. His contemporary Harold Macmillan had also served in the First World War and was prodigiously well-read.

Anthony was the third of four sons of Sir William Eden, a colourful figure with estates in Durham and Northumberland, an amateur painter and a considerable collector of art. Sir William amassed a fine collection of Impressionists, which had to be sold by the family. Otherwise they would have been immensely rich. He was born on 12 June 1897. Anthony was not, as some have suggested, the son of George Wyndham,* though he bore a striking resemblance to him. From Sir William, Anthony inherited something of a temper, which became a well-known feature of his career at the Foreign Office.

His mother was Sybil Grey, a society beauty and a great-niece of

---

1945, as managing director of Time-Life International between 1945 and 1949, and later as publisher of *Fortune* magazine; he was president of the anti-Communist Free Europe Committee between 1951 and 1952, and a speechwriter for Eisenhower on his successful presidential election campaign. Later he served as Eisenhower's liaison between the newly created CIA and the Pentagon.

* The Rt Hon. George Wyndham (1863–1913), Conservative statesman, man of letters and a member of the Souls. In later life he lived at Clouds, in Wiltshire. He was known to be close to Anthony's mother.

the Prime Minister, 2nd Earl Grey. He was brought up at Windlestone Hall in Durham. He went to Eton, and while there his brother John was killed (in 1914), and he lost his father in 1915. His brother Nicholas was killed in the battle of Jutland in 1916. Eden served in the King's Royal Rifle Corps, experiencing the full horror of bitter fighting in the trenches on the Western front. By the age of twenty he was a Brigade Major. In June 1917 he earned his Military Cross for rescuing his sergeant, Bert Harrop, in an exploratory raid across no man's land at Ploegsteert. Eden described Harrop as 'the best type of Greenjacket non-commissioned officer'. On their retreat, they were about fifty yards from their front line when Harrop was wounded in the thigh, bleeding profusely. Eden helped fix a tourniquet and called for a stretcher. They got him back safely but, as Eden wrote: 'To this day I do not know whether the enemy saw the stretcher and held his fire, or saw nothing in the flickering Very lights.'[4]

In the autumn of 1919 he went up to Christ Church, Oxford. His love of art was fostered in the Uffizi Society. Presently he began to collect – works by Constable and later by Degas, Braque and Picasso. Clarissa wrote of him that he had a first-class academic brain and high intelligence, but he was uninterested in the complexity of human beings. He did not analyse them. He put them into categories – 'honourable' or 'dishonourable', 'reliable' or 'unreliable' or 'You would or would not go tiger shooting with X or Y'. He read widely, constantly rereading the classics, and wherever he went he took his Shakespeare just as other men travelled with their Bibles.

He entered Parliament in 1923 as MP for Warwick, retaining the seat for the next thirty-four years. On 5 November that year he married Beatrice Beckett, whose father, Sir William, was a banker who owned the *Yorkshire Post*. In due course they had three sons, Simon, who died in Burma, a boy called Robert, who lived for only fifteen minutes in 1928 and Nicholas, born in 1930. Simon was closest to his father, and Eden told Clarissa that nothing was so awful for a parent as losing a child. Nicholas was closer to his mother.

He had a successful parliamentary career, and by July 1926 was parliamentary private secretary to Sir Austen Chamberlain, the Foreign Secretary. In the National Government after 1931 he was under secretary of state at the Foreign Office, the only Foreign Office representative in the House of Commons. At the end of 1933 he became Lord Privy Seal. In the next years he was something of a roving ambassador for the Foreign Office, meeting Hitler, Mussolini and Stalin. He entered the Cabinet in June 1935 as Minister for League of Nations Affairs (without portfolio), and after the resignation of Sir Samuel Hoare in December that year, he became Foreign Secretary, the youngest to hold that office since 1851.

Neville Chamberlain succeeded Stanley Baldwin as Prime Minister in May 1937. Eden mistrusted the new Prime Minister's view of Mussolini and got on less well with Chamberlain than he had with Baldwin. He resigned in February 1938 following a bitter confrontation in which he outlined the choice as Anglo-American co-operation versus a dubious settlement with Mussolini concerning his *de jure* recognition of the Italian position in Abyssinia. In his resignation speech he said: 'There are occasions when strong political convictions must override all other considerations.'[5]

While out of the political frontline Eden visited the United States, where he was well received by the Americans and by President Roosevelt. When war was declared in September 1939 he returned to government as Dominions Secretary, though excluded from the war cabinet, but when Churchill succeeded Chamberlain in May 1940 he became war secretary, and at the end of the year was once again Foreign Secretary. He served until July 1945. Clement Attlee told him later that their joint achievement had been to curb Churchill's wilder schemes. As early as 30 September 1940 Churchill had told Eden that he would be his successor and this pledge was reinforced in many ways over the years to come. In 1942 Eden was given the additional role of leader of the House of Commons. He declined the offer to become Viceroy of India in 1943. It was tempting, but there were overriding reasons for remaining as Foreign Secretary. In 1945 there was the Labour landslide and Eden was out of office.

By the time Clarissa met him again he was on his own. He had been living at Binderton, where he entertained friends from various strands of life, political, military and the arts. The visitors' book, adorned with a fine sketch by Rex Whistler, records the signatures of copious visitors between October 1942 and August 1952, many Edens and Becketts, aristocratic friends such as the Cranbornes (Salisburys), Lord Halifax and the Scarbroughs, diplomats such as Nicholas Henderson, and on 4 May 1952 Prince Philip and Lord Mountbatten stayed for a night. At Binderton he could play tennis, garden or walk in the nearby countryside. He continued to buy paintings, and whenever he went to Paris, he scoured the *quais* for books, and read them.

When Attlee called a general election for 25 October 1951, the Conservatives came back in with Churchill as Prime Minister again and Eden returned to the Foreign Office.

★ ★ ★ ★ ★

Early in his first marriage Anthony had discovered his wife's infidelities and, although wounded, had plunged himself into his 'prospering career', consoling himself with 'well-chosen ladies who loved him'.[6] Jim Thomas,* a fellow politician, and Lewis Douglas, American Ambassador to London from 1947 to 1950, were among his few male friends, while Noël Coward was a frequent visitor to Binderton.

Eden was exceptionally well dressed and he was attractive to women. He had been saddened that his divorce came through too late for him to marry Davina, Countess of Erne, whose husband had been killed in action in France in May 1940.† Davina had been a constant presence in his life for five years and was often at Binderton. He even tried to get his wife back, not because he loved her but because this was 'the cleanest thing to do'. Clarissa thought Davina would have made him 'an admirable wife'. That failure had left him 'bitter & lonelier than ever'.

Other women admirers included Rose,‡ wife of his nephew Fulke, Earl of Warwick (who nearly cited him in their divorce in 1938), Jane, wife of Kenneth Clark, and Lady Caroline Paget (by then Duff). Many believed Eden to have been the father of the child she had that died at birth.

In late 1949 he just succeeded in averting a serious scandal when he visited a lover in her London flat, only to find she had attempted suicide. He telephoned Jim Thomas who lived nearby. Being a

---

* Rt Hon. James Thomas (1903-60), later 1st Viscount Cilcennin. First Lord of the Admiralty 1951-6.

† Davina, Countess of Erne (1909-95). Clarissa had been a bridesmaid at her wedding. She was a daughter of Pamela, Countess of Lytton. Instead of marrying Eden, in 1945 she married Monty Woodhouse, later Lord Terrington, whom she met at a weekend at Binderton.

‡ Rose Bingham (1913–72). She appears in the Binderton visitors' book as Rose Fiske and as Rose Lawson, due to subsequent marriages.

bachelor, Thomas insisted on taking over, summoning a doctor and an ambulance, thus saving Eden from a crisis that would have ended his political career. The incident never reached the newspapers.

Then there was Dorothy, wife of 2nd Earl Beatty, whom Eden met at Ditchley Park, the home of her brother-in-law, Ronald Tree. She and Eden embarked on a four-year love affair, with the tacit acceptance of Lord Beatty. Her divorce was granted on 21 April 1950 and Eden's came through on 8 June. All of the above occurred before he and Clarissa began to see each other.

Clarissa's name appears with relative frequency in Eden's visitors' book. Besides 27–28 September 1947, she stayed from 24 to 25 January 1948 at the same time as the Nuttings and Dorothy Beatty. She returned in June with Lord John Hope and his future wife, Liza Paravicini, Somerset Maugham's daughter. Her line at that time was: 'I fear I should never make a politician's wife.'[7] She was back again in August. She was there alone from 3 to 4 October and back again with the Lambtons from 13 to 15 November. She spent Christmas 1948 there as Eden's sole guest, which she described to Cecil: 'My Christmas at Eden's was very dull & excruciating cold – no central heating & electric fires switched on a second only before you came into the room.'[8] She left to spend New Year's Eve with the Radziwills – a dinner for twenty-five with many Pagets and Coopers, leaving early to motor to the Rose Bower.

Unless she visited without signing, she did not go to Binderton again until 30–31 December 1950, or thereafter, before a spate of visits in 1952, in March, April and May. In March 1951 she went to see *Kiss Me Kate* with a 'rather self-conscious Eden', as she described him.[9] None of this suggests grand passion. Duff Cooper and James Pope-Hennessy encouraged the union, the latter believing that she would make a marvellous political hostess. On top of this, she was restless in her work, and disappointed when *Contact* was closed down in 1951, as there was nothing creative for her to do except work with trade magazines and annuals. Cecil Beaton monitored developments. He and Lady Pamela Berry set to work on Clarissa one weekend, attempting to persuade her to alter her life and take on the challenge of being a political wife. She told Cecil that Eden had no sense of humour, and was whimsical. Isaiah Berlin reported that he addressed his strawberries and raspberries as 'my darlings' and 'my dears' and enquired of them when they intended to appear above the surface of the soil.[10]

Clarissa's 1951 appointment diary is packed with the initial 'R' so that affair continued with its surreptitious meetings. Between 15 and 18 April 1951 she was able to sneak away to Bad Homburg with Raimund. Then Eden proposed to her and she turned him down.

There was a blazing row between Clarissa and Cecil when she dismissed the Australian Billy McCann,* generally considered a great personality, as 'a bore', a description she often attached to people. Cecil berated her angrily: 'Why don't you try to see him at his best? It's up to you to make some effort.' After the row, Cecil went to see her in her cottage for an intense meeting. Clarissa's criticism of Cecil was that he was 'too worldly & so censorious of her for not marrying someone whom it was impossible for her to marry'. He in turn told her he found her 'always bitter, soured, critical & selfish'. They kissed and parted friends.

Clarissa told Isaiah Berlin that she had been in great spirits since leaving Weidenfeld & Nicolson in July 1951: 'It is as if I have sloughed off 6 years of futile fussing and pretence, tiring myself out over meaningless and unpleasant chores. For the first time since these jobs began I feel receptive to experience and people, physically well, and happy.' She suggested that her holiday in Sicily and Venice in the summer of 1951 had been 'a dream of excitement and enjoyment',[11] yet tension between her and Cecil came to a head again in Taormina. At dinner one evening Clarissa told Simon Fleet, Lady Juliet Duff's walker, also with them, that she was 'sick' of Cecil 'feeling that she'd made such a mess of her life'. Nevertheless she went on with him to Venice to attend the Beistegui Ball at the Palazzo Labia, to lunch with Uncle Winston and Duff Cooper (separately), and to dine with the Radziwills. Raimund was on holiday in Austria with his family, returning in October, at which point

---

* William McCann (1910–94), a Catholic, son of Sir Charles McCann, agent general for South Australia, who had a large cattle business there and in Argentina. Fluent in French, Italian and Spanish, head of the anti-spy section of British Intelligence in Paris during the war, and later with Royal Dutch Shell. As a child he lived in Moscow Road, London, near Edith Sitwell and remained a lifelong friend of the Sitwells. He was a close friend of Robert Helpmann, the dancer. When he needed to escape the German occupation of France, Helpmann made him a member of his ballet company and they got away. He spent his summers in London and his winters in Sydney.

their lunches resumed, as did the furtive meetings, sometimes at 9.30 a.m. or later at 5.30 p.m.

Garbo

All they needed at this point was for Greta Garbo to arrive on British shores. She came to spend six weeks with Cecil, who was making an ill-advised attempt to marry the elusive Swedish star. She soon created jealousies, not only between Cecil and Clarissa but even between Clarissa and James Pope-Hennessy. As Cecil put it: 'Greta was an anxiety as well as a pleasure.' Referring to Clarissa, he noted: 'Slight jealousy of Greta, but we were both smitten by Greta – & who can resist the fascination of Greta when the allure is turned on & it was certainly turned on for Clarissa's benefit.'[12] Cecil, Garbo and Clarissa went to Salisbury to see the film *The Lavender Hill Mob*, and there were numerous Garbo encounters at lunches and dinners with Cecil, until the uncomfortable pair headed off to Paris, Garbo returning in due course to the ever-hovering clutches of George Schlee.*

Isaiah Berlin wondered if Clarissa had fallen in love with Garbo. She gave him her view of the star:

Miss Garbo – self-conscious?

Yes, but also no: considering she's not just a celebrity but a myth, a legend. Quite nice? Yes – epicene? Yes – but I hate women so it's a relief to me. Trivial? No, but very, very simple.

I think her quite incredibly beautiful, and possessing strong, magnetic and magical qualities that can infect a whole roomful of people with *désinvolture* – a most degrading experience, especially as one imagines she does not discriminate between ourselves and Gayelord Hauser† & his circle. But I liked her simply because, combined with these rather sinister attributes, she turned out to be

---

* Georges Schlee (1901–64), described by Kenneth Tynan as Garbo's 'Kafkaesque guard, escorting her to her next inscrutable *rendez-vous*'. He was a Russian émigré, who became a financier in New York. He was the husband of Valentina (Sanina) (1889/99–1989), the Russian dress designer. The three were engaged in a complicated ménage à trios. (*See* Hugo Vickers, *Loving Garbo* (1994) for the complicated intricacies of this tangled love triangle.)

† Gayelord Hauser (1895-1984), well-known promoter of healthy living.

kind and compassionate – a Swedish Ibsen troll with feet of good Swedish clay. She at no point in her complex and rather tricky visit to England behaved falsely – & I valued her for being true – something, for instance (say I, rounding sharply), that Nicolas Nab [Nabokov] is <u>not</u>.

Then she left us for Paris & Eric Goldsmidt-Rothschild.[13]

Meeting Garbo, James Pope-Hennessy considered his life 'wrecked by a very odd infatuation' for her. He told a friend that Cecil guarded her 'like an eagle, and nobody was ever allowed alone with her', and that Clarissa was 'almost equally mad about her'.[14] James wrote that he had been unable to do any work since he first saw her:

> Actually I find most of the magic goes when one doesn't see her. Her features at rest are almost those of a witch, and I now tend to regard her as the Troll King's Daughter – nothing else will explain that universal hypnosis and contagious passion she effects. I think it is some ageless mysterious figure from a northern forest that has got misplaced amongst us? I also find, on the other hand, the conversation boring & at times intolerable, as when she told me Selfridges was a sweet shop, Christmas a sweet time, Lady Bridget [Parsons] a sweet person, and your flat a sweet apartment; all within eight minutes.
>
> You will doubtless be at Warwick House on Wednesday? So, I hope, will not she.*[15]

Clarissa responded to this:

> Now listen – I am absolutely not going to <u>let</u> Miss G. come between us. We must make a rule never to discuss her again, or something of the sort, if it is going to be taken seriously . . . I mean I do adore her & think she is magical and also kind, but anything else is a social joke – so please let's start cooling off an overheated situation.[16]

★ ★ ★ ★ ★

* A general election had been held on 25 October 1951. This was a celebrated party given by Lady Pamela Berry to which Cecil Beaton brought Garbo, and people like Lord David Cecil fawned at her feet.

On 5 January 1952 Clarissa, Cecil and Frederick Ashton went to stay with Sir Robert and Lady Diana Abdy* at Newton Ferrers. Cecil asked: 'Does he [Abdy] still proposition girls at night?' Clarissa replied that he had done just that the night before. Not long afterwards Cecil was pleased to hear of 'a little peccadillo with Bertie Abdy'. There were several meetings between Abdy and Clarissa, prompting from him over twenty relatively tortured love letters, continuing until July (a month before Clarissa married). In some he spoke of a visit to Paris. She did visit Paris with him at the end of April, but in a late-life diary, she noted that she had made visits to Paris with Bertie, and with Stas Radziwill, neither of which involved sex.[17] Years later Clarissa thought that perhaps Cecil's mother had spotted them together in Broadchalke. She dismissed the affair as so unimportant that she never gave it a second thought.

In January 1952 the rotund American gossip columnist Elsa Maxwell was telling the world that Eden had enjoyed a dalliance with Lady Caroline Duff. Some newspapers in 1951 suggested (on no evidence) that he was about to marry the widowed Duchess of Kent, which, as Clarissa wrote to Duff Cooper, put him 'in a flutter'.[18] Elsa reported further that Eden had danced all night with the San Franciscan James Flood's pretty wife, Betty.†[19] But Elsa had not detected the growing presence of Clarissa in his life. On the other hand another diarist, Cholly Knickerbocker, had spotted Eden and Clarissa together. Cecil sent Clarissa the cutting and asked: 'Does this mean the end of Rose Bower?' She did not reply, but eventually told him that Eden had proposed to her again and this time she had accepted. He did so in February and she told him she would think it over. She wanted his son Nicholas to be happy about it.

At the end of 1951 the Raimund affair finally came to an end. There were no mentions of him in Clarissa's 1952 diary. As late as

---

* Sir Robert Abdy, Bt (1896–1976), a rich art collector with an eye for quality. He was then married to Lady Diana Bridgeman (1907–67). They divorced in 1962. She died in St Andrew's Hospital, Northampton, after a long illness, having suffered serious brain damage in a car accident.

† Elizabeth (Betty) Flood, née Dresser (1917–2011). Briefly a model for I. Magnin, her interests included driving her English sports car, rounding up cattle with cowboys, and making needlepoint rugs for her twenty-two great-grandchildren. She married James Flood at the Flood Mansion in San Francisco in 1938.

June 1951, Raimund had been writing: 'I miss you truly I miss you.'[20] And on 10 April 1952, he sent a message: 'I forgot to tell you how much I loved our evening.'[21] One of the last telegrams, within weeks of her wedding to Eden, stated: 'Don't worry about Pagets anymore ever.'[22] That did worry her as she told Duff Cooper: 'The whole of my future depends on there being no definite rumours – one word from Diana or even Caroline & it will be wrecked.'[23] According to Duff, Raimund was more than keen that Clarissa should marry Eden.

Of the Raimund love affair, Clarissa told Cecil: 'It's been a wonderful thing that I've never had in my life before, something unforgettable & it had to take all this time to get over. Like an illness – you can't decide to recover on a certain day. It had to run its course.'[24]

For six months Clarissa kept her engagement secret, monitoring how people reacted to her while oblivious of this development. Isaiah Berlin thought this was naughty of her: 'like some mysterious Caliph [she] used to learn people's true opinion of her husband when they spoke freely in front of her before they knew that he was about to marry her. It was not fair, but from her point of view amusing.'[25] Cecil ended his account with the conclusion:

I was surprised to find how little Eden seems to know of Clarissa. He thinks her a sweet little thing – & he may continue to think so – for he is not interested in people. He may well get along very well with her by dint of not noticing her moods – her vagaries. It is interesting to me to wonder what Clarissa's tactics will be with him for she is a fair & good person & I know she has decided to behave well – & is not indulging in a whim. She will make a success of the situation – & it is an important & powerful one as the wife of our next Prime Minister which will give an opportunity for her to broaden her horizons & give full play to her rare & unique qualities.

She is an independent creature, lonely, who has learnt to live alone. She has never come off her high pedestal & would never do so. No matter what company she keeps she has always maintained her innate dignity & grace. She now may well become one of the great characters of our age. She has had her bachelor fun of messing about in an unconventional world, making a little money & a life for herself that was filled with interesting characters, but now she is graduating to big things. Her mother took her away from school at her request a year earlier than was customary. The headmistress wrote & said we are sorry to lose Clarissa as expected great things of her & intend next term to make her a prefect. Now Clarissa [by then thirty-two] says after 20 years she is becoming a prefect at last.[26]

Clarissa read this analysis in 1983 after Cecil had died. She appended a private note to it: 'Cecil's analysis headed "Clarissa" of various periods shows shrewd insight in many ways but is vitiated by deliberately leaving out & denigrating a large chunk of my life which he did not like [the Raimund affair], but which formed a major clue to my character. I even wonder if he did not do this analysis in order to be able to change the emphasis.'[27]

Isaiah Berlin was also preoccupied with Clarissa's marriage, deeming Eden to be nice, dull and conscientious, and claiming that Clarissa told him he was 'almost dehumanised by patriotism': 'I doubt if she is in love with him, as for him I think he simply said to himself that he would marry the first girl he fell in love with. She loves him, I think, without being in love with him, if you know what I mean, pities him, regards him as pathetically inadequate in obvious social respects, and is determined to help him as far as she is able.'[28]

12. MARRIAGE

In her memoirs Clarissa wrote: 'In January 1952, I became engaged, secretly and to the surprise of all my friends, to Anthony Eden.'[1] Indeed, the engagement surprised everybody. The union of a divorced politician was lambasted in the *Church Times*, which used it as an excuse to denounce the lapse in moral standards and went so far as to compare it to the Abdication. In those distant days, a divorced politician was an issue, let alone a remarried one. Clarissa told Duff Cooper about it as early as April 1952 and he replied:

> I was going to tell you how proud I had felt that you should have
> told me your secret, and how glad I was about your future which has
> sometimes made me anxious, even while I admired the courage with
> which you faced it. You can be quite confident in my reliability. I
> shall certainly not tell Diana and I haven't seen and am not likely to
> see Caroline, whom I wouldn't tell either.[2]

Clarissa told Pope-Hennessy: 'Darling James, This is a matter-of-fact note to tell you that I'm getting married to Anthony Eden next week. You will be able to get hold of me in September by ringing up the Foreign Office WHI 8440 & then asking for our flat in Carlton Gardens, so please do that & we will meet soon, All my love always, Clarissa.'[3] James told her he was glad the rumours were correct:

> I think it is a brilliant idea, and it will make such an interesting sort
> of life . . . How pleased Lady Goonie would have been, would she
> not? I remember years ago, before the war, in Chester Terrace her
> saying she feared you would marry 'a Bohemian'; you are not doing
> this . . . From a selfish point of view, your letter has made me feel
> strangely lonely . . .[4]

Later he enquired: 'Has Miss G.G. reacted in some unexpected or delightful way?'[5] Needless to say, she had not. The nearest Clarissa came to hearing from her was in Cecil Beaton's telegram: 'Blessings and love from Cecil and I am sure from Greta too.'[6]

Garbo did respond a while after the marriage, suggesting to Cecil that, had they rented a house for the summer, 'Miss Churchill' might not have married. She would have been running around the beach with Cecil telling her to marry 'Mr Eden'. She hoped 'the little blond Mrs Eden' might have a child to 'make life fantastic'.[7]

Cecil told Clarissa he was thrilled by the news and sure that she and Eden had made up their minds that they could be happy:

> It is rare in life for people to have this full opportunity for expressing themselves. You are a very remarkable person with great qualities & I'm sure that they will now be given full scope. You are intelligent enough not only to make an interesting life but be able to spread abroad the true word, & thereby be of such general use.
>
> For my own selfish self there is a particular sadness because this will inevitably mean that I shall see much less of you in future, & it will be a wretched day when you leave Rose Bower, but I cannot but feel a deep & real rejoicing to know that you have been given an opportunity to expand your interests & gifts & to play such a large role in the life of your day. I'm sure you're going to have a wonderfully fulfilled & happy life.[8]

James and Cecil may have congratulated Clarissa. James sympathised with Cecil:

> I am glad you feel as I do about C: I am quite truthfully in <u>dreadful despair</u>, far more than I cd have imagined; she is effectually translated as if she had died, & to see one's oldest friend become the centre of all that obscene publicity, & exploited by that vulgar family [the Churchills] is unbearable to me.[9]

★ ★ ★ ★ ★

Clarissa did not tell Uncle Winston about the engagement because he was unable to keep a secret. However, a few days before the wedding she wrote to Clemmie who was in Capri. 'I am terribly happy about it, and only wonder and hope that I will prove capable of being of some help & comfort to him in his life.'[10] Clemmie at once flew home to prepare for the great day. As Mary Soames wrote their engagement and marriage created 'a considerable stir'[11] both inside and outside the Churchill family.

Eden and Clarissa hoped to marry quietly in August, but there being no news on which the media could focus, the romance between two political dynasties soon became the excitement of the summer. Lady Pamela Berry told her that the editor of the *Daily Telegraph* had 'cleared the whole front page'. She added that she was 'fascinated, happy and pleased . . . despite your inexcusable deceitfulness and slyness' and pointed out: 'I do think it is rather hard on all the other cabinet wives suddenly to have a beauty at No 10 – Sydney [Butler]* won't like it at all.'[12]

Appropriately, prior knowledge was given to Bluey Baker. Clarissa received a great many telegrams and letters, many of them sent to 10 Downing Street. There was no shortage of famous names adding their congratulations – David Niven, Chips Channon, the Droghedas, Julian Amery, Peter Quennell, Harold Nicolson, and from those who played their part in this story of her life – Frederick Ashton, George Weidenfeld, Rudolf Bing, Pamela Churchill, Alexander Korda, Ian Fleming (himself suddenly a father), Peter Brook, Valentine Lawford and even Stephen Tennant (marked 'urgent').†

Uncle Winston sent a cheque. hoping she would 'buy some souvenir of us with part of it'.[13] There were letters from former suitors, wishing her well – Trim Oxford, Jeremy Hutchinson (thanking her for her sweetness to him and admitting that he had not always been sweet to her), and Colin Tennant, apologising for not expressing himself well: 'I'm unusually interested to hear that you will shortly become a young married person: and I really hope you will be pleased & find it agreeable . . . I would have loved to go abroad with you, but

---

* Sydney Butler (1902–54), first wife of R.A. Butler, then Chancellor of the Exchequer.
† Of these the Earl of Drogheda was chairman of the *Financial Times* and later of the Royal Opera House, Covent Garden, Julian Amery was an MP, Rudolf Bing was general manager of the Metropolitan Opera in New York, and Stephen Tennant was living as an eccentric recluse at Wilsford Manor, near Amesbury.

I'm sure you are much better married: anyway, I enjoyed knowing you, may see you next week, & was always happy with you, & sad to loose [sic] another friend so soon . . .'[14]

It was nice to find my father and aunt writing to her, both having appeared in her 1936 diary. 'Having been so fond of your mother & father I felt that I would like to write to you,' wrote my aunt, praising Clarissa for her charm and for being 'an excellent hostess besides all your other talents'.[15]

Many of the messages were similar, but not everyone was pleased. Evelyn Waugh accused Clarissa of apostasy: 'Thousands have died and are dying in torture for the Faith you have idly thrown aside.'[16] According to Isaiah Berlin, Waugh wrote to her on the morning of her wedding accusing her of being 'in effect an adulterous renegade'.[17] This resulted in Clarissa's cousin Randolph choosing his moment to accost Waugh at the bar of White's when it was filled with aristocrats whom Waugh admired and denouncing him: 'It is interesting to observe that while the premier Catholic families of England received my cousin Clarissa's marriage with every mark of approval and sympathy, it took a lower-middle-class Catholic convert of recent date and dubious morals to defend the position of the Church.'[18] Waugh retreated in disarray. Ali Forbes telegraphed:

MY DEAREST CLARISSA, ALL SORTS OF EMOTIONS NOT ALL OF WHICH I CAN IMMEDIATELY IDENTIFY FILL ME AT THE NEWS OF YOUR FORTHCOMING MARRIAGE. I ALWAYS WANTED YOU TO COME TO LIVE NEARER EATON SQUARE SO THAT I COULD SEE MORE OF YOU BUT NOW I WONDER IF THAT WILL BE THE RESULT. PERHAPS I SHALL START THINKING THAT YOU ARE CUTTING ME NOW. ANYWAY NOW I CAN START ADMIRING ANTHONY WITHOUT DOUBTS FIRST FOR HIS TASTE AND SECOND BECAUSE THERE MUST BE MUCH TO ADMIRE IN ANYONE YOU HAVE SELECTED AS A HUSBAND . . . ALL LOVE ALWAYS ALI[19]

Duff Cooper, part instigator of the marriage, had lots to say:

> I was so glad to see the announcement yesterday. Diana said 'I
> thought she was a great friend of yours – Fancy her never telling
> you!' I said, 'Yes, just fancy!' I wonder what Liz said. You will find I
> expect that you have many more friends than you used to have. Even
> in London I heard echoes of things to come. 'I used not to like her,
> but she has become much nicer lately' I was saying to Mrs Slander
> and Lady Sneerwell and they both agreed.'

He added: 'I love you so much in a blameless way.'[20]

The Wedding

Clarissa was married from 10 Downing Street into which she had
been whisked the moment news of the engagement was released.
'The wedding week was like entering a typhoon,'[21] she wrote to Duff.
There was 'a whirlwind blast of cameras & telegrams & bouquets
until one felt quite bruised'.[22] A crowd of 500 gathered in anticipation
of the great day. Clarissa was thirty-two. Eden fifty-five.

On the day, 14 August, she lunched with Randolph. A small party
of friends joined them. Officially, her brother Johnny gave her away
– but he got somewhat sidelined in the proceedings. He even had to
append his signature as a witness in his smallest handwriting.*

The ceremony was performed swiftly at Caxton Hall, at 11.45 a.m.,
with a crowd of two thousand outside, such as might be attracted by
a film star. Clarissa wore a pale lilac silk shantung dress, pleated to the
waist, with a flared skirt, and a close-fitting pale lilac hat. Her corsage
spray was of white orchids. She was given a large square-cut emerald
engagement ring, surrounded by small diamonds set in platinum. As
the Edens left Caxton Hall, they were not sure who should go on
which side. Churchill told Eden: 'On the right, so that you have your
sword arm free.'[23]

The reception was held at Downing Street. Peregrine, Randolph,
the Salisburys, Lady Islington, Lord Brooke, the Sandyses, the

* Timothy Eden, Anthony's brother, and Fulke, Earl of Warwick, also signed the
register.

Beauchamps, the Soameses and young John Eden were all there. Uncle Winston made a speech. A while later Duff Cooper had a letter from Anthony's nephew, Fulke Warwick. He asked Clarissa: 'Is it true, as he tells me, that Winston in his speech at your wedding breakfast referred to "the marriage which we have just seen consummated"? Fancy if they had!'[24]

★ ★ ★ ★ ★

The most valuable part of Clarissa's somewhat guarded memoirs was her analysis of the man she married. She thought they were a 'surprising couple' with different interests – her friends were writers, critics or painters. His were politicians. Common ground was a shared love for art and books. She was impressed by his energy. She thought he would have been a good eldest son, caring for the family estates. She was aware that his father, Sir William Eden, possessed 'an exceptional character'. She wrote:

> Children with overwhelming parents often erect a protective shell. In Anthony's case it resulted in a debonair social manner, a preference for unexpanded relationships and a conventional reaction to human behaviour in general. He was not a complex man. To his legendary though brief tempers, the reaction of the budding diplomats and politicians under him can only be compared to huffy housemaids, however overworked they may have been.[25]

Service in the First World War had instilled in him a close sympathy for soldiers. He was good with 'the man in the street'. He once told her he was not really a Conservative, but an old-fashioned Liberal. He was not an intellectual or an orator, or an inspiring writer. Looking back years later at their marriage she wrote: 'He had had knocks at every phase of his personal life and, like many Englishmen, hadn't known intimacy. He was happy when it came to him later.'[26]

In conversation with Cate Haste years afterwards, she was more forthcoming. She admitted that Anthony could be 'irascible, fly off the handle'. He did so in private, but she never took it seriously. She thought all prime ministers did to some extent. Macmillan 'made people cower in the corner . . . Winston beat people up verbally'. She thought that Anthony trusted too many people, imagining that others behaved in the same way as he did. In that respect, he was 'terribly innocent in all sorts of ways'.[27]

Early Married Life

The happiness and contentment Clarissa and Eden came to share was by no means instant. It was hard for her to settle into married life, after so many years of independence. She wrote to Duff Cooper:

> I looked at my wedding ring & thought this is too nightmarish to last – & I can never take this thing off my finger as long as I live. Surprising it is that in spite of having seen so much of each other the last six months we both became suddenly ourselves only the day after the marriage. I am alarmed by his shortness of temper & general spoiltness . . . He [is] alarmed by my downrightness & kind of humour and inability to flatter'.[28]

She complained to Duff about political life. He sought to reassure her:

> Have confidence in your happiness. What doesn't bore you now because, as you say, it is all new will bore you less in the future when you know all about it and become good at it, as you surely will. Nothing one does well is boring. What you call 'the farce of modern politics' is no more farcical than politics at any other period, and most people become fascinated and absorbed by them.[29]

Fulke Warwick told Duff what he thought about Clarissa and her chances of a successful marriage. Duff passed this on:

> Anthony is deeply attached to Clarissa and I do believe will make a go of it, tho' of course it's a hell of a job to be married (he has certainly found it so) and he's not the easiest man' (vide Sir William) but she has experience of politics and public life' (I didn't know it) and seems terribly good and sane so I'm happy and sure they will be.' Very admirable and nephew-like sentiments.[30]

Among Clarissa's many surviving letters to Cecil Beaton, there is one marked: 'Letter to Cecil, not to be seen by Cate Haste'. It was written in the new year of 1953, after an inconsequential Christmas spent at the Rose Bower:

> The marriage goes very well with occasional stormy patches – but we are both happy & healthy & gay – & A has taken to entertaining, & I have even made him go to Pam Berry's in the interests of the *Daily Telegraph* – but there is still an unbridgeable chasm between us as regards people, & it is a question of suffering each other's friends alternately – though I am rather losing grip on mine, without making up for it by developing a grand Cabinet-wife manner, or throwing myself into official life either.[31]

The Edens had been to church on Christmas Day, 'but I disgraced myself by not knowing what to sing or where to find it all. The Catholic Church was much more restful in that way.' They visited Anthony's brother, Sir Timothy Eden, who lived at Fritham House School in the New Forest, finding him 'living on a hideous blasted heath only half an hour away from Broadchalke in a modern villa where one eats in the refectory & sits in the common room and all the girls' dormitories have Velázquez & Fabritius from the ancestral home in them, which infuriated A'.

Presently there was better news, seemingly before the letter quoted above. When Cecil Beaton saw her after the honeymoon, he noted:

> Still the same uncompromising character – great distinction – but surprising revelation in that suddenly she is in love. In two weeks she has come to accept the attitude of her husband regarding frivolous people, gossip, not leading a serious life. She has no wish to see any more the people she used to see for 'fun'. Instead of dreading the return home in the evening she is disappointed if her husband is half an hour late. She is touched by the sweetness of his character. They had a row (on the honeymoon – a terrible flare-up about the plum situation* in England) & their points of view are very different on many scores but later, having thought the matter over, he will come

---

* Crops were suffering from lack of rain that year. Victoria plums were noted to be small. Hard to see how this could have created a row on a honeymoon. On 20 August it was announced that surplus plums would be dried in Warwickshire.

to her, accept her wishes. It is a great instance of the flexibility of the feminine character, how we see the *mariage de convenance* of former periods has worked so well – a girl is made to marry a man for worldly reasons, & 9 times out of 10, within a few weeks of the honeymoon she has grown to love him.[32]

Clarissa was particularly impressed by the warmth and enthusiasm of the crowds when Eden visited Sheffield in early September 1952. Cecil noted that she had become conventional: 'The casquette that she wore as an art student has given place to a little black toque with a veil that might be worn by anyone from Mrs Chamberlain to Mrs R. A. Butler.'[33]

13. FOREIGN SECRETARY
1952–4

Cate Haste to Clarissa:

'You had been accustomed to having a private life and then suddenly you were flung into it, rather at the deep end, and you obviously coped with it extremely well, at every level. I mean at the constituency level as well as the business of suddenly having supper with various prime ministers . . .'

Clarissa:

'Well, but it's quite easy to do if everybody's kow-towing to you, terribly pleased to see you, isn't it? It's not very difficult. All you've got to do is to keep smiling.'[1]

The Edens lived in the Foreign Secretary's flat at 1 Carlton Gardens, which Clarissa thought was rather like living in a hotel. In those days the Foreign Secretary had the flat at the back and not the view over the Mall, so Clarissa was not excited by it. They had a cook, a butler, a kitchen-maid and a housemaid. Eden had a valet and she had a lady's maid. There was still rationing and she would get 'furiously upset' if the maid produced a new bar of soap before the old one was finished. The Edens paid their staff out of their own pocket. At Carlton Gardens, Clarissa did not have a chauffeur. She had her own Hillman Minx car. When Eden sold his shares in the Anglo-Iranian oil company at a low price, feeling them incompatible with his position as Foreign Secretary, he had to sell Binderton, after which 1 Carlton Gardens became their principal home; Clarissa retained Rose Bower in Wiltshire.

After 1954 they had Dorneywood, near Burnham Beeches, bequeathed to the nation by Lord Courtauld-Thomson, for use by a senior government minister.

Isaiah Berlin judged that she was 'not much approved of in Conservative Party circles, because she seems sour and proud to them'.[2] Clarissa was aware that people thought her assertive, but at first she deferred to the advisers and support team that surrounded Eden. He was a famous man, with 'people who had more of a hand on him' than she did and they were there the whole time, arriving in his bedroom first thing in the morning and still around at nightfall. Clarissa was depressed by the stream of government boxes.

Dorneywood

She knew little of politics. It did not occur to Eden to school her, least of all in constituency work. Sydney Butler, wife of R. A. 'Rab' Butler, the Chancellor of the Exchequer, was 'a great putter-downer' and berated Clarissa for 'being ignorant and not knowing how to behave'. In 1955 the Edens and the Butlers crossed the Atlantic together by ship. Clarissa was aware that Rab 'couldn't have been less Anthony's type of person in the world'.[3]

Clarissa found life as the Foreign Secretary's wife more fun than she would Downing Street later. She enjoyed meeting the great figures of the day. There were two or three big dinners each week, but it was not demanding. As for the constituency, Eden went there only once in August and again at Christmas. In the 1950s the locals took pride in their elected man being out in the world and rising up the political ladder, so he would make an important speech aimed at the outside world. The wife of the Foreign Secretary did not travel. Eden's line was: 'You'd be in the way. We won't be able to have all male dinners and get on with our work. There's no question of becoming involved in them.'⁴ Clarissa told Duff she was furious with Anthony for going to Yugoslavia without her, 'not discovering the existence of Jovanka [President Tito's new wife] beforehand – think of the delightful time us newly married brides could have had drinking Slivovitz together while A. ticked off Tito* for his Ogpu. Sickening.'⁵

When the Conservatives were in opposition in 1949, Bob Boothby told Cecil Beaton that Churchill was determined to cling to power. When Beaton suggested that another term of office would be an anti-climax, Boothby quoted Churchill saying: 'When I first came to the House of Commons, it was ambition that spurred me on. Just a lust for power. Now I want to continue out of anger.' He said that Churchill continued to make a fool out of an increasingly desperate Eden, chiding him with a side-long glance: 'How old was Mr. Gladstone when he formed his last cabinet?' Gladstone was eighty-two. Churchill was then seventy-five.⁶

Despite that, it was widely known that Eden was Churchill's anointed successor. The uncertainty and tension between 1951 and 1955 was that nobody knew when. Winston showed no inclination to step down. Clarissa was caught in the middle, between her husband with ever-decreasing patience, and her uncle lingering on, ageing, obstinate, yet tenacious.

The resignation issue had hung over Churchill's administration since he had taken over as Prime Minister in October 1951. Somehow there was always a reason for him to defer it. Churchill had served only three months in office when the King died. He saw it as his duty to help the new Queen find her feet. The same month he suffered a small arterial spasm, at which point his doctor, Lord Moran, discussed his future with Sir Alan Lascelles, the Queen's private secretary. Lord Salisbury wondered if Churchill might go to the Lords, remaining as PM with Eden leading the Commons. Lascelles did not want the Queen to be asked to suggest this. The

---

* Josip Broz Tito (1892-1980), Prime Minister of Yugoslavia 1944–63, and President, 1963–80.

swearing in of President Eisenhower in January 1953 gave Churchill another reason for staying* – he deemed himself the only man who could establish détente with the Russians, particularly after Stalin's death in March. Next, he wanted to be Prime Minister for the Coronation on 2 June.

In these early days of marriage, Clarissa decided to treat Anthony as 'a human being when everyone round him are such stooges . . . it is important to behave naturally with him . . .'[7] Now being a well-placed witness to affairs of state, she began to keep a diary, rather different from its only surviving predecessor in 1936. This one was focused on politics, politicians and world statesmen, rather than on herself. Thus she recorded Eden's views on Russia: 'Anthony said Stalin† was the best negotiator he had ever met. At Potsdam Winston said, "I think God is on our side," and Stalin replied "I think the Devil is on my side because of course the Devil is a Communist and God can only be a Conservative."'[8]

She recorded Eden's parliamentary private secretary, Robert Carr, warning him that Lord Beaverbrook was about to mount a serious campaign against him in the *Daily Express*, which prompted Eden to threaten to resign, saying he could no longer work with Churchill, who relied heavily on Beaverbrook and refused to break off relations with him.

Gradually she adapted to political life. At the State Opening of Parliament on 4 November 1952, she observed 'a Venetian scene' with peers huddled 'in heaps on the floor of the House all dressed in very creased red robes with Peter Pan collars of white rabbit tied under the chin with a tape'. Because the Queen had not yet been crowned, Lord Salisbury carried the Imperial State Crown on what looked like 'a tray of matches'. She saw Anthony come in from the Commons 'looking very pale and fingering his moustache'.[9] She liked listening to the debates in both Houses of Parliament.

Clarissa was depressed when Eden went to the United States to attend the UN General Assembly without her. In his absence, she lunched with

---

* Dwight D. Eisenhower became the thirty-fourth President of the United States on 20 January 1953.
† Joseph Stalin (1876–1953), General Secretary of the Communist Party of the Soviet Union 1922–53. He died on 5 March 1953.

Uncle Winston, who was struggling to understand some of the papers he had to read. She told him that Anthony could not do two jobs (Foreign Secretary and Deputy Prime Minister) and Winston said: 'I want him to get into training for when I go.'[10] But he did not go.

Clarissa also accustomed herself to a more prominent public life, asking Evelyn Shuckburgh,* Eden's private secretary, how she should comport herself at the Queen's dinner for the Commonwealth Conference on 3 December. He advised her not to ask questions or initiate strange topics. Shuckburgh was annoyed that she was not taken up to be presented to the Queen. In her turn she did not hesitate to berate Shuckburgh about an article that appeared to promote Rab Butler as a possible successor to Winston. Her complaint was that Eden was not getting a good enough press. Apparently Sydney Butler was going round expounding her curious theory that Eden could not be Prime Minister since the Archbishop of Canterbury had refused to officiate at their marriage.

Clarissa and Eden sailed to the United States on 26 February with the Butlers so that Eden could explain the results of the Commonwealth Conference to the Americans. But Clarissa could not get to bed when she wished, since Eden worked late into the night with his secretaries in his cabin.

Just as they docked in New York on 4 March, they heard that Stalin had had a stroke and was unlikely to survive. They flew to Washington where the press was out in force to photograph Eden. He was due to make a speech. Clarissa intervened when the British Ambassador, Sir Roger Makins, thought Eden should mention Stalin. She thought not. On the day Stalin died, 5 March, she went to see Anthony in his bath to advise him against saying he was 'sorry' that Stalin was dead. He took her advice. The next day Clarissa was invited to the White House, where Mamie Eisenhower presided over tea, the ladies in cocktail dresses: 'Like all celebrities, I find her much smaller than expected. Very dignified and grand atmosphere, which she combines with grimaces and wisecracks.' Mrs Eisenhower showed Clarissa round, ending by putting her arm round her: 'Well, anyway, it wasn't stuffy, was it?'[11]

On 9 March they flew to New York in a special plane and were

---

* (Sir) Evelyn Shuckburgh (1909–94), Eden's principal private secretary. In 1986 he published controversial diaries, *Descent into Suez*.

driven to the Waldorf Hotel in a procession of twelve cars. They had supper with Nin Ryan,* where Clarissa was relieved to find her friends, Rudolf Bing, Fulco di Verdura (the famous jeweller), Fulke Warwick, Ham Armstrong (the Foreign Affairs journalist) and Bill Paley (chairman of CBS), and his wife, Babe, 'shock-headed in a summer print and a white fur cardigan'.[12]

In New York, Clarissa was observed by Cynthia Jebb, wife of Sir Gladwyn Jebb, then permanent representative of the UK to the United Nations. Lady Jebb concluded that Clarissa was almost certainly 'happier leading a life where she could meet her own intellectual friends rather than a lot of dull people to whom she has to be polite'.[13] Others picked over the Eden marriage. Ava, Lady Waverley thought Clarissa should be more amiable and remember to smile. Isaiah Berlin thought that was impossible, that she had an 'Edwardian view of life with big romantic attachments' but he was certain that Clarissa would stick by Eden.[14]

While in New York, Clarissa rang the ever-reclusive Garbo and this time got straight through without the habitual nonsense. She noted: 'She's in bed today. Wants to lunch Thursday, but no doubt she will stand me up at the last minute.'[15] Clarissa was late for lunch and thought the less of Garbo for waiting under an umbrella in the rain just because she was now the Foreign Secretary's wife:

We go off to Maud Chez Elle, a very good French restaurant. Well, there she is, the same, but un-magical now, dressed in a plush great-coat, full of what Cecil calls cock-teasing, planning to holiday in Corsica with us. I say Mr Eden likes to play tennis. Then she will play tennis with him. 'I think I can give him some sort of a work-out.'

Shop at Altmans. As we walk down the aisles to the shoe department, all the sales girls say 'Good afternoon, Miss Garbo' and she is enchanted.[16]

The Edens were back in Britain on 16 March in time for the visit of President Tito of Yugoslavia the following day. This involved a visit to Buckingham Palace for Tito's audience with the Queen. A lot of

* Margaret 'Nin' Ryan (1901–95), daughter of the investment banker, Otto Kahn. Wife of John Barry Ryan; a keen patron of the Metropolitan Opera.

dignitaries stood around, including the Churchills and Attlees, then a gang of Yugoslavs:

> Chaos reigns and no one introduces us. Finally I go over to one man and introduce myself. The Queen enters in blue satin. Tito in sky blue with a red stripe on his pants. Princess Mary [the Queen's aunt] in beige shantung and the Queen Mother in a satin patterned in lilac blossoms.[17]

At the table Clarissa could hear Princess Margaret 'yelling' at Churchill, asking him if Eden had done well in the United States.

Queen Mary died at Marlborough House on 24 March at the age of eighty-five. Clarissa went to the lying-in-state and attended the funeral at Windsor.

Eden's Operations

Eden had been ill on and off since the marriage in 1952. Even before that, in June 1952, he had suffered from jaundice, which left him with bouts of pain. Indigestion from overwork was diagnosed; painkillers and bismuth were prescribed. He suffered an attack on their honeymoon and bad pains on his visit to Tito in the autumn of 1952, and at the Berlin conference in 1953. His doctor, George Rossdale, gave him morphine and he travelled with a hypodermic to inject himself. This he did once on a sleeper to Edinburgh. Only when he was examined by Dr Rossdale on 2 April was it discovered that the trouble was his gall bladder. Two days later he was seen by Sir Horace Evans,* the Queen's doctor, and Basil Hume,† a senior surgeon at St Bartholomew's Hospital. An emergency operation took place at 10 a.m. on 12 April.

D. R. Thorpe, Eden's biographer, unearthed an alarming series of mishaps that now followed. Churchill was causing havoc with the bulletins about Eden's condition, and harassing Hume about the gravity of having the Foreign Secretary on the operating table. The poor

---

* Sir Horace Evans (1903–63), later 1st Baron Evans, physician to Queen Mary, George VI and to Queen Elizabeth II (1957–63).

† (John) Basil Hume (1893–1974), anatomical surgeon. He retired in 1958. Not to be confused with Cardinal Hume.

surgeon was so alarmed over what should have been a relatively straightforward operation that he had to delay wielding the knife by an hour, until his own nerves were calmer. The operation took three hours and was overseen by sixteen doctors. In the panic Hume's knife slipped. An enormous amount of blood was lost and the bile duct was severed. This resulted in total jaundice from the non-functioning of the duct to the liver.

Guy Blackburn,* Hume's assistant, took over and Eden's life was saved but a second operation was needed. Eden remained in the London Clinic, visited each day by Clarissa. She wrote that this operation, on 29 April, was unsuccessful and 'followed by pneumonia & general deterioration of his condition. After trying to X-ray him again, severe shock & collapse took place. He was sent to Chequers in a hopeless condition.'[18] He was near death several times.

Eden was not well enough to attend the Coronation and the many lavish plans for entertaining during Coronation week, to which he and Clarissa had been looking forward, were cancelled. Instead, they sat in 'gloomy' Chequers, loaned by Churchill, and 'looking at the Ministry of Works flowers, which, as in St James's Park we are not supposed to pick'.[19]

Fortuitously, Dr Richard Cattell,† an American doctor, was in London addressing a medical conference. He was the world's leading expert on patching up gall bladders. Sir Horace Evans had the intelligence to contact him. Cattell pronounced that a third operation should be performed, and that Eden would have a better chance of survival if this were done in Boston with his own team of medics. Churchill intervened once more, claiming that this would reflect badly on English surgeons. Lord Moran was also against it. But sense prevailed.

Clarissa attended the Queen's Coronation and was then swept away from the Abbey with a police escort. Three days later the Edens flew to Boston, with Winston and Clemmie at the airport to see them off. Even as they boarded the plane, Churchill and Eden had a

---

* Guy Blackburn (1911–95), consultant surgeon. He never divulged details of this operation.
† Richard Cattell (1900–64), director of the Lahey Clinic; pioneering reconstructive surgeon in the fields of the biliary duct, pancreatic tract and thyroid.

talk about the merits of commercial TV. Clarissa thought: 'They never stop, do they?'[20] At this point Lord Salisbury became acting Foreign Secretary.

Eden underwent an eight-hour operation at the New England Baptist Hospital in Boston. Dr Cattell told him that he should now be able to lead a perfectly normal life and that one of his patients was even able to do some sailing. Clarissa's brother, Peregrine, confirmed that had he not gone to Boston he would certainly have died.[21] Eden wrote to Robert Carr, praising the operation. Clarissa added: 'Surgeon says it was one of the worst ops he has ever performed but that it has been completely successful.'[22] She wanted Anthony to recuperate until the end of the year.

If the Eden marriage had been difficult at the outset, this critical illness glued them together. Years later Clarissa wrote:

> When he decided to marry me (& I him) there was some trepidation on both sides. The marriage might well not have been a success but for three things. His extreme niceness, my capacity for devotion & his almost immediate illness. The latter was so appalling that it added ten years onto the marriage immediately & brought out the best characteristics in both of us. In him this was great courage, a determination to live, & a sweetness of nature under adversity. It also broke the gates for the first time, as he told me many times subsequently, & made the marriage a true & intimate one. Something he maintained he had never known before, masking any feelings of bitterness or reproach behind a decent & conventional façade.[23]

On 29 June Eden left hospital to recuperate at Moorland Lodge, the Newport Rhode Island home of Nin Ryan, shadowed by a Scotland Yard detective. Clarissa loved it: 'Very pretty & luxurious, with the pre-war kind of servants who are genuinely hard-working and amiable. Mr Ryan Jr seems intelligent, unembarrassed, efficient, and above all, mainly absent.'[24] Walter Monckton settled their expenses with government money.

While there, the Edens noted, in the *Daily Telegraph*, the guest list for a Downing Street dinner Winston had given for Alcide de Gasperi, the Italian Prime Minister. Two days later they read that the Bermuda Conference had been cancelled and that Winston had been ordered to rest. This put them in turmoil. Clarissa received a letter from Jock Colville explaining that Churchill had made a short speech at the dinner, but on leaving the dining room 'he suddenly lost control of his legs, and his speech became inarticulate and slurred. The guests were got rid of as quickly as possible, and Churchill got to bed. Next morning his left arm was paralysed, and he could walk only with difficulty.'[25] He had suffered a stroke.

Churchill struggled through the next day's Cabinet meeting, 'but his speech was slurred and his mouth drooping'.[26] Clemmie took him down to Chartwell, where his health declined sharply. For a while he lost the use of his left arm and left leg. Lord Moran believed the end was near, but just as contingency plans were discussed, Churchill rallied. Colville managed to prevail on the great newspaper magnates to gag the press. His message to Clarissa was: 'He says he will continue as Prime Minister for one reason alone – to give Anthony time to convalesce completely before taking over from him.'[27]

Randolph Churchill wrote to Clarissa, having seen his father on 27 June: 'As you can imagine, he was the gayest, most debonair and only natural person in the room.' He urged Clarissa that nothing must interfere with Anthony's convalescence: 'Everyone, and that includes above all Rab and Bobbety, is full of the feeling that it would be monstrous if Anthony were to lose his chance, because of his illness, particularly now when everyone appreciates that his troubles are behind him and that he is on the high road to better health than ever.'[28]

There was considerable political manoeuvring, one plan being that if Churchill stepped down, Lord Salisbury should form a caretaker government for six months. Eden thought this was a Palace plot against him, initiated by Sir Alan Lascelles (still the Queen's private secretary until the end of that year). He said: 'Why six months? And why a caretaker government? All that is necessary is for Bobbety to be acting PM until the autumn.'[29] They became more anxious when Walter Monckton, then Minister of Labour, and Jim Thomas both wrote pleading that Anthony should return as quickly as possible, preferably before the House rose.

Robert Carr assured the Edens of Butler's loyalty, the danger always being that he might make a bid for leadership. Robert Boothby wrote to let Eden know that the succession was assured and that sooner or later he would be 'elected by unanimous acclamation'.[30]

Though they had not wanted to return so soon, they became homesick and flew back on 25 July, Eden worrying about being photographed on arrival. As soon as he was home, he was seen by Horace Evans. They spent the weekend of 31 July to 4 August at Chartwell, during which Churchill, in siren suit and Stetson, teased Eden: 'What! Can't you drink? I can.'

Eden responded: 'Winston, you are very rarely ill and when you are you choose your illnesses very carefully.'[31]

D. R. Thorpe made the valid point that had Churchill retired after his stroke, and had Eden gone to the Lords at this time, Butler might well have become Prime Minister and Eden 'could have kept in contact with great events, taken on the role of the Conservative Party's beloved statesman, and influenced the progressive trend of domestic policy with regular speeches on the major international issues of the day. It would have been a fulfilled conclusion to a nigh-unblemished career.'[32] But, as ever, Churchill stayed on, the public largely unaware of the situation, and with Churchill's son-in-law, Christopher Soames, effectively running the country.

★ ★ ★ ★ ★

Anthony and Clarissa flew to Nice on 8 August 1953 for a recuperative cruise to Sardinia and Palermo, arriving in Gozo for three days under the aegis of the Mountbattens. They went on to Athens, Naxos and Rhodes. Churchill wrote that he was improving in health every day.

At the end of September, almost all at the same time, the Edens returned from Athens, Churchill flew in from Lord Beaverbrook's Villa Capponcina on Cap d'Ail, and the Queen came south from Balmoral. The return of Churchill and Eden was hailed as two great leaders returning to the fray. Eden declared himself rejuvenated, though doubts still lingered over his health. Lord Salisbury remained as acting Foreign Secretary until Eden resumed his post on 5 October. Two days later, Clarissa and Anthony lunched with Churchill: Winston drank two glasses of champagne, two of brandy and took an aspirin in the middle of lunch.

They went to Margate for the Conservative Party Conference, arriving at a dismal hotel – 'sordid bedroom with the gas fire unit and a window imperfectly tied up with string'.[33] The speeches were the challenge. Eden awoke to a depressing poll favouring Butler as the minister who had done the best job. He rose to his feet at 10 a.m. on 8 October. He received a good ovation, was judged to have spoken 'with vigour and assurance' and impressed the Conference with his vitality.[34] Clarissa thought it his best ever speech. On the last day Churchill spoke for fifty minutes, in a lower emotional key than usual, but exhibiting 'all his old humour and oratorical resource'.[35] He declared: 'If I stay on for the time being, it is because I have the feeling that I may well have an influence on what I care about above all else, the building of a sure and lasting peace.'[36]

Clarissa had remained in close touch with Duff Cooper since her marriage. She received a letter from him, written at Vaynol on Christmas Eve 1953, just before he set off on a sea voyage. He had seen her with Eden and applauded 'the heartiness of his appearance and the vigour and good sense of his conversation'. He highlighted a drama that would preoccupy Clarissa:

> Joe [Alsop*] had lunched that day with sweet little Pam Berry. When he told her that he was looking forward to seeing Anthony that evening, she said 'I fear you will find him much changed.' I repeat this not in order to make mischief but so that you may know who your friends are. Pam is almost pathologically disloyal. I don't think she means harm but is incapable of not doing it.[37]

To Clarissa's great shock, Duff died at sea from a haemorrhage on 1 January, before this letter and one other arrived. The Edens helped Diana bring her husband's body home for burial. Thanking them, Diana added: 'One day when I return I would love to talk to you, Clarissa, because Duff so dearly loved you & I can tell you comforting things that I cannot write.'[38] It is unlikely that such a conversation took place, but Clarissa did write to her:

> I understand the agony you suffer & must for a long, long time to come. I just wish to say that I am terribly unhappy. I loved Duff deeply and most tenderly. He was the best friend I ever had, perhaps the only one, for he was the sole person to whom I told all my thoughts and feelings.

* Joseph W. Alsop (1910–89), political journalist in Washington.

He was constant and vigilantly loyal – the last letter he wrote to me the day you sailed was a warning against false friends.

I admired him more than anyone – his way of life was unique and absolutely successful – successful because of his wisdom and sweetness of character.[39]

On 7 January the Edens joined Diana, the Churchills and many others (including Raimund and Liz von Hofmannsthal) for Duff's memorial service at St Margaret's, Westminster.

Lady Pamela Berry

The Pam Berry drama evolved from Duff's letter of warning. Clarissa claimed not to mind Pam disparaging Eden as 'dreary and stupid' and how she wished he would not become Prime Minister, but she resented her misleading Alsop to the point that he told Clarissa that 'had he not seen Anthony subsequently, he would certainly have gone back to America and told people they were saying in London that Anthony was finished'.[40] Pam, of course, denied having said anything of the sort. When they met at the Italian Embassy in October, Clarissa tried to talk to her, but Pam cut her dead professing herself hurt. In a further exchange Clarissa merely said she did not see why everyone should know they had quarrelled. She had had problems with Pam before. In 1952 they had gone to dress designers together, and Pam had 'continued to instil quite a lot of mischief into me by the end of the afternoon, which I afterwards began to resent'.[41] This was to lead to further trouble, when Pam became vociferous over Suez. Her daughter-in-law, Marina, was perceptive about her:

The word jealous does spring to mind. Pam was a great beauty and not outrageously modest and nor was she outrageously well behaved. She was a very strange woman and she was absolutely selfish and she could be disarmingly generous. You never knew what you were going to get. I realised that she was a bully from the start. The one thing that a bully wants is a victim. So if she said, 'The moon is made of green cheese,' I'd say 'How wonderful of you to notice.' You can't argue. If you want to bully someone you have to be telling them that they're wrong. The only thing to do is to agree with them.

Pam had a very strange intelligence. She read books and she had ideas but they always went in parallel lines. They never crossed and cross-fertilised. Pam, you see, considered herself to be a political influence. Because the house in Cowley Street was within the division bell she could have lunches. And she loved her lunches. And she never had couples. You went to her singly. She felt she was running this great show: 'And now so and so will tell us what he thinks about . . .'. She thought this was how political hostesses did it. And she ran her own show basically. She was one tough cookie.[42]

Miscarriage

Towards the end of January Eden went to the Berlin Conference, but Clarissa stayed at home because she was expecting a baby '& feeling extraordinarily unwell as a result'.[43] She spent her time at Rose Bower but could not go out because of impassable snowdrifts. Instead she read a lot, rested and was sketched by Henry Lamb. In March she lost the baby and recuperated in a nursing home in Queen's Gate. Aunt Clemmie wrote to her: 'Winston & I grieve that your high hopes & joyful expectations are for the moment disappointed. I was so happy when you told me last Friday . . .'[44] To Bluey Baker Clarissa wrote: 'We are very sad at present.'[45] Clarissa suffered a further miscarriage some time later.

She was well enough to accompany Eden to Switzerland for the Geneva Conference, keeping house for him at Le Reposoir, overlooking a park full of buttercups, with swallows dipping over the lake. Figures such as Bidault[*] and Molotov[†] were around, though to Clarissa's irritation when Molotov came to dinner, she was left in bed upstairs, reading the newspapers, while hearing screams of laughter from below. She succeeded in seeing the Russian and Chinese leaders however: 'Molotov looks made of the best quality wax, very wonderful, & the Chinese appeared in a dense horde, all tiny, delicate, dressed in loose blue uniforms, very terrifying in their apartness.'[46]

On 1 June Clarissa put a notice in *The Times* that she was to have

[*] Georges Bidault (1899–1983), President of the Popular Republican Movement, and former Prime Minister of France.
[†] Vyacheslav Molotov (1890–1986), Russian Minister of Foreign Affairs 1953–6.

a complete rest and spent ten days at the Bower. She suffered from gastric problems, exacerbated by her pregnancy, but avoided an operation. Anyone who doubted her love for Anthony could be assuaged by the kind of letter she wrote to him at this time, when he was away in Geneva and she was alone in her cottage:

> Shall I tell you how much I love you? It is a long time since we were separated for so many days at so great a distance & I realise now how immeasurably more I love you. I think of your sweet face all the time, and I lie in your arms at peace. I think of all my faults too – of how I grumble as a luxury – and how I am never calm and soothing at the right moments. I love you so much my darling and depend on you completely. Please be lenient if I am jealous sometimes – I am not jealous as some women are.[47]

A month later she was well enough to join Eden in Geneva. They stayed at Les Ormeaux, 'a bit dusty but bearable', with a better view of the lake. She met Molotov 'as waxen as ever,' was flown to Paris by Mendès-France,* 'a pale squat little man', and back in Geneva met Chou-en-lai,† 'much pinker and more shiny'[48] than she had expected. She was impressed that Chou had brought Ming china with him.

In October Emperor Haile Selassie of Ethiopia came on a state visit to Britain. Clarissa thought the Palace dinner dreary, and the ceremony at the Guildhall one of 'unparalleled boredom'. This was alleviated when two enormous elephant tusks that the Emperor was about to present to the City fell with a resounding crash just as they were about to be borne in. There followed an interminable lunch at the Mansion House, during which Churchill got 'rather tiddly' and Attlee fell asleep, his lit cigar falling onto the tablecloth. Michael Adeane, the Queen's new private secretary, spilt a glass of royal blue liqueur, and the guests endured the Emperor making a ten-minute speech in Aramaic. That night there was a dinner at the Ethiopian Embassy, and another Imperial speech in Aramaic, to which the Queen replied: 'Thank you.'[49]

On 20 October Eden was nominated a Knight of the Garter, an

---

* Pierre Mendès-France (1907–82), Prime Minister of France 1954–5.
† Chou-en-lai (1898–1976), Premier of the People's Republic of China 1954–76.

honour that he had declined after the war (as had Churchill). Clarissa recorded:

> Anthony goes to the Palace in the morning, returns with his Garter and all the trappings. We are both very excited. The news was on the ticker tape immediately. The Queen shook him by the hand and said how pleased she was and how she had wanted this for a long time. When we leave, lots of photographers there, all very pleased about it, and saying 'Just one more, SIR Anthony.'[50]

Eden could not be installed in 1955 as the Garter Ceremony was cancelled due to a national rail strike. His installation took place in June 1956, along with the Earl of Iveagh and Earl Attlee. Field Marshal Viscount Montgomery and Winston Churchill acted as his supporters at the Investiture. Clarissa was amused that Winston and Lord Iveagh were seated in adjacent stalls, and turned their backs on each other, due to a childhood incident in 1879 when the young Winston had lashed the young Guinness with a whip across the forehead during a game. The doctor applied caustic acid, which scarred him for life.

Clarissa was proud of Anthony's Garter, but as the years drew on, Garter Day was not an annual date that she looked forward to with any enthusiasm. Sitting next to the Duke of Wellington at lunch in the Waterloo Chamber one year, she volunteered that the Order was a witches' coven times two. The Duke was livid. He complained: 'The trouble with the Order of the Garter these days is that it is full of Field Marshals and people who do their own washing up.'[51]

On 30 November 1954 Churchill reached his eightieth birthday, which was copiously celebrated: 'Winston's speech good, containing many phrases that will become old tags, e.g. about the lion and his roar.' In Westminster Hall, his portrait by Graham Sutherland was unveiled. Churchill was horrified: 'Painful moment when the Sutherland portrait was revealed. "A remarkable example of modern art", whereupon the blimpish Tories let out a yell of laughter and Sutherland blushed.' To Cecil Beaton Clarissa expressed predictably heterodox views:

> The birthday, or days, passed off with great smoothness of organisation and curiously little emotion on the part of W. or anyone else. I thought

he would be constantly in tears. The Sutherland portrait is excellent both as a painting and as a portrait. It is extraordinarily lucky that the committee willy-nilly commissioned him – half of them no doubt thought he was another James Gunn.[52]

1955 dawned and Churchill was still Prime Minister. When Rab Butler dined with the Edens on 26 January Clarissa observed how 'self-important all politicians are'. She preferred 'Anthony's inverted conceit to this exhausting plugging of oneself that the others go in for'.[53]

The Edens spent a weekend with the Mountbattens at Broadlands, where Nehru* was a guest. In February the Shah of Persia came on a visit, 'unforthcoming on every subject'.[54] They flew to Egypt, where Eden had his famous (and only) meeting with Nasser,† annoying the Egyptian general by arriving in a dinner jacket, which he thought upstaged him: 'Great impression of health and strength. Terrifically broad and blooming. Very brown face and black hair.' Clarissa was not next to him at dinner: 'The General is thirty-five, has never been out of Egypt, is rather inscrutable and very polite with very indifferent English.'[55]

They went on to Bahrain, Karachi, Calcutta, East Pakistan and Bangkok. Clarissa visited Angkor Wat with Janet Foster Dulles, wife of the US Secretary of State, and was horrified that Janet read a paper-back all the way, without once looking out of the window. Janet became animated at the hotel: 'How did they know that Pears was my <u>favourite</u> soap?'[56] They flew to Kuala Lumpur and Rangoon, where Anthony paid a moving visit to the grave of his son Simon. They arrived in Delhi on 3 March, where Clarissa went sightseeing with Lady Clutterbuck, wife of the High Commissioner, and Indira Gandhi. She sat next to Nehru at dinner. In Baghdad she sat between King Faisal and the Prime Minister, Nuri.‡

Churchill did not hand over to Eden until April 1955, so he and

---

* Jawaharlal Nehru (1889–1964), Prime Minister of India, 1950–64.

† General Gamel Abdul Nasser (1918–70), President of Egypt, 1956–70.

‡ King Faisal II of Iraq (1935–58), king from 1939 when his father was killed in a mysterious car crash. Educated at Harrow, he reigned under a regency until 1953. He was murdered with many members of his family by Brigadier Abd al-Karim Qasim in a coup d'état in July 1958. Nuri al-Said (1888–1958), Prime Minister of Iraq, 1930–41 and 1946–58. He went into hiding after the King's assassination, then attempted to escape, dressed as a woman, but was found and shot.

Clarissa had to endure sixteen months of vacillation at any point of which Churchill might have gone but always found an excuse to stay. First, during the Chartwell weekend of August 1953 he went over to Royal Lodge to see the Queen and told her that he would decide to stay or go in a month's time, depending on how well he could manage in Parliament and whether he could make his major speech at the Conservative Annual Conference in October. Next he decided he could not go until the Queen came back from her Commonwealth tour in May 1954. In March that year Eden tried to pin Churchill to that; in June he tried to pin him to July. Churchill decided that the international situation was so unsettled that he needed to stay till the autumn.

After a garden party at Buckingham Palace, the Queen told Eden that 'Winston seemed less truculent about going.' But Churchill did not go. He became bitter towards Eden, taking the line that a prime minister should not be hounded out of office merely because his second-in-command wanted the job. He discounted the valid argument that Eden needed to be in charge for a clear year before a general election. His eightieth birthday would have been another ideal moment, but that passed, despite Macmillan warning him that Eden might leave politics altogether unless he did so. Before Christmas Churchill called a meeting at which ministers attempted to discuss the date of the next election. The Prime Minister was exasperated: 'It is quite clear that you are trying to get rid of me. I shall have to think this over and consider my position.'[57]

Over Christmas he skulked. When Jock Colville suggested he should go to Marrakesh over the holiday period, he replied: 'No. If I'm going to be a dog in the manger, I'd better stay in the manger.'[58] His 'cold hatred' of Eden intensified, but he was weakening.[59] Though he could still make a great speech, paperwork tired him. Even then he decided he was the only man who could deal with some serious threatened strikes.

Eventually it seemed that he was going. Clemmie invited Clarissa to inspect Downing Street. She was 'a little disappointed in the upstairs or bedroom floor. It is so very shabby and dirty.'[60] Just as the handover was settled, Clarissa came back from an exhibition to find Anthony 'in full crisis'. President Eisenhower had asked Churchill to meet him in Paris in May in order to save the Paris agreement to set up the Western European Union. The next day a letter arrived from Churchill announcing that he was staying on. Eden wrote back infuriated, saying he had never put 'party before country or self before either'.[61]

On Sunday, 13 March 1955, Macmillan and Lord Salisbury declared that they would resign should Eden do so. At a Cabinet meeting Eden 'burst out on a rather personal note', telling Churchill that this was the second time he had given a date and then broken his word. Churchill hid behind the Eisenhower telegram: 'They mentioned my name.' Mass ministerial resignations were threatened and Churchill agreed to go as planned. But on 29 March Jock Colville reported that Churchill had announced that the international situation was so bad that he could not resign after all. This provoked a row between Churchill and Butler.

The day came for the Edens to give a dinner for Winston. Clemmie backed out due to arthritis, and Churchill rang to say he had been delayed late at the Palace, which Anthony interpreted gloomily. At dinner Churchill asked her how she liked Downing Street, talked of going to Venice in June and to Sicily. Clarissa noted: 'So we assumed it is blowing over – until the next time.'[62] Jock Colville gave Eden the sound advice to be amiable rather than combative. Even so, as late as the morning of 30 March, Churchill told the Queen at his audience that he was contemplating putting off his resignation. He told Colville that he had asked the Queen if she minded, and she had said no.

Churchill tendered his resignation to the Queen on 5 April 1955. Eden became Prime Minister. As D. R. Thorpe wrote: 'The Crown Prince had at last ascended the throne.'[63]

14. PRIME MINISTER
April 1955–July 1956

An occupational hazard of being married to the Prime Minister was the officials that surrounded him, and the never-ending flow of government boxes.

Clarissa to Cherie Blair: *'We couldn't even share a bedroom without their presence because they were there till late at night, and they turned up first thing in the morning. It was absolutely impossible, all the boxes all over the place. It depressed me sometimes.'*

Cherie to Clarissa: *'There are times when I say I'm going to take my clothes off now if you don't go. It's amazing how it clears a room. I don't think they intend it to be an intrusion, it's just they're so geared up to what they think is important and what they are doing that they just have no conception of the other side of life.'*[1]

On 4 April 1955, the night before Churchill finally stepped down as Prime Minister, he and Clemmie invited the Queen and Prince Philip to a farewell dinner at Number 10. The guests wore full evening dress with tiaras and decorations. Clarissa and Anthony were there. Loelia, Duchess of Westminster inadvertently put her foot through Clarissa's train, prompting Prince Philip to comment: 'That's torn it in more than one sense.'[2]

Randolph Churchill was at the dinner. He had seen a policeman tagging a parking ticket to a car outside White's. 'The Eden terror has begun,' he declared melodramatically.[3] Randolph had decided that Eden would not make a good prime minister, and from that very day he launched a bitter vendetta against him, which was played out in the press. Resenting anyone who took over from his father, Randolph had long considered Eden 'a vain man, kept afloat by a certain anaemic charm'.[4] At this dinner he stormed up to Clarissa, as she recorded: 'Randolph comes up, huge, pale, sweating, blind drunk, and says: "I suppose you know I'm against the new régime." I say I guessed so, as he still had the integrity to keep away from me when he was vilifying Anthony . . .'[5]

Aware that in his drunken state Randolph would not remember his mean words, Clarissa wrote to him the next morning: 'I am sad that you should value our friendship below the pleasure you get from your cheap and futile campaign against Anthony in clubs, and no doubt, in print.'[6] She thought this could be of material advantage only to himself. As in her quarrel with Lady Pamela Berry, her line was that she was 'genuinely amused and curious' at attacks on Anthony in the press, but could not forgive 'sustained attacks from *friends*'.[7] She explained later: 'He wrote non-stop attacking Anthony. He became impossible. Therefore I couldn't speak to him any more.'[8]

At the end of a spectacular evening, Churchill retired to his room and sat on his bed, still bedecked with Garter riband and the Order of Merit. He said to Colville, with some vehemence: 'I don't believe Anthony can do it.'[9] The next day he went to the Palace to tender his resignation to the Queen.

Clarissa lunched at Wiltons with Cecil Beaton, Ali Forbes and Raimund. At the end of lunch, she said: 'I must be pushing along.' Ali never missed a trick: 'Haven't you pushed along far enough, dear?' he ventured. The Queen sent for Eden. They talked of all manner of things until Eden said: 'Well, Ma'am . . .' at which point the Queen said, 'I suppose I ought to be asking you to form a government.'[10] Churchill left Downing Street after tea, a rendering of 'For He's A Jolly Good Fellow'[11] ringing in his ears.

At the weekend the Edens went to Chequers, Anthony's country home now that he was Prime Minister, where they spent Easter, kindly inviting the recently widowed Rab Butler and his children. They found it a curious experience 'as if on a high peak'. During the weekend the Salisburys came, as did Clarissa's niece, Sally, 'a great success and seems amiable and forthcoming'. She got on well with Anthony's son Nicholas.

Chequers was not Clarissa's kind of house, with a pseudo great hall, a kind of pastiche, created by Sir Reginald Blomfield in 1909, 'the architect of the moment', complete with minstrels' gallery.

Chequers

She wanted the panelling stripped, but that did not happen. The park, the lie of the land, and the way the trees were planted did appeal to her, and she enjoyed looking through an album about the trees, made by Neville Chamberlain, a keen dendrologist. There was a grass tennis court, and she wished there had been a proper swimming-pool. She wanted to run the house, but did not discover until somewhat later that Clemmie had ordered the food in her day, chosen the chintzes, and tended the garden. Eventually Clarissa was able to plant a lot of old-fashioned roses, supervised by a kindly gardener.

The Queen invited them for the weekend at Windsor Castle from 16 to 18 April, where they slept in a Victorian bedroom, full of pictures of Prince Leopold.* The stay included a visit to Frogmore, where the Queen Mother, in ruched silk, showed Clarissa round Queen Victoria's mausoleum.

They moved into Downing Street on 25 April. Clarissa noted:

I am glad to be here – never liked Carlton Gardens with its pitch dark hall and sunless rooms. Anthony is miserable here because he hates the Mansard bedrooms and the downstairs rooms full of

* Prince Leopold, Duke of Albany (1853–84), haemophiliac son of Queen Victoria.

someone else's possessions. I am delighted to have two Turners in my sitting room. The view is heavenly. The Horseguards, the ugliest building in London, says Anthony, or the Admiralty opposite and St James's Park with the filmy sprig trees and the lake. Our garden is lovely too – a magnolia and cherries and narcissus and dicentra in the flowerbeds.[12]

10 Downing Street

They soon settled in. It took the servants longer. In those days pedestrians could walk right past the front door of Downing Street. Clarissa was able to slip out to places like Trafalgar Square to test the mood if there was a rally. Only occasionally did people recognise her and talk to her. Clarissa came to love Downing Street:

From our bedroom windows at night we look straight onto Wren's façade floodlit, and, beyond, Nelson and the Duke of York – pale cobwebby figures on their pedestals in the dimmer light. To the left the classical frontage of Carlton House Terrace in the lighting. By day the lovely planes of St James's Park are shaded with blue – bluer than usual because of so much rain earlier. In the Horseguards itself there is a perpetual parade.[13]

She had plans to have the house decorated in the appropriate period, which would have involved buying some Kent furniture, and copying damask patterns from Houghton, the seat of the Marquess of Cholmondeley in Norfolk. In order to redecorate the huge dining room she visited the Soane Museum in Bloomsbury, and noted the colours used there – 'a sort of creamy colour and amazing sort of red and crimson, and spinach green'. She told Cherie Blair years later that this would abrogate the need for each new resident to change the décor, as it would be in the style of the time.[14] However, a credit squeeze prevented this.

It raised Clarissa's spirits to entertain somewhat – the Palmelas,* the Mountbattens, Ivan Moffat, David Brooke, Ian and Ann Fleming, which was just as well since she could barely remember having a single meal alone with Eden during the time he was in office. She hardly saw her own friends, as she told Cherie Blair:

> I felt that I had to spend all my time making everything as easy for him as possible, because I had never seen anybody working like that in my life before, from dawn till two in the morning, and I just felt this is so awful, this life, that I must absolutely tailor my life to his, and the last thing he wants to see, when he comes up before dinner, is a lot of my friends lolling around on the sofas in the White Drawing Room.[15]

Nor did Clarissa make friends among the wives of the politicians who now peopled their world. The key figures were the principal members of the Cabinet, notably Lord Salisbury, Eden's close friend. The politician Clarissa viewed with the greatest suspicion was Macmillan: 'I never liked him. He seemed to me to be a sort of poseur and false and never said anything genuine. The opposite of Nehru. Winston used to say: "You ought to watch about Macmillan. He's very viewy." It was a wonderful sort of Winston word.' Macmillan's wife, Lady Dorothy, was a Cavendish by birth. 'Everybody loved and admired her. She was extraordinary. And she must have been rather marvellous-looking when she was quite young. All the Cavendishes are very tall.' Lady Dorothy had only one evening dress and out it came on every occasion.[16]

---

* Duke Domingos Maria do Espírito Santo José Francisco de Paula de Sousa Holstein-Beck (1897-1969), and his wife, Maria do Carmo Pinheiro de Mello, Duchess of Palmela.

Clarissa tried to fathom Rab Butler, Chancellor of the Exchequer until December 1955, then Lord Privy Seal and Leader of the House, a man with considerable intellectual influence over the Conservative Party, not least on account of his stewardship of the Research Department. When Butler stayed at Chequers for Easter, she wrote: 'I still find him all wrong. Nothing he says rings quite true. Also his mild boastfulness is irritating.'[17] On Budget Day Clarissa noted: 'Rab makes his usual "I – I – I" speech and the broadcast in the evening is even worse. "My policy has been . . ." as if he was PM.'[18] In August 1955 Butler came for another night. 'He accepts in the main Anthony's ideas but we know from his experience that he says one thing to one person and another thing to another. His trumpet-blowing gets worse and worse, but he seems so very nice that one can't mind, though one wishes he wouldn't.'[19] When Eden moved Butler to lead the House of Commons, Salisbury told Eden: 'You realise, of course, that Rab is done for now. He can never be PM after this.'[20]

There was formal entertaining – the Thai Prime Minister, Dr Adenauer of Germany at Chequers, Nehru at Chequers with Mrs Gandhi and Madam Pandit, President of the UN General Assembly. Clarissa saw Bluey Baker as often as possible, and occasionally David Jones, Ava Waverley (with mixed feelings) and Lady Juliet Duff. She felt that James Pope-Hennessy was too unreliable to appeal to Anthony. After an enjoyable evening in March 1955 James told her he no longer felt 'the awkwardness yr new life *did* inspire'. He continued: 'I also liked Sir Anthony quite immensely (I say kindly): I'd never seen him before and was tremendously taken by him.' He hoped she might come and dine at Ladbroke Grove: 'I don't dare to ask you to bring Sir A.'[21] Clarissa warned James: 'Anthony is very fond of you – I am surprised! Don't be offended if I say that you oughtn't to <u>interrupt</u> him so much XX C.'[22]

When the Edens stayed with Lord Lambton at Biddick, his Durham home, in April 1955, she wrote to James: 'Lord Lambton a charming & civilised host – Lady Lambton* mercifully not here, as I find her beastly and barbaric.'[23]

---

* Belinda, Viscountess Lambton (1921–2003), estranged wife of Tony Lambton.

The General Election, 1955

Eden announced there would be a general election on 26 May, fought on the issue: 'Will you go forward with us or backward with Socialism?'[24] The campaign began on 9 May and found them travelling the country, visiting Nottingham, Newark, Doncaster, Leeds, Sheffield, Newport and Cardiff, then Gloucester, Stroud – 'the whole town out to hear, every street jammed' – Bromsgrove, Warwick, Coleshill, Atherstone, Rugby, Wolverton, Bletchley and finally to Chequers for the weekend. At a meeting in London Communist supporters paraded with banners: 'Phoney Tony'. In a packed hall in Glasgow, Eden received thunderous applause.

It was a quiet campaign, a favoured theme being the 'property-owning democracy'. A successful new feature was the television broadcasts, and it was felt that Eden was the only person who gained in stature during those weeks. For his last broadcast it was noted: 'There was no pipe or cigarette, which are supposed to put some speakers at ease and to create a homely atmosphere but in fact irritate a great many viewers.'[25] Eden sat with arms on the table or hands clasped against a backdrop of books and flowers. His personal majority in Warwick rose. 'Well, back to work,' said his defeated opponent, to which his agent riposted: 'I should like to know what work *he* has ever done.'[26]

The Eden administration won a handsome majority of sixty seats at the polls on 26 May, the first time since 1900 that a sitting government had increased its majority in peacetime. Among those elected was my aunt, Joan Vickers, who defeated Michael Foot by 100 votes in Plymouth, Devonport. Churchill congratulated her on her 'brilliant victory'.[27] She was delighted to get his telegram:

> In 1936 you advised me at luncheon at Chartwell, if I was interested in politics, as a woman, to serve in local government. This I did for 9 years and now I am looking forward to serving under Sir Anthony Eden, but I am also thrilled that you will be in the House, so that I shall have the privilege of sitting there with the greatest Englishman in the history of our great country.

> Clarissa kindly wrote me a letter and I have only one regret and it

is that Jack, who gave me a generous donation towards my lost deposit in Poplar in 1945, is not able to share in this success.[*28]

★ ★ ★ ★ ★

On 16 July Clarissa accompanied Eden to Switzerland for another conference. The other first ladies were there, including Madame Faure:[†] 'argumentative, not very intelligent, and flat-chested. Why Mendès-France finds her more attractive than his heavenly wife is amazing. Mamie [Eisenhower] is rather nervous and terrifically American.'[29] They came back on 24 July.

On a commemorative regimental visit to Winchester, the Queen was rather taken aback to hear from Eden that Bulganin and the other Russian leaders were coming over.[‡] The Duke of Edinburgh took it better, relieved that, unlike Tito, they would not be their personal guests. Churchill came to lunch at Downing Street, Clarissa observing that he was in pain, that he spoke with difficulty and could not remember names.

The Press Secretary

Eden needed a press secretary. His eye fell on William Clark, an economist with a first in modern history from Oriel College, Oxford. In the early 1950s he had been diplomatic correspondent for the *Observer*. He lived in a set in Albany and belonged to the Athenaeum club. He was a bachelor and a gossip. His obituary stated: 'Though always coming across slightly larger than life and

---

* Not long afterwards Patrick Buchan-Hepburn told Clarissa that Harry Crookshank had sent a message to my aunt via Florence Horsburgh to instruct her not to dye her hair so blue. My aunt found that blue hair made her recognisable in her constituency. At times it became almost purple. She held Devonport until 1974, was made a Dame (DBE) in 1964, and Edward Heath put her into the House of Lords as a life peer in 1975. She died at her home in Wiltshire in 1994 – the house in which I wrote this book.

† Lucie Faure (1908–77), wife of Edgar Faure (1908–88), Prime Minister of France, 1952 and 1955–6; a novelist and editor in her own right.

‡ Nikolai Bulganin (1895–1975), Premier after Stalin, and Nikita Khrushchev (1894–1971), then First Secretary, were to visit Britain on a charm offensive seeking recognition by the West.

never one to underplay his own contribution to affairs, he achieved much in several areas.'[30] He provoked contradictory opinions. Robert Rhodes James, one of Eden's biographers, thought him 'a journalist of great charm and good humour, of unswerving honesty, with a strong internationalist outlook',[31] while admitting that his abilities were 'matched by deficiencies that included garrulousness and indiscretions, which found their way back to Downing Street'.[32] D. R. Thorpe considered his appointment 'a calamitous choice'. He was 'vain', with 'an exaggerated view of his importance in the scheme of things'.[33] Tarquin Olivier, Laurence Olivier's son, knew him well and thought him a man of considerable distinction.[34]

On 25 August Clark was summoned to dinner, and for the night, at Chequers by Philip de Zulueta, Eden's private secretary. He found himself in a room of 'stifling comfort'. Eden appeared, in a dark blue shirt and green scarf, and Clarissa 'very pretty and relaxed'.[35] Eden offered him the job, despite Clarissa's instant dislike of him: 'He is so bumptious that I find it terribly embarrassing and do not know where to look. It is like someone with hiccups. I hope I was not too brusque.'[36]

Clark's time at Downing Street was not a happy experience. The appointment went to his head. He had always admired Eden, but decried his time there as 'a story of disillusion', the mitigating circumstances being Eden's 'health, his colleagues, his party, his wife',[37] and his earlier political experiences.

Clarissa was the greatest of his woes. He found her considerable influence over Eden counter-productive. Macmillan told Clark that Clarissa fed Eden's sensitivity by showing him attacks in the press. Clark wrote: 'Macmillan's remark about Clarissa reinforced a hint I had just had that she might be going to cause me trouble.'[38] Her view was equally negative – that Eden never realized the danger of Clark, because he himself was 'terribly innocent in all sorts of ways'. She thought he should have got rid of Clark sharply: 'Anthony trusted too many people. He imagined people behaved like he did. Macmillan would have been on to that in a second and William Clark would have been shown the door.'[39]

One of Clark's problems was that Eden conducted much of his

business from his bed in their upstairs flat, which invaded Clarissa's personal space. If Clark went up after lunch she was often 'lying on a sofa reading the evening papers and spitting with fury'.[40] The garden at Number 10 was shared with Number 11, but Clark found Clarissa proprietorial of it. She was often outside, listening to the Third Programme on her wireless. One day she complained of interference and it transpired that the Commonwealth Prime Ministers' meeting in Downing Street was being relayed to her wireless, and also picked up by a passing taxi driver. Clark thought Clarissa had stirred up trouble by telling Eden that his reputation would suffer more than Butler's over the latter's budget (when he was still Chancellor). He told Clarissa that Butler was more criticised than the Prime Minister. She replied: 'Of course Rab is criticised more but that criticism is justified and the criticism of Anthony isn't.'[41]

Clark did not find Clarissa essentially political: 'But she was, partly because she was non-political, an extremist: she really thought that someone like Ian Jacob, the intellectual soldier in charge of the BBC, must be a red. She did not understand the *modus operandi* of politics. But she was forced into a horrid position by that wholly horrid man, her cousin Randolph Churchill. He used to ring up, always got through and left her invariably on the verge of hysteria, tears, and fury. My sympathies over Randolph's harassments were entirely with Clarissa.'[42]

Trouble in the Mews

On the night of 7 September Clarissa's elder brother Johnny and his wife Kathlyn (Kitty) were accused of creating a hullabaloo near their home in Adam and Eve Mews. Two meetings in the nearby Congregational church were disrupted, one the South Kensington British Legion and the other a gathering of Sunday-school teachers. It transpired that the Churchills were drunk, and when a mild-mannered caretaker went down to investigate, he was so provoked that he struck Johnny 'a glancing blow'. One of the teachers went down and heard 'a lot of unpleasant words', which were 'not in [her] vocabulary'. At the point of their arrest, Kitty told the police officer to call Downing Street. They were taken into custody where he howled like a dog, and she made cat noises.[43] They were remanded on bail of ten pounds after a two-minute court appearance. 'That was an unpleasant affair about Johnny,' wrote Bluey Baker, 'and there was a most unpleasant picture of the pair in the *Bulletin,* a sort of Scottish *Daily Mirror . . .'*[44]

On 6 October the case went to court. Johnny's defence was that, far from howling, he was singing the second act of *Fidelio* to symbolise his plight,* while Kitty said that cat language was a private one which she used to reassure him. Kitty said they rang 10 Downing Street purely for reasons of identification.[45] On 17 November the case was heard at Bow Street. The defence suggested that Johnny was a sensitive man, who had been hit over the head so felt he should not have been arrested. It did not wash. The Churchills were fined five shillings each, with ten guineas costs for being 'drunk and disorderly'. Johnny was fined a further five shillings for using abusive language.[46]

Johnny left a sanitised version of these events in his memoirs,† reporting that, though Uncle Winston was sympathetic, 'There was only a disapproving communication from my sister, and except on formal occasions I have not spoken to her or my brother-in-law since.'‡[47] Brother and sister had not been close for some years.§ The incident had one humorous postscript. When Randolph Churchill put his name forward as a candidate in Taunton, someone on the selection committee enquired: 'Is that the man who lives in a mews and barks like a dog?'[48]

Clarissa's other brother, Peregrine, remained on good terms with her. He noted a difference between Uncle Winston and Anthony if they were asked to lunch at 10 Downing Street. Churchill had always been very relaxed whereas Anthony was 'always jumping up and

---

* In the second Act, Florestan, a political prisoner, has been in a dungeon for two years. His wife, Leonore, arrives to rescue him.

† *Crowded Canvas,* pp. 207–10.

‡ Kitty died on 25 June 1957. On 5 July there was a memorial service. Clarissa was listed as one of those who were unavoidably prevented from attending.

§ On 24 June 1982 the Duke of Marlborough opened an exhibition of sixty-five paintings by Sir Winston Churchill at the Wylma Wayne Gallery at 17 Old Bond Street, the purpose of which was to raise money for Winston's daughter, Sarah, Lady Audley, who was selling some of her collection. Clarissa was there, as was I. She told me with some amusement that her brother Johnny, also present, had failed to recognise her.

down, a nervous wreck'. He would telephone the entire time. Once after lunch a man came in dressed in pin-striped trousers and a black jacket. They thought it was the butler. It was the Chief Whip, Edward Heath.[49] Occasionally the Edens could escape to Clarissa's Wiltshire cottage. Eden relished the summer weather: 'The cottage is lovely in flower & scene. I can never recall a place where one is so near the scent of flowers & shrubs & it is so strong. I have breakfast in the garden every morning. C is usually there too – & it is of course then that all is at its best and freshest – sight and smell.'[50]

Balmoral

On 1 October the Edens paid the traditional prime ministerial visit to Balmoral. They arrived in the midst of the drama over Princess Margaret's perceived wish to marry Group Captain Peter Townsend. This played out over the next month. The Archbishop of Canterbury wrote to the Princess asking her not to do anything until she had spoken to him. From the Downing Street point of view, the priority was to make sure it did not appear that either the government or the Church was putting pressure on her. She was genuinely trying to make up her mind. Simon Phipps, virtually an Anglo-Catholic, was her spiritual adviser. William Clark was not sure 'whether a round of dinner parties' with her close friend, Mark Bonham Carter, was the best way to help her resolve the marriage issue.[51] The Queen Mother insisted on an unfortunate statement from Clarence House that 'no announcement concerning Princess Margaret's personal future is at present contemplated',[52] which made matters worse. Both the Palace and Downing Street hoped she would not marry Townsend. Reports suggested that he had neglected his wife until eventually she abandoned him. Eden himself was more favourable towards Townsend, but Clark thought 'rather harsh' on Princess Margaret. His main worry was the effect this was having on the Crown. At some undisclosed point Eden saw the Princess and explained the position to her.

Clarissa worried that if Princess Margaret decided to marry Townsend, the Queen 'as Head of the Church' would be obliged to refuse permission: 'Anthony would also have to refuse and if Lord Monckton became Lord Chief Justice, there would be two divorced men refusing her.'[53]

The Edens headed north:

On arrival at Aberdeen we find we have to share a Daimler with a noisy naval equerry sent to meet us, and the captain of the aircraft. The landscape becomes progressively more sinister as we approach the castle – lots of pinewoods in a narrower and narrower valley. Found the Queen and Princess Margaret in the front hall. Everything very free and easy.* They are dressed in Royal Stuart Hunting Tartan, but with different shades of cashmere jerseys. No guests but courtiers, and Billy Wallace, Denys Dawnay[†] being in bed with some sort of insulin trouble. Anthony is immediately swept off by the Queen – the Duke of Edinburgh being out stalking – to start the discussions on Princess Margaret. I am left making conversation to her and Billy Wallace.

A charming suite of rooms done up in tartan chintz urine-coloured pitch pine with engravings by Landseer and Winterhalter framed in pine, and the bathroom papered like a pebbled house. Rather a chilly dining room, and the usual champagne or hock or burgundy goes round with the turbot. Afterwards a film in the ballroom. The Queen has chosen a French X film about gang warfare with a very loud soundtrack and shots of women with breasts exposed.[‡] We have the Principal of the Church of Scotland with us.

The next day they attended Crathie Church and went for a drive with Martin Charteris, the assistant private secretary. A consensus was reached about Princess Margaret's Civil List money, Anthony telling her that Parliament was unlikely to vote she got it, or all of it, but as Clarissa noted: 'The Queen told Anthony that George VI made a large settlement on her privately so she would have enough independent of the vote.'[54] Not long afterwards Princess Margaret published her statement that she would not marry Townsend.

---

* The Queen did not find Clarissa easy. According to Valentine Lawford, she was 'terrified' of her. She was advised to make a particular effort. At a wedding in the 1950s, Clarissa was surprised when she was tapped on the shoulder. She looked round. The Queen said: 'It's me.' (Valentine Lawford to author, 31 May 1981).

† Denys Dawnay (1921–83), versatile artist who became a close friend of George VI and later of Princess Margaret. He was the first person to suggest to Prince Philip that he should take up painting soon after the wedding in 1947.

‡ Probably *Razzia Sur La Chnouf*, a Jean Gabin film, released that year.

William Clark concluded: 'This drama stands out as the event that, for the last time, simultaneously and automatically brought into play all the pieces on the traditional English chessboard – Crown, Prime Minister, Archbishop, *The Times*, Lord Salisbury.'[55]

In the midst of this, the twenty-year-old King Faisal of Iraq and his uncle, the Crown Prince (formerly Regent), lunched at Downing Street on 5 October. Days later the Conservative Party Conference took place in Bournemouth. One evening Eden went to bed in some pain, and presently took pethidine. Then came the Portuguese State Visit, and issues were raised about the 1951 defection of Burgess and Maclean. On 7 December Attlee retired as leader of the Labour Party. When he came to see Eden, he asked for an earldom, telling him: 'That's the rate for the job.'[56] He duly went to the House of Lords and the following year joined Eden in the Order of the Garter.

Bluey Baker, Nicholas Eden, Clarissa's niece Sally, Fulke Warwick, his son David Brooke and the de Zuluetas joined the Edens at Chequers for the Christmas holidays. They also invited Rab Butler and his three children, forlorn in the first year after their mother had died. Butler told Clarissa that he was being done over in the press despite being 'the man who had saved the country during the last four years; the election was won because of him . . .'[57]

Another guest was Lady Bridget Parsons, daughter of the 5th Earl of Rosse, and a former Bright Young Thing. There was a move to steer Rab in her direction. Known to be exacting, she was not taken by him, remarking unfavourably on 'his forced gaiety'.[58] Clarissa informed Cecil Beaton: 'I don't know how Rab and Bridget hit it off. He asked Anthony a lot of questions about her, but he said to me that his bride was to be the House of Commons for the next few years.'[59] Rab confined himself to writing that he and his family had been much refreshed and invigorated by the stay.* Clarissa thought Bluey 'very old and deaf', finding the noise difficult, and was worried that she could not spend enough time with him until the other guests had left.[60]

---

* Rab married Mollie Courtauld, widow of the explorer August Courtauld, in 1959. Clarissa considered it a great tribute to him that two wives absolutely adored him.

Decline in Popularity

Pam Berry attacked in the new year, inspiring Donald McLachlan to pen a spiteful article on Eden in the *Daily Telegraph,* introducing the phrase that his leadership lacked 'the smack of firm government'. McLachlan wrote that there was a sense of anticlimax after the impressive election victory. No great policies had been implemented and the government appeared to deal in half-measures and frequent changes of direction. There was no clarity over Cyprus; Bulganin and Khrushchev had been offered a soft answer; and there was 'clumsy courtship of unfriendly and fickle Arab statesmen'. Eden relied on 'smoothing and fixing' in home affairs, minding about personal popularity and looking 'too much over the shoulder of his Foreign Secretary'. McLachlan compared him to Churchill: 'Very few of us are bulldogs, and collies cannot growl like a bulldog.'[61]

The phrase 'the smack of firm government' came to haunt the Edens. By 19 February, his friend Noël Coward was writing: 'Anthony Eden's popularity has spluttered away like a blob of fat in a frying-pan.'[62] Butler told them that the Birkenheads and particularly old Lady Birkenhead were fed up with Pam Berry, worried about her husband Michael, and convinced that McLachlan was a socialist. An article in *People* suggested Eden would resign in June. William Clark persuaded him to issue a denial, which was generally felt to be a mistake. Peter Fleming had hinted in the *Spectator* that there was a disloyal figure in the Eden camp. Randolph rang to tell Clarissa it was Clark.* This caused Eden to lose confidence in his press secretary, though Clark stayed on until after Suez.

Unwittingly, Clarissa added to her husband's problems. There was a tiresome fracas when she mentioned to Mrs Hill, the housekeeper at Chequers, that people in the cottage at the end of Lime Avenue on the estate hanging their washing out gave a bad impression. Mrs Hill interpreted this as an order to remove the washing. She rang the estate manager. The cottage dwellers rang the *Daily Mirror,* and unwelcome publicity ensued. Clarissa felt guilty that she had caused Eden harm. This inspired a flurry of cartoons in *Punch* and elsewhere.

The controversial excitement of that spring was the on-off visit of

---

* Clarissa's diaries include numerous examples of Clark's indiscretions.

Bulganin and Khrushchev, which finally happened in April, prompting yet another resignation threat from Lord Salisbury. The visit was a charm offensive by the Russians, and the first such visit to the United Kingdom of Russian leaders at a time when they were recovering from the war and had lately tested the Soviet thermo-nuclear bomb. The leaders arrived at Chequers on 18 April. Clarissa was driven from London, arriving just as Bulganin and Khrushchev were coming down for dinner. They nodded and smiled at her, and she took off her hat. Clarissa recorded the dinner:

> Dinner next to Khrushchev. He doesn't eat at all. A lot of jovial shouting across the table to Bulganin. No conversation of any importance. Issues dodged. After dinner I leave them to it.
>
> Up to now Anthony has found the going quite tough. At first talks in London they were adamant on their attitude to the colonies, and when Anthony referred to their satellite states they then said they were insulted, and anyone could ask the prime ministers of these states how independent they were. Anthony told them if anyone attacked the Gulf sheikhdoms, we would fight for the oil. Ugly silence.
>
> At dinner at No 10, Winston was very merry . . . came up and said he had just extracted Alan Lennox Boyd* from a tight corner with the Soviet Minister of Culture.
>
> Khrushchev said to Anthony tonight across the table: 'You are an island. You depend for your food and everything on your Navy and your ships. Submarines can cut you off in war. We have submarines that can surface and fire rockets inland.'
>
> Anthony replied that England was a porcupine, which could send back bombs and rockets to whoever attacked her. Selwyn [Lloyd] told me after that Gruenther† had been trying to find out if the Russians had rocket-firing submarines for ages.[63]

On 21 April, in the midst of the Russian visit, Clarissa made the long journey to Holkham in Norfolk for Colin Tennant's wedding to Lady Anne Coke. Colin wrote that he looked for Clarissa from the

---

* Alan Lennox-Boyd (1904–83), Secretary of State for the Colonies, 1954–9.
† General Alfred Gruenther (1899–1983), Supreme Allied Commander, Europe, 1953–6.

vestry but redeemed himself by saying that his bride was so beautiful that he felt it almost wrong to take her out of her surroundings.

Clarissa returned to Chequers. The following day the Russian leaders were up at 5.45 a.m.:

> There were more talks in the morning. On some subjects, such as religious tolerance, whereas on the first day they had been very prickly about it, now they were more reasonable — a much cosier atmosphere. Gaitskell,* Robens in royal blue, and Griffiths [Labour opposition leaders] came to lunch. Also, Khrushchev Junior and Nicholas . . .
>
> I get Bulganin this time who makes a great effort and flatters one. Afterwards there is a lot of horseplay on the terrace, which I take photographs of. Then the opposition go off for their talk with the Russians. They overstay their time and have to be asked, and then ordered, to stop. Guy [Millard] is ruffled by Gaitskell's manner.
>
> Next the Russians want to go for a walk. Anthony leaves for Windsor so Rab and I lead off through the daffodils in very slow motion. The security men miss us and only catch up later. We meet a policeman with an Alsatian. The Russians disappear on our return and reappear looking very smart in new black suits and clean shirts & different ties ready. So, goodbye . . .
>
> As soon as they had gone we rush to look at the presents. I have got a sable stole, though it will need remodelling. Poor Anthony has the most appalling conglomeration of writing accoutrements made of brawn-coloured marble with ormolu and agate, a sort of proletarian Fabergé with a lamp to match with yellow crêpe shade.
>
> The socialists weren't pleased with their talk, apparently. Anthony says that at the embassy the other night when he got up to speak, he asked Gaitskell if he should answer for him, too. Whereupon Gaitskell snapped: 'No, I speak for the opposition.' When he did, he said it would criticise both the government and the Russians if the opposition didn't like the result of the talks – to which Khrushchev said loudly: 'That's an easy thing to do.'
>
> Gromyko seems nasty. He told Ivone Kirkpatrick we were too lenient on the Germans, and Hitler's interpreter oughtn't to have been shut up for three years and then let out.

---

* Hugh Gaitskell (1906–63), leader of the Labour Party, 1955–63.

Apparently, after their visit to the Queen, the two Russians were very excited in the car going back to Claridge's, saying, 'The Queen said to me . . .' 'No, she said that to me . . .' and so on.[64]

There was an unfortunate postscript to the visit. Commander Lionel Crabb, a frogman, failed to return from a reconnaissance mission at Portsmouth around the Soviet cruiser in which the Russian leaders had travelled. Eden had specifically forbidden this frogman to explore its propellers, but his message was not relayed by the Admiralty. Eden did not want the Russian leaders to believe that 'while they were our guests on a friendly visit we had connived at espionage against the ships in which they had travelled'.[65] Clarissa recorded: 'The Russians have been very reticent about it. They say they saw him surface but will say no more. Eden wondered why Khrushchev kept on making jokes about cruisers being so obsolete. They must think us perfect fools.'[66]

The summer had its moments of magnificence. On 18 June there was the postponed service at which Eden, Lord Iveagh and Lord Attlee were installed as Knights of the Garter. On 26 June the Queen inspected three hundred Victoria Cross holders in Hyde Park for the centenary of the honour's creation, on the very spot where Queen Victoria had reviewed the original recipients. The Edens were on the dais with the Queen Mother, the Gloucesters, the Princess Royal and Princess Marina. The Queen and the Duke of Edinburgh arrived in an open landau, escorted by the Household Cavalry. Clarissa was, as ever, a sharp observer:

We stood in the sun for what seemed a long time waiting for the Queen. Then we saw the glint of the Life Guards' helmets coming through the trees and the royal carriages came slowly across the grass. Then she came up to the dais followed by the Duke who said, 'Morning, all.' The Queen Mother had been all smiles and shaken hands with everyone. At the end the wretched VCs paraded past with eyes right – the halt and the lame tottering by. It was astonishing, the huge proportion of them who were Gurkhas. We all cry except the Queen and the Duke. Poor Winston was sitting in the public stands in the full sun while we all lolled under a canopy.[67]

There was a dinner for the former US President Harry Truman, 'self-assured, very pale and flowery-looking, almost as if made up, with black shaded eyes', and his wife, 'a downright little dreadnought and quite attractive'.[68] The Edens entertained many of the Commonwealth prime ministers at Chequers – Nehru 'in very debonair spirits', the Hollands from New Zealand, St Laurent of Canada and others. On 27 June there was a dinner at Buckingham Palace for the Commonwealth Conference. Clarissa was shocked to see that Lord and Lady Mountbatten had insinuated themselves into the royal receiving line. She was even more shocked that she and Edwina had been given identical dresses by Worth. Clarissa sat next to J. G. Strijdom, Prime Minister of South Africa. He pressed her about the Royal Family, asking her about them one by one. His last question amused her. 'And what does the Duke of Gloucester do?'[69]

On the night of 26 July, Eden gave a dinner for King Faisal of Iraq at Downing Street. The Crown Prince and General Nuri al-Said were there, with Cabinet ministers, Air Chief Marshal Sir Dermot Boyle, and Eden's son, Nicholas. It was a men-only occasion, so Clarissa dined at Wiltons with her friend Anna Hägglöf, wife of the Swedish Ambassador, and went on to the Empire nightclub with Cecil Beaton and Frederick Ashton. When she returned home, Downing Street was in crisis mode.

President Nasser of Egypt had nationalised the Suez Canal.

15. THE SUEZ CRISIS
1956

'During the past few weeks I have felt sometimes that the Suez Canal was flowing through my drawing room'
Clarissa's speech to the Gateshead Conservative Association,
Opening Eden House
20 November 1956

The Suez Canal connects the Red Sea and the Mediterranean. It was built by the French Suez Canal Company, in partnership with the Khedive of Egypt, between 1859 and 1869 and stretches just over 120 miles. Although the canal belonged to the Egyptian Government, the shareholders in the Suez Canal Company were mostly British and French. Following the Anglo–Egyptian war of 1882, the British maintained a military presence in Egypt. Under the Anglo–Egyptian Treaty of 1936, the United Kingdom withdrew all its troops, other than the garrison force, which controlled and protected the canal. In 1954 the British Government pledged to remove its troops altogether.

Another issue concerned the building of the Aswan Dam, which was to be jointly financed by the United Kingdom and the United States. In 1952 General Gamel Abdul Nasser had led a revolution in Egypt. In June 1956 he was elected President. When he made overtures to Russia, British and American support was withdrawn from the Aswan Dam project. Nasser revoked the concession of the Suez Canal Company and placed it in the control of the Egyptian state-owned Suez Canal Authority. He claimed that the revenues to be raised were essential for the building of the high dam at Aswan.

The British wanted to retain control of the Canal, which had been of vital importance when Britain ruled India. As it belonged jointly to the British and French, Nasser was damaging British and French

interests and threatening the still essential trade route from the Far
East to Europe, needed for essential supplies of oil. Besides that, Eden
saw Nasser as a dangerous upstart dictator. The French wanted to
teach Nasser a lesson, to make clear to the Algerians that they could
not act with impunity and stop Nasser making a form of union with
them. The British had undertaken a similar action in attacking Iran's
Prime Minister, Mosaddegh* in 1952, largely to preserve Shell, the
British having big oil interests there.

Eden's principal error was to believe that the British could quell
Nasser independently of the Americans. Those days were over.
American support was crucial. He believed that support would come.
He can be criticised for not understanding President Eisenhower's
position over Suez. This was not the Panama Canal, which would
have exercised the Americans considerably more, and Eisenhower
was preoccupied with a presidential election campaign in November,
which he hoped could be conducted without any foreign turbulence.
The distinguished historian Simon Heffer explained:

> What Eisenhower didn't want when he was fighting a campaign was the
> distraction of a great international incident. The Americans had only
> just got rid of Korea. For them the Suez Canal was a pretty minor issue.
> They did not want to be dragged in as an ally of Britain and France.
>
> Eden had not quite accepted how diminished Britain was after the
> Second World War. We had won the war, but the Americans and
> Russians had helped enormously. That we weren't invaded made
> people think we were a powerful nation. We were an economic power
> diminished.
>
> Why Eden did not have talks with Eisenhower at head-of-state
> level I cannot understand. He did not have to rely on Macmillan. He
> was unwise to take Eisenhower for granted.[1]

In later years Clarissa hated having to think of the Suez crisis, but
in 1956, as the saga unfolded, she kept her own notes and diaries, and
followed the drama daily at Eden's side. Years later she told Cherie
Blair:

* Mohammad Mosaddegh (1882–1967), Prime Minister of Iran, 1951–3.
Overthrown in Operation Ajax.

Suez was so stressful, like entering into another dimension, so stressful that one wasn't conscious of it being stressful, a sort of non-stop crisis, day after day, week after week. His [Anthony's] actions were so out of character, not at all like any of his record before . . . I think I thought if this is what he wants, I must encourage him to do it. I have been accused of bolstering him up too much, encouraging him. I had no political motive . . . I find that people who think that Suez was a monumental hash think it can only have been because he was ill. But I think his judgement wasn't vitiated. I mean, if it was a hash, it was his hash. It wasn't because he was ill. I was with him the whole time and it seemed to me his judgement was perfectly normal until the last three weeks. He wasn't in any way behaving eccentrically because he was ill.[2]

On the evening of 26 July Clarissa noted a crisis meeting that lasted until 4 a.m., the assembled company disparately dressed, with Eden, Selwyn Lloyd, Lord Kilmuir,* Lord Salisbury and Harold Caccia all in evening tails; Lord Mountbatten and Sir Gerald Templer were called in, wearing black tie; Jean Chauvel (the French Ambassador) and one of his team were in lounge suits. Even then the possibility of military action was on the table.

The Pam Berry press campaign against Eden ramped up. William Clark felt the need to address the hostility of the *Daily Telegraph* at the time of Eden's Suez speech on 23 July 1956. He wrote him a note about 'Lady Pam and the general tenor of the paper – in particular her attempts to sow dissension between the senior members of the Cabinet'. Fleet Street was becoming known as 'Petticoat Lane' as a reflection of Pam's interference. Oliver Poole was cross with Clark for highlighting Lady Pam, believing that the *Daily Telegraph* represented a broad stream of opinion. Eden called a meeting of key colleagues to discuss the issue of the Party and the paper. Clark noted: 'The PM talking to me merely spoke of his disgust with the whole stinking press. Undoubtedly it hurts too much. "Anyway," he adds, "I don't think the Queen will send for Lady Pam if she gets rid of me."'[3]

---

* The Earl of Kilmuir (1900–67), Lord Chancellor, 1954–62, published his memoirs in 1964.

Eden held a meeting of the Cabinet and saw the 1922 Committee, keen to do so before the House rose for the summer recess. Clarissa recorded: 'Terrible 24 hours . . . Anthony and the Cabinet decided to fight, if necessary alone. The leave of the Home Fleet will be stopped but the Chiefs of Staff say they want *six* weeks to get the troops ready. Nehru sent a message to say how upset he was and what folly of Nasser etc.'[4] On 29 July William Clark thought it ominous that Clarissa told Eden at lunch: 'You will do a TV before sending the troops in, won't you?'[5]

Eden broadcast to the nation on 8 August at 10 p.m. to explain his stance. The speech was reported in forty-four languages, and afterwards the BBC received 'reports of excellent reception'.[6] He complained that the lights were too hot and too bright, and that he had to wear his spectacles. As a result Clarissa wrote Clark what he called 'a long and absurd note'.[7] She thought the interview had been a success, but that Eden was under considerable stress, made the point about the spectacles, that he could not see his notes properly so stumbled over certain words, and could not see where the camera was. The lenses of his glasses reflected the light making it hard to see his eyes: 'In the event this was just as well, since his eyes were made up like an early Charlie Chaplin. I am sure this was just stupidity and done because I had asked that his eye<u>lids</u> should be made up.' She made the following stipulations:

1. Investigate the lighting at ITV studios and find out why it is so much better.

2. From now on TV broadcasts must be made from No 10. This will make it easier to control the lighting. It will also be possible for the PM to go in and out beforehand testing it. It will also make it easier to eliminate the fiendish make-up girl.

3. Be quite sure that the lighting 'expert' who did this and the previous TV is not used next time. Quite apart from the brutality of the lights, the shadow cast in the shoulders showed great technical ineptitude.

4. Find out who lit Gaitskell, and who lights the ordinary newscasters – also <u>how</u> they are lit. I get the impression that they are enveloped in a dull glare, but not a blinding light, as the PM was. This would be preferable.

I am sorry to bother you about all this, but I consider it a scandal that the PM, wanting to give an important message to the nation, should be hampered by a handful of inefficient and conceited amateurs.[8]

Clark acted on her note. On 5 September they experimented with TV cameras in the upstairs room for further speeches. The Edens were much happier with the lighting, but Anthony was too short-sighted to read the teleprompter. Relations remained sour between Clark and Clarissa. When Clark wanted Eden to help with a *Time & Life* article, he telephoned Clarissa. By this time Clark was describing her as 'his unofficial and wholly bad press adviser'.[9] As a result Eden refused to do it.

Presently Clark heard from Norman Brook, the Cabinet Secretary, that Clarissa was upsetting the Prime Minister at every turn. Clark thought that despite this Eden's health was holding up well. He had been given various placebos on medical advice. Clark thought him alert and ready for action.

On 5 August Churchill rang up from Chartwell and asked whether he could come over. He arrived the next day. He told the Edens that he was far too interested in the unfolding saga to leave the country while this was on. He said: 'I must look up what Napoleon did when he invaded Egypt.' The visit upset Eden. He had hoped Churchill would give him courage. Instead he was worried, first by the gravity Churchill implied and then that Churchill would assume he had fore-seen nothing of how the campaign would play out. He had already worked out everything Winston addressed.[10]

The following day, to Eden's annoyance, Macmillan circulated a paper about how to arrange an invasion. Eden told him he had had no right to do that. There was the London Conference, which estab-lished an Eighteen Power Plan, with French and American repre-sentatives in August, Robert Menzies, the Australian Prime Minister, coming over to try to negotiate. He tried to deal diplomatically with Nasser – the Cairo Mission – but by 6 September this had failed.

On 25 September Macmillan visited Eisenhower at the White House. There were then secret meetings, which led to the so-called Sèvres Protocol, which was designed to give a *casus belli* – a reason to invade, and remove Nasser as an aggressor. Its plan of action was:

On 29 October Israel would invade Egypt in order to reopen the Straits of Tiran and the Gulf of Aqaba. They did so at 3 p.m. that day.

On 30 October an Anglo-French ultimatum would be issued.

On 31 October Britain and France would invade. They did so on 5 November. The United Nations General Assembly called for a cease-fire. This occurred at midnight on 6 November. The campaign was deemed to be a fiasco.

The options for force were discussed with members of the Cabinet, far from in unison. Clarissa noted:

At yesterday's Cabinet meeting, Walter Monckton [then Minister of Defence] suddenly burst out with a piece about his disturbedness about any use of force etc. Anthony pointed out that he had agreed with it weeks ago. Walter replied that things had changed since then. Harold says Walter had all this written down on a piece of paper. Today, Anthony received letters from Bobbety, Alan Lennox Boyd [Secretary of State for the Colonies] and Alec Home [Secretary of State for Commonwealth Affairs]. Alan said he was horrified by Walter's outburst, particularly as nothing has happened since the Cabinet had originally agreed on policy that anyone could not have foreseen.

Bobbety is worried and helpful. Alec is warning that Rab is wobbly to the point of lobbying as a result of which he says he has found seven members of the Cabinet who agreed with him.

Duncan [Sandys, Minister of Housing] is playing a sinister role. He complained to Anthony that the Cabinet has a right to know what was going on and he disapproved of what he had heard. Anthony said the Cabinet had no right to know when it concerned war and he wasn't going to tell them. Duncan then wrote a letter to Anthony with his complaints and views. Anthony did not answer. Duncan then asked three times in one day to see Rab, who made a great virtue of refusing to see him.[11]

The Edens spent the weekend of 24 to 27 August at Chequers. Macmillan came to lunch and littered his conversation with phrases such as 'Of course the situation is really like the Augustan Age' or 'So-and-so is really like Harold Bluetooth or Bolingbroke, or what have you.' Eden told Clarissa that these analogies particularly infuriated Lord Salisbury when they emerged in Cabinet. Salisbury's line was 'I really don't see any resemblance between us and Queen Elizabeth I.'[12]

On 5 September a telegram from Eisenhower appeared to ban the use of force. This brought Eden dashing back to London. He and Clarissa were able to undertake the traditional summer weekend visit to Balmoral, 8–9 September. Immediately after that, Robert Menzies, Prime Minister of Australia, came to London to report the failure of the Cairo mission. Guy Mollet* and Christian Pineau, the French Foreign Minister, came to London for talks. On 12 September Parliament was recalled for a special debate, Anthony's message being that there must be no appeasement. A second eighteen-nation conference opened at Lancaster House on 19 September.

Clarissa accompanied Eden and Selwyn Lloyd, the Foreign Secretary, to Paris for a twenty-four-hour visit from 26 to 27 September. The purpose was to cement Anglo-French unity over Suez and to discuss with their French counterparts the line of action to be adopted after the meeting of the Security Council. They arrived in drizzle and fog and stayed with Sir Gladwyn and Lady Jebb, now *en poste* in Paris, at the British Embassy. Clarissa was given the Pauline Borghese bedroom. She noted that Anthony came back from the first meeting 'very late and worried', finding Mollet 'good' but Pineau 'very violent and extreme', wanting force at any cost. Things calmed down the next day, and the visit was deemed to have been a success.

There was a dinner at the Quai d'Orsay at which Clarissa sat next to Pineau. He told her they wanted international management. Clarissa told him that in Britain one third of the Conservative Party was against the use of force, as was the entire Labour Party. But, she added, 'The people on the other hand, if it came to the point, would probably come along, so many of them were in Suez or had relations there and they loathe the Egyptians. What I don't understand about you and us is why you don't just create an incident.'

* Guy Mollet (1905–75), Prime Minister of France, 1956–7.

'Nasser is too clever to allow us to,' said Pineau.[13]

Clarissa's role in this crisis was widely discussed. Ava Waverley was critical as she told Cynthia Jebb:

Ava was evidently extremely worried – worried as to whom to back! She deplored Clarissa's ignorance and interference. It seems Clarissa is often present at private lunches and drinks and dinners, where important business has to be discussed with Anthony, and that she gives her opinion and advice. Worse still, Ivone [Kirkpatrick] has complained that she rings up Anthony at the last moment, tells him not to weaken, and interferes with whatever line has been agreed on. How dangerous all this sounds. Is it really a case of 'Infirm of purpose, give me the dagger'?[14]

D. R. Thorpe recorded that Clarissa's 'primary concern was for her husband's welfare. She was not a political figure but, like Clemmie Churchill, wanted her husband to know what people were saying.' Even he conceded: 'Sometimes this could be unintentionally counter-productive.'[15]

On 5 October it was clear that Suez was getting on top of the Prime Minister. He collapsed with a temperature of 106°F while visiting Clarissa, who was briefly in University College Hospital. He was well enough to go to Chequers, and soon busy sending messages to Guy Millard and Freddy Bishop.

On 11 October the Conservative Party Conference began in Llandudno. Clarissa noted a dinner, an agents' ball, a Young Conservative ball on the Friday night and a mass meeting at 2 p.m. on Saturday, 13 October. The day before, the Suez rebels had been making trouble, saying that Lord Salisbury had resigned in disagreement with the government. The truth was that he had suffered a heart attack. On the train to Wales Clarissa noted: 'Anthony looks pale and drawn and is desperately tired.' Macmillan and Butler were engaged in great rivalry, Butler 'staging a comeback and making speeches full of metaphors and quotations which the cleverer journalists adore'. Selwyn Lloyd telegraphed that Pineau was now against them. Eden had to change his speech: 'Anthony speaks for over an hour – terrible heat and glare from the television lights and he is sweating and so is everyone else. Rab is in the chair and I notice he stops the applause at the beginning by holding up his hand [and then] at the end, after a sidelong glance, by sitting down.'[16]

They took the conference train back, the Edens going as far as Watford. Eden and Macmillan discussed propaganda, Eden saying that Butler's only idea of propaganda was about himself. When Clarissa left the carriage, Macmillan said: 'You know Clarissa's quite right, it is always for himself. He was quite nasty about me at the conference.' There was a drama when the Edens arrived at Chequers: 'Telegram from Selwyn saying Pineau won't agree and is being difficult. Anthony bawls Ivone [Kirkpatrick] out for not knowing and [Anthony] Nutting for not being there.'[17]

On Sunday 14 October 'a mysterious Frenchman' who turned out to be Albert Gazier, Mollet's confidant, eventually beat his way through the fog, arriving with General Maurice Challe, the chief of the French air staff. Their 'plan' was that Israel wanted to attack Egypt to regain the Straits of Tiran and the Gulf of Aqaba, but not before the presidential election in America (on 6 November) and only if Britain approved. Clarissa noted: 'The idea would be that we and the French moved in to keep the Canal working.'[18] The French and British would break up the combatants and in the process take back the Canal.

The Edens were in London from 16 to 19 October. In the midst of this, Cecil Beaton brought Greta Garbo to visit Clarissa at Number 10 at five thirty on 17 October. There was to be a dinner for the President of Costa Rica that night, and the reception rooms were decked with flowers by the famous Constance Spry. They drank vodka and ice, and Garbo rose to the occasion by imitating the noises that kept her awake at Claridge's. Eden appeared, despite the pressures of government business. Clarissa murmured: 'He couldn't keep away.' As Cecil Beaton described it: 'The Prime Minister, looking utterly boyish & young, gangling like a colt – eyelashes flickering, teeth discreetly hidden' told Garbo that he had always wanted to meet her since seeing her in her 1927 film, *Love*. Garbo hated any mention of her films and said so politely. He moved on to talk about Sweden, another of her many forbidden topics. But, despite that, Cecil thought the meeting a success: 'Anthony lying back with legs stretched out told the people who needed him that they must wait.'[19] Garbo met various members of the Cabinet, but was upset to be caught by a random press photographer outside as they left 10 Downing Street.*

Selwyn Lloyd was sent over in conditions of great secrecy to meet the French and the Israelis at a villa at Sèvres, outside Paris, on 22 October. Eden insisted that the plan should not be interpreted as a response to a request from Israel. The Sèvres Protocol document was signed on 24 October. The essentials of this were placed before the Cabinet the next day, to which reactions were mixed. As a result Israeli forces entered Egypt on 29 October. Eden delivered his ultimatum, which Egypt rejected, so on 5 November the British and French invasion began. They succeeded in capturing twenty-three miles of the Canal. This secret act caused panic in Washington, at which point Eisenhower distanced himself.

The Americans did not support the invasion. Following a hostile response from them, the United Nations and the Soviet Union, a ceasefire was called within twenty-four hours. Churchill captured the mood of many: 'I would never have dared, and if I had dared, I would never have dared stop.'[20]

On 3 November there was another broadcast from Downing Street, in which Eden declared that all his life he had been 'a man of peace, striving for peace'. But he defended the invasion by saying: 'I am utterly convinced that the action we have taken is right.'[21] William Clark felt that it had been effective. Clarissa watched it with him as it aired. Clark recorded: 'This was the first fruits of all my efforts to get No 10 wired for TV and it was technically effective.'[22] The following day he noted good reaction to the speech, and even a letter of good wishes from Dirk Bogarde, the actor. But Clark described Eden as 'mad, literally mad'. On the point of resignation two days later, Clark was torn by his reaction to Eden: 'My mood towards him is extraordinary. I never see him, worn, dignified and friendly, but a surge of deep and almost tearful compassion surges up in me; I leave him and my violent bitter contempt and hatred for a man who has destroyed my world and so much of my faith burns up again.'[23]

---

* Garbo's visit coincided with Ulanova's famous performance at Covent Garden. Cecil Beaton and Oliver Messel both lived in Pelham Place. The press lay in wait for Ulanova dining with Messel, then realised that Garbo was in the house almost opposite. When she left Beaton's house, she had to run the gauntlet of photographic flashes.

On 4 November Israel and Egypt accepted the idea of the cease-fire, at which point Eden was relieved there would be no further loss of life. Anthony Nutting and Edward Boyle, economic secretary to the Treasury, resigned from the government. Clark resigned on 6 November.* On 8 November Clarissa wrote to Cecil Beaton: 'I hope we shall meet soon when it is less strained. It is like a bad illness in this house.'[24] Anthony was by then very tired.

Parliament was prorogued on 5 November. The government put these words into the Queen's prorogation speech, which fortunately she did not have to read in person:

> My Government have been gravely concerned at the outbreak of hostilities between Israel and Egypt. They resolved, in conjunction with the French Government, to make a quick and decisive intervention to protect the lives of our nationals and to safeguard the Suez Canal by separating the combatants and restoring peace. My Government have proposed that the United Nations should take over responsibility for policing the area, as a prelude to a satisfactory settlement in the Middle East. They earnestly trust that this purpose will be achieved.[25]

Clarissa wrote of Anthony:

> When he comes up for lunch he says he wants to go and see Eisenhower, who has just got in again. He rings him at lunch – it is incredible now that they have sub-ocean cable instead of radio – and Eisenhower says, 'Fine, fine,' but an hour or so later rings again and says, 'You aren't coming just to argue about the United Nations, are you?' Anthony

---

* In 1966 Clark published a novel called *Number 10*, which he protested was not 'a cryptic account of the Suez crisis'. On 13 October 1966 *The Times* judged: 'Mr Clark gets the atmosphere of it all pretty much right', but David Holloway wrote: 'The reader is left just a little unsatisfied.' (*Daily Telegraph*, 13 October 1966). His novel explored the relationship between the Prime Minister and his Cabinet during an international crisis. Is Julia, wife of the Prime Minister, based on Clarissa? She is not a sharply drawn character, but I can hear Clarissa saying: 'I've spent the whole morning ordering roses from Waterer's, and next year I am planning a whole bed of "Peace". Do you think it's quite safe?' He wrote that pundits would need to await the release of his Suez diary in the autumn of 2006. Clark died in 1985.

says, 'No.' Then he rings a third time and says he must wait to see the new Congressional leaders first etc. Then Anthony sends him a message about Russian intervention in the Middle East, which crosses with one from Eisenhower that ends by saying, 'Presumably we will withdraw our forces immediately and not wait for the arrival of the UN force.' Anthony very depressed.[26]

On the evening of 18 November Sir Horace Evans visited Eden at Downing Street, arriving late from Leeds at 9.30 p.m. An announcement was made at 11.45 p.m.: 'The Prime Minister is suffering from overstrain. On the advice of his doctors he has cancelled his immediate engagements.'[27] Clarissa observed Macmillan, waiting in the wings: 'Harold is playing a funny game. He is frantic at the thought of Anthony going away – Bobby Allan* thinks because the time isn't ripe for his own machinations.'[28]

Clarissa went up to the north and delivered her famous Suez Canal remark at the opening of Eden House, a care home in Gateshead. She stayed with the Lambtons and the next day attended a lunch at the Mansion House in Doncaster. She returned to London on 21 November. She was later greatly embarrassed by the line about the Suez Canal flowing through her drawing room – not least for the choice of the phrase 'drawing room'. When asked about Eden's health in Gateshead, Clarissa said: 'I need hardly tell you how much my husband minds having to take a break at this time. He is anxious to get his enforced rest over as quickly as possible. He really does need a holiday.'[29] The full speech is worth quoting, albeit from surviving notes and press reports, so possibly it is not precisely as delivered. She began by making reference to Eden's health:

He has had a tremendous strain put upon him during the past few weeks and is extremely tired. But otherwise there is nothing wrong with him. When I left home today he was certainly much better.

When we married my husband made me promise I would not make political speeches. And I have kept that rule ever since. I wrote one out on Monday for this occasion, but he would not let me make it.

* Robert Allan (1914–79), MP for Paddington and Eden's parliamentary secretary.

For the past three months I have felt as if the Suez Canal was flowing through my drawing room. So I would like to half break my rule and, in the most undiplomatic language, try to make one or two points clearer.

First of all, I do not believe it is generally understood why our forces have stopped exactly where they have in Egypt. As the Prime Minister explained on Saturday: 'We had said that we would cease all military action as soon as the Israeli and Egyptian governments accepted an unconditional ceasefire and the international forces arrived.' On 6 November both these governments had in fact promised to do so.

In the light of the undertaking which we had given, Her Majesty's Government could not have refused to conform in also ordering a ceasefire. We had already secured our main objective: to halt hostilities and thereby prevent their wider spread. Our two powers, Britain and France, working together in loyal comradeship could not have done more. Secondly, the government have never claimed that they went into this business in order to reveal a Russian plot to dominate the Middle East. What seems clear enough to most people is that their action has revealed the extent and the imminence of the plot. Russian tanks, Russian planes, Russian armoured vehicles, Russian ammunition and Russian rockets are reported to have been found in vast quantities. That a most sinister hornet's nest has been uncovered is surely evident from the violent reactions that have come from certain quarters in the last few days.

While dictatorships exist, left ones or right ones, big ones or small ones, we cannot risk a foreign policy that defers conflict on principle, that pacifies on principle those who act against the vital interests of our country or of peace itself.

The Conservative Government will always uphold Britain's vital interests and the peace of the world.[30]

Clarissa was pleased with the coverage of her speech. On the train from Doncaster two Americans sat down in her compartment. They did not recognise her until they saw her photograph in the newspaper and then wished Eden good luck. One said: 'I guess we've had time to think things over now.'[31] She returned to Downing Street to find Eden concerned because Macmillan was fretting about money and Lord Salisbury about Anglo-American relations.

By this time a hasty plan had been made for Eden to have a break. He was 'rather desperate at leaving'.[32] The plan was that the Edens should fly to Jamaica to stay at Goldeneye, Ian Fleming's bungalow at Oracabessa. Sir Horace Evans decreed that sunshine was essential. No doctors went with him but he would have two detectives. The fear of Norman Brook, the Cabinet Secretary, concerned 'the collusion witch-hunt' and the fear that Eden would be accused of running away.

Rab Butler, Lord Privy Seal, stepped in to run the government from 23 November until 14 December. D. R. Thorpe judged that Eden could perhaps have resigned at this point, garnering some sympathy. For two reasons he did not. He thought a restorative break in Jamaica would prove a turning point in his health. And, since the Suez engagement was his responsibility, he needed to see it through.

The Edens embarked on the twenty-hour flight in an American DC-7C airliner, *Seven Seas*, from London airport to Kingston at 7 p.m. on Friday, 23 November. The press were there to see them go. Eden said he was sure he would be better on his return: 'Our position has not changed.' There were meant to be no questions but a cheeky reporter asked Clarissa: 'Lady Eden, do you think that the Suez Canal will still flow through your drawing room in Jamaica?'

'Well, I hope not,' she replied wryly.

'Goodnight, everybody,' said Eden, as they headed to the plane.

In Jamaica they were greeted by Sir Hugh and Lady Foot* and were driven the seventy-six miles to Goldeneye to 'rest, rest, and then rest', as Eden put it.[33] At the outset of their visit, telegraphs for Eden had to be sent to Government House and then carried by messenger to the Prime Minister. Presently a teleprinter service was installed. Much was made by Noël Coward and others as to what the Edens had been expecting of Goldeneye – something magnificent rather than a bungalow.

Clarissa was never backward at complaining. She might have been polite to Ann Fleming – she was – but did not have to extol it to Bluey Baker:

* Sir Hugh Foot, later Lord Caradon (1907–90), Governor General of Jamaica, 1951–7.

Goldeneye

At the moment he [Anthony] is very fretful about being here and I have a bad cold.

I expect you have been to Jamaica because you have been everywhere. It is much nicer than I had imagined, but will be spoilt by hotels in about five years from now. It is a proper country, which I always prefer to an island, with a great hinterland and different kinds of vegetation. We had a long drive from the airport across a good deal of the island & it was enchantingly pretty . . .

I am hoping to make only two expeditions before we leave. One to Port Antonio, where one drifts up the local Rio Grande on bamboo rafts, & the other to the Blue mountains to see the Castleton Botanic Gardens. (The Blue Mountain coffee is delicious. I wonder why we don't drink it more in England.)

The house is very well done. Nice to look at, comfortable enough without deadening luxury, lovely garden full of violent-looking flowers and shrubs, banana orchard & grapefruit orchard, and a tiny private beach at the end, with creepers & palms to the shore. Warm turquoise water outside a coral reef.I haven't really explored the reef with a mask yet, because of my stupid English cold.

Food rather trying – they are very deep-freeze minded, which is frustrating when one can see the fishermen catching delicious lobsters in the open sea.

Heat perfect, though too much cloud, as it is early in the 'season'.

We are seeing no one, except perhaps the Governor, who is a brother of all those Foots, & seems nice.[34]

On 3 December the local doctor was called in on account of Clarissa's cold, but she was soon bathing again and taking on a limited number of social engagements. She enjoyed snorkelling round the reef.

While he was away, Eden missed a jibe from Khrushchev in Moscow: 'Eden fell ill. A doctor was called. The diagnosis after examination was – inflammation of the canal.'[35] There were plenty more jibes from Chips Channon and others. Randolph Churchill wrote spitefully: 'But even Hitler did not winter in Jamaica.'[36] Ann Fleming wrote to Clarissa that Pam Berry had given a dinner party for the Macmillans and others 'and put a huge notice on the dining room [table] saying "One big heave and he's out."* I gather from the Crawley[†] news service that the conversation was totally wrecked, everyone embarrassed and not amused and Michael [Berry] enraged.'[37] The main beneficiary of the holiday was Ian Fleming. It put Goldeneye on the map.

Macmillan was not idle during the Prime Minister's absence. Immensely ambitious, he knew this was his only chance to become Prime Minister. He was three years older than Eden. Soon it would be too late. On 22 November, while the Edens were away, Butler unwisely invited Macmillan to join him before the 1922 Committee. Butler made a lack-lustre appeal for unity. Macmillan then took over, as Anthony Howard described it. He delivered

A veritable political organ voluntary lasting thirty-five minutes – pulling out every stop and striking every majestic chord in his

---

* Harriet Cullen, Pam's daughter and author of her by no means uncritical biography, *Lady Pamela Berry: Passion, Politics and Power*, believes this to be an Ann Fleming exaggeration.
† Aidan Crawley and his wife, Virginia Cowles, the writer.

well-practised repertoire, including a *tremolo* on his own advancing years. Enoch Powell, who heard the speech, described it as 'one of the most horrible things that I remember in politics . . . seeing the way in which Harold Macmillan, with all the skill of the old actor-manager, succeeded in false-footing Rab. The sheer devilry of it verged upon the disgusting.'[38]

From Goldeneye Eden sent telegrams ordering the troop withdrawal from the Canal zone, which, on 3 December, Selwyn Lloyd announced to the House of Commons.

The Edens flew from Montego Bay on 13 December, touching down in London the next day. Eden declared himself 'reinvigorated' and ready to resolve the tasks ahead.[39] The next days were busy as they lunched with the Salisburys, Churchills and others. On 17 December Eden went to the House where he was greeted with muted politeness. 'The occasion defies description as either tragedy or comedy,'[40] wrote the *Daily Telegraph* reporter. The next day he spoke to a meeting of the 1922 Committee and answered questions. He had an audience of the Queen. On 20 December he answered questions in the House and, after a dramatic entrance by Black Rod to summon the Commons to the Lords to hear assent given to various bills, he spoke of the attacks on 26, 27 and 29 October: 'I wish to make it clear that there was no joint decision in advance of hostilities about the use of a veto. There was no joint decision about the use of the French air force in advance of hostilities.'[41] Eden's detractors claim that he lied to Parliament but the historian Robert Blake judged: 'No one of sense will regard such falsehoods in a particularly serious light. The motive was the honourable one of averting further trouble in the Middle East, and this was a serious consideration for many years after the event.'[42]

Since Jamaica, Eden had lost the confidence of Parliament. His health was not good. According to Clarissa: 'fevers increased accompanied by rigors'.[43] Only now did he take drugs.

Nehru came to lunch at Chequers on Christmas Eve before going on to the Mountbattens at Broadlands. For Christmas Clarissa invited Bluey Baker, her niece Sally and her brother Peregrine. On 1 January 1957 Eden went to London for more Suez talks. But it was over. The Suez Canal remained closed under the jurisdiction of the United Nations Emergency Force.

Most people on both sides of the political divide respected Eden as an honest man. But Suez damaged his reputation. He had mounted an invasion, then ordered a ceasefire. David Dilks* pointed out that Eden and the many members of the Cabinet who supported the invasion, would have done so with reluctance. Most had fought in the First World War, and many had lost family members in both World Wars. As Eden said, he was essentially a man of peace. For reasons of international security, just before he stepped down he misled Parliament about his prior knowledge of the invasion, claiming that he knew nothing of it. Clarissa believed that Macmillan had misled Eden as to the likelihood of American support, as a result of which Eden fell, with Macmillan becoming Prime Minister in his place.

Clarissa concluded: 'Tiredness brought on his illness. I was criticised for taking him to Jamaica. He would have got terminally ill if he had stayed. After we got back, then he was definitely ill, and that only lasted three or four weeks. I was a good wife to him, but I don't think I probably did the political side at all well.'[44] Eden's private secretary, Philip de Zulueta, summed up Clarissa's role: 'Inexperienced in, and not greatly enjoying, political life her touch was not always sensitive during the premiership, but without her Eden would not have survived then or lived to enjoy his long retirement.'[45]

The Suez crisis brought the curtain down on Eden's distinguished political career, one in which, until that point, his powers of diplomacy had received high accolades. The crisis divided the nation and continues to cause division decades later. It would haunt the Edens for the rest of their lives, in the same way that the Abdication hung over the Duke and Duchess of Windsor.

---

* Dr David Dilks (b. 1938), later biographer of Chamberlain and Macmillan.

PART THREE

16. EDEN IN RETIREMENT
1957–64

'Once he had retired, it was absolutely wonderful.
Then we were alone all the time . . .
Free, free at last.'
Clarissa to Cherie Blair, 6 December 2002

Eden asked the Queen whether he might visit her at Sandringham to warn her of his impending resignation. He and Clarissa took the train to Wolferton on 8 January. They stayed the night. Clarissa recorded these days:

> Anthony has to go through a Cabinet and listen to Harold prosing for half an hour. This almost puts him against recommending Harold. By train to Sandringham. Many photographers. Anthony looks shrunken and worn. We arrive into the hall where everyone is looking at the television. Ormsby-Gores, Dawnay and Bowes-Lyon.*
> Anthony goes off to talk to Adeane† and has his audience. I hang about for a while when they play games and put on the loud jazz, then to my room.
>
> Talking to Adeane, Anthony suggested Bobbety [Marquess of Salisbury], Kilmuir & Winston as advisers to the Queen.
>
> Anthony says he feels the waters sweep on over him now. The moment they know he is to go, they continue making their plans, and the machine grinds on.[1]

---

* David and Sissie Ormsby-Gore (later Lord and Lady Harlech), Denys Dawnay and Sir David Bowes-Lyon (the Queen Mother's brother).
† Sir Michael (later Lord) Adeane (1910–84), private secretary to the Queen, 1953–72.

No doubt many help themselves to royal writing paper. It was a surprise to find the Edens doing so, particularly when they had so much on their minds. From Sandringham Eden wrote to Churchill to tell him of his decision, the doctors giving him 'little hope that I can continue as I am doing without collapse'.[2] They left the following day:

> Dreary journey back to London. A large crowd of photographers at Liverpool Street. Horace [Evans] & Norman [Brook] come, and the announcement of resignation is made final.
>
> Anthony then tells Rab, who is completely taken by surprise – Rab says to me afterwards, 'What a shame. He's really quite popular in the country, you know', and Harold, who bursts into floods of crocodile tears. Norman is in real tears. Then the Cabinet. Bobbety reads out a little piece about their long association and his great love & admiration for Anthony but breaks down in the middle. Rab says a piece, so of course Harold has to say a piece too. Anthony then sees the junior ministers who are also very nice — even Nigel Birch.[*] Antony Head[†] comes up to Anthony's bedroom while he changes for the Palace and is very upset and understanding.
>
> Anthony goes to the Palace to give up his seals of office. The Queen says that when she became Queen she was told how lucky she was to have Winston as her Prime Minister. She doesn't think this advice was true. She has been fortunate in having Anthony. She thanks him for always being so helpful and making it nice for her. Anthony refuses an earldom. He tells Adeane what he wants is the OM.[‡][3]

Eden looked grim and hunched on his way to the Palace, but managed a thin smile as he was driven out. Some years later he made a private record of this audience:

> There are spurious reports (Kilmuir etc) that the Queen did not

---

[*] Nigel Birch (1906–81), caustic Secretary of State for Air, 1955–7.

[†] Antony Head (1906–83), Minister of Defence, 1956–7.

[‡] Order of Merit. This was given to Arthur Balfour in 1916, David Lloyd George in 1919, to Winston Churchill in 1946, and to Earl Attlee in 1951. Macmillan received it in 1976 and Margaret Thatcher in 1990. The Order is in the personal gift of the monarch.

consult me about my successor. Certainly she did. When I went to Sandringham and it was first realised what I intended, Michael Adeane quite rightly broached the topic at once. What are we to do, was the theme, there being no enthusiasm for either of the more obvious candidates, Rab or Harold. This led MA to speak of Menzies & the possibility of getting him over. I should have liked this above all things, but I had to point out that it was not practicable, which was accepted by MA, but only reluctantly. Years later I told Bob.

When I went for my final audience the Queen asked me formally & said what I repeated afterwards to MA. Rab had deputised for me when I had been away & I had no fault to find with the way he had done so. This, I thought, should be in the scales in his favour. On the other hand, this was a situation when the unity of the Cabinet was essential to the survival of the Govt & I thought that there should be informal consultations through an intermediary with at least the senior members of the Cabinet & in reply to a question I said that Bobbety was the obvious choice for intermediary since he could not succeed himself but was a most influential member of the Cabinet & respected by the party.[4]

A bulletin signed by four doctors, including Sir Horace Evans and Dr Ralph Southward, explained the resignation as his health no longer enabling him to 'sustain the heavy burden inseparable from the office of Prime Minister'.[5]

Eden did not return to Downing Street, but joined Clarissa at Chequers, where they stayed until they sailed. At dinner he asked his private secretary, Philip de Zulueta, several times if he had been unfair to Butler in not recommending him to the Queen as his successor. De Zulueta wrote: 'It was typical of his generous spirit to be concerned about this at such a moment in his life.' Many of those who worked for Eden had tears in their eyes that evening.[6]

Eden took no part in the events of the following day, which played out with some drama. Rab Butler began it thinking he would be appointed. But soundings had been taken – Lord Salisbury asking if it should be 'Wab' or 'Hawold'. Eden arrived at the Palace, followed by Churchill. Macmillan was summoned to the Palace, and his appointment as the next Prime Minister announced at 2.27 p.m., leaving Butler disappointed. Clarissa sent Butler a message, which he described as 'balm': 'Dear Rab, Just a line to say what a beastly profession I think politics are – and how greatly I admire your dignity and good humour. Yours ever Clarissa.'[7]

On 11 January Eden announced that he was stepping down from Parliament. On 13 January the Queen had to come down to London again to hear of Harold Macmillan's Cabinet changes. After that meeting Macmillan invited himself to dinner with the Edens at Chequers. Clarissa's diary recorded:

I go up to London dodging the press and all the main gates at Chequers. Awful day packing up. The puppies are in Anthony's bathroom now. It is the longest weekend I've ever spent. Dorothy Macmillan comes to see me on Saturday. I am furious that an *Express* photographer lies in wait as I am going out to lunch through the garden door. None of the servants want to stay with the Macmillans. Mrs Skit gives me a cooking lesson on Sunday morning and cries into the eggs.

We were horrified that Harold proposes himself to dinner at Chequers on Monday night. Bobbety and Betty [Salisbury] came to lunch when I was in London – Betty railing against Harold, Bobbety furious because he says Harold has not consulted him about any of the Lords' appointments or creations. He has already written one of his letters of resignation.

Harold arrives three-quarters of an hour late, extremely gracious to both of us. I mistrust him the most when he is like this. He talks of loyalty, the north country, our holiday. 'I'm sure you've had hundreds of letters,' etc. etc. We get information about the changes in driblets.

He sent for Rab and said to him: 'I will offer you anything you like, provided you do not intrigue against me.' Rab went away and came back saying he wanted the Foreign Office. Harold talked him out of that, which would have been a complete denial of Suez. Harold then said to us that of course Rab couldn't have it because we'd got to show Ike & Dulles we meant it, and so on – 'anyway for a few months'!

After I'd left the room, Harold breaks to Anthony that Lloyd George*

---

* Gwilym Lloyd George (1894–1967), son of David Lloyd George, created Viscount Tenby. The other sacked ministers were James Stuart, and Walter Monckton. Letters were exchanged and published, the ministers appearing to resign voluntarily, Macmillan thanking them sanctimoniously and frequently professing years of friendship.

is sacked, and Antony Head. Anthony is distressed, particularly about the latter. Harold says Alan [Lennox Boyd] won't last long. Head can have his job then.

After he's gone we ring up the Heads. Dot is very cagey, but Antony [Head] says he couldn't promise to slash defence, so he had to go.[8]

The following day Eden rang the sacked ministers. Patrick Buchan-Hepburn* told him he wanted the governorship of the West Indies. He was made a peer as Lord Hailes. Gwilym Lloyd George, the sacked Home Secretary, was 'sad'. Before they left, Clarissa secured a CBE for Cecil Beaton. She wrote to Bluey Baker:

Anthony is very heartbroken, but it was, alas, inevitable. The wonder is that he was able to carry on for so long after those operations.

I hope that a long holiday will prevent anything irreparable happening. We uproot ourselves now & hope to sail on Friday to Auckland, New Zealand, & after a bit, to the South Pacific Islands, New Hebrides, Samoa & so on, possibly not returning until after Easter.

I am so sad not to have seen you again before this upheaval. I will write frequently from our ports of call, and let you know any semi-permanent address we may have.

The new government looks very smart-alecky, doesn't it?[9]

The Edens sailed from the Royal Albert Docks in the Port of London aboard the liner *Rangitata* bound for New Zealand, a voyage that would take thirty-five days. There was a farewell party on board, consisting of Lord Home, Edward Heath (Chief Whip since December, and bearing a joint letter of good wishes from Macmillan and Butler), Oliver Poole (Chairman of the Conservative Party) and his wife, and Sir Michael Adeane. Eden spoke briefly to the press, largely wishing his successor well. Clarissa was presented with roses and lilac from the French Ambassador, and spring flowers from the staff at Downing Street. On the day she wrote:

* Patrick Buchan-Hepburn, 1st Lord Hailes (1901-74), Governor-General of the West Indies Federation 1958-62.

We drive to the docks from Chequers. The Pooles, Michael Adeane, Ted Heath, Alec, Waverleys, and so on are there to greet us. Ava, the skeleton at the feast, saying how well he looks, and she doesn't understand it etc., which upsets him. Our cabin is crammed with flowers. As we go down the Thames and Channel, all the ships are dressed overall and send messages of good luck. The boys on the Worcester training ship all line the rails to give 3 cheers and a submarine races along beside us, Anthony very unhappy.[10]

Four days into the voyage they had sunshine. They passed through the Panama Canal, the only option since the Suez Canal was closed. Their cabin steward was a young man called John Prescott, who morphed in later life into a pugnacious Labour cabinet minister. In Curaçao they dined with the Governor and passed Pitcairn on 12 February. While they were at sea, Macmillan told the House of Commons that he had been 'a close personal friend of his [Eden's] for the past 33 years when we entered the House together'.[11] Numerous friends wrote to Clarissa – Cecil Beaton and even Diana Cooper. James Pope-Hennessy asked Ann Fleming: 'Why couldn't they have been more natural, having taken this fatal & foolish decision? But then as John [his brother] says they are both neurotics.'[12]

The ship docked in Thailand. They visited Bangkok, Clarissa annoyed to find the canals filled in with concrete to please the Americans. While at sea Anthony swam with the captain and crew, played deck tennis or sunbathed. He suffered two fever attacks, one of them as they neared the Pitcairn Islands, but was well enough to address a press conference when they arrived in Auckland on 22 February after what Clarissa called 'wasted weeks'. She recorded 'fantastic reception with vociferous crowds at the Auckland docks and Sid Holland waiting to greet us . . . drive off in the scented air . . .'[13] There were cries of 'Go to it, Anthony,' from escorting vessels. Prime Minister Sid Holland and his wife took them for a stay at their holiday home in Waiwera.

In March Anthony suffered another high fever and delayed going to Otehei Bay, in the Bay of Islands, just south of Auckland, but when they got there, Clarissa loved it. She wrote to Cecil Beaton:

Picture the downs and combes of Ashcombe transplanted to the sea, with groves of ilex trees running right down to the beaches – in a

Anthony Eden by Konig, 1962

The wedding, 1952 – Aunt Clemmie, Anthony and Clarissa,
and Uncle Winston

Winston Churchill –
resting

Anthony Eden, with
his son Nicholas

The Edens in the South of France, photographed by
Bill Paley, 1953

Hugh Gaitskell & Bulganin,
Chequers, 1956

Nikita Khrushchev
at Chequers, 1956

The Edens with the Queen and Prince Philip, Balmoral, 1955

Anthony Eden at the Garter Ceremony, June 1956

Clarissa doing her bit at a Chequers fête

Anthony and Clarissa heading to Paris with Selwyn Lloyd
during the Suez crisis

Harold Macmillan with Anthony Eden
– poised to take over

Max Beaverbrook with
Anthony Eden

Lord Avon swimming
with Pamela Harriman,
Hobe Sound, 1976

Lord Avon with his
prize Hereford bull

Clarissa with Madame
Chou-en-lai, 1982

Lord Goodman –
the fixer

Clarissa photographed by the author at Cetinale, 1980

Diana. Marun Elizabeth R 1992 Philip

The Queen and her Prime Ministers at Spencer House, 1992
Back left to right – Clarissa, the Wilsons, Edward Heath, the Thatchers
Front left to right – The Callaghans, The Prince and Princess of Wales, The Queen and
The Duke of Edinburgh, the Majors

Clarissa hosting a dinner – Robert Harris and Jung Chang
at the table, 2010

Clarissa deep sea diving, 1988

Clarissa with the author on her
100th birthday, 28 June 2020

sub-tropical climate. Bay after bay of deserted sand and rocks covered with <u>oysters</u> – our garden full of hibiscus, bananas, peaches & figs. It is a revelation and a breathtaking combination of everything one likes most in scenery and climate. For several mad days we determined to stay here for ever . . . I feel very sad about everything – though old Nasser does seem to be playing up & showing himself to be all Anthony has always feared he was – and our mail is still terrific. The most dismal part personally is that I seem to have lost some of my very few friends in the process. I no longer feel able to be indulgent towards James's childishness and passionate ignorance, and though I love Ann [Fleming] for herself, she cannot understand why I may not want to meet Osbert Lancaster or James at dinner.[14]

Cecil agreed:

I'm afraid I've been out of sympathy with James for nearly a year now, & the awful thing is that he hasn't noticed it – so great is his egomania & arrogance. Perhaps *Queen Mary** has gone to his head & Lady Ebury† still wanting to marry him boosts his already inflated self-esteem. I'm just bored with friends that do nothing but accept kindness & hospitality without doing anything in return. Ann seems to be a bit fed up with James as she's tired of flattering him – the only way of getting a positive reaction from him. I'm really very fond of him, & I know you are too, but it'll take me some time to feel about him as I used to – & you too, no doubt.[15]

The idyllic holiday in New Zealand did not last. The doctors did not want them to go to Samoa for fear of Anthony's sudden recurring high fevers. Instead they flew to Boston for tests with Dr Cattell.

Eden looked frail on arrival. He went straight to the New England Baptist Hospital, where Cattell inserted a plastic tube on

---

* James was still writing the official life of *Queen Mary* (published in 1959).
† Anne Wignall (1912–82), married (1) 1933, 5th Baron Ebury (1914–57), a keen motor-racer, divorced 1941; (2) 1941, Henry Hoare (1901–81), divorced 1947; (3) 1947, Lieutenant Colonel Frederick Wignall (1906–56); (4), 1961, Anthony Marreco (1915–2006), a noted ladies' man. She wrote eleven books, invariably historical novels, romances or biographies.

the severed duct. Eden stayed in the hospital for a month. Clarissa was at the Ritz-Carlton and his only visitor. Although they had officially retired from public life, there was still considerable interest in them.

Sir Horace Evans had flown out to be present at the operation. He brought with him a letter from Aunt Clemmie to Clarissa, saying: 'My thoughts are constantly with you both. We are all miserable over here, and if concern, respect and affection could be the doctors, Anthony would soon be well . . . Dear Clarissa your courage and dignity in adversity are grand and I pray Hope and Happiness will come . . .'[16] The Queen was on a state visit to Paris and sent a message saying she was glad he had reached Boston and hoped he would have a speedy recovery: 'We are very greatly enjoying our visit to Paris which you did so much to foster.'[17]

While in Boston, they received about two hundred letters a day, mainly from Americans and mostly in favour of Suez. Many were ashamed of the part their government had played. There was a lunch for Clarissa at which Winthrop Aldrich's former assistant John Ames asked her why they had not gone on. She replied: 'How could we when your government instructed Wall Street to sell the pound to the tune of 40 million in one week?'[18]

The operation – for relief of a bile-duct obstruction – proved a success. On 29 April Eden left hospital, spent a week in a friend's house in Milton, and they then accepted Vincent Massey's invitation to stay with him in Ottawa.

Unhelpfully, Robert Allan, his former parliamentary private secretary, was quoted addressing the Primrose League: 'He is perhaps rather less well than we are apt to judge from reading the press. But he is in good heart.'[19] Government House Ottawa also put out a message to say he was 'still a very sick man and it will take a long time for him to get completely back to normal'.[20]

While staying with the Masseys at Government House, Clarissa wrote to Lord Beaverbrook with an update on Anthony's health, the aim of which was to clarify that Anthony would not be returning to politics:

At the moment he is, of course, completely weak. He was so exhausted before the operation and ravaged by the fevers, which began last October, that he didn't have a fair start. He took the operation very well & made a model recovery – but of course now he is terribly enfeebled and has relapses when he really feels like hell.

The doctors say they cannot predict when the same complaint will not start again. They think that it will, maybe in months, maybe years . . .'[21]

Soon after their return to Britain on 3 June they settled for a quiet spell at Rose Bower. Max Beaverbrook came to lunch on 10 June, with the message that Eden had done 'a fine and courageous thing'. He added that Macmillan was 'trying to make out that what Anthony had done was valueless'. Lord Head supported this. He said Macmillan 'had turned his back on Suez completely', that the country was on Eden's side, that he must use his 'terrific position' when better 'to oust the traitor Macmillan, the socialists and his own rotten ex-Cabinet – "You are young yet – you must never think of complete retirement" and so on'. Clarissa was emphatic that the American doctors had said Anthony must never do regular work again for fear of catching things that could lead to inflammation.[22]

In March 1958 Macmillan came to lunch. Clarissa had not seen him since the night at Chequers. She found him 'rather wary and frigid'. He continually said something and then decided it would have been better not to have said it: 'Foster thinks . . . the *Spectator* says . . . The Commonwealth trip was like a royal tour.' Beaverbrook proposed himself for tea the same day. When he appeared, Clarissa thought he was being mischievous again. The reason for his visit was never clarified.[23]

In September 1958, after living for a time at Donhead House, in Wiltshire, and at Donnington Grange, near Newbury, loaned by Daisy Fellowes, they bought Fyfield Manor, near Pewsey, from Hannah (Viscountess) Hudson. Their new home was a substantial pink brick house with a large garden, a wood, two lakes, an enormous ilex tree and a mulberry 'lying down like a leafy coffin'. The soil was 'solid chocolate' and perfect for gardening.[24] The house was hideously dirty when they first moved in, and the neighbouring fields were choked with weeds and nettles. Clarissa tackled that and soon they loved the place.

Fyfield Manor

If Clarissa was at last looking forward to having Anthony to herself, she was to be disappointed. He was writing his memoirs so there were researchers in the house. He managed the first volume, *Full Circle*, with the help of Alan Hodge,* editor of *History Today*, and Bryan Cartledge,† who tackled the non-Suez part. He was often at Fyfield for working weekends, tackling Eden's occasional tempers, during which he sent papers flying, balanced by his courteous apologies.[25]

Cartledge was succeeded by David Dilks who again lived at Fyfield while helping Eden with his second volume of memoirs:

Although steadily loyal to Eden, Lady A. understood that he could be unreasonable and unduly demanding; such moods passed quickly and meant nothing of substance. She would occasionally show by a glance or gesture that she understood the difficulties of a secretary or research assistant. In my early days I would sometimes reflect 'It must be dreary

* Alan Hodge (1915–79), English historian. He is said to have 'retired hurt' from the project, on which he worked in 1959. He also collaborated with Robert Graves, and made it possible for Graves to marry his second wife, Beryl.
† (Sir) Bryan Cartledge (b. 1931), later Ambassador to Hungary and Russia.

for her to give up all that fashionable life in London society for this regime of enforced quiet.' Slowly I realised that she far preferred the gardening, the meticulous ordering of the household, the vigilant attention to her husband's wellbeing, to the world of politics and perhaps even to the literary world. If ever a man was lucky in his second marriage it was A.E.; a fact of which he was well aware.[26]

During this time, Eden had to rest frequently. The fevers came on suddenly and laid him low. A friendly chemist in Marlborough was prepared to provide medication, sometimes late at night.

Years later it was suggested that all Eden's private papers relating to Suez had been lodged at the Westminster Bank in Salisbury. The issue arose in May 1986 when no one could find the British copy of the controversial Sèvres Protocol. It was thought that Eden might have destroyed it. Clarissa noted:

1) I was not privy to any secret diplomatic manoeuvres at any time during my husband's career. Quite rightly. I heard about the 'secret' Suez papers through the press & TV.

2) The idea that these papers wd be at a bank in S'bury seems ludicrous. All I can say is that in the course of writing *Full Circle* my husband came into the room one day white in the face with shock & said he had just asked Norman Brook for all the Suez papers & Norman told him they had been destroyed. The deduction from this I do not have the answer to.[27]

In the years that followed, the Edens did not greatly impinge on the national consciousness. Clarissa stood as godmother to Charles Tennant, infant son of Colin and Anne. In 1958 she and Anthony attended the memorial service for King Faisal, the Crown Prince of Iraq, and Prime Minister Nuri al-Said, who had been brutally murdered in Baghdad in July. Eden wrote to Robert Carr: 'What a terrible horror was that massacre in Baghdad. I don't think I have ever felt an international calamity more closely, certainly not since the death of Masaryk.'*[28]

Travel was their joy. They visited Mexico in the winter of 1958/9, the South of France in August 1962, Corsica for a fortnight in May

---

* Tomas Masaryk (1850–1937), President of Czechoslovakia.

1964, and stayed with Lord Astor of Hever in Grasse in November 1964. The Mexico trip took them to Cuernavaca ('ruined by the Americans . . . Everything & everybody is second-rate, shoddy & boring'),[29] and they lunched with Merle Oberon ('followed around by a pallid little husband who calls her Baby'.)[30] They went to Acapulco, just transforming from being a small fishing village to a well-known winter resort. In June 1959 they went to Honfleur, Clarissa twisting her left foot. They paid a summer visit to Paris, staying with the Ambassador and lunching with President de Gaulle.* In June 1962 Anthony particularly asked to see one of his favourite artists, Dunoyer de Segonzac.†They relished visits to Shakespeare plays at Stratford.

In December 1959 they travelled via Trinidad to St Vincent. They had not been happy at Mercer's Creek, Antigua, despite the beauty of the surroundings. Clarissa wrote to Cecil Beaton that the house was 'reminiscent of Dorneywood . . . It has been in the hands of several Americans & become proportionately de-soul-ified – with aubergine & persimmon & all the *House & Garden* coloured walls & quantities of colonial silver & colonial dumb waiters & colonial what-nots & rotten servants dolled up in turbans . . .'[31] Luckily Colin Tennant found them a house in Friendship Bay, Bequia: 'a shack made of shingles and 600 feet of beach (in West Indies parlance) . . . We shall be the only whites there.'[32]

Cecil wrote back: 'Friendship Bay sounds a splendid plan. I can imagine the dreariness of a West Indian Dorneywood, & there's nothing worse than a millionaire's club. However, you are wise to be away at this frustrating time of year.'[33] Eden described Bequia as 'beautiful but very primitive'.[34] The new house was greatly disapproved of by his doctor 'because of the 1½ hr rough sea passage & no airfield in a crisis'. But it was idyllic, cheap, private and had a beach.[35] It was not long before Clarissa was describing it: 'We think our bay the most beautiful in the world . . . exotic without being oppressive or sinister – & noble without being barren.'[36] They lived on lobsters and coconut milk, and she raced through volume after volume of Proust who put her in mind of James Pope-Hennessy.

* In June 1963 de Gaulle told Eden that he wished he would return to politics, but Eden said his health precluded this and he would not have gone to the House of Lords in 1961 otherwise.

† André Dunoyer de Segonzac (1884-1974), French painter and graphic artist.

Bequia

From Bequia the Edens were able to visit Clarissa's childhood companion and swain, Trim Oxford, by then administrator in St Lucia. She warned him that Anthony's health was such that if possible there should be no social life – other than perhaps a drink with the Chief Minister. The visit of the Queen's aunt, the Princess Royal, to the Caribbean got in the way somewhat: 'The Princess Royal is becoming a bugbear to us, she overshadows everyone & everything – so incongruous when one thinks of her inoffensive and unassuming personality.'*[37] They went on to Antigua, and home via Bermuda.

In 1961 Clemmie wrote that she was 'thrilled & rather horrified'[38] by an account Clarissa had given of their life on Bequia. Clarissa had told her aunt that Anthony had suffered 'a painful angina attack' two days after they returned from Barbados and Martinique. There being no electricity on Bequia, Anthony had to be taken by frigate to Barbados where the doctors advised them to resume their holiday but to see a

---

* The Princess Royal (1897–1965) was on a 13,000-mile voyage to the Caribbean in HMY *Britannia* between 15 January and 7 April, visiting British Guiana, Trinidad, Barbados, Antigua, St Kitts, the Cayman Islands, Turks & Caicos, British Honduras and the Azores. Colin Cowdrey presented the England team to her after the Test match. The team then had tea with the Edens.

specialist on their return to the UK. Back on the island, Anthony led a quiet life, but not for long: 'Unfortunately Carnival is about to break upon us, with its steel bands and general merriment,'[39] wrote Clarissa.

That year Lord Hailes visited them on 26 February, happily ensconced as Governor General of the Federation of the West Indies, and Winston came by on Aristotle Onassis's yacht. On their way back they lunched with Macmillan in Bridgetown. One of the joys of Bequia for Clarissa was snorkelling on the reef. Eden told Churchill: 'The fish are really fabulous, and since nobody ever disturbs them, curious rather than frightened.'[40]

In March 1962 Eden had had another operation in Boston, this time to remove a benign intrathoracic lesion. Cattell, then himself dying of leukemia, found that the plastic tube had disappeared. He enlarged the duct. Eden's departure to London was delayed by a day, due to fever. After a three-day visit to Martinique in February 1963, he suffered a heart attack. He was flown to Bridgetown on the evening of the fifteenth and returned to London on 20 March. The doctors finally told Eden that Bequia was too remote for safety.

Anthony Eden was ennobled as Earl of Avon in 1961 so that he could make occasional speeches in the House of Lords. In 1964 the Avons spent five weeks in Barbados, searching for a house there, and eventually finding the Villa Nova.

On the home front, books were published. In August 1959 there was Randolph Churchill's hostile Eden biography. Anthony was amused to run into Lord Attlee at a party Macmillan gave at Number 10 for President Eisenhower:*

> He spoke to me of the review he had done of Randolph's book about me (in the *Observer*). I thanked him. He said: 'That's all right. That book was a denigration. I don't like denigration.' He added that Winston had congratulated him on the review and had told him: 'If only you had been still rougher on Randolph.' Attlee chuckled with pleasure.[41]

---

* President Eisenhower was in the United Kingdom between 26 August and 2 September.

The first volume of his own memoirs was published in February 1960, while the Edens were in the Caribbean. *Full Circle* tackled the later years and Suez first, partly because the publishers were afraid that Eden might not live to complete the other two volumes.

On 12 July 1960 Bluey Baker died. He had been a constant in Clarissa's life while her mother was alive and in all the years that followed. His will revealed that he had left Clarissa three thousand pounds and his library of books. He was described in the press as 'an old friend of her parents'.[42] He also left her some land. It was only then that Clarissa came to wonder and finally accept that he was her biological father. She had never been particularly close to her accepted father so this was not an upsetting discovery.

On 30 May 1961 they dined with the Macmillans. They attended the Garter Ceremony in June, and in July lunched with Uncle Winston at 28 Hyde Park Gate. There was a more dramatic series of visits to Churchill in the Middlesex Hospital in August 1962. He had fallen in the Hôtel de Paris in Monte Carlo and broken his left hip and thigh. Against doctors' orders he was flown home and hospitalised for fifty-five days. He developed jaundice. The press monitored his progress. Asked about him on the way out, Clarissa said: 'He is getting sunshine into his room nicely this morning and he enjoys that.'[43] Eden left a private account:

We saw Winston three times during his illness in 1962, at the Middlesex Hospital. The second time was after his attack of jaundice, his hand was ice cold & he was very feeble. I feared we should never see him again.

The third time was a transformation. The nurse had warned us that he was rather tired, but far from it. He was more alert than we had seen him for months, if not for years, & more interested in current events. Whereas the first time he had been doubtful of my Warwickshire speech: 'It was not what you said, my dear, but the fact that it was you who said it.' But this time he seemed to have thought it over & made up his mind to approve. Several times during the 45 minutes he repeated: 'You are in a very strong position.' In vain I replied that I was in no position at all, simply living at Fyfield. He was not to be convinced. When Clarissa said that the Govt was in a difficult position he replied, 'Very difficult indeed.' He asked me about Selwyn Lloyd's dismissal & I told him what S had recounted to me, while he nodded in understanding & said, 'Too difficult.' He asked about the Common Market & I told him my apprehension lest Australia & NZ economies would not be safeguarded, as the Govt had promised & then added, but you have seen Harold, what did he say – W. replied 'He made himself very agreeable,' but clearly he had said nothing. W was very affectionate & did not want us to go, even after 45 minutes. When I said goodbye, he held my hand & kissed it.

Clarissa reminds me that W asked me about Africa & when I had given some account of Congo & Rhodesian & Kenyan events, American & other unhelpful activities, I asked what he thought. He sat up in bed & uttered vigorously: 'Damnation.'[44]

The summer of 1963 was a volatile time in British politics. The country was awash with scandal, not least the revelation that John Profumo, the Secretary of State for War, had been having an affair with a call girl, Christine Keeler. She had been peripherally involved with the Russian military attaché, Yevgeny Ivanov, so a potential security issue arose. Profumo lied to the House of Commons in a statement on 22 March and in June he resigned. Clarissa compared the atmosphere in London to Berlin in the 1920s. She did not like it.

Oliver Poole, then vice chairman of the Conservative Party, kept the Edens up to date with events. On 3 June 1963 the Pooles came to lunch at Fyfield and Lord Poole told them the party could not win the next election under Macmillan. He seemed determined not to step down, so Clarissa feared Harold Wilson as the next prime minister. At that time she and Daphne Poole hoped Lord Hailsham would lead the Conservatives. Eden and Lord Poole accepted that, with Edward Heath next and Reginald Maudling third. They all agreed that the party had lost its way. Poole said: 'Relations between members of the Cabinet were indescribable and unbelievable. They did not trust each other, it was all against all. Since the night of the long knives in which seven cabinet ministers were sacked, the surviving members felt they cd not be butchered & were less afraid, yet the rivalry prevented any working together.'[45]

Heath no longer trusted Macmillan, and Lord Poole recalled that years before Oliver Stanley had told him he would make no further serious contribution to a discussion when Macmillan was in the room as he would talk. Clarissa summed it up for Cecil Beaton, then in Hollywood, working on the film of *My Fair Lady*:

We went to Paris for a week – the Embassy is getting more depress-ing every time, with the doors & the enfilade permanently shut & lots of miserable & inefficient Spanish servants. Pompidou came to dinner & turns out to be, socially anyway, an oaf – Philippe de Rothschild had also been asked, the Dixons* not realising he wasn't the right Rothschild & pro Mendès-France, & both Anthony & I told him to pipe down & shut up independently, which was rather awful. He really is the French Randolph.

I took A. to see Marie-Laure [de Noailles], who was very paunchy & in her bedroom slippers & announcing that he was the one man she'd always wanted to meet all her life. Then Charles arrived & was very upset about the slippers.

General de Gaulle as delightful as always but [Gaston] Palewski said that at the Cabinet afterwards he was awful . . .

Then we lunched at Clarence House for Jock Whitney† – & after waiting for hours before lunch, in came the Queen & Profumo, who had been at a Privy Council together – this was the day before the balloon went up & Val‡ was in black with some prescience.

Selwyn's reaction to the scandal was 'I don't believe Jack did any of those things, married to a beautiful girl like Val.'

The whole place has gone quite crazy on the scandal – a sort of hysteria of gossip & salaciousness as if London were a small village. Everyone prays that Bill Astor will somehow get it in the arse, Marples is said to be the naked man in the mask, Duncan is said to be involved – also Soames – & Maurice Macmillan appears in a photograph although he says his face has been stuck on someone else's body by the Communists! It seems likely anyway that some-thing else is going to come out – someone else will be implicated. Harold insisting on this form of enquiry is thought to prove it.

Politically the rebels are increasing & absolutely furious because the meeting of the 1922 Committee was steam-rolled by the Whips

---

* Sir Pierson Dixon (1904-65), British Ambassador to Paris 1960-65.
† John Hay Whitney (1904-82), American Ambassador to Britain 1957-61.
‡ Valerie Hobson (1917-98), film actress, and wife of John Profumo.

& the motions of no-confidence in the PM not allowed. He is thought to have behaved badly in blaming MI5 & Norman Brook in the House. It's an unwritten law that the Minister always takes the blame. A. had to over that frogman & the Russians, even though he had given written instructions about it.

My view is that Harold will stick on & just refuse to go – but everyone else, including Oliver Poole, thinks he will have to go or there will be an upheaval in the Conservative Party.

I must say I cdn't have wished a more squalid exit for a man I have always disliked & distrusted![46]

Macmillan resigned on 18 October. It was clear, days before, that he was on the way out. From Hollywood Cecil Beaton wrote to Clarissa: 'I don't relish the sight of Rab Butler's face on the breakfast tray every morning,' adding later: 'Just seen the paper. So Mac's under the knife. I'm afraid his name will always be associated with Christine. It's rather unfair.'[47]

Clarissa filled him in:

We have been plunged in the last few days, by remote control over the telephone, into the prime ministerial crisis. We are rooting for Quintin (Hailsham), along with Randolph, Bobbety and Oliver Poole. Most, I fear, are for that toad-in-the-hole Rab, who looks more repulsive than he did 10 years ago, which I wdn't have believed possible, & who has got himself another madly ambitious wife.

Quintin was thought to have committed an error of taste by taking his baby to the Conference & mixing the baby food in the lobby of the Imperial Hotel, while the delegates marched the streets shouting, 'We want Hailsham,' & the Cabinet sulked in their bedrooms.

Harold is complaining that everyone is behaving as if he was dead. The S. Times even rang up Maurice Macmillan & said they presumed he wd be writing Harold's life & cd they have the serial rights.[48]

In retirement Harold Macmillan sometimes proposed himself for a visit to Wiltshire. Once Clarissa invited Field Marshal Lord Montgomery to lunch. A day or so before a man was spotted placing pointers to mark the way. On the day an outrider brought

Montgomery to her door at the appointed hour. But when Macmillan was expected he was nowhere to be found. He was eventually tracked down in Salisbury, where he had arrived, had been unable to find the Avons' telephone number and was sitting forlornly outside the station.[49]

Clarissa attended the first night of the James Bond film, *From Russia with Love*, on 10 October, after which Ian Fleming got up 'like an old man, pale grey in the face, sweat beading his forehead, swallowing pills, & apparently in a daze'. At the party afterwards, there was James Pope-Hennessy, as she reported to Cecil Beaton: 'I appear to have made it up with James. It's difficult not to when he comes sidling up – his eyes seem very bloodshot.'[50]

Ian Fleming died on 12 August 1964 and Clarissa went alone to his memorial service at St Bartholomew the Great, on 15 September. On 31 December the Avons postponed their flight by a day due to another of Anthony's fevers. They headed to Barbados for what was meant to be an eight-week stay in a rented house. Scarcely had their plane touched the ground than grave news reached them from London. They returned immediately.

17. EDEN'S LAST YEARS
1964–77

On 30 November 1964 Sir Winston Churchill attained his ninetieth birthday. He was just able to make a carefully staged appearance at the open window of his London home, to be photographed by the press. At the beginning of January 1965 he began to fade, gradually losing consciousness. Hyde Park Gate became the focus of the world's attention as Lord Moran, in a dark overcoat with a white scarf round the neck, read out the daily bulletins. The family watched and waited. Mary Soames took her mother out for walks in the park: 'killing time while time killed him'.[1]

The Avons flew home from the West Indies, staying at the Connaught and visited him at his home on the afternoon of 18 January, staying for about twenty-five minutes. On the morning of 24 January Churchill died. It was the anniversary of his father's death. There followed memorable days as his coffin lay in state in Westminster Hall, under a Union flag, surmounted with a dark blue velvet cushion on which rested the insignia of the Order of the Garter. On a glacially cold January day there was a procession through the streets of London to St Paul's Cathedral for the state funeral, attended by the Queen, nearly all of the Royal Family and heads of state from across the world. Wartime colleagues such as Dwight D. Eisenhower and Sir Robert Menzies joined the Kings of Norway, Denmark and Greece, Queen Juliana of the Netherlands and President de Gaulle of France in the cathedral.

Clarissa arrived at Palace Yard at 9.20 a.m. to travel in a carriage with the 10th Duke of Marlborough, while Anthony was one of the pallbearers at the Cathedral, along with ailing figures such as Lord Ismay, Earl Attlee, and the great war leaders – Alexander of Tunis, Montgomery of Alamein, and Portal of Hungerford. The Avons were on the train from Waterloo to see Winston buried at Bladon at 4 p.m., in distant view of his birthplace, Blenheim Palace.*

The Avons resumed their Caribbean holiday on 3 February. Not long afterwards Mary and Christopher Soames brought Aunt Clemmie to stay in Barbados with Ronald Tree. The Avons were staying there before moving into their new house. Clarissa described the scene to Cecil Beaton:

> Our fortnight at Ronnie's ('absolutely alone, I am finishing a book on Barbados, complete rest for Anthony' etc) unfortunately coincided with his having been unable to resist asking Clemmie & co, & with their surprisingly having accepted the suggestion. As she was in mourning, no one cd be asked in to relieve the strain, so we ate three meals a day (everyone down to breakfast. Have you ever seen Mary Soames at breakfast? It is the time of day when she feels her most vital & informative) – just the seven of us. For the first few days Clemmie appeared to be completely stunned. She sat there, not even answering questions, staring into space, and picking her teeth. Christopher told me they were afraid she was heading for a break-down. At the end of the visit we thought she had improved, though the Soameses didn't, but I thought they were a little hard on her for worrying about her maid's day off & whether she had enough Jamaican currency, because after all at 79 one does start worrying about things a bit.
>
> Mary, as you will have guessed, was perfectly intolerable in the nicest possible way, & Christopher was really rather endearing & a surprise to us all.[2]

Mary summed up the stay with her habitual guarded restraint: 'Clemmie, although ever pleasant and appreciative, seemed to be living in a world of her own, remote from us all.'[3]

In March the Avons took on the Villa Nova near St John's, finally moving in on 25 November 1965. The house had been built in 1831 following a famous hurricane, standing south-facing, surrounded by six acres of garden. It had a parapet roof designed to withstand hurricanes,

---

* On 19 September they were in Westminster Abbey for the dedication of Winston's memorial stone.

Villa Nova, Barbados

a white-shingled gallery, and latticework arches and fretwork. It excited Clarissa though she regretted they would not be able to afford to do it up as they wished. The house needed only a few Indian gauzes and some mahogany pieces. Soon they would have to leave Fyfield as it was too expensive: 'There are four servants there now eating their heads off.'⁴ But Anthony was ill again, had lost a stone, could not sleep for arthritis and neuritis, and suffered from a chronic temperature. In April she took him to Boston for a further check-up.

Back in England on 27 April there was the usual round of lunches, Garter ceremony, embassy dinners and a trip to Paris, a lunch with de Gaulle and a dinner for the Duke of Windsor at the British Embassy. In July Anthony attended the Foreign Affairs debate in the House of Lords.

They sailed from Southampton on 30 October to spend the winter in Barbados. Cecil Beaton was keen to see their 'romantic' plantation house: 'It must be very rewarding to plant a gardenia & to find it has become within a month, a vast flowering tree.'⁵ He came to stay from 5 to 8 February 1966:

It made me very happy to see you & Anthony enjoying your tropical home with such relish. And indeed how worthy this delightful little place is of its occupants. It has real charm, & exotic beauty of background, & you have given it your particular style. I loved staying in those large white airy rooms, & what you have done in the way of décor is worthy of Madame Errazuriz* at her best. It was a treat to wake up in those linen sheets & be given a tray with such glorious pieces of toast & a pristine pot of Cooper's Oxford marmalade. It was a joy to walk over acres of matting to the bath. Each meal was an event with tropical fish & fruit, & such relaxed & delightful company.[6]

There was a stream of visitors while they lived there between November 1965 and March 1971 – Isaiah Berlin, Claudette Colbert, Colin Tennant and his children, Roland Michener, Governor General of Canada, in 1969, along with many old friends, and figures from the political scene.

The highlight was the visit of the Queen and Prince Philip. They came to lunch on 15 February 1966, during their long Caribbean tour in *Britannia*. They both planted trees in the pouring rain and that night the Avons dined on *Britannia*. 'I wonder if Mrs Bannochie† has been supplying you with glorious exotics – & whether Audrey Hepburn‡ has yet recovered from the excitement of serving the Queen,'[7] mused Cecil Beaton. In November the Duke and Duchess of Kent came to Barbados to preside over the Independence ceremony. They came to the Villa Nova. Clarissa wrote: 'I was very impressed by the Kents who came to lunch. She seems to have taken a useful leaf out of the Queen Mother's book, & really does very well. Just the right word for everyone.'[8]

---

* High praise from Cecil. He greatly admired Eugenia Errazuriz (1860–1951). A Chilean of Basque origin, she was a patron of modernism. She believed that elegance meant elimination. Cecil wrote in *The Glass of Fashion*: 'Her effect on the taste of the last fifty years has been so enormous that the whole aesthetic of modern interior decoration, and many of the concepts of simplicity . . . generally acknowledged today, can be laid at her remarkable doorstep.' (Cecil Beaton, *The Glass of Fashion* [Weidenfeld & Nicolson, 1954], p. 167).
† Iris Bannochie (1914-88), celebrated Barbadian horticulturist.
‡ Classic Cecil Beaton: a maid who reminded him of the film star, Audrey Hepburn.

A regular visitor was the sprightly Princess Alice, Countess of Athlone, who came to lunch once a year. In January 1966 Dean Acheson was staying. He was most put out at the prospect of having to meet her. Within minutes the pair were in gales of laughter. A less welcome visitor was Randolph Churchill, who rented Laura Canfield's house. Clarissa wished to avoid him and knew it would be difficult. He was dying and, despite his vicious attacks on Eden in the press over many years, insisted on coming to see them, bringing his daughter Arabella and his friend Natalie Bevan with him. 'And we sat around in an awkward circle. He couldn't believe that it was not what anybody wanted,' recalled Clarissa.[9] Randolph died on 6 June 1968. Clarissa wrote to Aunt Clemmie, who replied: 'I am so glad that you have forgiven Randolph & that you share my sense of deprivation. I wish that you could come to the Memorial Service. He would have liked you to be there.'[10] Clarissa duly attended at St Margaret's, Westminster, on 2 July.

In February 1969 Anthony was laid low for many weeks in Barbados and only resuscitated by a brand new antibiotic. Princess Margaret was in Barbados 'happy to be away from Ld Snowdon, but demanding, unscrupulous & selfish nonetheless'.[11] Finally Clarissa decided she did not wish to remain in Barbados: 'Here we are, & frantic to sell & hating it. I dislike it so much now that I have shut all my senses off, & also don't give a damn if the servants do everything badly. The house & garden have in any case suffered from the fact that no one here expected to see us again.'[12] They last stayed at the Villa Nova in March 1971, selling it soon after. Instead they went to Portugal or Madeira in the winter.

★ ★ ★ ★ ★

In 1967 the Avons settled at the Manor House, Alvediston, purchased from Lady Glanusk. Since buying her cottage, Rose Bower in 1948, Clarissa had always loved Wiltshire. She was thrilled to return to the Chalke Valley and came to love Alvediston. Returning there in 2010, in her ninetieth year, she wrote: 'Lovely, lovely country . . . views, etc. Then on to Alvediston. At once I feel at home, out of the wooded valleys & into the green downs.'[13] Tracing it back, it was Stephen Tennant who had first invited Cecil Beaton to Wiltshire in 1927, then the wonderful Wiltshire novelist, Edith Olivier, who steered him to Ashcombe in 1930 and to Reddish House in 1947. Cecil's mother had found Rose Bower at Little London, near Broadchalke, for Clarissa.

Alvediston was a Grade II brick building, dating from the eighteenth century. It had an extensive lawned garden, a walled orchard and extensive outbuildings. This was to be Anthony's home until his death

Alvediston

in 1977, and Clarissa's until the autumn of 1984. Cecil was excited about it: 'Your house is a delight & I'm thrilled for you both to have something so worthwhile working on & I'm sure the garden will soon be quite remarkable. Soon <u>all</u> traces of Lady Glanusk will have disappeared.'[14]

Clarissa already had a coterie of friends nearby. In the 1960s and 1970s there was a good mixture of the aristocratic and the artistic. Cecil Beaton was the original draw at Reddish House, and there were three generations of Pembrokes at Wilton. Old Reggie had finally died in 1960; his son Sidney simplified the garden, divided the library into three rooms and used the breakfast room with Chinese wallpaper as the dining room. Juliet Duff had died in September 1965; Henry and Claire Herbert were living at Bulbridge until 1969, when Sidney died and Wilton was taken over by the 'beatniks', as Cecil Beaton called them. David Herbert materialised occasionally from Tangier, and his brother Tony was busy drinking himself to death at the High Post Hotel, near Amesbury.

Anthony's great friends Antony and Dot Head were at Throope; Michael and Anne Tree moved presently to Donhead St Mary, the David Cecils and various other Cecils were at Cranborne. The Crichel

Boys (Raymond Mortimer, Derek Hill, Desmond Shawe-Taylor and Pat Trevor-Roper) were at Long Crichel with a flow of guests.

Lord Avon was now officially in retirement, but he took pride in the herd of Herefords he established at Alvediston. And they were far from short of visitors. Thus they were able to observe the political world from a well-informed if remote vantage point. Even Aunt Clemmie came for a weekend in 1967.

In May 1967 the six-day war erupted in the Middle East. Nasser was once again in the middle of it. There was a revival of interest in Suez, with many people rethinking their position. 'I must confess that nothing in recent years has given me more pleasure than the letters which are now pouring in from all parts of the world about the events of eleven years ago,'[15] wrote Anthony to Robert Carr.

When they were staying at St Paul de Vence in May, Clarissa gave an interview to Graham Lord of the Sunday Express. Speaking of politics, she said: 'One misses the immediacy and excitement of events. On the other hand, being in the limelight was a great strain and sometimes it can be quite unpleasant. Now we are able to make exactly the life we want to lead and do exactly what we want to do.' She said she was glad that Anthony had been 'vindicated', 'proved right'. She was critical of recent books on Suez, which she found 'gossipy'. She explained: 'No one has done any serious research job on Suez. There have been two or three books lately, some of which purport to be historical. But they are not. It's a subject about which they feel they can write down rumours as historical fact.'[16]

Graham Lord left with the message that Clarissa considered herself lazy, but loved gardening, was out of touch with London, enjoyed swimming and read a lot. Anthony said his health was holding up, though after so many operations, he was inevitably weaker and tired easily. He made the occasional speech, as he had done in Nice on 25 May, and extolled his farm with his pedigree Herefords.

On 1 June Anthony made a speech in the House of Lords, one of his rare interventions. He was described as 'dapper as ever – legs propped languidly on the table, profile as handsome, grey hair with elegant wings, discreet flutter of white handkerchief in breast pocket – the same sway to and from the despatch box. He had to hold his notes a little nearer to his nose than he used to.' He did not mention Suez directly, but caused a ripple in the Chamber when he said: 'I'll be frank. I don't feel myself that it is ten years, but I feel very much in the thirties at the present time.'[17]

Macmillan, now in retirement, produced memoirs that Anthony and others found offensive. He particularly resented Macmillan's accusation that he had shown lack of leadership and that his negotiations with the European Defence Community had made entry into the Common Market difficult. He explained to Robert Carr:

What I most resent is that neither I nor any surviving colleagues was shown the text by Macmillan. Winston always showed me his proofs & nine times out of ten accepted suggestions. Winston saw all my three books in proof. If you are going to criticise a colleague whom you succeeded as FS & PM the least you can do is to tell him & show him . . . Naturally I don't want to be involved in a public brawl with my successor, but there is a limit to the extent to which one is prepared to see one's record distorted by those who do know better.[18]

In March 1970 Anthony was back in Boston for another operation, performed by Dr John W. Braasch, who inserted a catheter into the right duct. This took two hours due to the 'terrible scarring from previous operations'.[19] The Queen sent a message that she was glad it had been successful. Old friends and political allies died. In November they went to Paris for the funeral of General de Gaulle, and back in London, they attended the memorial service in St Paul's Cathedral. In 1972 Lord Salisbury died. On 1 November 1973 they watched Clemmie unveil the statue of Sir Winston in Parliament Square.

Clarissa was in Tenerife when she heard of the brutal death of James Pope-Hennessy at his home in Ladbroke Grove on 25 January 1974. In one version of the story James boasted he had received a substantial advance for a biography of Noël Coward and that his invaders believed they would find this in cash at his home. James had been violently beaten, a hairnet forced down his throat and a tie twisted across his mouth. Two men were jailed for seventeen and fifteen years respectively. Later, on appeal, their sentences were reduced to twelve and ten years. Lord Justice Scarman concluded that James had 'suffered only superficial injuries but tragically died after choking on his own blood from a lip wound'.[20] One of the men was

Sean Seamus O'Brien, who had recently been decorating Ann Fleming's house.

In his memoirs, Sir John Pope-Hennessy, James's famously aloof brother, confessed to mixed reactions. Clarissa approved of John's depiction, judging that it conveyed 'a combination of despair and affection'.[21] He identified the body: 'and when the trolley was wheeled out of the refrigerator and the sheet over his face had been turned down, I was appalled at the dissolute, almost evil expression on his face. It was as though one were participating in some unwritten Jacobean tragedy.'[22] He accepted Lord Goodman's offer of help with newspaper proprietors in getting the story removed from the front pages of the newspapers.

Peter Quennell summed up the last years when editing *A Lonely Business*, without spelling out the details, though these were widely reported in the press at the time:

> Whether alcoholism has a psychological or a physiological origin no authority had yet determined; in James's case its effects were frequently disturbing; and a succession of doctors had warned him that he must prepare to give up wine and spirits. For weeks and months he did his gallant best to put their counsels into practice; but he never quite succeeded; and, after his return to London, his financial and emotional problems allowed him very little peace. 'As you know well,' he had reminded a confidant in the mid-1940s, 'I find at times the gutter overpoweringly attractive,' and, in the 1970s, James's *nostalgie de la boue* often took him into dangerous company, where, like Oscar Wilde, he chose to 'sup with panthers' and associate with 'gilded serpents'.[23]

Clarissa was horrified, yet James's erstwhile Perdita adopted a harshly forensic tone when commiserating with Cecil Beaton:

> How appalling about poor James – we have all been saying for years that he'd be murdered one day, but when it really happens it is shudderingly ghastly – I can so imagine his rather tense cockiness when they tied him up, flashing eyes & the no-nonsense little voice – all to no avail, in that fragile little room. One is haunted by how long it must all have taken. It seems we are almost back at the level of the dark ages.[24]

She must have repeated the last line when writing to his brother John, for he replied:

Not, to me, the dark ages; it is rather as though one were suddenly projected into a Webster play, with its irrational violence and brutality. For more than five years one has watched James sliding ineluctably downhill – sometimes it was almost impossible to relate the elderly figure who came here, and to whose trembling hand one could scarcely entrust a coffee cup, with the enormously talented boy who dedicated those early books to you – and then last September, when I got back from Italy, I felt for the first time that a corner had been turned, and that solvency and self-control were within reach. The *Stevenson* is written with his old pleasure in words, and is untouched by the alcoholic over-emphasis that dogged the *Slave Trade* and *Trollope*. I think by and large he had an unhappy life, in the main because of an outsize capacity for self-deception about other people and about himself. It must be very difficult in middle life to reconcile oneself to the idea that one has an indecent quantity of talent, and not the genius one once thought, especially if you live as he did not in the present but in the past. There was absolutely nothing one could do about it except watch and hope, and I think that with the passage of time the achievement will prove to have been quite substantial, though much less than with a slightly different character, it could have been.[25]

Cecil Beaton wrote to Clarissa:

James's death hit me particularly hard as on the morning that his rather poetical romantic face appeared on the front page of *The Times*, a most delightfully friendly letter from him was on the breakfast tray. It conjured up all the charm & sweetness that he used to have & which so tragically he lost. For he really had become a mess – difficult to talk to, frenetic & either drunk or doped. And his looks had gone completely & he looked like the end of Dorian Gray. It is a terrible story. The man who murdered him was an Irishman that he'd brought to England after James had finished writing his book on Trollope. The man had been sent to prison for brawls in pubs & was a frequent visitor at James's. Len [Adams] took him in as part of a

team of house painters & he went to Ann [Fleming]'s home at
Sevenhampton where he climbed trees & brought down birds' nests
(a horrid thing to do but Ann 'adored' him). The night before he
died, James told the 'valet' he must get a carving knife, and when he
returned to Ladbroke Grove with the shopping & was set upon by
the three men who were ransacking James's flat for the 'advance' on
'Noël Coward', brought out the knife, stabbed one of the thugs & in
return had his hand almost severed & bad head cuts. He is still in
hospital . . .

It is awful that this should have happened when James was at last
'in the money', had an easy job & was getting out of Ladbroke, planning to turn over a new leaf & live in Switzerland . . . It is ironical
that it should take place just as he was about to touch 'home',
because he was quite a different person to the one I used to know
when the last time I saw him quiet & elderly & broad of beam week-
ending somewhat surprisingly at the Heads. I shall always be grateful
to him for bringing you & me together.[26]

Ann Fleming had not seen James much of late 'because he was so
drunken',[27] and, as related, she knew those involved – Len Adams, for
many years James's faithful companion and factotum, and O'Brien.
To Clarissa she wrote: 'John Pope-Hennessy said "If only it had been
Agatha Christie and not the Duchess of Malfi."' She wished John had
been more inhibited. Part of that letter has been published but not all:

It's all beastly and inexplicable for Sean must have known James well
enough to realise there was never any money in the house.

Len Adams and John [Pope-Hennessy] had never met the other
two men, and 11 a.m. is so unlikely for a sex orgy. The one the so
called 'valet' wounded was wearing James's coat and his gold watch.[28]

The full gruesome details of what happened on that fateful day will
probably never emerge.

★ ★ ★ ★ ★

Not so long after that there was an even more painful bereavement.
The names of Raimund and Liz were occasionally to be found in the
visitors' book at Fyfield and Alvediston. Time went by, and on 17

March 1974 Raimund von Hofmannsthal wrote to Clarissa from the London Clinic:

Dear Clarissa,

I was already in a bad way when your letter came on the day you suggested to meet at Claridge's. I could not let you know I was not coming. I have been here in the Clinic since, and tomorrow, Monday, I have a nasty operation. Please call me up at the end of the week, siesta time, 2–4, is the safest. Otherwise Pamela will know how I am. I shall be here at least three weeks so I hope you can come once or twice and bring a picnic lunch. They only serve tea or coffee.

I long to know how you are and what happened.
Love R.

On the envelope Clarissa wrote: 'Hofmannsthal last letter'. Two days later a telegram arrived at Alvediston: I WOULD LIKE YOU TO KNOW THAT RAIMUND DIED PEACEFULLY LAST NIGHT LOVE LIZ. It was 20 March 1974, marked in Clarissa's diary with a simple +. Raimund was nearly sixty-eight. Clarissa attended his memorial service at St Peter's, Eaton Square, on 3 April. Anthony did not accompany her.

★ ★ ★ ★ ★

Money running short, Clarissa sold Anthony's Monet of the Seine frozen in the hard winter of 1880 at Sotheby's. The Avons visited Gibraltar at the end of January 1975, staying there for most of February; they were back at the Lahey Clinic in Boston in May. As new leader of the Conservative Party, Margaret Thatcher was keen to visit Lord Avon. She arrived by helicopter on 28 August 1975. In November Clarissa's brother, Peregrine, mentioned that Anthony 'got very depressed these days – it's amazing he's still alive'.[29] He was suffering mild and infrequent fevers, and was diagnosed with carcinoma of the prostate.

On 5 April 1976 the Avons returned from a long winter in the United States, staying as usual with Averell Harriman and his wife Pamela, their days peppered with encounters with the likes of Mr and Mrs Douglas Fairbanks, Mrs Dean Acheson, and Mrs George Bush.

Anthony much appreciated the kindness shown to him, the comfort, the private plane that brought them from Miami, and the heated swimming-pool in which it was possible to swim whatever the weather. He saw guests for lunch, but dined in bed and there were numerous visits by the doctor.

The medical appointments did not relent on their return. Sometimes Anthony went every other day either to Salisbury or to Southampton. The drugs he was taking caused complications. 'The difficulty is over my blood following on the drugs I have been taking for the cancer. If they give me too much Warfarin (rat poison!) there is danger of haemorrhage; if they do not give me enough, the blood clots reappear.'[30] Dr Braasch from Boston diagnosed: 'His alkaline phosphatase was markedly elevated, probably due to widespread bone metastasis.'[31]

That year Anthony's last and most readable book, *Another World*, was published. The reviews were favourable, though Roy Jenkins criticised the military part. Anthony did not read that review but commented: 'What he knows about that topic from personal experience would not go very far.'[32] That particularly hot summer was enlivened by visits from Edward Heath, and Field Marshal Sir Gerald Templer with his wife. Once a week Clarissa 'clocked in', as she put it, to visit Cecil Beaton, recovering from the serious stroke which laid him low in 1974.

Anthony was well enough to attend the Garter ceremony, at which Harold Wilson was installed on 14 June.* They stayed the night before with Lord Caccia, provost of Eton, and his wife. Anthony summoned Lord Mountbatten from Windsor to pick a bone with him over remarks he had made to the author Robert Lacey about Suez. Mountbatten, ever the interferer, had briefed Lacey anonymously and Lacey had assured him that it would not be possible to identify him. Mountbatten's hand was all too evident. Mountbatten wrote to Lacey telling him that Lord Avon had protested most violently over his (in fact Mountbatten's) suggestion that the Queen had disapproved of his Suez policy. He told him that Lord Avon was threatening legal action.[33]

---

* The columnist, Bernard Levin, was in the congregation. 'I couldn't resist seeing Harold Wilson in a floppy hat,' he said.

On the Monday, Anthony sat next to the Queen Mother at the Garter lunch in the Waterloo Chamber. The Queen Mother looked across at the Queen and Wilson seated side by side, clearly enjoying each other's company. 'Isn't it wonderful,' said the Queen Mother, 'how she's tamed him?'[34] I observed Lord Avon entering and leaving St George's Chapel that day:

> The Duke of Beaufort modestly helped poor old Lord Avon, leaning on an elegant cane, with a fringe now, and a blotchy – possibly cancer-ridden seventy-nine-year-old face – and whom I was most surprised to see there. He has lost his sparkle. One year he was chattering away about how fine the sight was going down the steps. This year he came to the door and struggled to put his hat on, which he shouldn't have done. Gallant of him to come . . .[35]

On 7 July Anthony entertained Leonard Mosley,* a roving reporter, journalist and prolific author, but something of a maverick. He had visited the Avons over the years, even in Barbados. He told Lord Avon that he was looking well. 'I'm not, you know,' he said. 'I'm going to die. They have found a miracle drug for my cancer. But, alas, it clots the blood. One therefore prepares for the inevitable.' Mosley admired 'the cool, calm, considered serenity with which he was preparing for his end'.[36]

There were a handful more guests in July – his nephew, Fulke Warwick, Robert Carr and his wife, and Sir Alick Downer, the former High Commissioner for Australia, and his wife, then no more.

On 20 October the Avons left Britain for Bermuda, moving to Boston on 2 November where Anthony went immediately to the NE Baptist Hospital for tests which showed cancer of the prostate and in the chest, but under control. On 10 December they flew on to West Palm Beach to stay at Hobe Sound with the Harrimans, who arrived with Winston and Minnie Churchill on Boxing Day. Anthony weakened rapidly, suffering increasing pain. He got up for an hour or so each day and walked in the sunshine on two sticks. Anthony and Averell Harriman reminisced about the politics of the

---

* Leonard Mosley (1913–92), author of numerous books, including biographies of Emperor Haile Selassie of Ethiopia, Emperor Hirohito of Japan, and in 1978 of the Dulles family, including John Foster Dulles.

past and the politics of that time too. Anthony dictated a letter to Robert Carr:

> I have unhappily some dismal news about health. Every effort has been made by Lahey Clinic & others without coming to any firm conclusions about the cause of my troubles. Meanwhile I have too much pain & a partial return of my old bile duct trouble. We simply do not know how things will turn out, though we are being shown much kindness . . .

In his own hand Anthony added: 'Of course the above information is to be kept for ourselves. At the same time neither C nor I wish to spread optimistic information which is without foundation, as is unhappily the truth about myself at present.'[37]

Suddenly, on 31 December, Anthony's condition deteriorated. Dr John W. Norcross from the Lahey Clinic in Boston (where he had been treated before) flew down to see him on 2 January 1977. It was clear that he was gravely ill. He wanted to die in the land of his birth, but he was too ill to take a commercial flight. The family contacted the Prime Minister, James Callaghan, who sent an RAF VC10 to Palm Beach International Airport, Florida, and they were flown overnight to RAF Lyneham, arriving on the morning of Sunday, 9 January. Anthony was taken off the plane on a stretcher, semi-conscious and driven to Alvediston in a convoy of two ambulances. The press followed every move of the two-hour journey, noting that the ambulances slowed on sharp bends and on the rough roads over Salisbury Plain. There were even cameras poking over the wall to the Manor House. Anthony was carried into his home on a stretcher, in heavy rain. Clarissa was photographed outside, with a white hat under an umbrella.

Dr Richard Bayliss, the Queen's doctor saw him. So did Dr Christopher Brown from Broadchalke. Daily bulletins were issued. He was sleeping peacefully. He was getting weaker. Anthony died at 11.11 a.m. on 14 January 1977. The Queen immediately sent a message of sympathy to Clarissa from Sandringham:

> I am much distressed to hear of the death of Lord Avon. As a gallant soldier in the First World War and as a statesman in the Second, and

in many years of peace he gave outstanding service to his country. He will be remembered in history above all as an outstanding diplomat and as a man of courage and integrity.

The Duke of Edinburgh joins me in sending our sincere sympathy to you and to Nicholas.

The *Daily Express* rang Cecil Beaton, then recovering slowly, and he said: 'Clarissa has given up her life to care for him. She had no maids or outside nursing staff to help her. Life has been very difficult, but she never complained.'[38]

The numerous extensive obituaries hailed him as the last of the great statesmen on the international stage and a fine Foreign Secretary. Not all the press was favourable. *The Guardian* produced a spiteful headline: 'A lonely man and a disaster'. The article that followed made the point that was made so often:

> It is one of the personal tragedies of the twentieth century that Anthony Eden should be remembered for a single blunder in the century's second half than for the great deal of good that he did in the first.[39]

Leonard Mosley, who had lunched with Anthony in the summer, was quick to turn on him, partly because he was writing a book on the Dulles family. He described him as a broken man, who should be blamed not praised:

> Because even on his last days on earth, Eden remained blind to the monumental nature of his great error. In our last conversations together he continued to insist that it was not his own stupidity which brought disaster upon us in 1956, but the evil machinations of Dulles and his cohorts in Washington.
>
> Rancour came into his voice as he spoke to me about it. He had been right, right, right in everything he had done . . .[40]

In my own diary, I more or less got the message:

> He died at his own house, surrounded by his own 'Garden of Eden'. The news media were not quite sure what to do, I felt. In tributes they

described him as 'a great Foreign Secretary'. His premiership was at the time of Suez, 'which ended ingloriously'. Later in the day there was a certain amount on the television and radio. Lords Butler and Selwyn-Lloyd looked senile but spoke well. I had forgotten how long Anthony Eden had been at the centre of the life of the nation. He was of course a debonair figure as well.[41]

PART FOUR

18. BOHEMIAN WIDOWHOOD

'She has her place in history'
Kenneth Rose

Lord Avon's funeral was a family one in the church at Alvediston on Monday, 17 January. Two cars followed the hearse. In the first were Clarissa and Nicholas, now the 2nd Earl of Avon. In the second was Winston Churchill (the Prime Minister's grandson). Clarissa followed the coffin, her arm resting on that of her stepson. There were thirty-two members of the family in the church. Anthony was lowered into his grave in the churchyard.

Tributes were paid in the House of Lords and the House of Commons. James Callaghan, the Prime Minister, cited 'the matchless care and devotion of Lady Avon'. Margaret Thatcher, Leader of the Opposition, went further: 'Lady Avon, herself a remarkably gifted person, had dedicated her time to caring for him. To her we can only offer sympathy and admiration, however inadequate these feelings may seem in proportion to her grievous loss.'[1] Both Houses then adjourned despite a mean-spirited protest from Dennis Skinner, the Labour MP for Bolsover, complaining that the tributes had taken up valuable parliamentary time. In the media, Kenneth Rose was the most forthcoming in his praise of Clarissa:

> For his widow there will be more than the usual measure of sympathy. The niece of Sir Winston Churchill, she brought to their marriage a Churchillian stamina and affection which never faltered, even at the darkest moments of her husband's political life. She rekindled for him, moreover, that early interest in the arts – particularly in modern paint-ing – which his career had almost extinguished. Like Lady Churchill

and Mrs Gladstone, to mention only two of the great ladies of Downing Street, she has her place in history.[2]

Nicholas stayed with Clarissa until 19 January. Lord Avon's Garter banner was presented at evensong in St George's Chapel on 8 February. As the service ended, some Military Knights left the Quire, collected the banner and marched it up to the high altar rail, the stomp of their boots audible before they came into view. They gave the banner to the Dean, and he laid it on the altar. This simple act had been devised by George VI, and was less medieval than the robed procession each June. Clarissa was moved by it and greatly preferred it to the Garter ceremony. She presented the banner to Birmingham University.

Nicholas helped Clarissa organise the great memorial service in Westminster Abbey on 15 February, at which the Queen was represented by Earl Mountbatten of Burma, sent as a Knight of the Garter. The Queen Mother, Princess Alice, Duchess of Gloucester and Princess Alice, Countess of Athlone, were also represented. Five prime ministers attended – James Callaghan, Harold Macmillan, Lord Home of the Hirsel, Harold Wilson and Edward Heath, as well as Clarissa's Aunt Clemmie, along with a massive representation of diplomats, peers (including my aunt, by then in the House of Lords), MPs and members of the aristocracy. On 17 June she gave a big party at Alvediston for Edens and Churchills, on what would have been Anthony's eightieth birthday. Even her brother Johnny was invited.

There remained one last link to Clarissa's childhood from the earlier generation. In September she called on Aunt Clemmie, then living in a flat in Prince's Gate. Clemmie had been in declining health for some time and had been obliged to sell some of Sir Winston's paintings to make ends meet. On 12 December she lunched with her secretary at home, then died of a sudden heart attack. She was ninety-two. Clarissa attended the funeral at Holy Trinity, Brompton, on 15 December and the committal at Bladon the following day, after which there was the traditional lunch at Blenheim Palace. She was also present at the huge memorial service in Westminster Abbey the following January.

Not long after her death, Clemmie became the subject of controversy when it was revealed that she had commanded the destruction of Graham Sutherland's 1954 portrait of Sir Winston. In one of the tributes her daughter Mary Soames had written: 'One of Clemmie's principal characteristics was her impetuosity. She loved instant action and felt frustrated by procrastinations or delays.' As Frank Giles, editor of *The Sunday Times,* commented: 'We now know just what these words mean.'[3] In her biography of Clemmie, Mary was keen to point out that this not her only act of art vandalism: 'Although Clemmie greatly admired Sickert's work, and although he was a friend from her girlhood days, this had not deterred her from putting her foot through a sketch he had done of Winston some time around 1927.'[4] So that made it all right, then.

Lord Goodman

Early in Clarissa's widowhood, the mighty figure of Lord Goodman loomed. By then he was a respected negotiator, and known as an altruistic helper to members of the establishment and aristocracy – a universal fixer. As a formidable lawyer, he had defended Labour politicians, including Richard Crossman and Aneurin Bevan, in a famous libel case against the *Spectator*, in which they perjured themselves, and had become close to Harold Wilson. He had been sent out to negotiate with Ian Smith after he declared independence in Rhodesia. He would defend Jeremy Thorpe at the time of his trial in 1979. He was chairman of the Arts Council and numerous public bodies. Later he would be a conciliator between the Prince and Princess of Wales when their marriage broke down. In many ways he was at the opposite end of the spectrum from the Avons. Despite refusing to appear on television 'his huge frame registered with the public'.[5] *Private Eye* dubbed him 'Two Dinners'. For his obituary Clarissa wrote:

> He was essentially a man of peace, believing that few problems were incapable of solution, given only patience and goodwill and a willingness to compromise. Humour was a powerful weapon in his armoury. His clarity of mind enabled him to dispose of work in a fraction of the time required by others. He was in most respects rather larger than life.[6]

Clarissa was newly widowed, grappling with Anthony's affairs and her own. Significantly, and possibly alarmingly, Goodman had entered the lives of Sue Hammerson* and Ann Fleming at exactly this point, after the recent loss of their husbands. None of these ladies were familiar with the ways of probate, tax, insurance, or the finer points of wills and they all needed their personal finances resolved. Lord Goodman was a godsend, or so it seemed.

His relationship with Clarissa began formally, but at some point between June and September 1977, letters addressed to 'Lady Avon' and signed 'Goodman' became 'Dear Clarissa' and 'Yours ever, Arnold'. Invitations to the opera and to University College, Oxford, materialised and not long afterwards, a closer loving relationship developed.

Ann Fleming had recommended Goodman to Clarissa. Soon after Ian died, he had rescued Ann from her solicitors, found her a new doctor and invited her to the National Theatre. He became her closest friend in her later years. He even asked her to marry him shortly before she died on 12 July 1981. No one thought it was a sexual relationship, but they were close. Then he arrived in Clarissa's life and was soon resolving issues in connection with Anthony's will and insurance. He redrafted her will for her in September 1979 and she granted him a power of attorney in January 1980. The social and cultural invitations followed. Clarissa attended Jewish evenings with him on the grounds that few of her friends would see them there together. By 1979, as an outsider, I was aware of intense rivalry over him between Ann Fleming and Clarissa. This had prompted Lady Diana Cooper to nickname Clarissa 'Countess Dracula'. When Clarissa was on a visit to Australia in 1978 she wrote to him cryptically: 'I hope you've straightened things out with Ann & not hoped that nature will take its course, because it won't . . .'[7]

Soon after becoming a friend of Clarissa's in 1980, I met Lord Goodman. She took me to *Un Ballo in Maschera* at Covent Garden in January 1981. A small group went on to dinner with him afterwards

---

* Sarah (Sue) Waterman Hammerson, OBE (1914–2014), married 1938, Lewis Hammerson (1916–58), founder of Hammerson plc, one of the largest property companies in the United Kingdom. Sue and Arnold were soon close, telephoning each other on alternate mornings and even discussed marriage. The Hammersons had three children, two sons, David (1941–2023), Peter (1945–2021), and a daughter, Patricia (born 1943).

in the Savoy Grill, where he had a table, and for whom they opened the double doors to admit him. My first-hand impression was: 'His trousers come up to his breast, so that there are two buttons of shirt visible, where most men would have four. He wears a very thin tie.'[8] His voice was somewhat falsetto. They asked me about my recent book on Gladys Deacon:

> When I said that once Gladys* had thrown a glass of water over me, Lord Goodman said: 'It seems to me you paid a heavy price for your interest.' . . .
>
> He said that politicians eventually made fools of themselves on television. If they were wise, they would never appear. They didn't have to, but nobody has yet refused. I agree with him. People get thrown out, not voted in, so it's best to stay quiet.[9]

Lord Goodman loved the opera and was a considerable support to Covent Garden. At the end of a performance when dead bodies were piled up on the stage, covered with blood, he was inclined to say: 'There's nothing here that a good lawyer couldn't straighten out.'[10]

All Eden had wanted to do was to leave Clarissa well off. His pocket diaries chart financial transactions in minute detail, day by day. But there was concern. He only left £82,670. Lord Goodman came up with a plan to help Clarissa financially. He wasted no time in fixing a deal with Sue Hammerson. His plan was that Mrs Hammerson would buy furniture, pictures, silver and books from the Manor House, Alvediston, allowing Clarissa to keep these until she died. The original price, £250,000 in December 1978 was reduced to £231,054 by 14 February 1979. Payments were to be made in five annual instalments, four of £50,000 and one of £31,054.

Clarissa agreed to keep the items in good condition, to repair them if damaged, to resolve any issues if they were stolen, to insure them, not to dispose of any, not to lend them to any individuals, or to exhibitions without consent, and to have her executors release the chattels as soon after her death as feasible. A long schedule accompanied this

---

* I had told them about my visits to Gladys, Duchess of Marlborough, in St Andrew's Hospital, Northamptonshire. The glass of water was a low point in otherwise enjoyable encounters.

letter of agreement listing all the items and also clarifying which pieces were not part of the deal – mainly books and memorabilia connected with the Eden family.

In the schedule there was a considerable collection of Regency and Chippendale furniture. The most important picture was the Braque that Anthony had bought for Clarissa, but other paintings were by Picasso, Corot, Degas, Segonzac and Derain, not to mention works by Gwen John, Eric Gill, Jean-François Millet and Duncan Grant. There was a large quantity of antique silver, and many books, the most valuable being five volumes of *Flora Londinensis* by Curtis, Graves and Hooker, bound in full morocco.

Civil terms were more or less maintained between Clarissa and Mrs Hammerson over the long years that followed, though inevitably tetchiness crept in from time to time. A Troubetzkoy loaned to John Eden, was a point of contention. And there were issues that had to be discussed, mainly relating to insurance as the value of the items increased considerably. For example, between 1978 and 1993, the valuation of the Braque rose from £27,000 to £125,000. After Clarissa died it sold for £378,000. In the end the contents of her apartment were sold at Christie's for £2,702,196, the bulk of which went to the Hammerson family.

In conclusion, the Hammersons got a good deal, though they had to wait over forty years to realise it. Sue Hammerson never got the chattels because she died in 2014 just shy of her hundredth birthday.* Then one of her sons died of Covid in 2021. Clarissa lived on and on, way beyond anyone's expectations.

Clarissa kept Alvediston until 1984 but did not have a flat in London. At first she took rooms in the Cheyne Walk home of Nuala Allason. She gave dinner parties there for Mrs Thatcher and Walter Annenberg, one time American Ambassador, and his wife. At one such evening the diplomat, Sir Charles Johnston, whose wife Natasha was not well enough to come out late, found himself next to Mrs Allason: 'an ambitious, managing sort of lady, once married to a dull MP', who loaded him with flattery: 'But you're famous.'[11] In his diary Johnston noted 'Clarissa-isms'. In July 1982 he invited her to lunch

---

* She and Lord Goodman came to the Manor House, Alvediston, when it was sold in 1984, and she took some items. Clarissa took the rest to her London apartment.

on a Friday to help him entertain Vic Garland, the new Australian High Commissioner. She said: 'Just let me look in my book and see if I've got any engagements in London on Thursday. No, I haven't – so I'll be going down to the country then. There's no point in staying on an extra day in London – *for nothing.*' She did not understand why Sir Charles roared with laughter. He commented:

> With those icy blue eyes and a certain formality of manner, she seems the typical grand English dame of American and European legend. In fact, she isn't like that at all. One dines with her, and the place is full of Chinese and Indians she has picked up on her tours; they have done things for her out there, and she has said, 'You *must* come when you are in London', but untypically, she has really meant it.[12]

Later Clarissa took a lease on a flat in Montagu Square, before moving to her last home at 32 Bryanston Square. This was on the Portman Estate, on the recommendation of Lord Goodman. Whether he secured a good deal for her, or for himself, is unclear.

Clarissa stayed loyal to Arnold Goodman until he died. After Ann Fleming's death in the summer of 1981, she had him to herself. He never married. She was to the fore in organising a celebration for his seventieth birthday on 21 August 1983. It was decided to present him with a glass goblet engraved by Laurence Whistler, with a book containing the names of those who contributed to the present. Any surplus funds were to go to his charitable trust. Contributions flooded in, many expressing gratitude for his past kindnesses.

On 21 December 1986 there was a gala to honour him at the Coliseum, he having been chairman of the English National Opera for many years. Clarissa was part of an A-list gala committee. He was delighted at the prospect of the occasion, which was attended by Princess Alexandra, Lord and Lady Harewood and numerous VIPs. John Mortimer wrote the script for the gala. In February 1987 Sir Leonard Hoffmann reported that it netted £75,000 for the ENO. Lord Goodman was moved by the trouble everyone had taken on his behalf.

On his eightieth birthday Clarissa arranged a dinner party on Sunday, 22 August 1993. Princess Alexandra and Angus Ogilvy were among the guests, as were Edward Heath, Isaiah Berlin and Rupert

Murdoch. Clarissa was disappointed with the encomia. Kenneth Rose put a more positive spin on them in his *Sunday Telegraph* column, Albany: 'If it was a triumph for Goodman, so it was too for his friend and inspired impresario Lady Avon, who organised the entire affair in Lincoln's Inn with the same panache she brought to Number 10 nearly 40 years ago. She produced a harmonious seating plan, chose a delicious dinner with two Rothschild wines and saw that there was no undue exuberance of oratory.'[13]

The curious thing about the relationship between Clarissa and Arnold Goodman is that apart from the opera, the sparkling conversation and the advice he was on hand to offer (and it was frequently needed), she must have detested the residential seaside hotels he liked to stay in for the odd holiday. Yet she accompanied him on those depressing excursions, once again showing the quality of devotion that lurked beneath a cool exterior.

The later years were not kind to Lord Goodman. By the early spring of 1994 a leg had been amputated due to diabetes and he had trouble remembering names. He was confined to a wheelchair for the rest of his life. Clarissa confided the problems about this to me. She was not a relation so others took over. She volunteered: 'I sometimes think I should have married him.'[14]

Lord Goodman died on 12 May 1995, aged eighty-one. Some obituaries mentioned Ann Fleming and Clarissa as close female friends, though *The Times* judged he was probably closest to the older brother who predeceased him. There was a memorial service at the Liberal Jewish Synagogue in St John's Wood on 19 June with eulogies from Lord Annan and Sir Evelyn de Rothschild. Clarissa received many letters of sympathy. All stressed what a wonderful friend she had been to him, while recognising that his death had been a merciful release from pain and suffering. In 1996 she visited the Goodman School in Jerusalem, but was shocked that some children had sprayed graffiti on the wall of the brand new school hall.

Clarissa consistently turned down requests from biographers to talk about Goodman, unwilling to reveal that part of her life in widowhood. She refused Iris Freeman, who died before completing her work, and she would not cooperate with Dr Brian Brivati, even when he tried to provoke her help by saying that his book was being informed by Goodman's accusers, rather than his defenders. In June

1999, when allegations arose about Goodman's dealings with the Portman Estate, she wrote to David Astor: 'Is there any progress in refuting the story about Arnold now that Portman is dead?'[15]

* * * * *

Sarah Churchill, one-time runaway bride, died on 24 September 1982. Clarissa had observed her drunk at the sixtieth birthday dinner for Christopher Soames at the Ritz two years before, being carried out by her sister Mary, single-handedly over her shoulder, 'her legs dangling like a puppet'.[16] She wrote to Mary: 'So it has come to an end at last. I am sure you have had a heart-breaking time & have shouldered it all magnificently. I always thought Sarah had the greatest possible charm & allure & it was tragic to see how she literally destroyed herself . . .'[17]

Nicholas Avon died of AIDS on 17 August 1985, only eight years after his father. He had been in the Territorial Army, had enjoyed being appointed a Deputy Lieutenant for London, specifically for Kensington and Chelsea, and later a Lord-in-Waiting, and Under Secretary of State for the Environment. While his father was alive, much of his time was spent representing him at memorial services, which he appeared to enjoy. He ran a successful restaurant called Nick's. He and Clarissa were on the best of terms and were regularly in touch. She had not been pleased when Sara Morrison had been quoted saying he was gay – and many of his colleagues were greatly shocked when his death became headline news in the *News of the World*.[18] Margaret Thatcher wrote from Downing Street, and in a reply to a telegram from the Queen Mother, Clarissa wrote: 'As you can imagine, he was an ideal stepson . . . It is an additional sadness that his life sd have been cut short just when he was starting to do so well in the Lords.'[19] Clarissa arranged his funeral, the headstone and the memorial service. This was held at St Margaret's, Westminster, on 12 November. The Queen, the Queen Mother, Princess Alice, Duchess of Gloucester, Princess Alexandra and his friend from earlier days, Prince Henrik of Denmark, were represented.

Neither Clarissa nor Peregrine visited their brother, Johnny, in his last days, when he suffered from cancer of the throat. As far back as 1948 Peregrine had warned Clarissa that she and Johnny were 'too temperamentally different' to reconcile. This was not helped by

'misunderstandings over small things' that had grown out of proportion.[20] The incident in 1955 had been the last straw. Johnny died in
London on 23 June 1992. Clarissa attended his funeral.

In 1995 Winston Churchill sold the papers of his grandfather, Sir
Winston, in the Churchill Archive Settlement for £12.5 million, a
controversial business. Peregrine argued that part of that settlement
should rightfully belong to his side of the family because 'The Jennie
Papers', the papers of Lady Randolph Churchill, had belonged in
equal parts to his father Jack and to Winston. As ever it was a complicated legal issue. After Lady Randolph died in 1921, Winston took
most of her furniture and books to Chartwell, which he had just
bought. Jack took the Jennie Papers and the French books first to the
house in Cromwell Road, and later to the one in Regent's Park.
When that house was bombed in 1940, Jack, Clarissa and Peregrine
rescued what they could and the items were stored partly at Chartwell
and partly in Clarissa's flat in Rossmore Court. Some of those papers
were made available to Randolph Churchill when he was writing his
father's biography and became mixed up with the others. Suffice it to
say that the Jennie Papers were valued by Sotheby's in 1995 at between
£4.5 million and £6 million, none of which came to Peregrine,
Clarissa or to Sally, as Johnny's daughter. Sally's husband, Lord
Ashburton, assisted with legal fees but nothing came of it. Going to
court was considered unwise.

Clarissa was upset by this situation, but wished to avoid a public
quarrel with the Churchill family. She was unsure that anyone could
establish the exact ownership. Her proposal was that Pamela Harriman
should be asked to adjudicate. In January 1997 Winston offered
£250,000 as a full and final settlement and pointed out that Peregrine
had removed some Lord Randolph papers from Cambridge and sold
them for his own personal gain. Winston's line was that there was
£400,000 on offer. Eventually, unknown to Sally and others, Clarissa
wrote to young Winston, proposing to settle her part of it for
£100,000 because she needed the money. He agreed and paid her in
instalments of £20,000.

Peregrine died on 19 March 2002. Winston wrote to his widow,
Yvonne, and she replied bitterly: 'We are on different roads now. We
have <u>nothing</u> in common after your infamy.' Yvonne was never less
than nervous, even terrified, of Clarissa. This I had witnessed for

myself when I drove Clarissa to their home in Vernham Street for lunch. Yvonne kept diving into the kitchen and asking me, 'Is it going all right?' She died on 13 December 2010 and was buried at Bladon on 28 May 2011. I drove Clarissa to and from Bladon and Blenheim that day, and she showed me her mother's grave at Begbroke.

In contrast, figures from the past popped up unexpectedly. One such was the artist and painter John Merton, best remembered today for his meticulously painted triple portrait of Diana, Princess of Wales. He had been at Balliol and had known Clarissa way back in the 1930s. They used to sit out at dances together, and during her London season she had even asked him to declare his feelings. He had told her he loved her. At one time he had planned to paint her, but this idea was squashed by her mother. After Peregrine's funeral in 2002, Merton got in touch with Clarissa. He was eighty-nine and she was eighty-two. In 2003 he attempted to invite her to a private view of his pictures. The next year he pressed her to come and lunch with him at the Savile Club (not her sort of place). He reminded her that she had given him some Beethoven records when he married.

He tried to extract Clarissa's address from Nathalie Brooke.[*] She told him that when someone had been as beautiful as Clarissa had been in youth, they did not always wish to be seen in old age. Somewhat tactlessly, he passed this on to Clarissa, adding that he did not in the least mind what she looked like now. Nathalie described him as a 'SUPER-BORE' and refused to give him Clarissa's address, which infuriated him. But he found it and went on pressing her with invitations to lunch at the Savile Club. Finally Clarissa had had enough:

> I am really sad to have to say this to you, but I cannot lunch with you.
>
> I am truly sorry if I now offend you. We have nothing to say to each other. I am sure you realise this yourself and I wish you a happy life.
>
> Love Clarissa[21]

---

[*] Nathalie Brooke (1923-2019), daughter of Count Constantine Benckendorff, and widow of Humphrey Brooke, Secretary of the Royal Academy.

The most interesting aspect of this exchange is that she kept a Xerox copy of her reply.*

Travel

At the same time as seeking to resolve her finances and establishing a new base in London, Clarissa resumed many aspects of life that she had put aside while devoting herself to Anthony's care. As early as March 1977, she accepted an invitation from Aline Berlin, Isaiah's rich wife, to visit Israel. Later she wrote to Aline:

> Now that I have got into a different ambience I can realise more clearly than ever what a feat you performed for me during our week in Israel. Apart from the drudgery of organisation you coped with such kindness with my deadweight non-reacting mopiness. I some-times felt it wd surely make you impatient, though you never showed it, for which I admire you more than I can say.

She loved Israel: 'My feelings are perfectly genuine & perfectly dura-ble.'[22] Israel became a key point of call. She went back with Hugh Fraser in September 1978, after which she made a speech to the Conservative Friends of Israel, expressing her deep admiration for the country and saying how proud she was that Britain had created the state of Israel through the Balfour Declaration. She returned again with George Weidenfeld in April 1981 for the Jerusalem Book Fair. She became involved with the Ben-Gurion University of the Negev, at first from an interest in their desert research programme. She visited again in 1984 and 1988.

In November 1982 she went to New York on behalf of the Ben-Gurion University. By this time she was describing herself as a Zionist, and referring to Israel as 'the great romantic achievement of the 20th century'.[23] She spoke in New York and Boston at fundraising lunches in aid of the University's Scholarship Fund.

After her first trip to Israel she went to Siena and Rome and on to Tunisia: 'The country looks ravishing & we have seen dozens of lovely things, but I look at it all in a haze of hostility.'[24] She spent a month between New York, Washington and Blue Mountain Lake

* John Merton's wife died in 2009. He died aged ninety-seven in 2011.

between 13 July and 10 August (meeting Dr Henry Kissinger among others) and then in September she went to Italy for ten days. At the end of October she was in Paris.

Anne Glenconner invited Clarissa to a large house party with Princess Margaret at Glen, the Tennants' home in Scotland. Nicholas Courtney, Colin's biographer, was one of the guests:

> We went off in a minivan to the Edinburgh Festival. I was sitting next to Clarissa. Being a well-brought up lad I tried to make conversation. After a time with absolutely no response I was determined to find something to interest her. Total failure. When we arrived, Rupert Loewenstein [one time banker to the Rolling Stones], who was sitting behind us, said: 'Never have I heard anyone try so hard and receive so little response!' Princess Margaret, who was in front, overheard Rupert, put in: 'I often have that problem too!'[25]

Clarissa's mission was to see as much of the world as she could while she was still able to move easily, and even when mobility was an issue. She invariably found a friend to travel with her. She would alert the Foreign Office, so that they knew where she was going and could advise her that it was safe. Invariably this led to high-level diplomatic hospitality. The first big trip was to Australia with Mrs Coleman Glover (originally met in Hobe Sound) in the early months of 1978. They travelled to many parts, invariably staying in Government Houses, while Clarissa's status as a Prime Minister's widow ensured that the Governor General and the Prime Minister did their bit. Smart Australians jumped forward to entertain her, and Lady Casey remembered her from Garter ceremonies at Windsor.* She stayed at Jimbour House in Queensland: 'I am spending – and wish I wasn't – a weekend at this place, which is like a Tennessee Williams play, loopy son and all.'[26] From there she wrote to Lord Goodman:

> I have really jammed everything in all through Australia, thanks to all those Government Houses & their infinite facilities – with several

---

* Lady Casey had been delighted to meet Clarissa at the Garter Ceremony in 1969, 'on that enthralling day'. Anthony had looked 'so well and handsome'. (Maie Casey to Clarissa, June 1969).

sidekicks to the outback which I loved – even to Broken Hill where
I went one mile down the mine, no women allowed but me &
Margaret Thatcher – it brings bad luck to the miners. I expect you
forgot to tell your friend Murdoch to see me – anyway I haven't.
The Prime Minister [Malcolm Fraser] (conceited, arrogant, shy)
seemed to have the foreign sec. looks like Hollywood, & his wife has
left him for 'a Brit' they say continually. Sir Zelman [Cowen] came
through with a dinner for 50 in Canberra, followed by a tête-à-tête
the next day. He is a sweet man but rather boring.[27]

Presently she wrote to her secretary that she had now 'had about
enough of Australia, though it has all been a tremendous success thanks
to Sir Alick Downer's planning – & look forward to one more exotic part
next week, though having lived in the lap of luxury at all the Government
Houses etc we find hotels very complicated & expensive'.[28] She and Mrs
Glover went on to Indonesia, Bali, Singapore (invited to dinner by the
Prime Minister, Lee Kuan Yew), then to Malaysia and India.

Between 18 August and 1 September Clarissa visited Leningrad
and the Caucasus. Of this trip Marina Berry* (with whom she had
come from the opera on that Weidenfeld night in 1979) kept an illus-
trated diary. Clarissa travelled in a group of sixteen, led by Laurence
Kelly. Most of the others she did not know, but she certainly knew
the formidable and potentially forbidding Nathalie Brooke, who
acted as courier, or 'gruppenfuhrer, matron, hostess and mother', as
Marina put it, 'with such even temper'. One of Nathalie's particular
trials was looking out for Mr Bartsch from Minneapolis, a keen
gardener who was skilled at getting lost.

Clarissa had corralled Nuala Allason, then her London landlady, to
accompany her. Mrs Allason, being blonde, was forever being whisked
onto the dance floor by Russians in restaurants. Marina thought her
'as vain as a peacock'. She described her as Clarissa's 'friend and
companion'. In reality Clarissa could not stand her. In 1983 she said
to me: 'Everything is cold and calculated. Even when someone is
chewing her ear-lobe, she's thinking of the next move.'[29]

* Marina Berry, daughter of C. L. Sulzberger (1912–93), whose family owned the
New York Times. In 1967 she married the Hon. Adrian Berry (1937–2016), later 4th
Viscount Camrose.

Marina described Clarissa:

Clarissa is a marvellous eagle of a woman, in some ways very demanding in her expectations of perfect service and '*les petits soins*'. As she
herself put it: 'I'm not very matey', but she was extremely good
company, very funny and also very gallant. Although she complained
merrily about cockroaches and spiders and the lack of room service or
inedible food, she never once sighed about her arthritic hip which one
could see was giving her pain from the way she limped and had to sit
down frequently.

At one point Marina, Mrs Allason and Clarissa submitted to a massage
by a woman with but one tooth. Clarissa thought it would help to have
her hip gently rubbed, but the old woman grinned her one tooth, and
went on scrubbing: 'She scrubbed and Clarissa squealed and I nearly
drowned in the bath I was laughing so hard.' In a hotel in Pyatigorsk,
Clarissa, Mrs Allason and another couple had to share a bathroom.
Clarissa frightened them to such a degree that they did not dare go near
it. As it happened, the water came out drip by drip, and hot.[30]

The designer John Stefanides was a new friend of Clarissa's. She
had met him soon after Anthony died, finding him particularly
sympathetic, cultured, stylish and enjoyable to travel with – and he
saw her point. He came out to India to join Clarissa and Teddy
Millington-Drake, who was painting there. In Calcutta all three had
their hair cut by a barber, but Clarissa suddenly remembered a meeting with the Governor of Bengal and insisted they leave. Teddy rose
from the chair, one side of his hair cut, the other shaggy. They went
by arrangement to a hotel that had been a maharajah's palace, only to
find the imposing metal gates locked with a rusty padlock. They were
forced to take refuge in a pilgrim's house, 'empty of devotees, with
beds of coiled iron springs and no mattresses'. Their driver found
them scraps to eat and, wrapped in scarves, they slept on the rusty
springs. John recalled no complaints from his travelling companions,
'by nature gold-medal complainers'. When he related this to Ali
Forbes, the comment was: 'Class will tell.'[31]

Clarissa visited Vienna with John Stefanides in 1980, and was
disappointed that the Viennese did not match Raimund von
Hofmannsthal's pre-war charm – no bowing or hand-kissing. She

travelled to China and the South Pacific with the Countess of Wilton, New York in 1982 (where I ran into her by chance in Madison Avenue), Budapest in 1983, San Francisco in 1986, Oman and the Philippines for diving in 1987, Moscow (as guest of Sir Bryan Cartledge) and Prague (with Nathalie Brooke as tour leader) in 1988, Greece in 1991 (with Julian Amery), the Danube in 1992, Syria in October 1993,* masterminded by Serena Fass, Anguilla and St Barts in 1995, Australia with Lady Poole in 1996, and Morocco in 1999, along with many visits to Paris, Berlin, Italy and St Lucia.

In China she found my aunt on a parliamentary delegation. At the top of a pagoda, Clarissa said she saw first the black velvet bows, then the veil, then the blue hair. She continually ran into her, notably at a lunch at Government House in Hong Kong. My aunt, who did not think so negatively, commented to my father that it was odd only to encounter her in China since they both lived in Wiltshire but never saw each other. When Clarissa was in Mongolia she wrote one of her splendidly negative letters – it is not clear to whom, but probably Lord Goodman – in which she succeeded in making her plight entertaining:

> This letter is prompted out of sheer discomfort. We have reached a part of Mongolia where I was told there were Buddhist caves & temples, which there are. There are also icy winds off the steppes, an unheated hotel, damp bedclothes & swarms of little padded Chinese doing, I suppose, Mongolian business. The caves tastefully overlook a coalmine going full blast. After being taken over a factory tomorrow we go back to Peking & I shall continue.
>
> Your plans for the journey were a triumph. We were wafted into first class where they have seats that make a chaise longue. The Governor of Hong Kong was interesting & charming & I gave your shirt to a tailor. It appears John Keswick is giving us his flat & car for when we pass through on the way home.
>
> We shared our particular villa at the Government Guest House with Harold Brown, late Sec for Defence in America, and I have been treated as befits my station with a banquet in my honour by the

---

* The Duke and Duchess of Wellington were also on this trip.

Foreign Affairs director, 6 p.m., 14 filthy courses, toasts, & home by 9. Was received by Madame Chou-en-lai* at the Palace of the People & made her laugh, which the Ambassador says is rare. She is very old, very plain, very squat, with exquisitely fine hands, & a spittoon at her feet.

The Forbidden City is hideous, overpainted & overcrowded, but so is everything in Peking. They are pulling the entire place down & replacing it with Soviet style blocks. Millions of Chinese dressed only in blue or green bicycle up & down, & our guide is absolutely maddening & stupid & will get on my nerves very fast. The people are not as glum as in Russia, but it is all desperately primitive & drab, and so far has no atmosphere. We sneeze every day from dust & the corners of the streets are piled with mounds of wilted cabbages for sale.

The Peking opera was a crashing, squealing cacophony interspersed with acrobatics, as if Placido Domingo in a very elaborate costume suddenly stopped singing for a minute & did a double somersault.

I have made them change the programme, leaving out Mao's birthplace & stuff like that, & we now have a gruelling 2 weeks ahead, up at 6 & going all day. The Chinese say it is extraordinary, no Chinese lady <u>of my age</u> cd be as active! I enjoyed seeing a collective farm & cross-questioning them about their artificial insemination scheme (they haven't one).

It is 7.30 in Mongolia – all I was able to eat of the meal in the barrack was some nuts & a pear. I am sitting on the sofa of my room with a vest, a bedjacket, 2 jerseys, quilted coat, rug round my body & blankets on my feet. Can't go to bed at 7.30.

In 1986 Clarissa, then aged sixty-six, took diving lessons, achieving a novice-diver certificate the following year. She undertook many winter diving trips with Vane Ivanović, a Yugoslavian diplomat and sportsman, and a pioneer in scuba diving. He introduced her to the sport and she found him 'patient, but also tough, with amateurs' like

---

* Deng Yingchao (1904–92) widow of Chou-en-lai (1898–1976), first Premier of the People's Republic of China under Mao-Tse-Tung. She was the most powerful woman politically in China.

her.[32] She went to many places with him and only stopped when he died in 1999. Knowing Clarissa's ways, she clearly preferred the underwater company of the fishes to the humans on dry land, but she took no chances. She swam with a stick to fend off dangerous-looking fish, which amused Lady Penn,* who accompanied her on one of these trips. Lady Lambton was another deep-sea diver.

Thus Clarissa saw as much of the world as possible in her widowhood years.

---

* Prudence Penn (1926–2023), wife of Sir Eric Penn, comptroller of the Lord Chamberlain's Office.

19. KEEPER OF THE FLAME

John Stefanides thought Clarissa was caught in a dilemma in later life. On the one hand she was the remote rather bohemian character she had always been, and on the other she had a position to uphold as the widow of a prime minister. She did not especially wish to attend state occasions but neither did she like to be overlooked. She was present at the Queen Mother's eightieth birthday service in St Paul's Cathedral on 15 July 1980, at the evening reception at Buckingham Palace and wedding of the Prince of Wales and Lady Diana Spencer, at dinners for the Queen's prime ministers in 1992 and 2002, and other national celebrations. Despite her dislike of the man, she even attended the ninetieth birthday party of Harold Macmillan in 1984. Because she liked them personally, she invited Princess Margaret and Princess Alexandra to her dinner parties.

Her considerable preoccupation was protecting Eden's reputation and sometimes her own. Hardly was Anthony in his grave than the slurs on his character began. The laws of libel had protected him from such attacks during his lifetime. It now fell to Clarissa to take on the fight on his behalf, which she did with considerable energy. As early as June 1978 the journalist Leonard Mosley re-emerged with an article for the *Sunday Telegraph* entitled 'A Prime Minister at Breaking Point', an extract from his forthcoming biography of John Foster Dulles.* Mosley had inveigled himself into Lord Avon's favour, stayed with them in Barbados and talked to him as recently as the summer of 1976. His book averred that Eden was in no position to handle the tensions of Nasser nationalising the Suez Canal, that he had a sharp temper, was subject to 'fits of ungovernable rage',[1] displayed 'almost

---

* Leonard Mosley, *A Biography of Eleanor, Alice and John Foster Dulles and their family network* (Hodder & Stoughton, 1978).

Pavlovian frothing at the mouth' when Nasser's name was mentioned, called the detractors of his invasion plan 'weak sisters', and lashed out when John Foster Dulles expressed his displeasure – 'He would rather the Empire fell in one crash than be eaten away by mice.'

He suggested that Macmillan kept telling Eden that 'Ike' (President Eisenhower) would lie doggo and let the British get on with it. When Anthony Nutting wanted Britain to make overtures to neighbouring Arab nations in order to isolate Nasser, Mosley wrote that Eden rang Nutting: 'What is all this poppycock you've sent me? . . . I want him [Nasser] destroyed. Can't you understand?' He did not 'give a damn' if there was anarchy in Egypt as a result. Captain Basil Liddell Hart* was asked to produce a game-plan as to how the military campaign should be conducted. Eden rejected four versions. Liddell Hart submitted the original one as the fifth. Eden was said to have thrown a heavy old-fashioned inkwell at the captain. As the blue ink covered his summer suit, Liddell Hart responded by jamming a government wastepaper basket over the Prime Minister's head. Mosley concluded that Nasser, the Soviet Union and Dulles had 'made sure that the British lion had roared for positively the last time'.[2]

On 11 June Sir Frederick Bishop attacked Mosley on the grounds that his facts contained 'some fantasy as well'. Neither he nor any of his three colleagues at Number 10 could recall the Liddell Hart encounter: 'If any such meeting took place, and it had included such extraordinary events as are described in detail . . . then we would all have been bound to know it and to be able to remember it.'[3] The author responded, as authors do, that he had checked his sources and had merely cited that as one of 'the "rumours" circulating in London at the time'.[4]

The eccentric Peter Hoos, one-time stringer on the *Londoner's Diary*, wrote to Clarissa saying that Liddell Hart had told him at the time that he had been invited in by the Prime Minister to advise on Suez and that Randolph Churchill had refuted the story: 'One can only presume that this "poppycock" helped to sell serialisation rights in his book.'[5]

Clarissa entered the fray, adding that there were no government-issue wastepaper baskets in the Cabinet Room. More importantly,

---

* Sir Basil Liddell Hart (1895-1970), military historian.

there was no evidence of a Liddell Hart plan.[6] The *Sunday Telegraph* only printed part of her letter. She ended by denying that 'poppy-cock' was one of Anthony's words: 'Poppycock is a favourite word with Mr Mosley, I believe, and I would like to borrow it to describe this conversation . . . Voltaire wrote that history is a pack of tricks we play upon the dead. How right he was.'[7]

In November 1980 Bernard Levin wrote two provocative articles in *The Times*, quoting Lord Mountbatten's views on Suez, in a six-part series he had recorded for posthumous broadcasting. The Suez episode was blocked by the Cabinet Secretary, Sir Robert Armstrong, on grounds of serious 'breaches of confidential relationships . . . some of them involving people still active in public life'.[8] Levin was incensed by the suppression. His article made it clear that Mountbatten had been against Suez, but that Eden had been determined to go ahead even though Nasser had done nothing illegal in nationalising the Canal. Lord Hailsham, then Lord Chancellor, who was mentioned, was quick to point out that 'Lord Mountbatten's memory must have played him completely false by the time that the programme was recorded'.[9] Armstrong could do no more than apologise to Clarissa.

Clarissa spent much of her later life restraining authors and editors from libelling her in their books and excising passages from letters by or to her that she wanted kept private. She exercised the right of censorship, freely offered to her by editors such as Artemis Cooper, when producing her grandfather Duff Cooper's correspondence, and Mark Amory when editing Ann Fleming's letters. Her wishes were respected. When Amory was editing Evelyn Waugh's letters, she pointed out that he often exaggerated to amuse his correspond-ents. When he was editing Ann Fleming's letters, she took advice from Lord Goodman, and wrote to Amory: 'This is really much worse than I anticipated, because I had not realized how little the general reader was likely to understand about one's ways & our jokes. Also, when you came to see me you said the book would stop at 1952 . . .' She added: 'I must say I am distressed at what the rest of the book may be like. Is all this what Ann intended & is it in her best interests?'[10]

Guy Burgess

Her earlier acquaintance with Guy Burgess caused her trouble in later life. She had been part of his set and she had known Donald Maclean in Paris in the late 1930s. James Pope-Hennessy and Burgess had had an affair in 1941, at which time Pope-Hennessy was certainly seeing a great deal of Clarissa. Some even went so far as to suggest she had been engaged to Burgess.

This became an issue when the author Barrie Penrose telephoned her in 1985 about his book, *Conspiracy of Silence*, a biography of Anthony Blunt. Penrose told her that the director of MI5, Sir Percy Sillitoe, had told the Security Service, in front of his son, 'Anthony Eden has a lot to answer for' in connection with Burgess and Maclean. He alleged that Sillitoe had told the Home Secretary that Clarissa 'must have tipped off Burgess & Maclean'. He wanted to write that around 1942/1943 Burgess was telling his mother and friends that he would marry Clarissa and that this was 'the only way out'.[11]

Clarissa informed Penrose that 'these reports were grotesque. They are absolute nonsense but also the gravest possible libel.' She threatened legal action unless he assured her that none of it would appear in his book.[12] Penrose wriggled. He told her he proposed to quote her saying: 'I hardly knew Burgess. I met him, I suppose, about half a dozen times. James Pope-Hennessy was a friend of mine and I met Burgess with him.'[13]

Clarissa was not satisfied. Lord Goodman advised her quietly in the background, but could not formally represent her as he was acting for Penrose on another legal matter. Instead she enlisted the help of Sir Max Williams of Clifford-Turner. She warned Penrose that she would have 'no hesitation is asking Sir Max to seek the protection of the law'. The book was published in 1986, and contained her line about hardly knowing Burgess, but nothing more.[14]

Much later in her life, on one of the car journeys with her niece Sally, she said she had got bored with Burgess, deeming him only interested in her because she was Winston's niece. She was unaware that he was a traitor or homosexual. She had no idea that he had been suggesting he might marry her.

The matter did not end there. On 30 August 1989 an *Evening Standard* reporter rang Clarissa to check allegations in a forthcoming book by Richard Deacon – *The Greatest Treason*. Deacon was an alias for Donald McCormick, a somewhat dodgy journalist and historian with an eye for stories involving espionage and conspiracy theories. He alleged that Burgess and Maclean had been enabled to escape to Russia 'when [Guy] Liddell tipped off the (still alive) wife of a government minister, who, herself a lesbian, was a close friend of Burgess'.[15] The implication was that this was Clarissa. The next day she issued a writ and an injunction was served against the book.

Clarissa had to prepare a detailed affidavit as plaintiff, in which, among other things, she pointed out that Anthony 'was most critical of and exasperated at the incompetence of the relevant authorities in allowing Burgess and Maclean to operate for so long undetected and to escape so easily after they had been exposed as spies'. She admitted she had met Burgess through James Pope-Hennessy during the 1939–45 war, and that she had known Maclean. She had never heard of Guy Liddell until he surfaced in books in the 1980s. She maintained (not strictly accurately) that she had met Burgess only with Pope-Hennessy and never alone. Neither had she attended 'wild parties'.

The publishers defended themselves stating that there were plenty of other wives of distinguished Conservative politicians. Clarissa drew up a list of them, including figures such as Mollie Butler, Anne Nutting and Valerie Profumo. She described the publication of the book as 'a hideous and outrageous allegation for which there is not a shred of truth'.[16] She was paid substantial damages and all her legal costs by the publishers.[17]

The allegations were, however, republished in a number of newspapers, the *Daily Express*, the *Evening Standard* and the *Sunday Correspondent*, and again in the *Glasgow Herald* on 25 September 1991 – 'in even clearer terms than in the book'. In March 1990 Patrick Moloney, QC, advised her that the point had been made in a clear victory against the publishers, and that it would be best not to stir things up with further legal action.

A curious postscript to this was a long series of rambling letters from Robin Harbinson Bryans, a casual partner of Burgess, and prolific travel writer, born in Belfast, who spent his later years accusing public figures of crimes unimaginable. In 1970 he had been imprisoned in contempt of court for three years because he threw a jug of water at a barrister in court. In the late 1980s he was living at 58 Argyle Road, a detached house in Ealing.

Clarissa received a barrage of letters from him between 1989 and 1991. Writing to her lawyer she began: 'This man has struck again . . .' but she was disinclined to prevent him from writing to her 'in order to know what he may say in the future' and also because she thought him 'obsessive & malicious & I wd not want to annoy him & thus draw his malice. So far it has suited him to be on my side.'[18]

In 1996 the author, Miranda Carter, wrote to Clarissa, seeking an interview for her forthcoming biography of Anthony Blunt. Clarissa declined: 'I only saw Anthony Blunt once, from about 10 yards' distance, and have never spoken to him.'[19] In 2005 Michael Dobbs, the politician and author, wrote to her about Burgess. She first replied that she had almost no recollection of Burgess. Dobbs pursued the matter, asking her if she could verify a story that had appeared in Peter Wright's controversially banned book, *Spycatcher*: 'that Burgess was instructed by his masters in Moscow to create a cover for his espionage activities by trying to marry you! He was, allegedly, warned off by James Pope-Hennessy brandishing a revolver.' Dobbs softened his request by stating that Wright was a 'far from unimpeachable source' and that the story appeared to have emanated from Blunt.[20] Clarissa replied: 'I have no idea whether Burgess was asked by Moscow to marry me – judge for yourself. (I have heard the story once before – perhaps from you?)'[21]

A later book on Burgess by Stewart Purvis and Jeff Hulbert in 2016 went further and quoted a letter from Burgess found in the National Archives, addressed to 'Dear Clarissa' and apologising for having given Tom Driberg Anthony Eden's letter of thanks to him for look-ing after him in Washington in November 1950.[22] This letter was illus-trated in full in Driberg's book on Burgess.[23]

There is very little to add to the Burgess issue. Clarissa had the name of Guy Burgess in the 'address book' section of her pocket diaries, listed at 5 Bentinck Street in 1941 and 1942. There are mentions of lunches and dinners with him, sometimes with James Pope-Hennessy. From 1943 she was involved with Raimund von Hofmannsthal and there was then no place for Burgess, if ever there had been one.

The Eden Biographies

In 1971 Anthony had given the bulk of his papers to Birmingham University, where he had been Chancellor. Some years after his death Clarissa sent them the remaining papers from Alvediston. She also sent them a collection of sometimes magnificent but often deeply unpractical and certainly unwanted official gifts presented to the Edens in connection with their official life. 'I handed them all over to Birmingham whether they wanted them or not,' she recalled. Clarissa was Anthony's literary executor and was consulted whenever authors wished to research in the papers.* She was invariably supportive to the many requests from biographers of other political figures, and academics assessing areas of history in which Eden had played a part. But all too often she had to rebuff allegations and smears on his character in books and TV programmes, and on her own involvement, sometimes having to resort to litigation.

A key issue was the appointment of an authorised biographer. Four biographies of Eden were published after his death. Clarissa authorised two. It had been hoped that Sir John Wheeler-Bennett[†] would be the authorised biographer but he had died in 1975. The following year she asked Isaiah Berlin's advice: 'We want an historian who will be sound but not sycophantic & with whom I will not have disagreeable or shocking relations.'[24] Martin Gilbert, then at work on his multi-volume biography of Winston Churchill, was next approached within Eden's lifetime and confirmed posthumously by the Trustees of the Avon papers on 23 March 1977. But he was so preoccupied with Churchill that Lord Goodman arranged an amicable termination of his contract. The next author was Philip Magnus. He did not last long. By July 1980 Clarissa had dropped him, citing his deteriorating eyesight. Evidently, behind Clarissa's back, Lord Goodman had approached Magnus and set up a plan whereby he would be assisted by a junior co-author, Richard Davenport-Hines, later to become a distinguished biographer, to provide him with 'the raw material which he would convert into majestic prose'. When Clarissa found

---

* In the last years of her life, when she could no longer attend to this, I took on the role on her behalf, acting as her future literary executor.

† Sir John Wheeler-Bennett (1902–75), historian and biographer of George VI.

out about this, she promptly vetoed the scheme.*[25] Shocked by this, Magnus's agent, Andrew Best, recommended the historian, Piers Brendon, but that idea did not run.

In the meantime Dr David Carlton's highly critical biography of Anthony appeared.† He had studied history at the London School of Economics and would go on to write several books with an Eden or Suez theme. Clarissa allowed him limited use of copyright material, but no access to the Avon or Churchill papers. She was unhappy about a rumour that suggested the book might have been authorised, an accusation that Carlton strenuously denied. It was a substantial work, hampered by an essential dullness, as one reviewer put it. D. R. Thorpe described it as 'a devastating critique'.[26] Gunnar Hägglof, formerly Swedish Ambassador in London, wrote indignantly to *The Times* to complain that the unpleasant exercise had been carried out 'in the spirit of a prosecuting attorney'.[27]

Sir Robert Rhodes James

Clarissa then appointed Robert Rhodes James, one of his missions being to mount a defence against the Carlton hatchet job. Rhodes James had written a number of political biographies, including one on Lord Randolph Churchill, and on Winston Churchill, and he had edited the original Chips Channon diaries. Clarissa chose him 'on the basis that he was a well thought of historian, though I had heard that his life of Rosebery had been badly received by the family. R. J. told me he was very much an admirer of Anthony's and wanted to do a book about the man, rather than the politician accompanied by a mass of documents à la Gilbert.'[28]

Weidenfeld & Nicolson offered an advance of £60,000, some of which would go to Clarissa. Lord Goodman challenged the amount of commission being taken from her cut. When Anthony Sheil, the literary agent, explained it, Goodman wrote: 'I deplore discord on vulgar matters like money but, alas, the dear lady must live.'[29]

---

* Richard Davenport-Hines recalled: 'Goodman gave me a large cheque as a solatium, drawn on a private account, using monies that I now suspect had been illicitly siphoned from Lord Portman's funds.'

† David Carlton, *Anthony Eden – A Biography* (Allen Lane, 1981).

One of Clarissa's stipulations was that she should be consulted about her 'personal relationship' with Anthony, and although she did not want to impugn Rhodes James's integrity, that he should not include matters which might be embarrassing to herself or her family. By May 1981 negotiations were complete. Serena Booker, who had researched for Alistair Horne on his official Macmillan biographies, was chosen to go through Eden's papers still at Alvediston. An attractive and intelligent girl, she annoyed Clarissa by plying her with numerous personal questions, which Clarissa declined to answer. Clarissa found her personality 'irritating' and thought Rhodes James should be asking the questions himself. Not long afterwards Serena went to Thailand and was shockingly murdered.*

There was a delay of two years, due to Rhodes James still serving as an MP. The book was finally published in the autumn of 1986, George Weidenfeld telling Clarissa that he was 'extremely proud that this magnificent volume should be the crown of our rich and prolific autumn list'.[30] Clarissa disagreed as she told the author:

> I lived with Anthony for 25 years in terms of complete intimacy, the only one intimate relationship he ever had, according to him. I am not boasting – I have had several. I wd have been more than happy to talk to you about his character & the way he functioned – he was a far more interesting person than anyone knew or than you have portrayed. It has surprised me all these years that you did not want to question me. I said to you with some irony a few weeks ago that I thought it was time you did.
>
> You arrived with a completed mss of the last 20 years of his life & asked me no questions at all.[31]

Clarissa thought the book lacked tautness of style and was sloppily written. She was annoyed to find that he had used some private letters from her to Anthony, which she had not wanted him to see. She took him up on a number of points: 'I thought one of the reasons Butler

---

* Serena Booker (1954–82), sister of Christopher Booker. She was in Thailand on her way to Burma, travelling on local buses, to visit a deserted Buddhist monastery. Bandits came out of the trees and killed her. Laurence Whistler engraved memorial windows in memory of her and her sister.

failed to become PM was because of his gross disloyalty at time of
Suez – <u>Many</u> people said they cdn't stomach it. Surely you saw Antony
Head?'; 'Clark & barrack room language. I thought this was a chest-
nut that had been cracked, even denied by Eisenhower himself.' In a
private note she wrote:

> I wd have accepted any judgments on Anthony, but not the senti-
> mental and over-simplified ones in the book. Those he was deter-
> mined to make, in spite of information to the contrary supplied by
> friends & relations. I was also wounded that I was given no credit for
> giving Anthony twenty-five years of great happiness (or so he said)
> and for saving his life.[32]

The book sparked a row with the ever-touchy Isaiah Berlin. He
objected to Clarissa inadvertently letting Rhodes James see a letter he
had written in support of Suez, an issue over which he later changed
his mind.* Clarissa rebuked him archly: 'I no longer remember what
your letter said, but [you] having written it, I am saddened by your
embarrassment, because it means that you no longer stand by its
contents.'[33] Such spats caused Clarissa to tell Berlin's biographer that
she thought Isaiah 'had allowed himself to become a salon conversa-
tionalist, an intellectual acrobat in the society circus'.[34]

The Conservative Government in 1986 used Rhodes James's book
as a conduit to save themselves from being accused of withholding
evidence about Suez.† They authorised Sir Patrick Dean and Sir
Donald Logan‡ to tell the author that Eden had tried to have the
French copy of the Sèvres Protocol destroyed and that he had wanted
nothing written down. Clarissa realised that the government did not
have a copy of the Sèvres Protocol or a record of the Dean-Logan
visit to Paris, and was displeased that the Secretary of State took the
line that the advantage of proceeding in that way 'probably outweighs

---

* This resulted in a line on page 552, stating that Berlin had 'supported' the
government.

† Rhodes James wrote: 'There are occasions when an historian, especially dealing
with sensitive matters that are so relevantly recent, has to use his discretion on
sources. This is one of them.' (Footnote, page 530.)

‡ Sir Patrick Dean (1909-94), diplomat, later Ambassador to the USA; and Sir
Donald Logan (1917-2009), then assistant private secretary to Selwyn Lloyd.

the disadvantages of suggesting that a previous Conservative prime minister might have been somewhat duplicitous'.[35]

By and large the reviews were favourable. Tony Lambton took a swipe at Harold Macmillan, who had exaggerated the dangers of Britain's economic situation at the time of Suez:

> He was the Iago of the drama, who saw his opportunity to become prime minister. Indeed it is sad, if just, that the crafty old man of Birchwood [Birch Grove] should find his last dawns disturbed by the perching of yet another roosting cockerel on the end of his bed. It joins those who already sit there, every morning, crowing unanswered, unanswerable choruses which lament his past deceptions and make a mockery of his boastful belief that he was a saviour of this country.[36]

The postscript to this biography was that Rhodes James failed to return many original papers, unwisely loaned to him, and those that did come back were 'in total chaos'. When the papers reached Birmingham, the librarian identified that some letters between Eden and Macmillan, which had been quoted in the book, were missing. Rhodes James professed his innocence to the last and claimed to have searched and searched again. His conclusion was that he was sad that a biography which had had such remarkable success should end on such a sour note. Clarissa remained unforgiving, but wrote a letter of sympathy to his widow when he died in 1999. By then his health had been greatly damaged by an extreme reliance on alcohol.

The next book to appear was David Dutton's *Anthony Eden – A Life and Reputation* (Hodder, 1997), a series of essays drawing on a wealth of international scholarship, and therefore full of good material. It was curious that the front-cover photo of Eden was printed back to front. Dutton was senior lecturer in history at Liverpool University. His book was welcomed as a long overdue look at Eden, published at the time of his centenary. It was well researched and praised for cutting through much of the detail of his political career to give a portrait balancing light and shade. And then came Richard Thorpe.

D. R. Thorpe

Dissatisfied with what she called Rhodes James's 'rather silly "official" biography'[37] Clarissa turned to D. R. Thorpe, a full-time history master at Charterhouse, whom she first met in 1986 when he consulted her for his biography of Selwyn Lloyd. In January 1989 he mooted the idea of editing her Suez diaries. These she had sealed until ten years after her death, but she agreed he could come and discuss them. In 1991 Clarissa allowed him to listen to some tapes under strict embargo, confirmed by a contract devised, as ever, by Lord Goodman. Nothing came of the tapes, partly because Thorpe felt they lacked a sense of continuity, but the idea morphed into a biography, which Thorpe would tackle after his life of Alec Douglas-Home came out in 1995. On 21 May 1991 Clarissa wrote to him: 'I have also seized on the idea that you might one day contemplate what I wd consider the official biography. I am not interested in a hagiography but in a professional, thorough assessment of his life & work.'[38]

Thorpe welcomed the proposal as 'a most attractive proposition and a great challenge'.[39] He was able to conduct dual interviews on Home and Eden as he finished off the Home biography. In relation to Eden, Clarissa was aware that 'the big fish'[40] were now dead, and that many books relied on private secretaries and junior civil servants. She forged numerous introductions for him, and was especially keen that he should talk to people who had known Eden in Europe and elsewhere. She wanted his book to have 'a cosmopolitan view rather than a public records view, outside looking in'.[41] The publishers were hoping for a 'light' book, but Clarissa wanted a 'definitive comprehensive one', which she knew he could produce.[42]

In his acknowledgements, Thorpe thanked Clarissa 'for her unfailing help in making available new material and for providing introductions to so many people, whilst at no time seeking to influence my interpretations'.[43] He had been worried that she might exert undue influence on him but, unlike his predecessor, he went to great lengths to consult and inform her of every move in his research. While she did not influence Thorpe's interpretations, she took an active and positive interest in the book, sending him her habitual corrections and suggestions.

To help Thorpe, Clarissa investigated Anthony's medical condition. In 1996 she consulted Sir Frederick Bishop, Eden's principal private secretary, and Sir Guy Millard asking them for their recollections, since there were persistent rumours that Eden was on uppers and downers during the Suez crisis. She remembered that he had been given Sparine (an American brand of tranquilliser) to help him sleep, and some Benzedrine after his return from Jamaica, in the last days of the premiership. Bishop recalled his boss as 'remarkably calm and steady'[44] during the crisis, while Millard declared drug rumours as 'complete nonsense' and attributed the persistent rumour to 'political enemies, Tories of the Nutting, Astor, Gilmour tendency, FO Arabists & others like Shuckburgh, etc., including real vipers like the absurd [Alastair] Forbes. Someone like the latter would be the most likely source.'[45] Dr (later Sir) Nigel Southward confirmed that his father, Sir Ralph Southward, never prescribed stimulants.

Eden was published by Chatto & Windus in March 2003, and proved considerably more to her satisfaction. Roy Hattersley described it as 'a biography of almost unqualified excellence'.[46] Simon Heffer's verdict was: 'This magnificent biography . . . will profoundly alter our judgement of a much caricatured and underestimated man, and it is unlikely to be surpassed.'[47] Anthony Howard considered it: 'the best life of this ill-starred politician that we are likely to get . . . Some of the disclosures . . . are pure, unalloyed joy.'[48] Andrew Roberts declared that 'Thorpe's 80 page analysis of the [Suez] Crisis' was 'quite the best compressed account of it'[49] that he had ever read.

Richard Thorpe went on to write a life of Harold Macmillan. He sent it to Clarissa and she turned immediately to the Suez chapter, done this time with Macmillan in full frame. She thought it masterly. Later Thorpe edited two volumes of Kenneth Rose's diaries, which proved something of a damp squib. He was planning to write a book on prime ministers' wives in which Clarissa would have featured, but his health let him down.*

★ ★ ★ ★ ★

* Thorpe greatly encouraged me to write her biography. He asked me to alert him when she died, which I attempted to do, but by then he had lost his memory and retired to a nursing home. He died on 2 February 2023.

In 2002 Cherie Blair published a book called *The Goldfish Bowl.** Having been in Downing Street since 1997, Cherie thought it would be interesting to write about the prime ministers' spouses in the Queen's reign, since in varying ways, they had all had similar experiences. Mary Soames had written effectively about her mother, Clementine, so she started with Clarissa, and to help put it together, she worked with Melvyn Bragg's wife, Cate Haste. Cherie found Clarissa 'an unusual character, reserved, though forthcoming in relation to the book.' She was aware that Clarissa had come from a different generation: 'She had not been able to go properly to university, had no on paper qualifications, and had not been able to develop her skills.' She had to play the role of 'decorative wife.' But ever the keeper of the flame, Clarissa 'cared about her husband and wanted to set the record straight'.[50] They had two long interviews and Clarissa was unusually open with her reminiscences.

The following year, Cate persuaded the surviving prime ministers' wives, Mary Wilson, Clarissa and Norma Major to take part in a documentary. Clarissa had not wanted to do it, and at Edward Heath's funeral in 2005, she discovered that the other two had not wanted to do it either.

It was a short programme, and Clarissa only played a small part. She was filmed in her London flat, and revisiting Downing Street. As usual she expressed herself succinctly. When inspecting the drawing room, she could not resist pointing out that it had been much cosier in her day, quickly adding that she thought it one of the finest rooms in London.

The collaboration between Clarissa and Cate Haste led to a close friendship. Clarissa got on well with Cate, and at one time noted that she opened up to her in a way to which she was unaccustomed: 'I asked her what else she knew about me & she said only that George [Weidenfeld] had mentioned R. [Raimund] as the reason (rightly) why I had married so late. I found myself telling her all about the relationship – something I never do to anyone.'[51]

For many years Clarissa had resisted Weidenfeld's entreaties to write a memoir. Suddenly she was bombarded with a barrage of

---

* *The Goldfish Bowl – Married to the Prime Minister 1955–1997* (Random House, 2004), co-authored with Cherie Booth.

attention, seated next to him at his dinner parties, and telephoned endlessly with silken words of flattery. She succumbed but on condition that the book was done in collaboration with Cate.

The resulting book proved disappointing to those who knew Clarissa. She was capable of better. She gave away nothing of herself, but whenever a name was mentioned she launched into an interesting character sketch. There was a cavalcade of the talented, unusual, and globally famous.* Among the notes was the occasional sealed envelope marked 'not to be shown to Cate Haste'.

Cate was a thorough and experienced researcher. She scooped in and organised copies of Clarissa's letters from libraries all over the world. They had excellent, open conversations, but their backgrounds were different. 'I am having problems with the word – *lounge*,' Clarissa said disparagingly, on several occasions. The fundamental problem was that Clarissa was disinclined to share her thoughts openly with the world. Cate could only go so far with her, and no further, so the book revealed just enough to get itself published, but not a word more.

Scholars and academics such as Vernon Bogdanor and D. R. Thorpe were consulted. I tried to persuade Clarissa to say more about her distaste for Macmillan. She would not go far:

> Harold Macmillan played no personal role in my life either before or during the Suez Crisis, though inevitably I formed an assessment of his character from the wings. I only observed him close to after he had resigned as Prime Minister, on his constant visits to Anthony in the 1960s down in Wiltshire. *I would have to meet him* at Salisbury station, where the stationmaster was waiting for the train in full rig, as Harold was a gold card holder (having been on the board of the old GWR), and drove him home *in as much silence as possible*. He only came for some specific reason: once it was to ask Anthony to back his return to politics as prime minister. Nothing came of that.†52

As I had read the Profumo letter (*see* pages 255–6), this was disappointing, but she would not budge. She maintained that the reader would get the point. I am not sure that they did.

---

* This was not wholly unpleasing as it left plenty unsaid for this biography.
† The italics are mine.

Age was a factor. The memoirs were published in 2007, by which time Clarissa was eighty-seven. They were gently and favourably reviewed by her friends and she enjoyed the book's reception. The best thing that came from it was a close friendship with Cate Haste, one of her most constant visitors in her last years, taking her on expeditions to see snowdrops and bluebells and lightening the longueurs of her old age. Clarissa became genuinely devoted to her.

20. THE LAST YEARS

*'In Proust's final volume the enchanting, youthful creatures
of the belle époque become in their middle age and old age
monsters unrecognisable as what they once were.'*
Noel Annan[1]

I was a witness to Clarissa's last years. The friendship that developed
so strongly in 1980 survived until the end. We were both in New
York in December 1982. I lunched with her at the Regency. Her
suite was a bower of flowers. 'These hostesses send you flowers *before*
the dinner,' she said. Night after night she had been to dinners, and
was funny about the moment when 'the inevitable spoon hits the
glass and the host rises to his feet'. One night she was given four
glasses of Chablis and nothing to eat when suddenly the host called
out 'Countess!' She had to make a speech on an empty stomach. She
found the people in the streets very rude: 'They say, "Excuse me," as
they bash into you.' Her old friend Sir Rudolf Bing had been to lunch
but was so senile that he asked the same question over and over. Later
we went for a walk and looked in various stores. In FAO Schwartz,
she was infuriated to see a Mountbatten doll set next to a Winston
Churchill. 'Is there no stopping him?' she said.[2]

In the summer of 1983 I drove her from Milan to Athens and we
crossed to Patmos for a ten-day stay with the artist, Teddy Millington-
Drake. The eleven-day drive from Athens back to London was long.
Clarissa was an exacting passenger, with a cloth over the left-hand
window, her cushion, her selective approval of music to be played,
and never any question of her taking the wheel. I had miscalculated
how long the trip was going to be and was anxious to get back to
London. We were not totally in tune with what we liked to see. She
was right and I was wrong. She relished ancient monuments. If there

was a mosque to be seen, she did not mind how long it took to get there or how great the detour. I preferred the Villa Miramare in Trieste, where the Coburg Emperor Maximilian of Mexico had lived, or seeing Tito's house in Belgrade. She surprised me from time to time with her vocabulary. 'Oh, come on, buster!' she said, when a driver blocked the way.

Twice I returned to Cetinale with her, in 1990 and 1998. I enjoyed the spark-off between her and Tony Lambton – his outrageous remarks parried by her reserve as when at breakfast he expounded on Pamela Harriman's dexterity with ice cubes. 'I see,' she commented, as she might have done had some mathematical conundrum been explained to her. And there was no better pairing when the findings of the Monica Lewinsky report came through sheet by sheet from the fax machine in London. These were passed from hand to hand, with spicy reaction to the unconventional uses to which cigars had been put in the White House in the days of President Clinton.

Back in London, there were excursions to the opera, the cinema or to dinner. She took me twice to dinner parties given by Lady Colyton* for Margaret Thatcher in the late 1990s. In 1997 I told Lady Thatcher how the Labour Foreign Secretary Robin Cook had lately mucked up the Queen's state visit to Pakistan and India. Her riposte was: 'Robin Cook is just as foxy in his mind as he is in his looks.'[3] Clarissa took me to the after-dinner party at the French Residence, given by President Mitterrand in 1983 at which the Queen and the Royal Family were present, and many guests in white tie and decorations (not all of them correctly worn). We went to a Harold Pinter play at the Royal Court Theatre and she came to stay at my house in Hampshire. I never knew why she chose me as a friend, but it worked.

★ ★ ★ ★ ★

Between 2005 and October 2012 Clarissa kept a diary, recording incidents between the ages of eighty-five and ninety-three. Three volumes survive. She had lost none of her powers of concentration. In the first little book she noted: 'This diary is written as an aide memoire and is therefore not elegant or witty.'[4] There followed a flow of observations

---

* Barbara Colyton (d. 2004), formerly Barbara Addams of the Addams Family, widow of Lord Colyton, and a close friend of Margaret Thatcher.

and musings, all the better for this unselfconscious approach. She plucked from daily events aspects of life and human behaviour that amused her,* and was more self-revelatory in the diaries than in her memoirs. One such was that she often employed a trick. She would remain silent, not speaking, and wait to see how long it took until the other person spoke. She tested Lucian Freud and he finally broke the silence after two minutes.

In widowhood, new friends peopled Clarissa's world. Mercia Tinker had married the actor Rex Harrison, as his sixth wife in 1978. She was able to cope with Rex, not the easiest of men, reducing his intake of alcohol and even getting him into a gym. When Rex died, I wrote his obituary for the *Independent*, coining a phrase later used in more than one of his biographies: 'A man who was guilty of the most ungentlemanly behaviour to colleagues and to ladies in everyday life came to represent on stage the most virtuous and courageous of Englishmen.'[5] Mercia succeeded in getting Rex a knighthood in 1989. To secure this, he returned to the British stage in several productions. 'She left no stone unturned,' said Clarissa. Lady Harrison frequently entertained Clarissa and she in turn would have her to lunch. According to Clarissa, she did not have many friends in Britain, but she thought this was because Rex had made himself so unpopular. She remembered that Claudette Colbert had loathed him when they were in Frederick Lonsdale's *Aren't We All* at the Haymarket Theatre in 1984.

In widowhood Pamela Harriman advanced the career of Bill Clinton in Washington and was sent to Paris as US Ambassador. Clarissa saw her there: 'How calm and determined she was in the mastery of the job, coupled with the well-tried ability to enchant men. That tour of duty was her apotheosis. As the president of the Académie Française, Maurice Druon, said of her end: '*Quel chance, pas de déclin.*'[6] Pamela Harriman lost consciousness beside the swimming-pool at the Ritz in 1995. Inevitably a line was formed: 'She died staring at the ceiling of the Ritz – as so often in life.'

I made appearances in the diaries and might have got off lightly since she was aware that one day she would entrust them to my care.

---

* An enterprising publisher could do worse than publish them in full. They give an intriguing portrait of key figures of the twentieth century in the twilight of their lives, some in decline, some bravely vigorous.

At Grange Opera when she was in her late eighties, she wrote: 'Hugo's wife very sweet, he as always, in Ian Fleming's bow tie, or so he says, & a cloak. Full of amusing bits of information.' There was a dinner at Occo, a restaurant near Bryanston Square: 'downstairs where there are sofas & cushions & the most delicious food & a sweet girl waiter. H. as usual rather tortured – what to work at to pay for his children's education. He can only think of a book on Mrs Simpson!'*

In September 2007 I put on a play:

To the Windsor Festival. Hugo has arranged a performance about Stephen Tennant, based on his letters & acted by 'Charley Duff'. He had no notice, so has to read the lines, but does it well, not overacting the camp stuff & Stephen was v. intelligent & the material was clever & interesting. This took place in the mews of Cumberland Lodge & dinner was in the house itself. This was where I used to come as a child to play with Alathea [Fitzalan Howard] . . . I enjoyed my evening as everyone seemed pleased to see me . . . Hugo's son Arthur was flitting around all the evening like a little sprite.[7]

Clarissa also made friends with the author, Robert Harris. He recalled:

Clarissa was one of the most striking people I ever met, very sharp, no sentimentality or self-pity, with piercing eyes and manner. She didn't at all dwell in the past, but if you asked her about it, she could tell you things which literally no one left alive could do. I remember her describing a lunch with Churchill, just the two of them, in May 1940. Her voice and style and vocabulary were a link with the vanished age of the 1930s and 1940s, but her sensibility was modern. She was always on the lookout for new friends with the latest news. She came to the premiere of my film The Ghost in 2010 and cut a swathe through the crowd, wearing a black leather jacket. She was still very beautiful in her nineties – in fact perhaps even more so than she was when she was younger.[8]

* Duly written and published as Behind Closed Doors (2011).

Dégringolade

There was no shortage of friends in decline. They died, often in their nineties, and she lived on. Just as Cecil Beaton turned to his diary to describe himself and his friends in old age, so Clarissa did likewise in hers. She thought that losing her balance, dropping or endlessly mislaying objects could be irritating for others. She was acutely aware that her memory was failing. Also, she suffered from aches and pains in her back and neck and from arthritis. But she compared her plight favourably to that of 'Lucian [Freud] gaga & Debo [Devonshire] blind' and thought perhaps she was not so bad. She was pleased when after a lunch party given by Trim's daughter, Katie Page, a guest wrote: 'For someone in their eighties he had never met anyone so razor-sharp & quick in their reactions.'[9] A few days before, she had had her brain tested to learn what the future might hold. In her late eighties, and early nineties, she frequently had falls, sometimes small ones, sometimes more serious, more than once hitting her head as she fell back in the street.

Trim Oxford was back home at Mells after long years overseas as a colonial governor. Clarissa heard news of him from his nephew, John Jolliffe, in 1996: 'Trim retains his magisterial calm & we are shooting together next week – not bad for 80.'[10] When Clarissa lunched with his daughter Katie at East Knoyle in 2007, she noted: 'Dear Trim had come from Mells, very red in the face, but very sweet, affectionate & gentle.' A while later Katie told her that he stayed up all night, went to bed at 8 a.m. and that his favourite TV entertainment was *Coronation Street*. Trim's wife Anne died in 1998. Neighbours walking their dogs on the hills behind Mells would see the light shining from the one room in which he lived. He died on 16 January 2011, aged ninety-four. Clarissa was unable to attend his funeral.

Colin Tennant, who had become Lord Glenconner in 1983, came to see her when he was in London, on one visit wearing 'a terrible brown zip-up jacket, sandals' with 'Virgin airline cotton socks, pale blue', another time 'dressed as a tramp'. She found him looking old, any benefit from a recent face lift having worn off. They went to a Thai café in Crawford Street called 'Monkey & Me' where he was 'extremely rude to the charming waitress'.[11] He brought his factotum Kent Adonai with him as he could not bear to be on his own. Kent could neither write nor read so the menu had to be explained to him. Colin could eat only slops and was concerned that his false teeth might fall out during lunch. He complained that had he not sold his enormous estate in Trinidad he would have been a billionaire. He proposed moving into two rooms belonging to Kent in Saint Lucia (bought with Colin's money). In his last year, it was revealed that Colin had produced a son with Henrietta Moraes, the muse of Francis Bacon (though Lucian Freud thought the boy was his, and Colin's wife Anne Glenconner expressed doubts). In June 2010 Colin went to lunch with Clarissa, sporting a goatee beard, and gave her a conch shell for her ninetieth birthday. He made it to the birthday party, and died on 27 August that year.

Nathalie Brooke, who had been the stalwart mainstay of the trip to the Caucasus in 1978 and kept John Merton at bay, moved into a care home in Roland Gardens in South Kensington, from which she was at least able to emerge for concerts, exhibitions and parties. But Clarissa found it depressing: 'Lunch with Nathalie Brooke in a restaurant opposite her care home. The horror of her "home". Two nurses rush out to help her up the steps near a bench on which is sitting a completely gaga vacant old woman. Natalie has just one room to live in.'[12] Nathalie died on 16 September 2019, aged ninety-six.

Isaiah Berlin had died in 1997. His widow, Aline, was also in a care home. Clarissa was a regular visitor, finding her increasingly weak, walking but a few yards with a zimmer frame, deaf and speaking in a whisper. In January 2010, on a 'nightmare' visit, she found Aline recounting 'incomprehensibly' how she had extricated herself from her first husband in order to marry Isaiah. She wanted Clarissa to write it down. Clarissa excused herself. In September 2011, she noted: 'She is unable to enunciate so all she says is incomprehensible. She is no longer remotely interested in the outside world or anything I might have done in it. So after the regulation ½ hour one leaves.'[13] Aline died on 25 August 2014, aged ninety-nine.

Clarissa paid a last visit to Tony Lambton and Claire Ward at Cetinale in the summer of 2006: 'Three & a half days to get through – the talk, a combination of Claire & Diana Wilton is stupefying & Tony of course worse in real life than one cd imagine. He asks a question about somebody or something. You reply. Pause. Then the same question & on & on.' Tony died on 30 December that year.

Mary Soames had been a constant in her life since childhood, when they had holidayed in Switzerland or when Clarissa went to Chartwell. Of a late-life encounter in 2008 she noted: 'Mary Soames is really old. Seeing me across the room she crossed over, barged between me & [John] Carey, unsmilingly kissed me & steamed on. Is she like this w. everyone or has she a complex about me?' Clarissa was struck by how fat Mary had become, whereas she had retained a trim figure. At a Churchill reunion, the invitation stated 'Decorations'. No one wore them except Mary, who sported ten medals. Clarissa found her very deaf. Mary died on 31 May 2014, aged ninety-one, and her life was celebrated with a packed memorial service in Westminster Abbey, which Clarissa attended in a wheelchair.

She had known George Weidenfeld since the 1940s. At the book launch of her memoirs in 2007, 'George looked like death & before the end, which admittedly was at 9 o'clock, retreated to his study & slumped in a chair.'[14] In 2012 the Weidenfelds gave her a lift home from an event: 'George completely wonky, & his face collapsing, but mentally OK, so apparently still rushing about the world.'[15] He lived to be ninety-six and died on 20 January 2016.

She was most admiring of Harold Pinter, his talent and good looks. He declined gravely. Clarissa would take the ladies to her bedroom briefly at the end of a dinner party at her flat. At one such, he was 'on the dangerous verge of outbursts, which apparently did happen when I had taken the women to my room when he shouted where were the women & quite soon appeared in the door of my bedroom menacingly'. Not long afterwards she was staying with the Ashburtons, when the news came on the radio that he had died (on 24 December 2008): 'I feel a shock go through me. Another man gone,'[16] she wrote.

Lady Thatcher looked younger than anyone at Sir Edward Heath's funeral in Salisbury Cathedral in 2005, but 'vacant' and she arrived late for an Andrew Roberts book launch in 2008 'looking stuffed, surrounded by agitated admirers'. James Fairfax, her Australian philanthropist friend, downed a martini, white wine, red wine and a Cointreau at lunch at Mark's Club and 'was consequently smashed'.[17] He died on 11 January 2017 aged eighty-three. Lucian Freud had been getting increasingly old, but was well cared for by David Dawson. He died on 20 July 2011. The following night, his lawyer, Diana Rawstron, telephoned Clarissa. 'Cancer had come back, but he drifted away, thank goodness,' wrote Clarissa. 'He was absolutely the last of my old friends.'[18]

During these years, Clarissa stayed in England with her niece Sally and her husband, John (Lord Ashburton) near Winchester, or with John Eden (Lord Eden of Winton) and his second wife Margaret Anne (M.A.), on the Shaftesbury estate in Dorset. From time to time she went to Gay Charteris's home near Stanway in Gloucestershire. In France she was a regular guest of Mollie (Marchioness of) Salisbury at her 1770 Château de Saint-Clou in the Vaucluse, Provence, once the home of the uncle of the Marquis de Sade. These generous hosts and hostesses came under particularly intense scrutiny, the more so since she stayed with them so often.

Clarissa was rather disapproving of her old friend from Oxford days, Gay Charteris, judging her life sad. Gay spent hours cooking, washing up and attending to laundry and only wanted to discuss the political news in the papers. Had she not married Martin and become involved in court life, she would have been completely devoted to 'left wing Strachey stuff'. Gay had loved 'Nicko' Henderson* when they were at Oxford. When he died in March 2009, she, Clarissa and Mollie Salisbury were driven to his funeral at St Swithin's Church, Combe, by the Wykehamist chauffeur, who regularly drove John and Sally Ashburton:

> Gay wears an old hat with brown fur, & Mollie an Edwardian suit, a saucer hat well forward over forehead, with a veil . . . I am unfairly irritated by both Gay & Mollie. I suppose they are the two women left alive who I can call friends, though I do not have much in common with either of them. I have more affinity with Cate [Haste], thanks to her knowing everything (or almost everything) about me. Today was typical – Mollie's ridiculous appearance & her bigoted conversation, & Gay's grotesque clothes & her calm narrow mindedness. She never developed after marrying Martin. In their lack of 'bolshiness' they resemble each other.[19]

Gay Charteris died aged ninety-seven on 14 March 2017.

It was at the Henderson funeral that Clarissa first met Jung Chang. She reserved for authors that she admired a particular respect.

---

* Sir Nicholas Henderson (1919-2009), Ambassador to Paris and also to the USA.

I witnessed her go over to Angus Wilson's table in a restaurant once to tell him of her admiration for his works, somewhat to his surprise. It was thus with some diffidence that she invited the author to dinner. Jung Chang observed: 'She was unusually sharp-minded, and a word-smith. There were no superfluous words. She had a great interest in international politics, and was interested in personalities. She told me she had been impressed by Chou-en-lai until she read my biography of Mao at which point she modified her view [learning that Chou was worse than Mao – 'Mao gave the orders, but Chou actually carried them out'[20]].[21]

Robert Salisbury had died in 2003. When staying with his widow Mollie in France, Clarissa recorded her displeasure at the dogs: 'snapping, barking, yapping, barking again'.[22] In the summer of 2009 the holiday became a disaster when Mollie was heard scream-ing, having fallen and broken her hip. She was taken to a nearby hospital, Katie Page a faithful bedside visitor, the matter so serious that her son Robert (Marquess of Salisbury), flew out. The follow-ing year Mollie found a huge support in Mandy Harrison-Allen who joined the house party and smoothed the life of the château. Clarissa soon corralled her into driving her about. In the summer of 2011 she pulled Mandy aside. Gwen (Lady) Dartmouth had arrived expecting a vast château and grand dinner parties. 'She arrived with *eight* suitcases,' Clarissa pointed out. Mollie died on 12 December 2016, aged ninety-four.

Clarissa's niece, Sally, had known Clarissa since she was in her teens, and found her 'demanding, kind, intelligent, beautiful, easily bored, terse', as well as 'elegant, always soignée.' As a shy seven-teen-year-old, she had been, not unnaturally, in awe of the Edens' 'sophisticated milieu'. Due to the fall-out between her father, Johnny, and Clarissa, she did not see so much of her aunt until later life. Clarissa invited her to drinks on her seventieth birthday at 32 Bryanston Square, and as she aged, Sally stepped in, overseeing carers, coping with fast-failing finances, and looking after all aspects of her life. Sally would have Clarissa to stay at Lake House, near Winchester, driving to London to bring her down. During these journeys of two hours, Clarissa was warm and forthcoming, chat-ting freely to her niece on aspects of her life which she did not normally discuss. In her diary Clarissa observed: 'I think Sally is

very lucky that, after what must have been a childhood of pillar &
post & no real love, she now has security & can be surrounded by
children & grandchildren.'[23]

Sally wrote:

> It wasn't exactly a close relationship but I became very fond of her
> and admired her courage and determination and her caustic wit
> which often hit the button with a thump . . . Her wit sometimes
> took an unusual turn. On arriving at our house in Hampshire for
> Christmas one year, she marched up to my husband John and said:
> 'Hello, John. Tell me how long have you lived in this dump?' It star-
> tled the attendant grand-children who couldn't help laughing. She
> felt encouraged to continue in this vein and told my other aunt* she
> looked as though she hadn't got long.[24]

This coincided with Sally's seventieth birthday party:

> An Indian tent done with no taste or style. Ld Sainsbury apparently
> enjoyed sitting next to me. At lunch next day there was Angela
> [Sally's mother], instantly recognisable but lost her marbles. Then a
> bent, pale, wrinkled figure who to my horror turned out to be
> Janetta [Sally's aunt], the man killer, who hasn't lost her marbles.[25]

Clarissa once made the mistake of leaving her diary behind at Lake
House. In it she complained that no one made an effort to talk to her.
Sally could not resist reading it. She told Clarissa that *she* made no
effort, so the young thought she disliked them. Subsequently Clarissa
engaged more, and everyone was happier.

Clarissa also stayed with Anthony's nephew, Lord Eden of Winton
and his wife, M.A., in Dorset. She prevailed on John Eden to drive
her all over Dorset and Wiltshire, which she greatly enjoyed, and,
depending on her mood, he was variously described as 'a sweet man'
or 'a v. kind silly man'. She considered him lucky to have M.A. who
created around him an atmosphere in which he could shine. John
Eden was concerned about certain family treasures in Clarissa's possession. In the end he predeceased her, dying on 23 May 2020, aged

* Janetta Parladé (1921–2018), born Janetta Woolley, much married.

ninety-four. After her death, the probate lawyers sent all her possessions including the Eden items, to the saleroom.

Clarissa was able to go out, to attend concerts and give dinner
parties until 2013. Then old age caught up with her and the carers
moved in. To quote Maurice Goudeket as he wrote about his wife,
the novelist Colette: 'Her memory detached itself from the recent
events so that it might better hold the deeply graven traces of the
past.'[26]

On 28 June 2010 she reached the great age of ninety. The
Ashburtons hosted a birthday party at the Tite Street home of John's
daughter, Lucy Vaughan. It rounded up the most eclectically interesting group of guests, ranging from Mary Soames and Mollie Salisbury,
Colin and Anne Glenconner, to Lucian Freud, Colin Thubron, Barry
Humphries and Robert Harris. Had a bomb dropped that night, a
bumper edition of *Times* and *Daily Telegraph* obituaries would have
been required. It provided evidence, should any have been required,
of Clarissa's personally chosen friends. Few would have bored her. Of
the evening Clarissa wrote:

> My 90th birthday – try to spend the day resting. Impossible because
> the doorbell rings 5 times with flowers (Aline – Jung [Chang] –
> Weidenfeld's) & a very good pashmina (Diane [Lever]).
>
> Party is in large studio room in Tite Street. Some relation of John
> or Sally – the wife says how beautiful I am. I enjoyed it all – sat with
> Lucian for a bit. David D. [Dawson] has brought a huge, huge bucket-
> ful of pink peonies for L. to give me. Nice to see Vidia [Naipaul],
> Colin Thubron, Robert Harris, Jung Chang & so on. Colin
> Glenconner looks grotesque with his new pointed beard . . . Mary
> Soames v. gracious.[27]

On 24 January 2015 Janet Binnersley, Clarissa's housekeeper, drove
her to Bladon for a service to mark the fiftieth anniversary of Winston's
death. They left at 9 a.m. and returned at 4 p.m., after which Janet
and the night nurse helped her undress. On 30 January, the fiftieth
anniversary of Winston's state funeral, there was a commemoration in
Westminster Hall, with a service and tributes from the Speaker (John
Bercow) and the Prime Minister (David Cameron). Clarissa left with
Janet at 8 a.m. It was her last formal excursion. She was ninety-four.

A 2017 diary kept by the nurse records frequent excursions to Regent's Park or the Serpentine: 'L.A. was up very early, very talkative and happy, took her to Hyde Park in the a.m., sat watching the ducks & swans, but sleepy late afternoon.'[28] Clarissa liked to go to the Wallace Collection. Cate Haste visited often. Sally took her to stay in Hampshire until it became too difficult to move her. Clarissa was most content when lying on her bed reading the newspapers. There were good days and bad days. Her carers were fond of her. They respected her because she was decisive, and they admired her courage.

It was still possible for Clarissa to preside over a small lunch, and she could sparkle with reminiscences. As late as 2019 she chatted to the author Tom Roberts about James Pope-Hennessy. I spent a happy afternoon looking through Gladys, Duchess of Marlborough's photograph album with her and her concentration never wavered. At other times she was confused. She believed she was living in the country, not recognising the familiar surroundings of her London flat.

On Saturday, 23 February 2019 I took Antonia Fraser to see her. We had lunch at a small table in Clarissa's bedroom. Clarissa was not well that day, and there was much uncomfortable coughing. Antonia never forgot it: 'I even remember the menu. I remember her lying looking like an angel in white, and saying to you, who were her greatest friend: I know you.'[29]

Living to a great age is expensive and Clarissa had carers round the clock for more than six years. While Clarissa herself did not worry about the expense of all this, it was of considerable concern to Sally, who oversaw all the arrangements at a time when her husband John was also in poor health. As early as 1991 a friend wrote to John Major, then Prime Minister, complaining that Clarissa did not receive a pension as the wife of a long-serving MP, one of the longest serving foreign secretaries and prime minister. He replied that it would require primary legislation and a parliamentary debate to institute a retrospective pension improvement.[30]

In April 2019 Jennie Churchill (now Mrs Laurence Geller) introduced me to a young American author, Catherine Katz, who wanted to meet Clarissa as she was writing about Sarah Churchill, Kathleen Harriman and Anna Roosevelt for her book, *The Daughters of Yalta* (Houghton Mifflin Harcourt, 2020). By that time Clarissa's memory was clouded, but there seemed no harm in Catherine coming to see her. At least they would meet, even if Clarissa remembered little, and it would give the carer a little time off. Catherine duly arrived at Bryanston Square. Clarissa was in bed. Catherine perched beside the bed and asked her: 'What was it like living in Downing Street?'

'Did I?' This was disappointing – one of those afternoons, then.

Catherine tried another tack: 'You must have known Averell Harriman?'

At that point Clarissa leant back and proclaimed: 'I always thought he was the most frightful bore!' This was not what Catherine was expecting. As we left, Clarissa took Catherine's hand in hers and pronounced dramatically: 'I shook the hand of the woman responsible for the deaths of a thousand men.'[*]

In December 2019 Sally brought a couple from Québec to see Clarissa. As a young boy, Mark Schofield had met her years before as his parents were friends of Peregrine. Mark's son, Julian, proved by DNA that his father was, surprisingly, Peregrine's illegitimate son. Mark confessed that he had been rather in awe of the meeting, but Clarissa was welcoming and accepting of this unexpected development.[†]

By 28 June 2020 time's ever-rolling stream had carried most of Clarissa's old friends away. Due to the pandemic lockdown, which had been in force since March that year, obliging people to stay at home, she was denied the spectacular hundredth birthday party she deserved. Only a small socially distanced lunch was possible. There is something a bit depressing about such a birthday. Flowers and telegrams arrived and Clarissa had to be told who they had come from. Sally had decorated her dining room with balloons and created a festive air. In due course Clarissa was wheeled in, looking dignified in her pretty housecoat, her pure white hair swept back, her

---

[*] Catherine recalls: 'And then we stood outside her house puzzling over whether she was confusing me with someone else, making a literary or historical allusion that escaped both of us (something like Helen of Troy, perhaps), if she was referring to Pamela Churchill (who we had been discussing with her), or if she had placed a hex on me! I certainly hope not!' (Catherine Katz to author, 14 December 2023.)

[†] Peregrine lived with Cecil and Valerie Schofield as a more or less permanent lodger for nine years until 1953. Mark does not know if Peregrine was aware that he was his father. Peregrine stood as his godfather when he was baptised a Catholic (Mark Schofield to author, 18 July 2024).

features finely sharpened by age, her eyes monitoring the passing show. She was slightly displeased to accept that she was a hundred.

Cards were shown to her, and she received the statutory celebratory card from the Queen (with the wrong date on it, due to Buckingham Palace inefficiency). We were a small group, Sally, her son P.J. (Clarissa's godson), Mrs Jonathan Stone, the ever faithful Janet and her carers, eating smoked salmon sandwiches and drinking champagne. I presented Clarissa with a specially made birthday cake. But otherwise we had to keep our distance, so Clarissa found it hard to hear us. Extraordinarily, from somewhere in the depths of her memory, she produced the information that as a child she had called herself 'Cissa', something she had never told us before. I confess I left with a heavy heart, and when I got home, I felt sad and depressed, thinking back over the forty years to the person she had once been. I was able to see her twice more.

On 6 October she was in her chair in the library. I told her that Sally could not leave John just now. Clarissa showed uncharacteristic concern in worrying if Sally would be all right should anything happen to him. I showed her the video of the Queen knighting Captain Tom,* which amused her. Later that day John Ashburton died at the age of ninety-one. On the next visit, on 25 October, Clarissa was lying in bed, 'a tiny head on the pillow, very calm & comfortable, but talking so faintly it was hard to hear her'.[31] Sally and her daughter Bel came. Clarissa's money was fast running out. It was hoped that she could stay at home in Bryanston Square.

The last time I saw her was at a small lunch with Sally on 18 April 2021, the day after Prince Philip's funeral. She had taken in that Prince Philip had died, and it had upset her. She was determined to tell us that she was not a hundred. 'I'm ninety-nine,' she declared. A few days later Cate Haste died aged seventy-five. I don't think Clarissa was told. On her hundred-and-first birthday, Sally had one of her regular FaceTime calls with her aunt. This time Clarissa asked Sally: 'How old am I?'

'A hundred and one.'

'Well, she looks a hundred and ten,' she commented, with customary verve.

---

* Sir Thomas Moore (1920-2021) who raised millions for the NHS by walking up and down outside his house at the age of 99.

Clarissa died peacefully on 17 November 2021, nearly five months after her hundred-and-first birthday. The last words she spoke were to her carer as Sunday night drew to a close. Amina said to her: 'I love you.'

With a twinkle, Clarissa replied: 'Well, I don't love you.'

I end this book as with the last words from the eulogy that it was my privilege to give at her funeral at St Mary's Church, Alvediston on a cold, rather wet afternoon:

To live to the age of 101 is a challenge. That she was able to stay in her apartment in Bryanston Square involved lots of hard work behind the scenes. In particular she was lucky to have her niece Sally, who worked tirelessly to make sure she was able to stay at home, had her to stay and visited her at every opportunity. She was beautifully looked after by Janet, who was with her for so many years, by Patricia, her house-keeper of seventeen years, and by her devoted carers, Vanya and Amina. Those who saw her in the last years will remember that, though her memory may have been spasmodic, she was never short of a crisp observation.

Finally, to have a chocolate soufflé and a glass of champagne on a Sunday night at the age of 101, then not wake up the next morning is surely an enviable way to go.

Now she has come home, to rest at Anthony's side, in a remote churchyard in the green downs of the beautiful Wiltshire countryside.

We who loved her will miss her more than it is possible to say.[32]

Acknowledgements

My first debt is to Clarissa Avon, whose friendship I enjoyed for 41 years, and who appointed me her literary executor in July 1985 and entrusted her papers into my care. It is my hope that these papers will join Anthony Eden's at Birmingham University, where some of her papers are already housed. It is important that they are preserved for posterity.

Never have I received such kindness and help over a book. Clarissa's niece, Sally, Lady Ashburton, has been supportive throughout and read the book in draft. So too did Simon Heffer and Charles Duff and all three contributed important advice and guidance. The primary source for this book was Clarissa's archive, but I made three particular excursions – to Mells Manor where Lord Oxford kindly allowed me to read Clarissa's letters to his father; to the Bodleian Library to delve into the papers of Sir Isaiah Berlin, William Clark, Robert Carr (Lord Carr of Hadley) and Hon David Astor; and to Churchill College, Cambridge for the papers of Sir Winston Churchill, Clementine Churchill, Mary Soames, Peregrine Churchill, Duff Cooper, and Lady Gladwyn. Allen Packwood, Director of the Churchill College Archives also allowed me access to the digital archive of the Churchill papers. I am grateful for help at Churchill College from Jessica Saunders, and, at the Bodleian Library, from Jeremy McIlwaine, Vanessa Wright and Oliver House. Also to Mark Eccleston, Head of Collections at Birmingham University, where the Avon papers live.

Many were kind enough to talk to me about Clarissa – Sally, Lady Ashburton, Cherie Blair, Marina, Viscountess Camrose (Marina Berry), Sir Bryan Cartledge, Jung Chang, Nicholas Courtney, Hon Harriet Cullen, Richard Davenport-Hines, Patric Dickinson, Dr David Dilks, Lord Dobbs of Wylie, Charles Duff, Lady Antonia Fraser, Anne, Lady Glenconner, Robert Harris, Mandy Harrison-Allen, Simon

Heffer, Hon John Jolliffe, Catherine Katz, Michael Mallon, Hon Sara Morrison, Sir David and Lady Newbigging, Juliet Nicolson (Anson), Viscountess Norwich, Hon Tarquin Olivier, the Earl of Oxford & Asquith, Lady Katharine Page, Hon Mrs Mary Pearson, Tom Roberts, Mark Schofield, Nicholas Shakespeare, Julian Spencer-Churchill, Octavian von Hofmannsthal, John Stefanides, Graham Viney and Victoria Zinovieff, and if quoted directly, their quotes are published with their kind permission.

During Clarissa's lifetime, in the course of many years, I also talked to Mrs Humphrey Brooke, Lady Charteris of Amisfield, Minnie Churchill, Peregrine Churchill, Lady Diana Cooper, Lord & Lady Eden of Winton, Alastair Forbes, Lady Gladwyn, Cate Haste, Robert Heber Percy, Felix Hope-Nicholson, Eileen Hose, Lord Lambton, Valentine Lawford, Laura, Duchess of Marlborough, Kenneth Rose, and D.R. Thorpe.

At Hodder, I am grateful to Rowena Webb for commissioning this book, and for her early editing, also to Susannah Otter for being so supportive as the book came to fruition. Once again Hazel Orme was a great help, and Lucy Buxton masterminded the production side. My agent, Clare Alexander, played a vital role in making this book happen.

Additionally, at various points, I am grateful to Robert Craig, Joan Darling, Marilyn Darling, Sybilla Jane Flower, Elizabeth Lane, and Harrison Goldman. Mike Kleyn spoke to me about Mells.

I am most grateful to another Juliet Nicolson (Miles) for help transcribing certain documents.

Copyright Permissions

I am literary executor to the Countess of Avon, Sir Cecil Beaton, Sir Charles Johnston & to my aunt, Joan Vickers, so am able to give myself permission to quote them. Clarissa's parents, John S. Churchill and Lady Gwendeline fall within this. I am grateful to the following for permission to quote from private letters and diaries:

The Earl of Avon – Sir Bryan Cartledge
Sir Isaiah Berlin – Henry Hardy

Sir Winston Churchill & his son Randolph Churchill – reproduced with permission of Curtis Brown, London on behalf of The Estate of Winston S. Churchill © The Estate of Winston S. Churchill

Baroness Spencer-Churchill & Lady Soames – The Master, Fellows and Scholars of Churchill College, Cambridge

John Spencer-Churchill & Angela Culme-Seymour – Sally, Lady Ashburton

William Clark – Lord Hemingford

Duff Cooper & Lady Diana Cooper – Artemis Cooper

Ann Fleming – Mary Gibson

Alastair Forbes – Miia-Mari Forbes

Lord Glenconner (Colin Tennant) – Anne, Lady Glenconner

Lady Hartwell (Lady Pamela Berry) – Hon Harriet Cullen

The 2nd Earl of Oxford & Asquith (Trim) – The 3rd Earl of Oxford & Asquith

James Pope-Hennessy & Sir John Pope-Hennessy – Michael Mallon

Raimund von Hofmannsthal & Lady Elizabeth von Hofmannsthal – Octavian von Hofmannsthal

David Wallace – Lady Howell of Guildford & her sister, Laura Morland

Other quotes fall within fair dealing. The author apologises to anyone he has failed to trace and will correct omissions in subsequent editions.

Picture Acknowledgements

All photographs are from the private collection of the Countess of Avon, now in the possession of the author, with the exception of:

Inset 1:
p. 2, centre right: © KGPA Ltd / Alamy Stock Photo.
p. 7, below: © Album / Alamy Stock Photo.
Inset 2:
p. 2, above: © PNA Rota / Hulton Archive / Getty Images.
p. 3, above: © Kate Cushing Paley.
p. 7, above: author's private collection.
p. 8, above: with kind permission of David Dawson.
p. 8, below right: © Sally, Lady Ashburton.

Select Bibliography

A. G. Macdonell was suspicious of bibliographies. He wrote: 'Nothing is easier than to hire someone to visit the British Museum and make a most impressive list of authorities, which will persuade the non-suspecting that the author is a monument of erudition and laboriousness.' Suffice it to say that I have quoted a little from a great number of books. All these are listed in the source notes with appropriate details of publisher, etc.

Therefore, I propose only to mention certain books here, which I found particularly helpful, in order to recommend further reading, along with a few to avoid.

Clarissa herself

Clarissa wrote a book of memoirs with Cate Haste – *From Churchill to Eden* (Weidenfeld & Nicolson, 2007). She appears as a character in James Pope-Hennessy's *London Fabric* (Batsford, 1939) & Lord Berners, *Far from the Madding War* (Constable, 1941). She also appears in my memoir of researching Cecil Beaton, *Malice in Wonderland* (Hodder & Stoughton, 2021). Cecil Beaton's was a parallel life. Clarissa appears in my biography, *Cecil Beaton* (variously published between 1985 and 2020).

Lady Gwendeline Churchill

There is a privately printed volume of tributes – *G.S.C. – The Seventh of July 1941*.

Anthony Eden

I relied primarily on D.R. Thorpe, *Eden* (Chatto & Windus, 2003). There were biographies by Robert Rhodes James, *Anthony Eden* (Weidenfeld & Nicolson, 1986), which Clarissa disliked, & David Carlton, *Anthony Eden – A Biography* (Allen Lane, 1981), generally deemed hostile.

A yet more unpopular book was Randolph Churchill: *Eden* (MacGibbon & Kee, 1959).

Eden himself wrote three volumes of memoirs: *Full Circle* (Cassell, 1960), *Facing the Dictators* (Cassell, 1962), and *The Reckoning* (Cassell, 1965). In 1976 he wrote a delightful book about his childhood and First World War experiences: *Another World 1897–1914* (Allen Lane, 1976).

Sir Winston Churchill

The eight volumes of official biography of Sir Winston Churchill by Randolph Churchill and Martin Gilbert, along with the various Companion Volumes proved especially valuable. There was also Lord Moran's controversial *The Struggle for Survival* (Constable, 1966), and John Colville's *Fringes of Power* (Hodder & Stoughton, 1985). Mary Soames edited the letters between her parents, *Speaking for Themselves* (Transworld Publishers, 1998).

Clementine Churchill

Mary Soames wrote the best biography of her mother: *Clementine Churchill* (Cassell, 1979), reissued by Transworld Publishers, 2002.

Randolph Churchill

There are several biographies of Randolph, notably the one by his son, Winston S. Churchill: *The Life of Randolph Churchill* (Weidenfeld & Nicolson, 1996).

Mary Soames

Her memoirs are *A Daughter's Tale* (Transworld Publishers, 2011).

John Spencer-Churchill

Clarissa's brother wrote *Crowded Canvas* (Odhams Press, 1961).

William Clark

Clark wrote *From Three Worlds* (Sidgwick & Jackson, 1986).

Lady Horner & Mells

Life at Mells is well covered in Frances Horner, *Time Remembered* (William Heinemann, 1933), John Jolliffe, *Raymond Asquith – Life and Letters* (Collins, 1980) and his memoir, *The Spice of Life* (Brunton Books, 2008), and Georgiana Blakiston, *Letters of Conrad Russell 1897–1947* (John Murray, 1987).

Sir Isaiah Berlin

Michael Ignatieff wrote the biography: *Isaiah Berlin: A Life* (Pushkin Press, 2023), and Henry Hardy edited the four volumes of letters: *Flourishing – Letters 1928–1946* (Cambridge, 2004), *Enlightening – Letters 1946–1960* (Chatto & Windus, 2009), *Building – Letters 1960–1975* (Chatto & Windus, 2013), and *Affirming – Letters 1975–1997* (Chatto & Windus, 2015).

Raimund von Hofmannsthal

There is a privately printed tribute: *A Rosenkavalier* (Hamburg, 1975).

Source Notes

Unless otherwise stated, the main sources come from the papers of the Countess of Avon, currently in the possession of the author. The other holdings are as follows:

Birmingham University

> Papers of the Earl of Avon
> Certain papers of the Countess of Avon

Churchill College, Cambridge

> Sir Winston Churchill
> Clementine, Baroness Spencer-Churcill
> Mary Soames
> Duff Cooper
> The diaries of Lady Gladwyn

The Bodleian Library, Oxford

> Archive of David Astor
> Papers of Sir Isaiah Berlin
> Archive of (Leonard) Robert Carr, Baron Carr of Hadley
> Archive of William Clark

The Getty Museum, Los Angeles
> Papers of James Pope-Hennessy

St John's College, Cambridge
> Papers of Sir Cecil Beaton

Mells Manor, Somerset (private collection)
Letters from Clarissa to 2nd Earl of Oxford & Asquith

Hugo Vickers (private collection)
Diary of Sir Charles Johnston

Harriet Cullen (private collection)
Papers of Lady Hartwell

Mary Pearson (private collection)
Papers of Lady Charteris of Amisfield

Key to the initials
AE – Anthony Eden
C – Clarissa
CB – Cecil Beaton
Clark – William Clark
Clemmie – Baroness Spencer-Churchill (aunt)
Duff – Duff Cooper
DW – David Wallace
G – Lady Gwendeline Spencer-Churchill (mother)
HV – Hugo Vickers
IB – Isaiah Berlin
Jack – John Spencer-Churchill (father)
JH – Jeremy Hutchinson
JPH – James Pope-Hennessy
JV – Joan Vickers
RVH – Raimund von Hofmannsthal
Trim – Earl of Oxford & Asquith
WSC – Sir Winston Churchill (uncle)

Introduction

1 HV diary, 31 August 1975.
2 HV diary, 8 December 1977.
3 HV diary, 16 December 1979.
4 HV diary, 25 March 1980.
5 HV diary, 25 July 1980.
6 HV diary, 2 August 1980.
7 HV diary, 5 August 1980.
8 HV diary, 6 August 1980.
9 HV diary, 28 August 1980.
10 HV diary, 1 September 1980.
11 HV diary, 15 October 1980.
12 HV diary, 25 September 1983.
13 HV diary, 4 March 1982.

Part One

1. Winston, Jack and Goonie

1 C to Cate Haste, 10 June 2006.
2 John Spencer-Churchill, *Crowded Canvas* (Odhams Press, 1961), p. 20.
3 Angela Culme-Seymour, *Bolter's Grand-daughter* (Bird Island Press, 2001), pp. 42–3.
4 *Crowded Canvas*, p. 86.
5 *Crowded Canvas*, p. 59.
6 Gladys, Duchess of Marlborough, to author, 1976.
7 JPH to C, Chatham, 8 October 1940.
8 Simon Heffer (ed.), *The Diaries of Henry 'Chips' Channon 1918–38* (Hutchinson, 2021), p. 917.
9 Julian Spencer-Churchill to author, Zoom from Montréal, 16 April 2024.
10 *The Times*, 12 March 1928.
11 *The Times*, 12 January 1998.
12 *The Times*, 9 July 1941.
13 Cynthia Asquith, *Remember and Be Glad* (James Barrie, 1952), p. 88.
14 *The Times*, 18 July 1941.
15 *The Times*, 11 July 1941.
16 *The Times*, 11 July 1941.
17 *Bolter's Grand-daughter*, pp. 42–3.
18 WSC to Lady Randolph Churchill, Trimulgherry, Devon, 4 November 1896; Randolph S. Churchill, *Winston S. Churchill, Youth* (Heinemann, 1966), p. 296 (CHAR 28/22/18–23).
19 *Winston S. Churchill, Youth*, p. 544.

20 Randolph S. Churchill, *Winston S. Churchill, Young Statesman* (Heinemann, 1967), p. 252.

21 Mary Soames, *Clemmie Churchill* (Doubleday, 2002), p. 59.

22 John Pearson, *Citadel of the Heart* (Macmillan, 1991), p. 110.

23 Anne Sebba, *Jennie Churchill* (John Murray, 2007), p. 276.

24 G to WSC, Coombe Abbey, Coventry, 9 August 1907 (CHAR 1/66/3).

25 WSC to G, Tring Park, Tring, to Coombe Abbey, Coventry, 11 August 1907.

26 WSC to Pamela Plowden, near Colenso, 21 February 1900, quoted in Randolph S. Churchill (ed.), *Winston S. Churchill, Companion Volume I, Part 2 1896–1900* (Houghton Mifflin Company, Boston, USA, 1967), p. 1151.

27 G to WSC, Eaton, Chester, 14 August 1907 (CHAR 1/66/6-8).

28 WSC to G, 12 Bolton Street, London W., to Newnham Park Oxford, 24 August 1907.

29 G to WSC, Wytham Abbey, 27 August 1907 (CHAR 1/66/15), quoted in *The Times*, 29 December 2014.

30 WSC to G, 12 Bolton Street, London W., to Wytham Abbey, Oxford, 27 August 1907.

31 G to WSC, Wytham Abbey, 28 August 1907 (CHAR 1/66/3).

32 G to WSC, Wytham Abbey, 7 September 1907 (CHAR 1/66/22-24).

33 Countess of Lytton (Pamela Plowden to WSC), Knebworth, 14 September 1907, quoted in Randolph S. Churchill (ed.), *Winston S. Churchill, Companion Volume II, Part 2 1907–1911* (Houghton Mifflin Company, Boston, USA, 1969), p. 677 (CHAR 1/66/27).

34 WSC to G, HMS Venus, Red Sea to Wytham Abbey, Oxford, 15 October 1907.

35 WSC to G, Great Lake, to Wytham Abbey, Oxford, 18 November 1907.

36 Jack Churchill to WSC, Bath Club, 34 Dover Street, 14 November 1907 (CHAR 1/66/48-50), quoted in *Winston S. Churchill, Companion Volume II, part 2 1907-1911*, pp. 695–6.

37 Jack to WSC, Bath Club, 34 Dover Street, 14 November 1907 (CHAR 1/66/48-50).

38 Jack to WSC, 28 Throgmorton Street, 21 November 1907 (CHAR 1/66/48-52-53), quoted in *Winston S. Churchill, Companion Volume II, part 2 1907–1911*, p. 705.

39 Lady Randolph to WSC, 21 November 1907 (CHAR 1/66/54-55), quoted in *Winston S. Churchill, Companion Volume II, part 2 1907–1911*, p. 705.

40 G to WSC, Coombe Abbey, 26 November 1907 (CHAR 1/66/59-61), quoted in *Winston S. Churchill, Companion Volume II, part 2 1907-1911*, pp. 709–10.

41 G to WSC, Wytham Abbey, 16 December 1907 (CHAR 1/66/66-68).

42 WSC to G, White Nile, to Wytham Abbey, Oxford (forwarded to Coombe Abbey, Coventry), 22 December 1907.

43 Jack to WSC, Marlborough Club, Pall Mall, SW, 19 December 1907 (CHAR 1/66/71-3).

44 WSC to Jack & G, 12 Bolton Street, W. [undated but April 1908] (CHAR 28/152B/215).

2. Bored at Boarding School, 1920–35

1   Clemmie to WSC, Brookside, Sutton Court [1918] (CHAR 1/125).
2   Hon. Arthur Bertie (brother) to G, Headington End, Oxford, 2 July 1920.
3   WSC to G, War Office, Whitehall, SW1, 28 June 1920.
4   John Spencer-Churchill, *Crowded Canvas* (Odhams Press, 1961), p. 39.
5   *The Times*, 30 July 1960.
6   *The Times*, 30 July 1960.
7   Frances Horner, *Time Remembered* (William Heinemann, 1933), p. 187.
8   John Pearson to author, 20 October 1991.
9   *Crowded Canvas*, p. 41.
10 C to John S. Churchill, Brighton, 1928.
11 Mary Soames, *A Daughter's Tale* (Transworld Publishers, 2011), p. 40.
12 JV to WSC, 1947 (GBR/0014/CHUR 1/43).
13 *Crowded Canvas*, p. 91.
14 G to C (undated, but 1931/1932).
15 C to G (undated, but April 1932).
16 Angela Culme-Seymour, *Bolter's Grand-daughter* (Bird Island Press, 2001), p. 55.
17 G to C (undated, but May 1934).
18 C to G, 1930 or 1931.
19 C to G, Wroxham Hall, Norwich, 3 January 1932.
20 C diary, 2 May 1933.
21 Mary Soames, *Clemmie Churchill* (Doubleday, 2002), p. 263.
22 G to C, 25 July 1935.
23 Obituary of Mrs E. L. Houison Craufurd, *The Times*, 18 December 1950.
24 Anne Glenconner, *Lady in Waiting* (Hodder & Stoughton, 2019), p. 27.
25 G to C, 28 September 1934.
26 Clarissa Eden, *From Churchill to Eden* (Weidenfeld & Nicolson, 2007), p. 11.
27 C to Cherie Blair, 13 November 2002.
28 C to Winston S. Churchill, 11 March 1997.
29 G to C, May 1935.
30 G to C, 7 November 1935.
31 Sally Bedell Smith, *Reflected Glory* (Simon & Schuster, 1996), p. 37.
32 C to G, 9 October 1931.
33 G to C, October 1934.
34 C to G, Blenheim Palace, 25 December 1934.
35 C to G, Himley Hall, 29 December 1934.
36 C to G, Himley Hall, January 1935.
37 G to C, 22 October 1935.

38 G to C, 1 November 1935.
39 G to C, 14 November 1935.

3. *The Narcissistic Diary, 1936–7*

1   *From Churchill to Eden*, p. 4.
2   Mary Soames, *A Daughter's Tale* (Transworld, 2011), p. 65.
3   C diary, 31 December 1935, 2 and 4 January 1936.
4   C diary, 2 January 1936.
5   C diary, 9 January 1936.
6   C diary, 21 January 1936.
7   C diary, 24 January 1936.
8   C diary, 30 January 1936.
9   Mary Soames, *Clementine Churchill – The Revised and Updated Biography* (Doubleday, 2002), p. 276.
10 C diary, 16 February 1936.
11 *Clementine Churchill – The Revised and Updated Biography* (Doubleday, 2002), p. 276.
12 *A Daughter's Tale*, p. 65.
13 C diary, 19 February 1936.
14 C diary, 14 March 1936.
15 C diary, 17 July 1936.
16 C diary, 1 April 1936.
17 C diary, 14 July 1936.
18 C diary, Easter Day, 1936.
19 C diary, 17 May 1936.
20 C diary, 20 March 1936.
21 C diary, 16 April 1936.
22 C diary, 26 January 1936.
23 C diary, 21 January 1936.
24 C diary, 13 March 1936.
25 C diary, 23 April 1936.
26 C diary, 11 September 1936.
27 C diary, 31 May 1936.
28 C diary, 28 November 1936.
29 C to JPH, Holworth House (undated, but 1938).
30 *From Churchill to Eden*, p. 13.
31 C diary, 21 August 1936.
32 C diary, 7 August 1936.
33 C diary, 22 November 1936.
34 C diary, 3 October 1936.
35 C diary, 11 December 1936.
36 C diary, 1 January 1937 (in 1936 diary).

37 *From Churchill to Eden*, p. 13.

38 G to C, 42 Chester Terrace, 4 May [1937].

39 G to C, 42 Chester Terrace, [15] June 1937.

40 G to C, 42 Chester Terrace, 5 May 1937.

41 G to C, Holworth House, Dorset (undated but 18 April 1937).

42 G to C, Chartwell (undated, but 13 or 20 June 1937).

4. *Aspirant Lovers*

1 *The Times*, 20 November 2007.

2 Clarissa Eden, *From Churchill to Eden* (Weidenfeld & Nicolson, 2007), p. 23.

3 JPH to C, Tuesday 7.15 (undated but June 1940).

4 JPH to C, Sheed and Ward Publishers, 31 Paternoster Row, 25 November 1937.

5 JPH to C, 74 Avenue Road, NW8, 28 September 1938.

6 JPH to C, Sheed and Ward Publishers, 26 September 1938.

7 James Pope-Hennessy, *London Fabric* (Batsford, 1939), p. 5.

8 *London Fabric*, p. 14.

9 *London Fabric*, p. 12.

10 *London Fabric*, p. 148.

11 *London Fabric*, p. 154.

12 G to C, Mells, 12 January 1938.

13 *From Churchill to Eden*, p. 6.

14 C to JPH, Mells (undated, but January 1939).

15 Robert Gathorne-Hardy (ed.), *Ottoline – The Early Memoirs of Lady Ottoline Morrell* (Faber & Faber, 1963), p. 178.

16 *From Churchill to Eden*, p. 5.

17 Trim to C, Mells, 16 August 1938.

18 C to JPH (undated, but 23 November 1939).

19 C to JPH, Dyrham Park, Chippenham, Wilts, Saturday [28 November 1939].

20 C to Trim, Lenzerheide, 8 January 1938.

21 C to Trim, Lenzerheide, 7 January 1938.

22 Trim to C, The Old Palace, Oxford, 21 February 1938.

23 Trim to C, Mells, 24 March 1938.

24 C to Trim, Pinewood Studios, Iver Heath, 4 April 1938.

25 C to Trim, Holworth, 8 April 1938.

26 *The Times*, 15 June 1938.

27 C to Trim, Crab Wood (undated but summer 1938).

28 C to Trim, [summer] 1938.

29 G to C, Chartwell (undated but 8 August 1938).

30 Clemmie to G (undated fragment, but August 1938).

31 Trim to C, 89 St Aldates, Oxford, 10 November 1938.

32 C to Trim (undated but November 1938).

33 Trim to C, 89 St Aldates, Oxford, 17 November 1938.

34 Trim to C, 89 St Aldates, Oxford, 29 November 1938.

35 Trim to C, 89 St Aldates, Oxford, 29 November 1938.

36 C to Cate Haste, 10 June 2006.

37 *From Churchill to Eden*, p. 19.

38 7th Marquess of Lansdowne to C, White Horse Hotel, Wincanton, 13 November 1939.

39 Lansdowne to C, Woodborough, Nottingham, 29 January 1940.

40 *The Times*, 5 February 1945.

41 DW to Clarissa, 14a Broad Street, Oxford, 26 February 1938.

42 DW to Clarissa, 14a Broad Street, Oxford, 26 February 1938.

43 DW to Clarissa, Hotel Imperial, Karlsbad, 26 August 1938.

44 C to Trim, Lavington Park, Sussex, 15 September 1938.

45 DW to C, Élysée Park Hotel, 2 Rond-Point des Champs-Élysées, Paris, 28 January 1939.

46 *From Churchill to Eden*, p. 15.

47 G to C, The Manor House, Mells, Tuesday 11 (January 1938).

48 DW to C, King George Hotel, Athens, 30 March 1938.

49 JH to C, Hôtel du Quai Voltaire, Paris (undated but April 1939).

5. *Paris Pre-war*

1 C to Trim, 27 October 1938.

2 C to Trim, Blenheim Palace (undated but 26 December 1938).

3 *From Churchill to Eden*, p. 24.

4 C to Trim, London, January 1939.

5 G to WSC, 42 Chester Terrace, 29 January 1939 (CHAR 1/125).

6 Trim to C, 89 St Aldates, Oxford, 26 January 1939.

7 C to JPH, 104 rue de Rennes, Paris (undated but January/February 1939).

8 C to JPH, 104 rue de Rennes (undated but January/February 1939).

9 C to JPH, 104 rue de Rennes (undated but January/February 1939).

10 C to Trim, 104 rue de Rennes, circa 8 February 1939.

11 C to Trim (undated).

12 C to Trim (undated but February 1939).

13 Trim to C, 12 February 1939.

14 Mrs Auberon Herbert, quoted in a letter, G to C, 42 Chester Terrace, Thursday [9 February 1939].

15 Quoted back to C to G, 42 Chester Terrace, Sunday [5 March 1939].

16 C to Trim (undated but February 1939).

17 C to Trim, 26 March 1939.

18 C to Trim (undated but March 1939).

19 C to Trim, 29 April 1939.

20 Jack to WSC, I Throgmorton Street, 4 July 1939 (CHAR 1/344/36).

21 C to Trim, 19 April 1939.

22 C to JPH, 104 rue de Rennes (undated but May 1939).

23 G to C, Chartwell, Saturday before dinner (29 April 1939).

24 G to C, Chartwell, Saturday before dinner (May 1939).

25 C to JPH, Grand Hotel, Venice (undated but May 1939).

26 C to JPH (undated but end of July 1939).

27 C to JPH (undated but end of July 1939).

28 C to JPH (undated but end of July 1939).

29 C to JPH, Grand Hotel, Venice (undated but May 1939).

30 C to JPH, Corcova, Strehaia (26 August 1939); and C to Trim (undated).

31 C to Trim, Posada, Romania, 19 August 1939.

6. Oxford, 1939–40

1 C to Trim, 31 July 1940.

2 C to JPH, Oxford, Monday (undated but autumn 1939).

3 C to Trim, 63 St John's Street, Oxford, 25 October 1939.

4 *From Churchill to Eden*, p. 34.

5 Simon Asquith to C, Rockbourne, Fordingbridge, 2 October 1938.

6 C to JPH, Holworth, 27 September [1939].

7 Lansdowne to C, Egypt, 21 September 1940.

8 Trim to C, Mells, 12 November 1939.

9 C to Trim, 63 St John's Street, 25 October 1939.

10 C late-life diary, 2005–7.

11 C to Trim, 63 St John's Street, 9 November 1939.

12 Trim to C, November 1939.

13 C to Trim, 63 St John's Street, July 1940.

14 C to Trim, 16 December 1939.

15 C to JPH, 63 St John's Street, 26 [October] 1939.

16 Trim to C, Northampton, 12 August 1940.

17 C to Trim, August 1940.

18 Brian Roberts, *Randolph: A Study of Churchill's Son* (Hamish Hamilton, 1984), p. 228.

19 *Spectator*, 6 May 1989.

20 Winston S. Churchill, *Memories & Adventures* (Weidenfeld & Nicolson, 1989), p. 20.

21 Diary, 18 March 1942, quoted in James Lees-Milne, *Ancestral Voices* (Chatto & Windus, 1975), p. 36.

22 C to JPH, 63 St John's Street, 26 [October] 1939, Getty Research Institute.

23 JPH to C, Long Barn, Weald, Sevenoaks, 29 February 1940.

24 JPH to C, 7 April 1940.

25 C to JPH, 63 St John Street, 21 May 1940.

26 JPH to C, Tuesday (undated but circa 16 April 1940).

27 Conrad Russell to Lady Diana Cooper, 2 March 1940, quoted in Georgiana Blakiston (ed.), *Letters of Conrad Russell 1897–1947* (John Murray, 1987), p. 180.

28 Trim to C, Mells, 3 March 1940.

29 *The Times*, 4 March 1940.

30 JPH to C, Long Barn, Weald, Sevenoaks, 6 March 1940.

31 Conrad Russell to Lady Diana Cooper (26 December 1940), quoted in *Letters of Conrad Russell 1897–1947*, p. 193.

32 Russell to Diana, 27 December 1940, quoted in *Letters of Conrad Russell 1897–1947*, p. 194.

33 Russell to Diana, 2 September 1941, quoted in *Letters of Conrad Russell 1897–1947*, p. 200.

34 JH to C, HMS King Alfred, Hove, Surrey, 8 August 1940.

35 C typed note with the Hutchinson letters (undated).

36 JH to C (undated, postmark 27 September 1940).

37 C to JPH, 63 St John's Street, 5 October 1940.

38 JPH to C, Chatham (Tuesday) 8 October 1940.

39 C to Trim, late summer 1940.

40 C to Trim, Crab Wood, 7 September 1940.

41 Trim to C, Chatham, 18 September 1940.

42 Trim to C, Kettering, 5 October 1940.

7. Drifting, 1940–41

1 C to JPH, 63 St John's Street, Tuesday 26 (October 1939).

2 C to Trim, 42 Chester Terrace, 1 April 1940.

3 C to JPH, 63 St John's Street, 5 June 1940.

4 C to JPH, 42 Chester Terrace (undated but late 1939).

5 JPH to C, Sunday morning (undated but 26 January 1941).

6 C to JPH, 63 St John's Street, Friday (undated but June 1940).

7 C to JPH, 63 St John's Street, 30 January 1941.

8 Lady Antonia Fraser to author, 2 December 2023.

9 C to Trim, circa 2 July 1940.

10 Clarissa Eden, *From Churchill to Eden* (Weidenfeld & Nicolson, 2007), pp. 38–9.

11 *From Churchill to Eden*, p. 42.

12 C to JPH, 63 St John's Street, Friday (undated but June 1940).

13 C to JPH, 63 St John's Street, Friday (undated but June 1940).

14 Mark Amory, *Lord Berners – The Last Eccentric* (Chatto & Windus, 1998), p. 189.

15 Lord Berners, *Far From the Madding War* (Constable, 1941), pp. 4–5.

16 Berners to C, Faringdon, 4 August 1941.

17 C to Gay Charteris, Faringdon, March 1941 (Mary Pearson Papers).

18 Valentine Lawford to author, New York, 31 May 1981.

19 C to GC, 24 Yeoman's Row, London SW3, 16 December 1940.
20 C to GC, 24 Yeoman's Row, London SW3, 16 December 1940.
21 C to GC, 24 Yeoman's Row, London SW3, 16 December 1940.
22 C to GC, Crab Wood, 18 December 1940.
23 C to Gay Margesson, December 1940.
24 JPH to C, Avenue Road, 23 December 1940.
25 C to Gay Margesson, December 1940.
26 C to GC, Crab Wood, 22 December 1940.
27 G to C, probably from Crab Wood, Thursday (January 1941).

8. London, 1941–4

 1 G to C, Crab Wood, 8 February 1941.
 2 C to a friend, January 1941.
 3 JPH to C, Sunday morning (undated but 26 January 1941).
 4 JPH to CB, 2 December 1940 (CB Papers, St John's College, Cambridge).
 5 C to GC, Faringdon, March 1941.
 6 CB analysis of C, unpublished diary, 1952.
 7 Trim to C, Middle East Forces, 39 January 1941.
 8 C to Trim, Rockbourne, Fordingbridge, August 1941.
 9 C to Trim, Rockbourne, August 1941.
10 C to Trim, Rockbourne, August 1941.
11 C to Winston S. Churchill, 11 March 1997.
12 *The Times*, 18 July 1941.
13 C diary, September 2007.
14 Anne, Lady Islington to C, Dyrham Park, 7 July 1941.
15 George Cornwallis-West to WSC, Branksome Tower Hotel, Bournemouth, 11 July 1941 (CHAR 1/361/38).
16 Countess of Lytton to C, Knebworth (undated but 1941).
17 Trim to C, Syria, 2 October 1941.
18 C to Trim, Rockbourne, August 1941.
19 Isaiah Berlin to Alice James, 6 June 1953; Henry Hardy and Jennifer Holmes (eds), *Enlightening – Letters 1946–1960* (Chatto & Windus, 2009), p. 377.
20 C to JPH, Rockbourne (undated but August 1941).
21 C to CB, Chequers, 10 September 1941.
22 Quoted in CB to C, 8 Pelham Place, SW7 (undated but 23 September 1941).
23 CB to C, Ashcombe, Friday (undated but September 1941).
24 Trim to C, M.E.F., 15 March 1942.
25 Trim to C, Beersheba, Palestine, 8 December 1944.
26 CB to C, Plaza, New York, 21 January 1948.
27 CB to C, 20 December 1950.
28 C to CB, Dorchester Hotel, 20 April 1942.

29 C to CB, Dorchester Hotel, 20 April 1942.

30 Diary for 2 August 1942, quoted in James Lees-Milne, *Ancestral Voices* (Chatto & Windus, 1975), p. 83.

31 Diary for 1 August 1943, quoted in *Ancestral Voices*, p. 219.

32 C to CB, Dorchester Hotel, 20 April 1942.

33 Diary 15 April 1942, quoted in Simon Heffer (ed.), *Henry 'Chips' Channon, The Diaries 1938–43* (Hutchinson, 2021), p. 767.

34 Diary 7 July 1949, quoted in *Henry 'Chips' Channon, The Diaries 1943–57*, p. 573.

35 C to CB, 124 Rossmore Court, 23 February 1944.

36 C to CB, 17 April 1944.

37 C to Berners, quoted in Mark Amory, *Lord Berners – The Last Eccentric* (Chatto & Windus, 1998), p. 189.

38 *The Times*, 9 September 1944.

39 *The Times*, 25 October 1944.

40 Lansdowne to C, M.E.F., 11 September 1943.

41 *The Times*, 5 February 1945.

42 Lady Colum Crichton-Stuart to C, Bowood, 27 January 1945.

9. Raimund, 1943–51

1 Charlotte Mosley (ed.), *The Mitfords – Letters Between Six Sisters* (Fourth Estate, 2007), p. 273.

2 C late diary [post 2007].

3 C to Cate Haste, 8 June 2006.

4 CB diary, Clarissa – Her Engagement – May 1952.

5 *Raimund von Hofmannsthal – A Rosenkavalier 1906–1974* (Hamburg, privately printed, 1975), p. 15.

6 Diana Cooper, *The Light of Common Day* (Rupert Hart-Davis, 1959), p. 67.

7 *A Rosenkavalier 1906–1974*, p. 19.

8 *A Rosenkavalier 1906–1974*, p. 54.

9 *A Rosenkavalier 1906–1974*, p. 28; originally 'Mr Raimund von Hofmannsthal' (supplement obituary) – *The Times*, 26 April 1974.

10 *A Rosenkavalier 1906–1974*, p. 30.

11 *A Rosenkavalier 1906–1974*, p. 40.

12 Charles Duff, *Charley's Woods* (Zuleika, 2017), pp. 122–3.

13 George Weidenfeld, *Remembering My Good Friends* (Harper Collins, 1995), pp. 162–3.

14 Charles Duff to author, 7 August 2023.

15 Octavian von Hofmannsthal to author, London, 22 November 2021.

16 Laura, Duchess of Marlborough to author (1980s).

17 RVH to C, 21 January 1944.

18 C late diary.

19 C to CB, 124 Rossmore Court, 23 February 1944.

20 C to CB, 124 Rossmore Court, 7 April 1944.

21 C to CB, Faringdon House, Berks, 17 April 1944.

22 RVH to C, Dorchester Hotel, 12 July 1944.

23 RVH to C, London, 10 August 1944.

24 JPH to C, 9 Ladbroke Grove, 23 November 1944.

25 JPH to C, 9 Ladbroke Grove, Good Friday (undated but April 1946).

26 C to CB (undated but January 1946).

27 *A Rosenkavalier 1906–1974*, p. 60.

28 C to CB, 9 September 1946.

29 C to CB, 9 September 1946.

30 C to IB, Mas de Fourques, Lunel, Hérault, 22 September 1946 (1–826), Oxford, Bodleian Libraries, Papers of Sir Isaiah Berlin 1897–1998.

31 C to IB (undated).

32 RVH telegram to C, 18 October 1947.

33 RVH to C, Time International, Rockefeller Center, New York, 13 June 1950.

34 Duff Cooper to C, 69 rue de Lille, Paris, 9 September 1952.

35 Duff to C, Travellers Club, Paris, undated.

36 C to Duff, London Film Productions, 146 Piccadilly, 22 August 1947. (DUFC 12/3).

37 Duff Cooper diary, 19 October 1947 (DUFC 15/1/37).

38 Duff Cooper diary, 4 February 1948 (DUFC 15/1/39).

39 Duff Cooper diary, 16 June 1948 (DUFC 15/1/40).

40 Duff Cooper diary, 7 September 1945 (DUFC 15/1/34).

41 Duff Cooper diary, 13 September 1945 (DUFC 15/1/34).

42 Duff Cooper diary, 25 November 1945 (DUFC 15/1/34).

43 Duff Cooper diary, 1 February 1948 (DUFC 15/1/39).

44 Duff Cooper diary, 12 February 1948 (DUFC 15/1/39).

45 Duff Cooper diary, 6 March 1949 (DUFC 15/1/43).

46 C to Duff, from Weidenfeld & Nicolson, 7 Cork Street, London W1, 21 March 1951 (DUFC 12/3).

47 C to Duff, from Weidenfeld & Nicolson, 7 Cork Street, London W1, 25 March 1951 (DUFC 12/3).

48 Duff to C, Château de St Firmin, 26 March 1951.

49 Alastair Forbes to author (1980s).

50 Clarissa late diary.

10. *Condé Nast, Korda and Weidenfeld, 1945–52*

1 C to JPH, Chequers, 14 July 1945.

2 C to JPH, Chequers, 14 July 1945.

3 C to JPH, 124 Rossmore Court, NW1 (undated but January 1945).

4 C to Duff, 20 July 1945 (DUFC 12/3).

5 *Vogue*, February 1946, p. 62.

6 Berlin Letter, *Horizon*, March 1946, pp. 188–94.

7 C to Duff, 1 January 1946 (DUFC 12/3).

8 Quotes from 'Spotlight' in *Vogue*, July to October 1946.

9 CB to C, Cort Theatre, Broadway, 14 November 1946.

10 JPH to C, 9 Ladbroke Grove, London W11, 25 July 1944.

11 Emma Soames (ed.), *Mary Churchill's War* (Two Roads, 2021), p. 297.

12 Lord Horder, University College Hospital, Grafton Street, WC1, to WSC, 1 May 1945 (CHAR 1/386/72, Churchill College, Cambridge).

13 JV to WSC, 1947 (GBR/0014/CHUR 1/43).

14 C to Duff, 124 Rossmore Court, 7 March 1947 (DUFC 12/3).

15 C to IB, 13 March 1947.

16 C to IB, 13 March 1947.

17 C to Duff, 124 Rossmore Court, 30 March 1947 (DUFC 12/3).

18 C to Duff, 124 Rossmore Court, 7 March 1947 (DUFC 12/3).

19 *From Churchill to Eden*, p. 99.

20 CB diary, January 1947.

21 CB diary, January 1947.

22 C to CB, London Films, 146 Piccadilly, 15 November 1947.

23 C to CB, London Films, 15 November 1947.

24 C to CB, London Films, 15 November 1947.

25 C to Duff, South Wraxall Manor, Bradford-on-Avon, 4 August 1947.

26 Simon Harcourt-Smith, 'Is Vivien Leigh better than Greta Garbo?' *Picture Post*, 24 January 1948.

27 C to Cate Haste, 19 February 2003.

28 Diana Cooper to John Julius Norwich, Dorchester Hotel, 24 January 1948, quoted in John Julius Norwich (ed.), *Darling Monster* (Chatto & Windus, 2013), pp. 244–5.

29 Colin Tennant to C (undated).

30 Colin Tennant to C (undated but February 1948).

31 C to CB, London Films, SW1 (undated but late 1948).

32 Harold Baker to C, Athenaeum, 19 July 1949.

33 *Sunday Times*, 22 June 1947.

34 C to IB, Hotel Österreichischer Hof, Salzburg, 19 August 1949 (Mss. Berlin, 1–826).

35 C, quoted in Sofka Zinovieff, *The Mad Boy, Lord Berners, My Grandmother and Me* (Jonathan Cape, 2014), p. 285.

36 George Weidenfeld, *Remembering My Good Friends* (Harper Collins, 1995), p. 138.

37 Lady Antonia Fraser to author, 2 December 2023.

Part Two

11. The Path to Marriage, 1947–52

1 C to Duff, Binderton House, Chichester, 6 June 1948. (DUFC 12/3).
2 CB diary, analysis of Clarissa, 1952.
3 John Julius Norwich (ed.), *The Duff Cooper Diaries* (Weidenfeld & Nicolson, 2005), p. 453. (Diary for 24 November 1947.)
4 Anthony Eden, *Another World* (Allen Lane, 1976), pp. 87 and 91.
5 *Hansard 5C, volume 332*, p. 42.
6 C's note in response to Rhodes James biography.
7 C to Duff, Binderton, 6 June 1948 (DUFC 12/3).
8 C to CB, Broadchalke, 1 January 1949.
9 C to CB, 124 Rossmore Court, 29 March 1951.
10 IB to Rowland Burdon-Muller, 7 October 1952, Henry Hardy and Jennifer Holmes (eds), *Enlightening – Isaiah Berlin Letters 1946–60* (Pimlico, 2009), p. 323.
11 C to IB, 4 January 1952. (Mss. Berlin, 1–826).
12 CB diary, June 1952.
13 C to IB, 4 January 1952. (Mss. Berlin, 1–826).
14 JPH to Nolwyn de Janzé, 9 Ladbroke Grove, 2 December [1951], quoted in Peter Quennell (ed.), *A Lonely Business* (Weidenfeld & Nicolson, 1981), p. 78.
15 JPH to C, 9 Ladbroke Grove, 25 November 1951.
16 C to JPH, 124 Rossmore Court, Thursday (undated but 27 December 1951).
17 C diary (2), 2008–2010.
18 C to Duff, 26 February 1951 (DUFC 12/3).
19 Elsa Maxwell, *The Temptations of Anthony Eden*, widely syndicated in newspapers, 6 January 1952.
20 RVH telegram to C from New York, 20 June 1951.
21 RVH telegram to C from London, 10 April 1952.
22 RVH telegram to C from New York, 27 May 1952.
23 C to Duff, 124 Rossmore Court, undated but 1951 (DUFC 12/3).
24 C to CB, undated.
25 IB to Alice James, 6 June 1953, quoted in *Enlightening – Isaiah Berlin Letters 1946–60*, p. 377.
26 CB diary, analysis of Clarissa, 1952.
27 C note: 'Comment on Cecil Beaton analysis of my character' – C. Avon 1986.
28 IB letter to Rowland Burdon-Muller, 7 October 1952, quoted in *Enlightening – Letters 1946–1960* (Chatto & Windus, 2009), p. 323.

12. *Marriage*

1 *From Churchill to Eden*, p. 110.
2 Duff to C, Château de St Firmin, 11 April 1952.
3 C to JPH, 124 Rossmore Court, Saturday (undated but 9 August 1952).
4 JPH to C, Mottisfont Abbey, Monday (11 August 1952).
5 JPH to C, 9 Ladbroke Grove, London, 1 September 1952.
6 CB telegram to C, 14 August 1952.
7 Garbo to CB (undated, but summer 1952).
8 CB to C, Redditch House, Broadchalke (undated but 1952).
9 JPH to CB, 9 Ladbroke, Grove, Thursday (undated but circa August 1952).
10 C to Clemmie, undated, but 1952 (CSCT).
11 Mary Soames, *Clementine Churchill* (Transworld, 2002), p. 471.
12 Lady Pamela Berry to C, Cross Farm, Kidmore End, Monday (11 August 1952).
13 WSC to C, Chartwell, 10 August 1952.
14 Colin Tennant to C, Glen, 8 August 1952.
15 JV to C, 18 Albion Street, London, 12 August 1952.
16 Evelyn Waugh to C, White's, London, 2 September 1952.
17 IB letter to Rowland Burdon-Muller, 2 December 1952, *Enlightening – Letters 1946–1960*, Pimlico 2009 p. 339.
18 IB letter to Rowland Burdon-Muller, 2 December 1952, *Enlightening – Letters 1946–1960*, p. 339.
19 Alastair Forbes telegram to C, 13 August 1952.
20 Duff to C, Cap Ferrat, 13 August 1952.
21 C to Duff, British Embassy, Lisbon, 26 August 1952 (DUFC 12/3).
22 C to Duff, British Embassy, Lisbon, 26 August 1952 (DUFC 12/3).
23 *Daily Telegraph*, 15 August 1952.
24 Duff to C, 69 rue de Lille, Paris, 24 September 1952.
25 *From Churchill to Eden*, p.121.
26 *From Churchill to Eden*, p.122.
27 C to Cate Haste, 19 February 2003.
28 C to Duff, 26 August 1952 (DUFC 12/3).
29 Duff to C, 69 rue de Lille, 9 September 1952.
30 Duff to C, 69 rue de Lille, 24 September 1952.
31 C to CB, 1 Carlton Gardens, (undated but early) 1953.
32 CB, undated diary (but late in 1952 or 1953).
33 CB, undated diary (but late 1952 or 1953).

13. *Foreign Secretary, 1952–4*

1 C to Cate Haste, 19 February 2003, p. 42.

2 IB to Arthur Schlesinger, 30 May 1953, *Enlightening – Letters 1946–60* (Pimlico, 2009), p. 371.

3 C to Cate Haste, 19 February 2003.

4 C to Cate Haste, 2003.

5 C to Duff, 1 Carlton Gardens, 17 September 1952 (DUFC 12/3).

6 CB unpublished diary (undated), 1949.]

7 C to Duff, Warwick Castle, 3 October 1952 (DUFC 12/3).

8 C diary, 1 November 1952.

9 C diary, 4 November 1952.

10 C diary, 25 November 1952.

11 C diary, 6 March 1953.

12 C diary, 9 March 1953.

13 Letter to MJ, 23 March 1953, quoted in Miles Jebb (ed.), *The Diaries of Cynthia Gladwyn* (Constable, 1995), p.153.

14 *The Diaries of Cynthia Gladwyn*, p. 157.

15 C diary, 10 March 1953.

16 C diary, 12 March 1953.

17 C diary, 17 March 1953.

18 C's report on Anthony's illnesses and operations (Avon Papers, AP39/3/461).

19 C to Duff, Chequers, 29 May 1953 (DUFC 12/3).

20 C to Cate Haste, 2003.

21 Peregrine S. Churchill to author, London, 25 November 1975.

22 Edens to Robert Carr, New England Baptist Hospital, Boston, 22 June 1953 (Mss. Robert Carr, Bodleian Library, Ms. Eng c. 7300 [1–165]).

23 C's note on her marriage, in response to the Rhodes James biography.

24 C to Ann Fleming, Moorland Lodge, Newport, Rhode Island, 31 June 1953.

25 C diary, July 1953.

26 John Colville, *The Fringes of Power* (Hodder & Stoughton, 1985), p. 668.

27 Colville to C, 26 June 1953.

28 Randolph Churchill to Clarissa, Oving House, Aylesbury, 28 June 1953.

29 C diary, July 1953.

30 C diary, 15 July 1953.

31 C diary, 27 July 1953.

32 D. R. Thorpe, *Eden* (Chatto & Windus, 2003), p. 392.

33 C diary, 7 October 1953.

34 *Daily Telegraph*, 9 October 1953.

35 *Daily Telegraph*, 12 October 1953.

36 *Daily Telegraph*, 12 October 1953.

37 Duff to C, Vaynol, N. Wales, 24 December 1953.

38 Diana Cooper to AE and C, British Embassy, Madrid (undated, but January 1954).

39 C to Diana Cooper, 1 Carlton Gardens (DIAC 1/5/3).

40 C to Lady Pamela Berry, March 1954 (Harriet Cullen Papers).

41 C to Ann Fleming, 1 Carlton Gardens, 5 September 1952.

42 Marina, Viscountess Camrose to author, 1 February 2024.

43 C to CB, Rose Bower, 24 February 1954 (Avon Papers, Birmingham University).

44 Clemmie to C, 10 Downing Street, 9 March 1954 (Avon Papers, Birmingham University).

45 C to Harold Baker (undated, but 11 March 1954) (Avon Papers, Birmingham University).

46 C to Cynthia Jebb, Hôtel Beau-Rivage, Geneva, 27 April 1954 (Cynthia Gladwyn Papers, Churchill Archive Centre).

47 C to AE, Rose Bower, Sunday (undated but June 1954).

48 C diary, 19 July 1954.

49 C diary, 15 October 1954.

50 C diary, 20 October 1954.

51 C to author, August 1980.

52 C to CB, Rose Bower, 4 December 1954.

53 C diary, 26 January 1955.

54 C diary, 18 February 1955.

55 C diary, 20 February 1955.

56 C diary, 20 February 1955.

57 C diary, Xmas 1954.

58 C diary, Xmas 1954.

59 John Colville, *The Fringes of Power* (Hodder & Stoughton, 1985), p. 706.

60 C diary, 10 March 1955.

61 C diary, 12 March 1955.

62 C diary, 29 March 1955.

63 D. R. Thorpe, entry for Anthony Eden in *Dictionary of National Biography*.

14. Prime Minister, April 1955–July 1956

1 C to Cherie Blair, 13 November 2002.

2 *The Fringes of Power*, p. 708.

3 Kay Halle, *Randolph Churchill, The Young Pretender* (Heinemann, 1971), p. 166.

4 *Observer*, 30 October 1960, quoted in *Randolph Churchill, The Young Pretender*, pp. 185–6.

5 C diary, 5 April 1955.

6 Winston S. Churchill, *His Father's Son – The Life of Randolph Churchill* (Weidenfeld & Nicolson, 1996), p. 332.

7 *His Father's Son*, p. 333.

8 C to Cate Haste, 19 February 2003.

9 *The Fringes of Power*, p. 708.

10 C diary, 6 April 1955.

11 *Daily Telegraph*, 21 April 1955 (retrospective due to a national newspaper strike).

12 C diary, 27 April 1955.

13 C diary, July 1955.

14 C to Cherie Blair, 13 November 2002.

15 C to Cherie Blair, 13 November 2002.

16 C to Cherie Blair, 13 November 2002.

17 C diary, 9 April 1955.

18 C diary, 19 April 1955.

19 C diary, 22 August 1955.

20 C diary, 22 December 1955.

21 JPH to C, *Times Literary Supplement*, Printing House Square, 25 March 1955.

22 C to JPH, 10 Downing Street, 2 December 1955.

23 C to JPH, Biddick Hall, Co. Durham, 2 April 1955.

24 *Daily Telegraph*, 30 April 1955.

25 *Daily Telegraph*, 23 May 1955.

26 C diary, 27 May 1955.

27 WSC to JV, 26 May 1955 (CHUR 2/137).

28 JV to WSC, May 1955 (CHUR 2/137).

29 C diary, 17 July 1955.

30 *The Times*, 29 June 1985.

31 Robert Rhodes James, *Anthony Eden* (Weidenfeld & Nicolson, 1986), p. 406.

32 *Anthony Eden*, p. 411.

33 D. R. Thorpe, *Eden* (Chatto & Windus, 2003), p. 444.

34 Hon. Tarquin Olivier to author, 24 May 2024.

35 William Clark diary, 20 September 1955 (Oxford, Bodleian Libraries, Archive of William Clark) (CMD ID 7010, 12146).

36 C diary, 25 August 1955.

37 William Clark, *From Three Worlds* (Sidgwick & Jackson, 1986), p. 146.

38 *From Three Worlds*, p. 155.

39 C to Cate Haste, 19 February 2003.

40 William Clark diary, 15–16 October 1955 CMD ID 7010, 12146.

41 *From Three Worlds*, p. 156.

42 *From Three Worlds*, p. 157.

43 *Daily Telegraph*, 7 October 1955.

44 Harold Baker to C, Crab Wood, 14 September 1955.

45 *Daily Telegraph*, 29 October 1955.

46 *Daily Telegraph*, 18 November 1955.

47 *Crowded Canvas*, p. 208.

48 C diary, 25 March 1956.

49 Peregrine S. Churchill to author, London, 25 November 1975.

50 AE diary, 2 September 1955, (Avon Papers AP20/1/24-28, Birmingham University).

51 Clark diary, October 1955 (CMD ID 7010, 12146).

52 *Daily Telegraph*, 15 October 1955.

53 C diary, 2 October 1955.

54 C diary, 2 October 1955.

55 *From Three Worlds*, p. 159.

56 C diary, 29 November 1955.

57 C diary, 27 December 1955.

58 C diary, 27 December 1955.

59 C to CB, Chequers, 26 December 1955.

60 C diary, 27 December 1955.

61 *Daily Telegraph*, 3 January 1956.

62 Noël Coward diary, 19 February 1956, Graham Payn and Sheridan Morley (eds), *The Noël Coward Diaries* (Weidenfeld & Nicolson, 1982), p. 308.

63 C diary, 18 April 1956.

64 C diary, 22 April 1956.

65 Sir Anthony Eden, *Full Circle* (Times Publishing, 1960), p. 365.

66 C diary, 5 May 1956.

67 C diary, 26 June 1956.

68 C diary, 26 June 1956.

69 C diary, 27 June 1956.

15. *The Suez Crisis, 1956*

1 Simon Heffer to author, 17 January 2024.

2 C to Cherie Blair, 13 November 2002.

3 William Clark diary, 24 July 1956 (CMD ID 7010, 12146).

4 C diary, 27 July 1956.

5 Clark diary, 29 July 1956 (CMD ID 7010, 12146).

6 *The Times*, 9 August 1956.

7 Clark diary, 9 August 1956 (CMD ID 7010, 12146).

8 C to Clark, 9 August 1956 (Avon Papers, Birmingham University).

9 *From Three Worlds*, p. 187.

10 C diary, 6 August 1956.

11 C diary, 25 August 1956.

12 C diary, 27 August 1956.

13 C diary, 27 September 1956.

14 Cynthia Jebb diary, 14 November 1956, quoted in *The Diaries of Cynthia Gladwyn*, p. 191.

15 D. R. Thorpe, *Eden* (Chatto & Windus, 2003), p. 500.

16 C diary, 14 October 1956.

17 C diary, 13 October 1956.

18 C diary, 14 October 1956.

19 CB diary, [17] October 1956, quoted in Hugo Vickers, *Loving Garbo* (Jonathan Cape, 1994), p. 194.

20 Martin Gilbert, *Never Despair: Winston S. Churchill, 1945–1965* (Orion, 1988), p. 1222.

21 *Daily Telegraph*, 5 November 1956.

22 Clark diary, 2 November 1956 (CMD ID 7010, 12146).

23 *From Three Worlds*, p. 209.

24 C to CB, 8 November 1956.

25 *The Times*, 6 November 1956.

26 C diary, 7 November 1956.

27 *Daily Telegraph*, 20 November 1956.

28 C diary, 20 November 1956.

29 *Daily Telegraph*, 21 November 1956.

30 C's Gateshead speech, draft notes, 20 November 1956 (Avon Papers AP3/2/1-3 Birmingham University).

31 C diary, 24 November 1956.

32 C diary, 24 November 1956.

33 *Daily Telegraph*, 26 November 1956.

34 C to 'Bluey' Baker, Goldeneye, Oracabessa, Jamaica, 28 November [1956] (Avon Papers, Birmingham University).

35 *Daily Telegraph*, 30 November 1956.

36 Robert Rhodes James, *Anthony Eden* (Weidenfeld & Nicolson, 1986), p. 583.

37 Ann Fleming to C, 16 Victoria Square, SW1, Friday 20 [in fact Thursday 20 December 1956].

38 Simon Heffer, *Like the Roman: The Life of Enoch Powell* (Weidenfeld & Nicolson, 1998), p.210.

39 *Daily Telegraph*, 15 December 1956.

40 *Daily Telegraph*, 18 December 1956.

41 *Hansard*, 20 December 1956.

42 J. P. Mackintosh (ed.), *British Prime Ministers in the Twentieth Century, Volume 2: Churchill to Callaghan* (Weidenfeld & Nicolson, 1978), Robert Blake, pp. 112–13.

43 C's note on AE's illnesses (Avon Papers, PP39/3/461).

44 Philip de Zulueta, 'Thirty Years On', *Spectator*, 11 October 1986.

45 C to Cherie Blair, 6 December 2002.

Part Three

16. Eden in Retirement, 1957–64

1 C diary, 8 January 1957.

2 AE to Sir WSC, Sandringham, 9 January 1957 (CHUR 2/216).

3 C diary, 9 January 1957.

4 AE private diary.

5 *The Times*, 10 January 1957.

6 Philip de Zulueta, 'Thirty Years On', *Spectator*, 11 October 1986.

7 Quoted in *The Art of the Possible – The Memoirs of Lord Butler, KG, CH* (Hamish Hamilton, 1971), p. 196.

8 C diary, 13 January 1957.

9 C to Harold Baker, Chequers, 14 January 1957 (Avon Papers, Birmingham University).

10 C diary, 18 January 1957.

11 *Daily Telegraph*, 23 January 1957.

12 JPH to Ann Fleming, 9 Ladbroke Grove, 18 February 1957.

13 C diary, 18 January 1957.

14 C to CB, Otehei Bay, Northland, New Zealand, 16 March 1957.

15 CB to Clarissa, Reddish House, 29 March 1957 (Avon Papers, Birmingham University).

16 Clemmie to C, 28 Hyde Park Gate, SW7, 12 April 1957.

17 *Daily Telegraph*, 13 April 1957.

18 C diary 10 June 1957.

19 *Daily Telegraph*, 23 May 1957.

20 *Daily Telegraph*, 24 May 1957.

21 C's draft letter to Lord Beaverbrook, Government House, Ottawa, 18 May 1957 (Avon Papers, Birmingham University).

22 C diary, 10 June 1957.

23 C diary, 14 March 1958.

24 C to CB, Donhead House, Shaftesbury, 5 September 1959.

25 Sir Bryan Cartledge to author, 27 March 2024.

26 David Dilks to author, 24 June 2024.

27 Note by C on memo from Sir Bryan Cartledge to Secretary of State, Telo 549, May 1986.

28 AE to Robert Carr, Fyfield Manor, Pewsey, 17 October 1958 [Oxford, Bodleian Library, Archive of (Leonard) Robert Carr, Baron Carr of Hadley].

29 C to CB, Quinta Cala, Cuernavaca, 17 January [1959].

30 C to CB, Uxmal, Yucatan, 2 February [1959].

31 C to CB, Mercer's Creek, Antigua, 13 February 1960.

32 C to CB, Mercer's Creek, Antigua, 13 February 1960.

33 CB to C, 7 Pelham Place, SW7, 20 February 1960.

34 AE to Robert Carr, Government House, St Lucia, February 1960, Ms. Eng c. 7300 (1–165)].

35 C to Trim, Dian Point, Antigua, 26 February 1960.

36 C to CB, Friendship Bay, Bequia, 7 February 1961.

37 C to Trim, St Vincent, 4 February 1960.

38 Clemmie to C, 28 Hyde Park Gate, 3 February 1961 [Avon Papers, Birmingham University].

39 C to Clemmie, Friendship Bay, 23 February 1961 (CSCT).

40 AE to Sir WSC, Friendship Bay, 20 February 1962 (CHUR 2/518).

41 AE private diary.

42 *Daily Telegraph*, 17 November 1960.

43 *Daily Telegraph*, 3 August 1962.

44 AE private diary.

45 C to CB, 23 June 1963.
46 C to CB, 23 June 1963.
47 CB to C, Bel Air Hotel, Los Angeles, 10 October 1963.
48 C to CB, Fyfield Manor, Pewsey, 16 October 1963.
49 Peregrine S. Churchill to author, London, 25 November 1975.
50 C to CB, Fyfield Manor, Pewsey, 16 October 1963.

17. *Eden's Last Years, 1964–77*

1 Mary Soames, *Clementine Churchill* (Cassell, 1979), p. 491.
2 C to CB, Yeoman's Point, St James, Barbados, 21 March 1965.
3 *Clementine Churchill*, p. 548.
4 C to CB, Yeoman's Point, St James, Barbados, 21 March 1965.
5 CB to C, 30 December 1965 (Avon Papers, Birmingham University).
6 CB to C, Heron's Bay, Barbados (undated but 1966) (Avon Papers, Birmingham University).
7 CB to C (undated but circa March 1966) (Avon Papers, Birmingham University).
8 C to CB, Villa Nova, Barbados, 4 December [1966].
9 Clarissa to Cate Haste, 2003.
10 Clemmie to C, Flat 26, 7 Princes Gate, SW7, 20 June 1968 (Avon Papers, Birmingham University).
11 C to CB, 14 February 1969.
12 C to CB, Villa Nova, Barbados, 12 January [1971].
13 C diary, circa May 2010.
14 CB to C, 8 Pelham Place, 3 October [1967].
15 AE to Robert Carr, Alvediston, 20 June 1967 (Mss. Robert Carr, Ms. Eng c. 7300 [1–165]).
16 *Sunday Express*, June 1967.
17 *The Times*, 2 June 1967.
18 AE to Robert Carr, Alvediston, 25 May 1969 (Mss. Robert Carr, Ms. Eng c. 7300 [1–165]).
19 C's note on AE's operations (Avon Papers, Birmingham University).
20 *Daily Telegraph*, 6 May 1975.
21 Quoted back to her by Sir John Pope-Hennessy in his letter to Clarissa, 28 via de Bardi, Florence, 18 June 1991.
22 John Pope-Hennessy, *Learning to Look* (Heinemann, 1991), p. 228.
23 Peter Quennell (ed.), *A Lonely Business* (Weidenfeld & Nicolson, 1981), p. xix.
24 C to CB, Hotel Loro Parole, Puerto de le Cruz (undated but January 1974).
25 Sir John Pope-Hennessy to C, 41 Bedford Gardens, W8, 10 February 1974.
26 CB to C, 8 Pelham Place, SW7, 8 February 1974.
27 Ann Fleming to Patrick and Joan Leigh-Fermor, 6 February [1974], in Mark Amory (ed.) *The Letters of Ann Fleming* (Collins Harvill, 1985), p. 410.

28 Ann Fleming to C, Chatsworth, 16 February 1974.

29 Peregrine S. Churchill to author, London, 25 November 1975.

30 AE to Robert Carr, Alvediston, 3 May 1976 (Mss. Robert Carr, Ms. Eng c. 7300 [1–165]).

31 John W. Braasch, *Anthony Eden's (Lord Avon) Biliary Tract Saga – Annals of Surgery*, Vol.238, no 5, November 2003.

32 AE to Robert Carr, Alvediston, 3 May 1976 (Ms. Eng c. 7300 [1–165]).

33 Derived from correspondence between Earl Mountbatten of Burma and Robert Lacey, 9 March 1976, 2 August 1976 and 4 February 1977 (K20 file, Hartley Library, Southampton).

34 C to author, 1980.

35 HV diary, 14 June 1976.

36 Leonard Mosley, 'The Last of the Old School', *Daily Express*, January 1977.

37 AE and C to Robert Carr, Box 308, Hobe Sound, Florida, 22 December 1976 (Ms. Eng c. 7300 [1–165]).

38 *Daily Express*, January 1977.

39 *Guardian*, 15 January 1977.

40 'The Last of the Old School', *Sunday Express*, January 1977.

41 HV diary, 14 January 1977.

Part Four

18. Bohemian Widowhood

 1 *The Times*, 18 January 1977.

 2 *Sunday Telegraph*, 16 January 1977.

 3 'A Great Lady's Sad Mistake', *Sunday Times*, 15 January 1978.

 4 Mary Soames, *Clementine Churchill* (Transworld, 2002), p. 550.

 5 C's tribute to Lord Goodman for the *Daily Telegraph*, partly published 12 May 1995.

 6 C's tribute to Lord Goodman for the *Daily Telegraph*, partly published 12 May 1995.

 7 C to Lord Goodman, Jimbour House, Queensland, (undated but circa 19 March 1978).

 8 HV diary, 26 January 1981.

 9 HV diary, 26 January 1981.

10 Sir Charles Johnston unpublished diary, April 1986.

11 Johnston unpublished diary, 25 May 1980.

12 Johnston, unpublished diary, 7 July 1982.

13 *Sunday Telegraph*, 29 August 1993.

14 HV diary, 24 March 1995.

15 C to Hon. David Astor, 32 Bryanston Square, 22 June 1999 (Mss. David Astor, Bodleian Library, Oxford).

16 HV diary, 18 October 1980.

17 C to Mary Soames, 26 September 1982 (Churchill College, Cambridge).

18 *News of the World*, 23 August 1985.

19 C's draft reply to The Queen Mother, August 1985.

20 Peregrine S. Churchill to C, 2 Lord North Street, Westminster, 29 May 1948.

21 C to John Merton, 32 Bryanston Square, W1, 12 October 2004.

22 C to Lady (Aline) Berlin, Tuscany (copy), 19 March 1977.

23 *Jewish Week*, 10 December 1982.

24 C to Lady (Aline) Berlin, Tuscany (copy), 19 March 1977.

25 Nicholas Courtney to author, 27 February 2024.

26 C to Lord Goodman, Jimbour House, Queensland (undated but circa 19 March 1978).

27 C to Lord Goodman, Jimbour House, Queensland, (undated but circa 19 March 1978).

28 C to Mrs Kay Burleigh, Barrier Reef, 31 March 1978.

29 C to author, 7 October 1983.

30 Marina Berry, Private illustrated diary, Leningrad and the Caucasus, 18 August to 1 September 1978.

31 John Stefanides to author, London, 1 May 2024.

32 C to June Ivanović, April 1999.

19. *Keeper of the Flame*

1 *Sunday Telegraph*, 4 June 1978.

2 *Sunday Telegraph*, 4 June 1978.

3 Sir Frederick Bishop letter, *Sunday Telegraph*, 11 June 1978.

4 *Sunday Telegraph*, 25 June 1978.

5 Peter Hoos to C, Brooks's, St James's Street, 9 June 1978 (Avon Papers, Birmingham University).

6 C letter, *Sunday Telegraph*, 9 July 1978.

7 C copy letter to *Sunday Telegraph*, 3 July 1978 (Avon Papers, Birmingham University).

8 Sir Robert Armstrong to C, Cabinet Office, 18 November 1980 (Avon Papers, Birmingham University).

9 *The Times*, 7 November 1980.

10 Draft replies by C to Mark Amory, 1984.

11 C note on Penrose business.

12 C to Barrie Penrose, 14 May 1986.

13 Quoted in Penrose to C, 28 May 1986.

14 Barrie Penrose and Simon Freeman, *Conspiracy of Silence* (Grafton Books, 1986), p. 348.

15 Richard Deacon, *The Greatest Treason* (Century, 1989), jacket copy. This book was withdrawn from publication.

16 Draft for Plaintiff, 30 January 1990.

17 Goodman, Derrick (TJL) to Anthony Sillitoe, 1 October 1991.

18 C to Jeffrey Mansell, Goodman Derrick, undated draft note.

19 C to Miranda Carter (fax), 3 September 1996.

20 Michael Dobbs to C, 8 August 2005.

21 C to Michael Dobbs, 30 August 2005.

22 Stewart Purvis and Jeff Hulbert, *Guy Burgess – The Spy Who Knew Everyone* (Biteback Publishing, 2016), pp. 352–3.

23 Tom Driberg, *Guy Burgess* (Weidenfeld & Nicolson, 1956), p. 77 and opposite p. 39.

24 C to IB, 13 May 1976 (Mss. Berlin).

25 Richard Davenport-Hines to author, 24 September 2023.

26 D. R. Thorpe, *Eden* (Chatto & Windus, 2003), p. 599.

27 *The Times*, 4 September 1981.

28 C's comments on Rhodes James biography.

29 Lord Goodman to Anthony Sheil, 9 July 1981.

30 Lord Weidenfeld to C, 7 September 1986.

31 C to Robert Rhodes James (draft letter), 14 March 1986.

32 C's comments on Rhodes James biography.

33 C to IB, 24 September 1986, 1–826 (Mss. Berlin, Bodleian Library).

34 Quoted in Michael Ignatieff, *Isaiah Berlin: A Life* (Pushkin Press, 2023), p. 215.

35 Confidential Deyou 34129-1 to Sir Bryan Cartledge, from the private secretary to Geoffrey Howe, May 1986.

36 Antony Lambton, 'This Other Eden', *Literary Review*, November 1986.

37 C to Martine de Courcel, 27 September 2000.

38 C to D. R. Thorpe, 20 May 1991.

39 Thorpe to C, 21 May 1991.

40 C to Thorpe, 20 March 1992.

41 C to Thorpe, 30 May 2000.

42 C to Graham C. Greene, 20 October 2000.

43 D. R. Thorpe, *Eden* (Chatto & Windus, 2003), p. xxv.

44 Sir Frederick Bishop to C, 22 June 1996.

45 Sir Guy Millard to C, 21 June 1996.

46 *New Statesman*, 2003.

47 *Literary Review*, 2003.

48 *Sunday Times*, 16 March 2003.

49 *Sunday Telegraph*, 16 March 2003.

50 Cherie Blair to author, 27 June 2024.

51 C diary, 2006.

52 *From Churchill to Eden*, p.126.

20. The Last Years

1 Noel Annan, 'The Man I Loved', quoted in Hugh Lloyd-Jones, *Maurice Bowra – a celebration* (Duckworth, 1974), p. 54.
2 HV diaries, New York, December 1982.
3 HV diary, 14 November 1997.
4 C diary, 2005.
5 *Independent*, 4 June 1990.
6 C to Winston S. Churchill, 11 March 1997.
7 C diary, 2007.
8 Robert Harris to author, 12 June 2024.
9 C diary, May 2006.
10 John Jolliffe to C, Shepton Mallet, 22 December 1996.
11 C diary, 2008.
12 C diary, autumn 2007.
13 C diary, 7 September 2011.
14 C diary, 1 November 2007.
15 C diary, 9 July 2012.
16 C diary, 26 December 2008.
17 C diary, early 2006.
18 C diary, 21 July 2011.
19 C diary, March 2009.
20 *From Churchill to Eden*, p. 159.
21 Jung Chang to author, 13 June 2024.
22 C diary, New Year 2009.
23 C diary, New Year 2009.
24 Sally, Lady Ashburton to author, 4 March 2024.
25 C diary, March 2005.
26 Maurice Goudeket, *Close to Colette* (Farrar, Straus and Cudahy, 1957), p. 240.
27 C diary, 28 June 2010.
28 Nurse note in appointment diary, 5 October 2016.
29 Lady Antonia Fraser to author, 2 December 2023.
30 Clifford Henderson to John Major, 18 July 1991, and John Major to Clifford Henderson, 12 November 1991.
31 HV diary, 25 October 2020.
32 HV eulogy for C, 24 November 2021.

Index

INDEX